Spring 75

PSYCHE & NATURE
Part 1 of 2

A JOURNAL OF
ARCHETYPE
AND
CULTURE

Fall 2006

SPRING JOURNAL
New Orleans, Louisiana

CONTENTS
PART 1 OF 2

JUNGIANA

FILM REVIEWS

BOOK REVIEWS

REVERSION

Opening the book, its pages turn back
into a forest; each word flowering
into leaf, bird, or deer.
Language resumes its purpose of being,
regains its covenant with the earth.
The reading lamp-light has become
the last glimmers of the day's sun,
brushing the tree bark;
a swarm of gnats is busy
before the gathering dusk.
So much to say that will never be said.
The book is no longer a book,
but seamless with the world.
Returned, I am present with things;
the forest within and around me,
as if I too were coming into leaf.

—Michael Whan

Psyche and Nature: Tower and Lake, Yin and Yang, Archetype and Earth

GLEN A. MAZIS

> There is nothing without spirit, for spirit seems to be the inside
> of things. ...
> Whether that is our own psyche or the psyche of the universe we
> don't know,
> but if one touches the earth one cannot avoid the spirit.
> ——*Interpretations of Visions*[1]

I. Psyche and Nature

For the modern post-Cartesian worldview, psyche seems in opposition to nature, the realm of the subjective versus the objective, the realm of spirit versus matter. For the classical Greeks, psyche and *phusis* were of a cosmos in which matter was "ensouled" and humans were intermeshed in an order in which there

Glen A. Mazis teaches philosophy and humanities at Penn State, Harrisburg, PA, where he is Full Professor and director of the interdisciplinary humanities Masters program. He is also a poet who gives readings and performances, and he has published about 70 poems in leading literary reviews. He is the author of *Emotion and Embodiment: Fragile Ontology* (Lang, 1993), *The Trickster, Magician and Grieving Man: Returning Men to Earth* (Inner Traditions, 1994), and *Earthbodies: Rediscovering Our Planetary Senses* (SUNY, 2002), as well as numerous essays on imagination, art, film, dreams, and embodiment. He is currently at work on *Humans, Animals and Machines: Blurred Boundaries* and *Merleau-Ponty and the Dream World of the Senses*.

was a process of growth of all things from beginning to end.[2] Nature was this encompassing present order whose denomination derived from roots that meant "growth,"[3] and psyche as *psuchē* derived from the verb *psuchein*, "to breathe, to blow," and was the "life" within all things as well as consciousness.[4] Lao Tzu, at the same time in history, articulated the world as a "way," or *Tao,* of continual transformation where human and nature, spirit and matter, were interpenetrating and yet distinctive. Like Heraclitus, for Lao Tzu and Taoists there is the "fairest harmony" between unlikes, and this mysterious going together of what shouldn't go together logically is the motive force of all things, including human articulations and actions. Even more to the point, this inseparability of the "ten thousand things" and the "eternal Tao" as yet another face of matter and spirit or nature and soul, when taken to heart, is the coming into presence with that of which we are a part. It is the call to meditate upon this mysterious going together of what is both separate and inseparable that is called the "gateway" to the mystery, the human's way to become open to the depth of meaning and wonder of existence that is asked of the reader of the *Tao te Ching* in its initial verse.

For C. G. Jung, the disjunction of psyche and nature that occurred in the subjectification of psyche and the despiritualization of nature were keys to the modern human's loss of spiritual values and "the break-up in world-wide disorientation and dissociation."[5] This dissociation betokened a loss of a precious dimension:

> Thanks to our one-sided emphasis on so-called natural causes, we have learned to differentiate what is subjective and psychic from what is objective and 'natural.' For primitive man, on the contrary, the psychic and the objective coalesce in the external world.[6]

Not that we in the year 2006 can return to the world of *participation mystique* or forsake our gains in rationality, but our one-sidedness forecloses the possibility that for Jung was a foundation for the depth of meaning of our lives that we had forced into unconsciousness. It was a task that Jung left as a challenge for modernity to recapture at least partially the way that

> primitive man experienced the psyche. To him the psyche appears as the source of life, the prime mover, a ghostlike presence which

> has objective reality. Therefore the primitive man knows how to
> converse with his soul; it becomes vocal within him, because he
> is not simply he himself and his consciousness. To primitive man
> the psyche is not, as it is with us, the epitome of all that is
> subjective and subject to the will; on the contrary, it is something
> objective, self-subsistent, and living its own life. (*CW* 8 § 666)

Insofar as we look for psyche internally, as a spirituality that is human-centered, that is accessible only subjectively, we distort the spirit, the soul, and impoverish it. Again, as Jung phrased it, "Natural life is the nourishing soil of the soul. Anyone who fails to go along with life remains suspended." (*CW* 8 § 800) This suspension was described by Jung as an increasing velocity towards nebulous goals that appear often in the guise of acquiring ever more gadgets. Within this uprooted whirligig, humanity begins to feel dispirited, disoriented, and bitterly and cynically resigned.

Psyche is to be found within an encounter with nature. This insight hearkens back to the cultural legacy of the Greeks. Yet, the legacy as part of the collective consciousness encountering our shared planet goes beyond the Greeks. Soul as life-breath is a widespread recognition. Unlike the turn that Greeks and Europeans took, however, towards the dissociation of soul from body, Jung saw that, in archaic cultures, soul taken as "life-breath" meant "that the soul was essentially the life of the body." (*CW* 8 § 800) The body here evoked is the body whose boundaries are the boundaries the earth gestures forth by its motive power of unfolding and enfolding, which takes us into its rhythms and significance as the vital breath or spirit that infuses all beings. These are bodies I have called our human "earthbodies" as "part of a dynamic process" and are "sensual, perceptual and feeling conductors through which richer meaning flows than we can grasp intellectually."[7] This sense of embodiment as an open element in the life-breath of the planet was articulated eloquently by Merleau-Ponty in describing how our bodies were not objects or entities but an open flesh that touches only in being touched or sees only in being seen as part of "the flesh of the world."[8] Spirit as disembodied would be the agent of apprehension, but would not be really in time and space. The embodied self is a reciprocal relationship of being of the same stuff as what it apprehends, so that as often quoted by Merleau-Ponty, Cezanne asserts that he can only paint Mt. St. Victoire because the mountain paints itself through him—the mountain is the motive force of his hand as much as the artist, and the artist is given a sense of himself through the vision of the mountain.⁹ However, the mountain is the mountain, and the artist is the artist: their boundaries entwine and reverse in the process of painting, perceiving, and expressing, but remain distinct.

Psyche and nature may well be inseparable in their unfolding in Greek myth, cosmogony, and etymology, as Gerard Naddaf claims in *The Greek Concept of Nature*, and so be at the heart of European cultural legacy and languages. This same view of nature and psyche may also be embedded in archaic peoples' existence and at the heart of the collective unconscious as our living legacy, yet how we postmoderns are to bring this to experience in a felt recognition remains a daunting challenge. Even if we heartily agree with Jung's declaration, "I am fully committed to the idea that human existence should be rooted in the earth,"¹⁰ how we are to allow the world's breath to enter our being more fully, to make it palpable in order to experience its vitality, and then to become able to express this realm is far from obvious.

It is in quest of this path that we might ask why Jung built a structure—the tower at the side of the lake—in order to truly experience the "repose and renewal" that nature could infuse into his spirit and to open depths of self and expression beyond the "number one self" of modern humanity. As Jung said, "People who have got dirty through too much civilization take a walk in the woods or a bath in the sea," explaining at the same time that the sense of dirt or of being dirty only comes when civilization misplaces matter, puts matter in the "wrong place."¹¹ Realizing this, the modern beleaguered person, feeling both drained of spirit and distanced from nature, at odds with the unconscious and at odds with others, flees from a world cluttered with matter in wrong places, in superfluous objects of consumption, and in crowded environments of soulless structures into the cleansing of the woods or the waters of the sea. In the decades since Jung's death, there is an explosion among Americans and others of the global modern urbanized civilization venturing off into places we believe will wash away the dirt of civilization and return us to "nature." These journeys may help break the crust of our ego-centered unknowing about nature, and certainly Jung himself told how his earliest spiritual stirrings were not from the human, cultural world, but from "rivers, lakes, trees, flowers and animals" and that "trees in particular were mysterious and seemed to me direct embodiments of the incomprehensible meaning of life."[12] Yet, there is the lingering dissatisfaction that for many travelers into the wild there is no regeneration of the vitality of soul. Is it a matter of leaving "culture" for "nature?" Are nature and culture necessarily opposed or are they interdependent in the depth of their recognition and expression? Sojourns "into nature" might seem like what is the most "natural" and most direct way to restore the vitality and depth of psyche that comes from "touching the earth," but is this necessarily so?

Paradoxically, often the "walking through" or "bathing in" the natural world is *not* really to *encounter* nature, nor does it find the way psyche is nature in the depth of an unconsciousness that needs to infuse and ground the modern psyche while simultaneously keeping a certain distance, a distinctness within unity, in order that there be a bringing to consciousness. The plant does not become the soil, it is not just immersed in the soil, but to get nourished by the richness the soil has to offer, it roots itself, a process of projecting itself, of growing outwards that allows a flow back inward and into. It is a becoming enmeshed that takes time and process. For humans, there is a need to move beyond the immersion in nature for "as long as we are still submerged in nature we are unconscious" (*CW* 8 § 750) was Jung's conclusion. There is no going back to an earlier state of being and consciousness, for "reduction to the natural condition is not an ideal state or a panacea." (*CW* 8 § 94) Achieving rationality is vital, but so, too, is not losing our rootedness. We cannot find ourselves in things, which are mere objects to us, both those of the natural world and those of our making. Rationality does not have to lead to a state of isolation from the surround, yet it has:

> [T]he conscious mind becomes more and more the victim of its
> own discriminating activity, the picture we have of the world
> gets broken down into countless particulars, and the original
> feeling of unity, which we integrally connected with the unity
> of the unconsciousness, is lost. (*CW* 11 § 443)

This is what struck Jung with pessimism, this "rootless condition of consciousness," which "becomes a real danger."

This is the postmodern world we live in, when approaching hurricanes like Katrina seem like they are unreal, either becoming an occasion to have a party and "ride out" its violence in a dissociated sort of carnival atmosphere or to watch on TV as another happening, if not in harm's way. If the breath of the planet is in all things, then we might feel the pain and turbulence of a Katrina as a disturbance in our shared spirit and circulations of energies on the planet. Yet, even as such storms vent their fury, it is hard for others to fathom the power and the chaos of soul and body that is engulfing land, creatures, people, and the pulse of the planet. Within the confines of their rationalized, objectified, fragmented relationship with the world, people struggle to feel the shift in the global community that nature expresses as the tsunami of 2004 engulfs portions of the earth and swallows hundreds of thousands. However, it might be more the case that *only* the violent upheavals, like other manifestations of the return of the repressed, may drag postmodern humans back into a momentary connection with the sense of the earth and other humans as part of the earth household. More to the point is the everyday beckoning of landscapes passed on the way to work or the gradual, tragic melting ice caps or widespread drought that is barely seen, filtered through our ego consciousness and disconnected sense of self. To become rooted again is not a return to the unconsciousness of primal existence. Yet, the disconnection of everyday postmodernity, where only the fury of what is repressed gets noticed, will not allow psyche to find its larger sense in the natural world.

We need to find the soul of nature from within, which means both that humanity is caught up in something larger, yet the natural world also gains from humanity a fullness through our consciousness of its manifestations. On his trip to Kenya and Uganda in 1925, Jung had this realization watching gigantic herds of animals—gazelle, antelope, gnu, zebra, warthog, and others—stretching out to the horizon, "herds moving like slow rivers." Jung was grasped by the melancholy cries of a bird of prey and thought

> this was the stillness of the eternal beginning, the world as it had always been, in the state of non-being; for until then no one had been present to know that it was this world. (*MDR*, 255)

It was then that there swept over him Jung's felt recognition of humanity's place in giving an excellence to the world by recognizing it, by taking it in the flow of spirit all around us in the natural world, and bringing it to stand. This is humanity's "invisible act of creation" by making things come to shine forth in their presence. For this encounter that truly brings us face to face with the breath in all things to occur, rather than keeping the world at a fragmented distance, humans must return to what I have called their earthbodies, the way in which our flesh is of the world's flesh or gesturing matter, or as Jung declared: "For it is the body, the feelings, the instincts, which connect us to the soil."[13] For this realization to occur, Jung had to be in the presence of these herds flowing around him and feel their movement in his own viscera. He had to be swept along kinetically in the fullness of perception and take them in through a unity of sound, sight, imagination, and emotion as an embodied being, not as a disembodied spirit looking on from some other realm outside time and space. To return to the psyche in its depth as found in the depths of the world around us, and particularly in the natural world, requires a return to the body-self, the sense of embodiment which is interwoven with the landscape. Yet, why we need to make this turn and how to turn towards this sense of embodiment that allows the level of psyche and openness to the natural and material world around us as meaningful to come into the depths of our soul is also obfuscated in our postmodern world of materialistic consumption and disposable objects, where even a city like New Orleans, which has been home to hundreds of thousands (and also home to this journal) can be jettisoned by many, if the breath within nature is labeled too unruly to be controlled rationally.

II. Lake and Tower, Yin and Yang, Nature and Culture

In Jung's work and life, there is an answer to how our psyche—spirit—soul—the marrow of our spiritual being—encounters itself in its deepest form within nature, and yet is not swallowed up by its mothering matter, but is played with creatively to give the person depth and vitality. At the same time that our larger identity is midwived through this emergence from within nature, we lend to nature an appearance, a coming to be fully, in the light of being and as shaped. Aspects of nature become recognizable and encounterable as we do in the same stroke. It is mutual midwifery. It can also be looked at as the thought or letting be (*Gelassenheit*) of the hand, as referred to by Heidegger, when he states in *What is Called Thinking?* that the hand can allow what is within the material that it shapes to come forth and be itself: "all the work of the hand is rooted in thinking."[14] This is the kind of the work of the hand, Heidegger tells us, of those craftsmen who worked with wood and came to apprehend its meaning, its way of being, that could be expressed through the shaping, the cutting, the polishing that let the wood be:

> he makes himself answer and respond above all to the different kinds of wood and to the shapes slumbering within the wood— to wood as it enters into man's dwelling with all the hidden riches of its nature.[15]

So, for example, the wood of a library—shelves, walls, tables, chairs, and ladders—might be worked by the understanding hand in such a way that the embracing, fruit-bearing stillness and solid, sheltering quietness of the grain, texture, and the hue of the wood—something also of the life of trees distilled and captured in matter in a shapeable way—breathes forth as psyche in a surround of thoughtful reading and musing over texts.

There is a certain kind of concentration, with its distinctive pace and felt depth engendered by this woody environment worked a certain way by the hand. It is the particular nuance of creativity and fidelity to the psyche or soul of wood that might be symbolized by the "green man" of myth, whose expression and work is inseparable from the spirit permeating wood and forest. This faithful dedication to a realm of matter and nature is also a bringing forth of corresponding dimensions of the psyche of the person. This experienced mutual manifestation of qualities within perceiver and perceived is the "reversibility" of embodied perception as Merleau-Ponty designated it when he referred to Michelangelo's assertion that each block of marble told him what to sculpt and his hand only followed these beckonings, or as Paul Klee declared,

> In a forest, I have felt many times over that it was not I who looked at the forest. Some days I felt that the trees were looking at me, speaking to me … I was there listening.[16]

As we have already stated, to get beyond the confines of the modern civilization with its dissociation from both nature and depths of psyche, rather than just walk through nature, it is necessary to "touch nature from the inside." Perhaps, Jung uses the word "touch" here with purpose.

To touch is the way to access the knowledge of the hand, of the embodied subject, for whom touch is the most openly reciprocal perception with the world.[17] In other words, there is an indirectness, a mediating process and material encounter that allows the psyche of nature and human to emerge in mutual transformation and embodied understanding.

Jung was a man of his hands. In his late forties, although he felt that all his writing and speaking had expressed who he was, that although his visions and even unconscious realizations had been given through his scientific work a "solid footing" in the world,

> words and paper, however, did not seem real enough to me; something more was needed. I had to achieve a kind of representation in stone of my innermost thoughts and of the knowledge I had acquired. Or, to put it another way, I had to make a confession in stone. That was the beginning of the 'Tower,' the house which I built for myself at Bollingen. (*MDR*, 223)

To carve stone, to place stone, to build with stone was for Jung a way to solidify who he was, to shape himself in shaping the stone, and to work with himself in working with the stone. When Jung contrasts walking through nature or lying in the grass or bathing in the sea as a way of entering nature from "the outside," he says that the way through dream is to enter nature from the inside. Often, we think of dream as only what we do when asleep, but do the hands also dream? Is the concentrated shaping of matter when following matter's own psyche or life-breath, its own trajectory towards expression in concert with felt, deep, inner psychic need of the human artist or shaper, is that dream? Each time Jung added another section to the original tower, adding a second tower, then a loggia and a courtyard, and finally an upper story at four-year intervals, he felt beckoned to do so. Looking back on his efforts, he realized that "I built it in a kind of dream." (*MDR*, 225) As psyche, there is an oneiricism of matter that the sensitive hand can release in collaboration with a deeper embodied understanding, the dimension of matter to which Bachelard hearkened so sensitively:

> The hands dream. Between the hand and the things, a whole psychology unfolds. ... For things, as for souls, the mystery is inside.[18]

To work with the hands to contact the force within the matter of nature as it resonates with the felt psychic need of the maker to extend and unfold is to dream with the hands. The dream is the place where the psychic depths of the person find expression. Things within nature have their dreams, too, if they are also psyche. The encounter with nature that can give humans back their depths of soul occurs in the material dialogue of embodiment and surround. Words are material, too, but even though they are part of the flesh of the world, they are different, as Merleau-Ponty phrased it:

> It is as though the visibility that animates the sensible world were to emigrate, not outside of every body, but into a less heavy, more transparent body, as though it were to change flesh, abandoning the flesh of the body for that of language, and thereby would be emancipated but not freed from every condition.[19]

This lighter, thinner body of language fuels the agility of thought, but may not forge the depths of psyche as within the life breath of the denser material body of the natural world or of Mother Earth, as Jung always reminded us of the source of the sense of matter. Nearing midlife, Jung felt a gratitude and satisfaction with how words, texts, and thoughts had brought forth into expression and consciousness much of what he had to become, but at that time he felt a need for something denser and something located within the matrix of the natural world around him to bring forth the fuller depths needed for the greater unfolding of individuation. Jung felt the need for substantiality and an expression in the natural realm that would meet him in a particular kind of thickness and enduring solidity:

> From the beginning I felt the Tower as in some way a place of maturation—a maternal womb or a maternal figure in which I could become what I was, what I am and will be. It gave me the feeling of being reborn in stone. It is thus a concretization of the individuation process. (*MDR*, 225)

If we look closely at this construction of the tower in its stages at the side of the lake as recounted by Jung in *Memories, Dreams, Reflections*, there is remarkable coming together of nature and psyche, self and world, male and female, past and present, past and future, spirit and matter, time and timelessness, birth and fulfillment, which are at the heart of the possible depths to be found in the interweaving of psyche and nature.

Jung relates that his earliest memory that emerges from vagueness was one of an indescribable sense of well-being of lying in his pram, in the shadow of a tree on a fine, warm summer day of "the sky blue, and golden sunlight darting through green leaves" and a pungency of sky, golden warmth, and the "sun glittering through the leaves and blossoms of the bushes" that infused his psyche with a sense of rightness and wonder. Another very early memory is of staying by Lake Constance, and the sun "glistening on the water," the sand under the water "curled into little ridges by the waves," and the stretching away into the distance of the water infusing him again with a source of "inconceivable pleasure," and "at that time the idea became fixed in my mind that I must live near a lake; without water, I thought, nobody, could live at all." (*MDR*, 7) So when Jung felt the need to express in stone who he had become and was still becoming, he also needed to hearken back to his earliest beginnings of first feeling most himself sparked by the natural life around him. His shaping of stone was a way of calling back into focus this felt interconnectness with nature and had to be juxtaposed to the glistening, fluid power of water. Tower/water are a figure together, a mandala, and could also be seen as a variation of the circle symbol of yin/yang of the Tao. Jung reminds us that "mandala means circle" whose center is "a kind of central point within the psyche ... by which everything is arranged and which is itself the source of energy ... manifested in the almost irresistible compulsion and urge to become what one is." (*CW* 9i § 357) As Jung stated in *Memories, Dreams, Reflections*, the tower from the beginning was the maternal womb, hearth, or figure which would allow him to be himself. This becoming could only be achieved by shaping himself within the felt substantiality of matter, the Mother earth of the natural surround.

Having shaped stone and placed dwelling in the landscape in an arrangement that concentrated the energy of nature into a felt sense of psychic wholeness, Jung declared, "At Bollingen, I am in the midst of my true life, I am most deeply myself. Here I am, as it were, the 'age-old son of the mother.'" The four stages of construction that Jung undertook after successive four-year periods, from central round hut that had a feeling of familial hearth, to central tower annex with its room of solitude and spiritual concentration, to the courtyard and loggia open to sky, lake, and natural surround, to the final upper story of ego-personality giving way to "an extension of consciousness achieved in old age" reflected in stone and landscape the quaternity of individuation of self. This becoming who he was meant to be was permeated with a sense of further integrating at Bollingen "the personality number two" Jung had always experienced as a second dimension to who he was, a being of the wisdom of having always been and always will be, a son of the maternal unconsciousness. As Jung stated, "in my fantasies he took the form of Philemon, and he comes to life again at Bollingen." Previously, Philemon in Jung's life had been the pagan voice who spoke for the power of psyche not being the individual's, but rather being of the natural surround. A decade before this, Jung had imagined conversations with Philemon who corrected him that the thoughts Jung had taken as his thoughts, the creations of his subjectivity, had to be reconsidered: "in his view thoughts were like animals in the forest, or people in the room, or birds in the air." (*MDR*, 183) In other words, this spirit that Jung felt came to life for him at Bollingen in the persona of Philemon was Jung's personal messenger declaring that psyche is *phusis,* the life within all things.

However, it was not only at Bollingen that Jung had the realization of what he called the "objectivity" of psyche—that spirit is in the landscape and within other beings around us insofar as it emerges from within us—but the shaping of stones and construction of the tower allowed opening even more fully a felt kinship with the natural world. Being at Bollingen, Jung confessed:

> At times I feel as if I am spread out over the landscape and inside things, and am myself living in every tree, in the splashing of the waves, in the clouds and the animals that come and go, in the procession of the seasons. There is nothing in the Tower that has not grown into its own form over the decades, nothing with which I am not linked. Here everything has its history, and mine; here is space for the spaceless kingdom of the world's and psyche's hinterland. (*MDR*, 225-6)

In this building in stone, a sense of space of psyche becomes manifest that is both internal and external, that is most individuated and most linked with the lives of other beings and infused throughout nature, and that is most palpably interwoven through the unfolding in time. What emerges in this unfolding in time is a sense that one inhabits all time through penetrating to the material and psychic core of the natural world. Here again is the upsurge of that sense of eternity that Jung experiences looking out over the vastness of animals surging to the horizon of the African plains.

Yet, at Bollingen, this sense of timelessness has also been brought into unity with culture through the ability of humans to shape things, to write who they are through the stones of nature. What emerges is neither one nor the other, but somehow becoming both more intensely through the identification with the other. This has happened through enlivening matter from its dormancy as the mere objectified matter of modern humanity that opposes us. This deeper sense of matter is the marrow of nature and yet is shapeable:

> But the word 'matter' remains a dry, inhuman and purely intellectual concept, without any psychic significance for us. How different was the former image of matter—the Great Mother—that could encompass and express the profound emotional meaning of Great Mother. In the same way, what was the spirit is now identified with the intellect and thus ceases to be Father of All.[20]

Through bringing the materiality of the natural world into an encounter with the thinking and feeling of the hand, an integration of the psyche and natural depth of culture has been brought to a stand. The masculine shaping and inscribing that is so much of the work of culture has been brought together in the embracing, sheltering of the maternal sense of nature and matter to giver a deeper sense of the embodied psyche interwoven with nature. The person shaping matter to open up psyche and nature in their mutual revelation experiences himself or herself as simultaneously most individual and most collective, and most purely present in encounter and as most timeless in being present in all times. This is the logic of yin/yang, the mutual transformation of the energies of the opposed and inseparable.

Stepping back to gaze on Jung's tower at the side of the lake and taking to heart the image and energy cast by this juxtaposition, it is interesting to note the Tarot card of the major arcana, the "Tower," symbolizing the self as unfolding through embodiment as spirit plunges from the height of the tower into the material world. The image depicted shows lightning striking the tower as the male and female parts of the self fall to earth towards the stone base of the tower. The task indicated by the card is to regain the crown of spirit, the power of the lightning, but in the embodied, material realm—bringing together these dimensions of psyche. Through his construction of the four-fold tower during a dozen years, Jung achieved an integration, but one occurring at the level of what he felt modern humanity had lost, where for the earlier human "in his world, spirit and matter interpenetrate each other, and his gods still wander through forest and field." (*CW* 8 § 682) Jung felt modern humanity had forgotten that "the *lumen naturae* is the natural spirit" and that we cannot "pitch nature out with a fork." (*CW* § 229) In alchemy, Jung was to discover a parallel creative thought of the hands and the body immersing themselves in the material matrix of the world's elements. Yet, alchemy is more culturally inscribed, symbol laden, contained, and concentrated soul-working. It is interesting to ponder how much of the efficacy of soul deepening in alchemy, writing, and artistic expression is initially opened by this shaping of material matrix within nature's space of all spaces and the time of all times which, as Jung put it, is psyche's "hinterland." Succinctly put, Jung declares, "Nature is not matter only, she is also spirit." (*CW* § 229)

In 1937, two years after Jung had added the fourth element of the tower and the "quaternity" of self "had arisen," Jung gave a lengthy analysis at the Eranos conference of the visions of the third century alchemist, Zosimos. He revised and completed this analysis in 1954, right before adding the final upper story of the tower that he said signified the extension of consciousness in old age. Zosimos dreamed of a temple that was a stone in the heavens. Jung sees the stone as the divine in the human, that sense of self beyond the personality. In that "single stone" of the temple, Jung sees "the round wholeness, the stone, is a guarantee of vitality." Jung, of course, references both the philosopher's stone of alchemy and the omphalos of Delphi and other oracles that were always the "navel" of the earth and the point of connection with the divine, represented by a stone. Jung himself had at Bollingen in 1950 made a monument to the meaning of the tower by carving in a four-sided block of stone on one side a poem in reference to the philosopher's stone, on a second a Greek verse about the play of time everywhere and in dark and light, and on the third, a Latin inscription whose words ended with a homage to psyche's ubiquity:

> I am one, but opposed to myself. I am youth and old man at one and the same time. I have known neither father nor mother, because I had to be fetched out of the deep like a fish, or fell like a white stone from heaven. In woods and mountains I roam, but I am hidden in the innermost soul of man. I am mortal for everyone, yet I am not touched by the cycle of aeons. (*MDR*, 227)

After carving the fourth side with his own name and age as a "thanks offering," he was puzzled by the compulsion he felt in the carving in stone and its meaning, but knew it was a manifestation of who he was and his message to the world. After relating this tale of carving the stone in *Memories, Dreams, Reflections*, Jung remembers being at the tower when it was just completed, putting a kettle on the hearth, and being fascinated for more than an hour by the kettle's boiling water singing a music that was both inside and outside the tower, that was the music of culture, hearth, and orchestra and also the music of water, wind, and "all the discords of nature." The tower and the carvings in stone were mandala, were yin/yang, were an example of the way that Heidegger articulates how humans come to work with earth in order to both encounter its natural qualities as home for and manifestation of spiritual values, but always in a *strife* of *inseparable* unfolding—unities of opposition.

However, even though the stone of the tower and the stones around the tower had this significance as they were worked by Jung, it is especially in the relation of tower and lake that can be seen a fuller significance of the archetypal symbol of the relationship of psyche and nature. In reflecting on Zosimos' visions, Jung speaks of the interplay of stone and water, for they are juxtaposed in the visions. Of the water, Jung states, "Water and spirit are often identical." In juxtaposition to the stone as temple, the stone can be seen to be the inner self seeking spirit as water. When water takes on this function as spirit, as "divine water," it becomes the "quintessence of things." Jung hearkens back to where our meditation began, with the Greeks and their cosmogony, and relates "when the celestial waters were animated by the spirit, they immediately fell into circular motion, from which arose the perfect spherical form of the anima mundi" (*CW* 13 § 102). Insofar as the world around us is psyche, is ensouled as a totality, this is symbolized by the movement of the waters, especially in a circle. In addition, in one of the only references to the symbolic significance of lakes in the

Collected Works, Jung states that in the inorganic world, one of the two most common symbols of the deeper self are lakes and they "transcend the scope of the ego personality in the manner of a daimonion." (*CW* 9 ii § 226) If the stones of the tower and around it can be seen as shaped in seeking an interweaving with the deeper spirit of the surround, this is perfectly signified by the juxtaposition with the lake. When water is symbol of spirit in juxtaposition to stone, Jung states there is a duality always emphasized within the water as the "two principles balance one another, masculine and feminine, which constitute the essence of creative power in the eternal cycle of birth and death." (*CW* 13 § 105) Jung's sense of the coming together of these principles in the tower is symbolized by tower/lake as circular yin/yang in motion and mutual transformation.

Again, there is a fascinating continuity between Jung's work and insights and his own journey of individuation. In 1944, after he broke his foot, then had a heart attack, and then fell into delirium and visions, he reports experiencing himself high up in space when he encountered a "tremendous dark block of stone," also floating in space that was "about the size of my house, or even bigger." (*MDR*, 290) As the vision progresses, the stone is a temple of sorts, and as Jung approaches it everything extraneous from his psyche is stripped away, and he is one with the stone in such a way it consists of his history and "this is what I have been." The rock temple promises the answers to Jung's spiritual questions, and in it he "would learn why everything had been thus and not otherwise." Of course, fortunately for us, Jung does not enter the rock and returns down here to his earthly existence. In discussing Zosimos' visions and the parallel floating stone that is a temple, Jung looks at the Navaho myths in which the stone goddesses, besides being symbolic of the maternal earth, "at the same time symbolizes self." In this light, Jung quotes an ancient alchemical text about the "the secret of the philosophy" found in the mediating power of the stone: "how the highest demands the lowest, and how the lowest ascends to the highest, and how the midmost draws near to the highest, and is made one with it." The midmost is the mediating power of the philosopher's stone to draw together the opposites. Yet, stone is not just any material but at the core of self and at the core of the substantiality of the maternal body of the natural world. Stone calls for water to be activated, to be drawn into the mediating center of human and nature, of psyche and *phusis*.

III. EARTH AND ARCHETYPE

Given the mentalistic and dualistic tradition of European thought, it is easy to interpret the archetypes as mental structures or at least as universal *a priori* structures of subjectivity, yet the relationship of psyche and nature that we have been exploring in Jung's work and life would lead us to take seriously that the archetypes are found within the historical unfolding of humans in the larger field of the natural and material world. In his commentary upon the "The Secret of the Golden Flower," Jung concludes that the West is challenged by the "cult of consciousness" and in need of a "new integration" of psyche. (*CW* 13 § 71) In his "attempt to build a bridge of psychological understanding between East and West," Jung hopes we can move towards a shift in which "the subjective 'I live' becomes the objective 'It lives me.'" By this, Jung is certainly not endorsing the destructive embrace of an objectivity of natural causality, which is the correlative of seeing nature and matter as opposed to us, but rather means a "feeling of reconciliation with all that happens, for which reason … the gaze of one who has attained fulfillment turns back to the beauty of nature." (*CW* 13 § 78) In his collaboration with Wilhelm and his reading of Taoist texts, Jung not only found inspiration for developing his ideas of synchronicity and alchemy by returning to their rich history in the Western tradition, but he also took heed of the contrasting destructiveness of the West's overvaluing the intellect: "The intellect does harm to the soul when it dares to possess itself of the heritage of the spirit." (*CW* 13 § 7) Recognizing this danger is how Jung commences his commentary on "The Secret of the Golden Flower." Jung takes heed to how the Taoist logic of the yin/yang opens "its eyes to spirit" as it simultaneously "obeys the laws of the earth." In one of the few passages where Jung discusses explicitly the notion of yin/yang, he recognizes that for the Taoist, the power of the intellect in its striving "towards the shining heights" finds a balance in the whole: "Opposed to this *yang* principle is the dark, feminine, earthbound *yin*, whose emotionality and instinctuality reach back into the depths of time and down into the labyrinth of the physiological continuum." In his formulation, there is the suggestion that by returning to embodiment and earthiness, the West could come to a balance of psyche and nature. The depths of time are in the earth and the way the body is rooted in the earth.

Jung was also greatly impressed by the writings of Nietzsche and especially by *Thus Spoke Zarathustra*. That work opens with the cry that humanity's spirit "must remain faithful to the earth."[21] Like the Taoist texts, like Jung's sense of archaic humanity, Nietzsche too felt for the grounding of psyche in the earth and the natural world humanity has to recognize the "body is the great reason" or, as Jung puts it, Zarathustra's great insight was "the union of the pairs of opposites, spirit and body."[22] In Nietzsche, Jung found another who believed that in European and American modernity, "the thing people are most afraid of is not so much the soul ... but the body." Part of the prejudice of the ascendancy of the intellect and subjectivity is that in the realm of psyche "the body is excluded and has nothing to do with it." If we in the West are driven towards the light as our conception of the psyche, then embodiment must be shunned for "the body is darkness."[23] Yet, we then become dissociated from the deepest reaches of the psyche. Jung comments in contrasting the current state of Christianity with the spirituality expressed by Nietzsche in *Zarathustra*: "Our idea of the spirit has become quite lamed; in late Christianity it is lame and abstract." By contrast, in Nietzsche's work, Jung appreciates that

> the body and what one called the 'spirit' have come together in a revelation that really comes to him from the body. So, it is a sort of redemption of the body, something which has been lacking in Christianity, where the body, the here-and-now, has been depreciated.[24]

A key for both Jung and Nietzsche for the reviving of modernity's spiritual life is the embrace of the body.

The return to the unity of body and psyche is the return to the union of psyche and nature as earth. The body opens us to a spirituality that remains faithful to the earth. If the body is of "the flesh of the world" or if there is a "knowing of the hands" that releases the oneiric dimension of matter, then this kind of alternative knowing opens us to the life-breath of psyche as infusing nature. In interaction with the larger body, that of the earth, the products of the interweaving with the collective psyche of humanity emerge, as Jung states eloquently:

> … the archetypes are, as it were, the hidden foundations of the conscious mind, or, to use another comparison, the roots which the psyche has sunk not only in the earth in the narrow sense but the world in general. … They are thus, essentially, the chthonic portion of the psyche, if we may use such an expression—that portion through which the psyche is attached to nature, or in which its link with the earth and the world appears most tangible. (*CW* 10 § 53)

In Jung's own life, his shaping of stone in the mandala of lake/tower was an opening to the natural world, to the chthonic powers of the interweaving of earth and collective wisdom of humanity. Tower and lake in juxtaposition both embody and represent the yin/yang of the depth of natural world and soul emerging in archetypal consciousness.

If the world has a soul, the *anima mundi* is not of a detachable spiritual realm that merely "participates" in the earth. Its marrow is in the mutual interpenetration, in the way that the yin/yang symbol should be drawn with arrows around the outside to indicate that in the unfolding of time, opposites interweave and become each other. That is why this primordial depth contains all time: it is an unfolding in its process that weaves into itself the significance of the history of the planet. The formed contents of our deepest psyche, Jung reminds us, are not just structured but also are *dynamic*, and "the archetype consists of both—form and energy." (*CW* 9i § 187) In "Mind and Earth" (or perhaps it could be also translated as "Soul and Earth" [*"Seele und Erde"*]), Jung begins the essay with considering the import of this long history (*CW* 13 § 49-53), and concludes its presence is not the accumulated effects in time of a series of causal interactions, but rather an interweaving of identity in time: "The psychic influence of the earth and its laws is seen most clearly in these primordial images." (*CW* 10 § 53) When Jung's own consciousness integrated lessons of hearth, family, music of the spheres, work, and identity, he shaped stone into a circular structure, into tower, courtyard, rock monuments, and the formed psychic contents broke over his soul like waves coming in from the lake transmitted through the stone and showered from the sky and trees around.

I believe that in the thought of Jung and in his handiwork are the realizations of a deeper sense of psyche and nature in the indirect work of humanity's shaping of the material world as embodied. This shaping intensifies and extends

> the need to project ourselves into the things around us. My self
> is not confined to my body. It extends into all the things I have
> made and all the things around me. Without these things ... I
> would not be a human being.[25]

Shaping is more powerful than the mere walking into the natural
world, for the earth so formed brings the psyche face to face with us
through the body. This is Heidegger's message in "The Origin of the
Work of Art," when he is speaking of the building of a Greek temple
and says,

> the temple-work, in setting up the world, does not cause materials
> to disappear, but rather causes them to come forth for the very
> first time and to come into the Open of the work's world. The
> rock comes to bear and rest; metals to glitter and shimmer, tones
> to sing, the word to speak. All this comes forth as the work sets
> itself back into the massiveness and heaviness of stone, into the
> firmness and pliancy of wood, into the hardness and luster of
> metal ...[26]

For Heidegger, the "world" of which he speaks is the ultimate sense of
values or meaning of a person's place in the scheme of things and the
significance of their actions in relation to others. These meanings come
about through setting back into the earth these manifestations of spirit.
For Heidegger, too, earth and world only come to be through their
inseparability *and* never-ending strife—the dynamic turning of the
Taoist yin/yang.

   Another way to see this indirect path of mutual emergence of
psyche and nature or self and world is through the light-heartedness
of Wilhelm's Taoist story of the rainmaker that Jung loved to tell to
anyone who would listen to him repeat it again (as Sabini relates in
her wonderful collection, *The Nature Writings of C. G. Jung*).[27] The
essence of the story is after many failed attempts of spiritual leaders to
end the drought in a province, the rainmaker, a dried-up old man,
was fetched from another province. He asked for a quiet little house
somewhere and locked himself in for three days. On the fourth day,
an unseasonable snow storm came. When explaining himself, the
rainmaker said when the world is out of Tao and disordered, he set
into order his small space and returned to the Tao. Jung explains that

"Tao is in the room and nothing wrong can happen." For Jung, this was an example of synchronicity or thinking without direct causality. However, the story can also be understood to say that if we work with something smaller and shapeable, the right spirit of the whole will become manifest—not as a direct demand, but as an expression of patterning among the ten thousand things. Just as the rainmaker would never claim he "caused" the rain to fall, I would not claim that Jung's insights "came" and that the insights of his work have manifested a dimension of psyche in our modern world that were "caused" by Jung's construction of the tower and its monuments by the lake. However, tower and lake can be envisioned as shaped as a Taoist inscription of a ring of stone and water. They archetypally express how we move in a cycle in which psyche is nature and nature is psyche that preserves the darkness of both—fissures and dangers—and also the fair harmony of both—inseparability and mutual nurturance.

NOTES

1. C. G. Jung, *The Earth Has a Soul: The Nature Writings of C. G. Jung,* Meredith Sabini (ed.) (Berkeley: North Atlantic, 2002), 81 (quoted from *Interpretations of Visions*). Sabini's collection of Jung's writings on this topic is skillfully and evocatively done.

2. Gerard Naddaf, *The Greek Concept of Nature* (Albany: SUNY Press, 2005), 64.

3. *Ibid.*, 64.

4. *Ibid.*, 66.

5. C. G. Jung, *Man and His Symbols* (Garden City: Doubleday, 1964), 97.

6. C. G. Jung, *Collected Works*, 10 § 128. Since the *Collected Works* are cited extensively throughout this essay, future references will use the abbreviation "*CW,*" followed by the volume number and paragraph number, all within parentheses in the body of the text.

7. Glen A. Mazis, *Earthbodies: Rediscovering Our Planetary Senses* (Albany: SUNY Press, 2002), 1.

8. Merleau-Ponty's life-long articulation of this sense of embodiment culminates in the unfinished work, *The Visible and the Invisible,* especially in the chapter, "The Chiasm," trans. Alphonso Lingis (Evanston: Northwestern University Press), 130-55.

9. Maurice Merleau-Ponty, "Cezanne's Doubt," in *Sense and Non-sense,* ed. Patricia and Hubert Dreyfus (Evanston: Northwestern University Press, 1964), 17.

10. Sabini, 156 (quoted from the published interviews with Jung).

11. *Ibid.*, 207 (quoted from the published notes of the dream analysis seminar, 1928-30).

12. C. G. Jung, *Memories, Dreams, Reflections*, trans. Richard and Clara Winston (New York: Vintage, 1965), 67-8. Since *Memories, Dreams, Reflections* is cited extensively throughout this essay, future references will use the abbrevation "*MDR,*" followed by the page number, all within parentheses in the body of the text.

13. C. G. Jung, *Seminar on Nietzsche's Zarathustra* [Abridged], ed. by James L. Jarrett (Princeton: Princeton University Press, 1998), 373.

14. Martin Heidegger, *What is Called Thinking?,* trans. by Fred Wieck and J. Glenn Gray (New York: Harper and Row, 1968), 16.

15. *Ibid.*, 14.

16. Maurice Merleau-Ponty, *The Primacy of Perception*, ed. John Wild (Evanston: Northwestern University Press, 1964), 167.

17. Glen Mazis, "Touch and Vision: Rethinking with Merleau-Ponty Sartre on the Caress," *Philosophy Today,* vol. xxiii, 4 (1979), 312-318.

18. Gaston Bachelard, *The Poetics of Reverie,* trans. Daniel Russell (Boston: Beacon Press, 1971), 72.

19. Merleau-Ponty, *Visible and the Invisible*, 153.

20. Jung, *Man and His Symbols*, 94-5. Jung's use of 'maternal' and 'paternal,' as well as 'masculine' and 'feminine' are problematic, of course, but a nuanced discussion of this would necessitate another essay.

21. Friedrich Nietzsche, *Thus Spoke Zarathustra*, trans. by Walter Kaufmann (New York: Viking, 1977), § 3, prologue.

22. Jung, *Seminar Zarathustra*, 192.

23. Sabini, 169.

24. Jung, *Seminar Zarathustra*, 193.

25. *Ibid.*, 155.

26. Martin Heidegger, *Poetry, Language, Thought*, trans. by Albert Hofstadter (New York: Harper and Row, 1971), 46.

27. Sabini, 211.

The Unsaying of Stone

in

Jung's Psychology

MICHAEL WHAN**

Nature loves to hide. — Heraclitus, fragment X[1]

1. The stone is a stone. 2. The stone is not a stone. 3. Despite being not a stone, it is not anything else nor simply nothing at all, but nevertheless a stone. And only as this *in itself* (innerly) negated stone is it *the philosopher's* stone.

—Wolfgang Giegerich, "Once More 'The Stone Which is Not a Stone:' Further Reflections on 'Not'"[2]

An epigraph such as the two above can be either an inscription on stone, on a statue, a coin, or at the head of a book chapter. Inscribing stone points to the complex and subtle relationship

Michael Whan is a Jungian analyst in London. He has published previously in *Spring, Harvest, Chiron, Dragonflies,* and elsewhere. His most recent publication is a chapter called "Supervision as self-questioning: the contribution of Jung's *Psychological Types* towards theory in supervision," in *Supervision and the Analytic Attitude,* edited by Christine Driver and Edward Martin.

**I dedicate this essay to the memory of Daniel C. Noel, friend, teacher, author, and much more. — Michael Whan between meaning—signs, symbols, writing—and nature in its elemental form and substance as stone. The interface between inscription and stone marks the ambiguous place between human and nonhuman nature. From prehistory, stone has received our inscribing gestures, our restless urge "to leave a mark." Whilst in the course of time and weather (we can now add the effects of erosion caused by human industrial and agricultural pollution), human inscription has been removed from its nonhuman surfaces. Stone both allows (impermanently) and resists being used as the material for scripture. Stone is more ancient than meaning, more original, finally outlasting what we mark upon it.

Such inscriptions can be understood as concrete forms of what depth psychology terms "projection." To project in this sense is to mark something on the earth's stonitude. But if we can appropriate stone in the service of the human symbolic, so stone can also "petrify" us, turn us to stone. Projection can work in a dual direction. In his critique of the notion of projection, Dan Noel recalls

> one of my graduate school mentors once remarked in this regard, 'primitive' humans could not have experienced a stone anthropomorphically without at the same time experiencing *themselves* 'petromorphically.'[3]

Many notions of the projection onto stone appear at the heart of Jungian psychology. Most Jungian thinking around such matters remains within an anthropological framework of "animism:" the projection of human subjectivity and primitiveness onto the "animate" and "inanimate" world of nature. Even though in *Memories, Dreams, Reflections*, Jung gives a graphic notion of what Noel refers to as *petromorphication*, as far as I have found, discussions of projection tend to focus mainly in terms of the anthropomorphizing of stone: making stone over in the images of the human imagination.[4]

When depth psychology speaks of the meaning of stone, it intends the stone as a symbol, as something "substituting" for something else; stone then provides for metaphorical equivocation, as a way of saying something about something else. Von Franz in an essay, "The Process of Individuation," for instance, recounts an analysand's dream, in which a "dark oval stone...probably symbolizes the dreamer's innermost being, his true personality."[5] Here, clearly, the image of stone acts as a metaphor for human individuation, though in doing so, stone becomes the image *by which* we apprehend the notion of individuation. That is to say, the image of stone means we symbolize individuation *petromorphically.* Elsewhere describing a woman's active imagination, the "Self" is said to appear as a "deer," that is, "the connective animal," because, as it depicts itself, "I connect people, animals, and even stones with one another if I enter them. I am your fate or the 'objective I.'"[6] Pointing to the "just-so-ness" of stone, von Franz suggests that its aptness as a symbol of the Self indicates "the still unknown relationship between what we call the unconscious psyche and what we call 'matter.'"[7] Stone symbolism carries the "stuff" of psyche and nature, reminding our awareness of the hidden or underlying connection between them. The power of stone to turn us into an image of itself, that is to say, the counter-movement of projection, may free us from the one-sided binding that the notion of projection can generate. Open us to how things shape our subjectivity.

Thus, Jung's psychology contains an implicit counter-movement in that its notion of interiority goes beyond the subjectivized, humanized idea of psyche, in which the soul's interiority is conflated with that of human subjectivity. This counter-movement is to be found, for instance, in Jung's mysterious, speculatory concept of synchronicity. Synchronicity, or what Jung referred to as "meaningful coincidence," an acausal idea of meaningful correspondences between the "inner" and "outer," implies not only the subsisting of meaning in nature and the "material," "external world," but counter-wise, the subsisting of nature in meaning. The stone symbol of the Self bespeaks a mineral psyche, a "mineral Self:" hence, not only the "spirit in the stone," but the "stone in the spirit." An interiority that encompasses stone.

In her essay, "Symbolism in the Visual Arts," Aniela Jaffe draws on the psychology of projection to "explain" the religious and artistic uses of stone. She writes:

> Man, with his symbol-making propensity, unconsciously transforms objects or forms into symbols…We know that even when stones had a highly symbolic meaning for ancient and primitive societies. Rough, natural stones were often believed to be the dwelling places of spirits or gods, and were used in primitive cultures as tombstones, boundary stones, or objects of religious veneration. Their use may be regarded as a primeval

> form of sculpture—a first attempt to invest the stone with a more
> expressive power than chance and nature could give it.[8]

Here, clearly, Jaffe's language (in English translation, at least)—
"unconsciously transforms," "believed to be," "a first attempt to
invest"—characterizes the animation of stones in terms of a
psychological theory of projection. The "meaningfulness" of stone derives
from the "symbol-making propensity" of human subjectivity "projected"
onto and into stone. The "spirit" in the stone is not truly the spirit of
the stone, rather a projected or "displaced" content of the human
psyche. For as Jaffe stresses, the "expressive power" of stone has a source
other than "chance and nature could give it."

Having claimed that the "animation of the stone must be explained
as the projection of a more or less distinct content of the unconscious
into the stone," Jaffe describes a very different counter-wise, more
participatory conception, which allows for "'the self-expression' of the
stone; to use the language of myth, the stone is allowed to 'speak for
itself.'" Jaffe then cites a letter from the artist, Max Ernst. Referring to
"granite boulders, large and small, from the moraine of the Forno
glacier," Ernst observes how

> [w]onderfully polished by time, frost, and weather, they are in
> themselves fantastically beautiful. No human hand can do that.
> So why not leave the spadework to the elements, and confine
> ourselves to scratching on them runes of our own mystery?[9]

For Ernst's sensibility, nature surely can and does have such "expressive
power." What Jaffe is intimating in these passages goes beyond the
notion of projection; or, at the very least, makes it problematic. The
animation of stone cannot solely be reduced to the hand of human
subjectivity. Stone has an expressive life of its own, and *affords* to the
sensitive eye and hand of the artist (a *primordial sensibility,* perhaps)
the handiwork of the elements. Ernst is working *with* stone, not *on* it,
giving way, yielding and responding, to its selfsame power of "self-
expression" (though, of course, in using this latter term, I've put the
whole thing back into the language of human subjectivism).

What then of stone in Jung's life and work; what relevance, if any,
does it have for his formulation of depth psychology and the legacy of
his theory and practice? What of the waystones along the way, the *herm*
in "Jungian" hermetics and hermeneutics? My particular concern here

is how stone in Jung's work might be intimating an inkling of a philosophy of nature. Or better, what such a philosophy of nature has critically to confront in the relations between psyche, psychological thought, and nature?

Many stones make an appearance in Jung's psychology. There are many and one. Do all the different stones finally come together, transformed into the One that is the philosophical stone of alchemy; or are all the seemingly many stones really the particular reflections or refractions of this one philosophical stone? The placing of the Philosopher's Stone at the heart of Jung's psychology suggests a petromorphizing of his psychological intuitions. Interiorizing becomes a stonelike self-containment, self-subsistence, an hermetic standing wholly within itself. Thus, in its self-showing lies a selfsame self-concealing. As a stone reveals itself by its very virtue of being a stone, it withdraws into itself. A stone gives and withholds itself. So too, Jung's psychology, as it articulates its conception of psyche and psychology at the selfsame time it conceals its own self-generating mystery. Its form of knowing rests upon an unknowing, upon a grounding in groundlessness.[10] To be underway to being psychological requires that Jung's psychology not remain exempt from itself. It knows its practice as a creation or self-expression (*logos*) of the soul. As such, it must go by way of self-interiorization, it has to get right inside itself, to enter truly its own inner depths, reflecting the psyche *from* which it speaks and not only *about* which it speaks. The philosophical stone of Jung's psychology is uroboric, circular; a hermeneutic circle. The "personal equation" of psychology, its deep subjectivity, is the soul in search of itself, reaching evermore deeply into, underway, to self-relation.

The Philosopher's Stone is no ordinary stone. For the alchemists, in whose labors Jung perceived a proto-psychology of his own, spoke of the "spirit in the stone." The stone, Jung tells us, is not an actual stone, but a symbolic one. Rather, it is the "'Stone that hath a spirit,'" "'the stone that is no stone.'" This *lithos ou lithos*, this unstonely stone, is not then to be taken literally. It is full of symbolic meaning. Speaking of the stone symbol in relation to the domain of spirit and specifically Christian spiritualization, Jung understands it as a complication, an *aporia*. He writes: "The very concept of 'stone' indicates the peculiar nature of this symbol."[11] For, he notes, it signifies "the essence of everything solid and earthly." As "matter," says Jung, "this concept intrudes into the sphere of 'spirit' and its symbolism." It is "a concretization, a 'materialization' that reached down into the darkness of the inorganic realm or even arose from it."[12] The aporetic nature of stone becomes essentially the *aporia of nature* for the spiritualized (Christian) metaphysics of Western thought. From Plato through Christianity to modern philosophy, truth and meaning are predominantly laid claim to from the standpoint of spirit. But the intrusion through alchemy of the stoniness of the philosophical stone makes for a contradiction, a rupture, breach, and resistance to the spiritualizing appropriation of Christian metaphysics. The *alchemical lapis,* and through it Jung's psychology, requires that truth and meaning have to take account of the world of nature. The alchemists, in Jung's view, worked with a perception of the interiority of the natural world, the "spirit *in* the stone." They worked with the depths, the inwardness, at the heart of matter. They sought the redemption of nature in order to overcome the tearing apart of nature and spirit, which occurred through the diremptive praxis of Platonic-Christian-Cartesian metaphysics.

Jung's reference to the alchemical *lapis*, his assertion that its "essence" expresses "everything solid and earthy," and its intrusion into "the sphere of spirit," brings the whole problem of nature, of materiality, into his psychology. How does his psychology take up the split between spirit and nature? For the diremption remains intimately connected with his concept of "psychic reality." Jung identifies the severance between nature and spirit as a consequence of Western philosophy, indeed, to the point that it is also the condition for the historical emergence of psychology at all. He writes:

> The development of Western Philosophy during the last two hundred centuries has succeeded in isolating the mind in its own sphere and in severing it from its primordial oneness with the universe. Man has ceased to be the microcosm and eidolon of the cosmos and his 'anima' is no longer…the *Anima Mundi*, the World Soul.[13]

Jung's words resonate with those earlier of Schelling, who held that, "[the]whole of modern European philosophy since its beginning (with Descartes) has this common defect, that nature does not exist for it at all and that it lacks a living ground."[14] The coming into being of psychology, according to Jung, has also meant a radical transformation of our experience of nature. The notion of psychology, of the soul's inwardness or interiority, has taken shape through the tearing apart of nature and spirit. As Jung puts it:

> The gulf that Christianity opened out between nature and spirit enabled the human mind to think not only beyond nature but in opposition to it, thus demonstrating its divine freedom, so to speak. This flight from the darkness of nature's depth culminates in Trinitarian thinking, which moves in a Platonic, 'supracelestial' realm.[15]

The inward turn of the Christianized soul consists at the same time as a turn away from the world, a disenchantment of nature. Hence, the process of interiorization led to "a new and independent relation to nature whereby the foundation was laid for natural science and technique..." But the price paid has been that "the world has not only lost its God...but also to some extent has lost its soul as well."[16] Christian spirituality and Western metaphysics as the ascetic inward turn have generated the epistemological conditions for depth psychology. Depth psychology rests upon the notion of the psyche, of "psychic reality," of interiorization; corresponding to which we undergo a deep change in how we perceive nature. The psyche, states Jung, "has attained its present complexity by a series of acts of introjection. Its complexity has increased in proportion to *the despiritualization of nature*."[17] Depth psychology emerges and evolves through this disenchantment of the world. Jung even posits it as one of psychology's tasks, for its disenchanting logic appears to be the form psychology takes to deepen and interiorize itself. Jung declares the need to "de-psychize nature," to "take back all archaic projections."[18]

For Jung, this separation between nature and spirit belongs to the very essence of psychic life and further to the very condition for understanding, especially psychological understanding, at all. In his essay, "Basic Postulates of Analytical Psychology," Jung observes that the "conflict between nature and spirit is itself a reflection of the paradox of psychic life. This reveals a physical and a spiritual aspect which appear a contradiction because, ultimately, we do not understand the nature of psychic life itself." So, to be able at all to grasp something which we have not or cannot understand, then we have to "be willing to contradict ourselves, we must pull this something into its antithetical parts in order to be able to deal with it at all. The conflict between the physical and the spiritual aspects only shows that psychic life is in the last analysis an incomprehensible 'something.'"[19] Jung goes on to give the following description concerning the spirit and nature split and its relation to psychic reality:

> If we try to penetrate more deeply into the meaning of this concept ['psychic life'], it seems to us that certain psychic contents or images are derived from a 'material' environment to which our bodies belong, while others, which are in no way less real, seem to come from a 'spiritual' source which appears to be very different from the physical environment. Whether I picture to myself the car I wish to buy or try to imagine the state in which the soul of my dead father now is—whether it is an external fact or a thought that concerns me—both are psychic reality. The only difference is that one psychic happening refers to the physical world, and the other to the spiritual world. If I shift my concept of reality on to the plane of the psyche—where alone it is valid— this puts an end to the conflict between mind and matter, spirit and nature as contradictory explanatory principles.[20]

Comparing the two passages, it seems as if Jung is contradicting himself. On the one hand, the conflict between nature and spirit features as in Jung's own words, "a reflection of the paradox of psychic life." Whilst otherwise, he says that when the "concept of reality" is moved onto "the plane of the psyche," the conflict between "nature and spirit as contradictory explanatory principles" is put to "an end." What does this mean? Does it mean that beyond psychology and its "plane" of consciousness, the worlds of nature and spirit, *in themselves*, remain rent apart? Or is Jung saying rather that it is the "contradictory explanatory principles" that themselves have arisen from the "paradox" of psychic life, that have polarized nature and spirit? Namely, is it our thinking which has sundered their underlying connectivity. If the scission between nature and spirit is *overcome conditionally* through the concept of psychic reality, does this mean that at the level of "transpsychic reality" the division remains? If Jung is speaking of the overcoming as conditional on "psychic reality," then he is implicitly acknowledging the limits of his psychology. For at those differing levels of my existence which are "physical" and "spiritual," I am left in a state of self-division. I must suffer this in my modes of experience as a "consumer" with my car-buying wishes and as a "spiritual being." My life of material consumption, at bottom, appears to be in conflict with my spiritual life. Yet, according to Jung, when I treat each of these differing aspects of existence as "psychic contents or images," then the conflict between them is put to "an end." But is this so only for the "I" that "picture[s] to myself the car I wish to buy" or that tries to "imagine the state in which the soul of my dead father now is"?

In saying that the division between spirit and nature reflects the "paradox of psychic life," isn't Jung stating that this "contradiction" belongs to the soul's dialectic, that necessary "pulling" of something, in his own words, "into its antithetical parts in order to deal with it at all"? If so, then what we speak of as nature and spirit are, as Jung puts it, already interiorized, already within the soul's encompassment. Then they are not "derived from a 'material environment to which our bodies belong,'" nor "from a 'spiritual' source which appears to be very different from the physical environment." What Jung is trying to say here becomes clearer when we understand it in terms of the overcoming of what could be called a "natural consciousness." The conflict between spirit and nature, as an essential element of psychological consciousness, consciousness of psychic reality, is seemingly not found in that sensibility which we call "natural." In other words, the apparent confusion in these passages belongs to the difference between the "immediate experience" of "psychic life" and the medial difference of the soul in search of itself; namely, psyche's self-consciousness.

We get a glimpse of the peculiar and radical nature of Jung's idea of psychological awareness in the following almost Hegelian way of regarding psychology. Psychology, says Jung "actualizes the unconscious urge to consciousness," and, he continues, it is actually "the coming to consciousness of the psychic process, but it is not, in the deeper sense, an explanation of this process, for no explanation of the psychic can be anything other than the living process of the psyche itself." Jung then emphasizes the problematic and sublating character of psychology underway to itself:

> Psychology is doomed to cancel ['*aufheben*' in the German text] itself out as a science and therein precisely it reaches its scientific goal. Every other science has so to speak an outside; not so psychology, whose object is the inside subject of all science.[21]

Two key elements in these lines are the "self-cancelling" and the absolute movement of interiorization. Psychology has no "outside," psychology is wholly the matter of interiority. Thus, the "stone that is no stone" is not the "stone" of "natural" consciousness. The alchemical stone that serves at the heart of Jung's psychology belongs to the absolute interiority of psychological consciousness. It belongs to the essence of "the inside subject" of psychology, It cannot be found in "the external" world, the "outside" of the other sciences. The "stone that is no stone" is the boundary-marker, the *herm*, that delinates the difference (Giegerich's "psychological difference") between the immediacy of psychic life and the psyche's self-mediation. Hence, the alchemical *lapis* of Jung's psychology is the negation of the "stones" of so-called "natural" consciousness. The "self-cancelling," the sublative movement, is the dialectical self-overcoming by psychology of itself in order to reach its *telos* as psychology. As psychology it has to overcome the immediacy of psychic life, it has to suffer self-division, a rupture of psychic life within itself.

Jung posits immediacy of experience as our utter enclosure by psychic reality, we are wrapped around completely by psychic images, including this image of absolute interiority. Because of this immediacy, he argues, "primitive man puts spirits and magical influences on the same plane as physical events." Psychic life in this immediacy of experience accordingly comprises an animistic experience of nature, for, Jung asserts, the so-called "primitive" has "not yet torn his original experience into antithetical parts. In his world, spirit and matter still interpenetrate each other, and his gods still wander through forest and field." When Jung speaks of the primivity of "immediate experience" and the reverse, his designation of this notion is logically conditional upon the tearing apart of "original experience." One can speak of "immediate experience" in this sense only after its tearing apart into nature and spirit through the psychological movement from immediacy to mediation. Both terms, nature and spirit, then belong to reflective consciousness, to the soul's self-interiorizing self-mediation. Jung goes so far as to assert that this event of consciousness is foundational for the fateful appropriation of nature in Western thought: "When this aboriginal world fell apart into spirit and nature, the West rescued nature for itself."[22] The tearing or falling apart led or was itself an event in consciousness of the rescue of nature: what can this mean?

Hidden in the alchemical Philosopher's Stone is an incipient philosophy, or better, a theology of nature, but one that carries with it a *pathos.* The West, says Jung, "was prone by temperament to a belief in nature, only became the more entangled in it with every painful effort to make itself spiritual."[23] The alchemical *lapis* was one such cultural site where "spiritualizing" thought suffered (the "painful effort") a greater entanglement, a contradictory pull, with and into nature. The *pathos* of this entanglement was at the same time the rescue of nature. Consciousness found rescued nature not "outside" itself, not as exteriority, but within itself. The "stone that is not a stone" contains nature and its negation within; and through the Stone's intrusion into the realm of spirit, a second negation. This leads to the *concept or idea of nature* as idea in itself. In alchemy, as elsewhere, there is a developing underlying metaphysics of nature. As Dews has put it, as a "form [that] can be appropriately characterized as 'metaphysical,' since it would strive to give us at least some intuition of how nature must be constituted '*an sich.*'"[24] Nature like matter "is not an empirical visible fact. It is already a thought, an abstraction. It is sublated things."[25]

The alchemists, through the notion of the Stone and the other substances of its *opus,* moved consciousness of nature onto a level other than the "natural" or the simplistically *empirical,* the nature of "immediate experience" in the sense of the identity of subject and object—as given in Jung's description of the so-called "primitive." In this way and no doubt others, alchemy's work with nature constitutes an *opus contra naturam.* For alchemy—and Jung's psychology too— had necessarily to work with nature through the *opus contra naturam,* the "work against nature," because alchemy takes the form of a complex of opposites. Alchemy, as Giegerich has pointed out in his *The Soul's Logical Life,* bridges between the ancient and modern worlds with their differing modes of existence and forms of thought.

The "spirit in the stone" and the "stone that is not a stone" embody dialectical tensions which have complexified the idea of nature. The "rescue of nature" of which Jung speaks finds an historical expression in alchemy. Alchemy took up the work with nature through its "work against nature," an "against" that is at the same time a "rescue." When Jung describes Mercurius as a "nature spirit," it is not in the same sense as in the ancient world. For alchemy represented already a radical transformation in our relationship to nature, a radical transformation that expressed itself through its dialectical idea of nature. That is to say, an idea of nature that held together nature as "natural" and yet *not* so. Nature in alchemy, and in psychology, as moments in the history of the consciousness of nature, is not solely what is *given*, "creation," as the *materia* of the alchemical work, it is *open*, still "in the making" ("incomplete," "imperfect"). In alchemy, nature is subjected to its "Promethean ambitions."[26] It undergoes a transformation, a suffering, through the alchemical "against nature," in which nature is subjected to the *artifices* of its praxis and becomes itself an *artifact*.

To speak then within its idea of nature of the "spirit in the stone" or the "stone that is not a stone," alchemy gives recognition to nature as a *nonhuman subject*. The very notion of nature's suffering through subjugation to the alchemical process, the *mortificatio*, suggests the subjectivity of pathos, the suffering spirit or soul of nature.

Yet alchemy, aside from its personifying ways, treats nature, *materia*, as an object; alchemy objectifies. Alchemy's dealings with nature make of it *both* subject *and* object and *neither* subject *nor* object. Its "work against nature" pushes off from the encounter with nature's materiality; its language is drawn from nature's physicality.

Hence, the description of the Philosopher's Stone as the "stone that is not a stone" contains within itself the stonitude of what it negates and transforms to another form of meaning. The actuality of stone is broken down in its discourse and transformed into the alchemical discourse, yet pieces of stone, *fragments*, remain in a way that they cannot be completely assimilated, dissolved, into an alchemical symbol. The materiality of nature, the mystery of its being *resists* appropriation, whilst that very mystery, what is *unsayable,* what remains unsaid, is precisely what the alchemical discourse is pointing towards. The saying of the "stone that is not a stone" undoes itself, is the unsaying of stone, which has always and already incorporated into itself the stone that has become "not a stone." By "becoming," I don't mean a temporal "coming to be," but one that emerges through alchemical logic.

When alchemy speaks of nature, it speaks of what it cannot say, of what cannot be told. A double negation or "not" haunts its *theoria* in the sense that its does not fall into a straightforward silence, but the silence of indirect language. It speaks instead of the *natura abscondita* which alchemy sought to release.[27] Alchemical language, whilst speaking of its *material*, keeps the secret of its mystery.

In his seminal essay on Jung's phallic self-image, Noel recalls for us the many stones in its genesis.[28] Stones figure with Jung's phallic self-image, sometimes as attendants close at hand, sometimes the phallus itself, its symbolic representation. Through his life, work, and writings, Jung allowed a space for the "material imagination" (Gaston Bachelard). With Jung there appears an intimacy and affinity between stone, flesh, and soul, an intimacy and affinity that animate his psychology. At first, there was the dream of early childhood of the underground phallus, "a subterranean God 'not to be named' [negation]," a "mystery of earth," which inhabited "a dark, rectangular, stone-lined hole in the ground."[29] Next came the manikin and his "smooth, oblong blackish stone from the Rhine...painted with water colours to look as though it were divided into an upper and lower half" carried around by the schoolboy Jung.[30] In the psychologically turbulent period after his break with Freud came the return of childhood memories, the recollection of playing with stones. To re-establish a connection with "that child's life," Jung overcame his resistance to playing again with stones as a grown man. He collected stones from the lake shore and its water, building "cottages, a castle, a whole village." Yet when it came to the church's altar, a hesitancy befell Jung. In these activities lay the touchstones of memory. Whilst walking the lake shore, he found "a red stone" worked by "the action of the water," elements of the solid and fluid, permanence and erosion, the effects of a time that has nothing of the human, a time of nature, a pure contingency ("a pure product of chance"). This "red stone" served as the altar, and with it, says Jung, he "recalled the underground phallus of my childhood dream."[31] Then, in later life, building the Bollingen Tower, another stone appeared upon which Jung carved a number of alchemical inscriptions and an eye with a "tiny homunculus" corresponding to "a kind of Kabir, or the Telesphoros of Asklepios."[32] Finally, on its back face, Jung inscribed "*Le cri de Merlin!*" For the stone reminded Jung of "Merlin's life in the forest, after he had vanished from the world. Men still hear his cries, so the legend runs, but they cannot understand or interpret them." Through the stone, Jung claimed a lineage and a legacy that runs from the Merlin figure, whose spirit has withdrawn into nature's depths, through to alchemy and its duplex Mercurius, culminating in his own psychology:

> This cry that no one could understand implies that he lives on
> in unredeemed form…the secret of Merlin was carried on by
> alchemy, primarily in the figure of Mercurius. Then Merlin was
> taken up again in my psychology of the unconscious and—
> remains uncomprehended to this day![33]

The Bollingen stone, this unremarkable remarkable stone, carries upon
its various faces Jung's memorializing work of inscription, the *re-marking*
of an incomprehension that materialized in his psychology, something
obliquely, revealing and concealing itself. In the stone (nature) Jung
marks time (history). The stone gathers to itself different modalities of
time, the elemental weathering, the "once-upon-a-time" of myth, fable,
and legend, biography and historical narrative. Written in stone, Jung
weaves meanings. Yet time also erodes its textures of meaning, time
deconstructs, wears them out. For the stone points to something fleeting
(Mercurius), withdrawn and uncomprehended (Merlin and his cry).

When the writer, Maud Oakes, sought out the "inner meaning"
of the Bollingen stone whilst visiting Jung, she declared "the stone is
Hermes."[34] With such a self-assured assertion, Oakes spoke as if the
collapse of alchemy had never happened, as if "the symbolical unity of
spirit and matter" had not, as Jung observed, fallen apart, resulting in
that estrangement in which "modern man finds himself uprooted and
alienated in a de-souled world," or that it could be simply overcome
by an hermeneutic assertion.[35] As if one could simply take up again
the alchemical and mythic meaning and appropriate it for depth
psychology. Oakes tells what Jung himself said to her of the stone: "The
stone is nothing. I am not an artist; I did it to amuse myself. It is a
holiday thing—as if I sang a stone."[36] How can the one interpretation—
"the stone is Hermes"— be matched to the other — "The stone is
nothing"? Oakes doesn't even say, "the stone *as* Hermes," she affirms a
positivistic interpretation: it *is* Hermes! Jung counters this with his
negation, as self-amusement. Jung speaks right out of the diremption
between spirit and matter, where there was meaning, now
meaninglessness. Indeed, is there not something about the temporality
of stone that breaks through Oakes' unmindful, unhistorical claim the
way elemental time interrupts the continuity of human time? The
ancientness of stone "is of the order of the always already. Stone comes
from a past that has never been present, a past unassimilable to the
order of time in which things come and go in the human world; and

that nonbelonging of stone is precisely what qualifies it to…memorialize such comings and goings."[37] The "nonbelonging" of stone signifies its belonging to the earth as that which withdraws, but which sustains historical time, meaning, symbol, hermeneutics, alchemy, psychology, and so on. It belongs to an originary time, which as Jung shows by his answer, is no stay against the loss of meaning, cannot be appropriated to human time, but which can etch its passage, bear the record of its being and passing. Oakes' affirmation conceals the "unassimilable" antiquity of stone. Were psychology to follow, it would assimilate stone into its own likeness, convert it into a similitude, hiding its alterity, its otherness. Both Hillman and Giegerich, in their different ways, have caught hold of this. Hillman puts it: "the stone does not allow itself to be held in meaning…Its capacity to resist mental penetration is the primary wound to human hybris."[38] And Giegerich:

> 'brokenness' can be seen most blatantly in such phrases as '*lithos ou lithos*' which unmistakenly bring out into the open the incision or wound recklessly inflicted by reflection upon the intactness of the naïve, spontaneous image (here of 'the Stone'). In this phrase, reflection shows in the *ou* ('not'), which cuts into the word in question, negating its very meaning.[39]

One more biographical anecdote: in *Memories, Dreams, Reflections*, Jung recounts how in his garden in childhood "was embedded a stone that jutted out—my stone." A curious dialogue ensued with this interlocutory stone:

> Often, when I was alone, I sat down on this stone, and began an imaginary game that went something like this: "I am sitting on top of this stone and it is underneath." But the stone also could say "I" and think: "I am lying here on this slope and he is sitting on top of me." The question then arose: "Am I the one who is sitting on the stone, or am I the stone on which *he* is sitting?" This question always perplexed me, and I would stand up, wondering who was what now. The answer remained totally unclear, and my uncertainty was accompanied by a feeling of curious and fascinating darkness. But there was no doubt whatsoever that this stone stood in some secret relationship to me. I could sit on it for hours, fascinated by the puzzle it set me.[40]

Elsewhere, Jung elucidates his experience further. When his Mother recalled his childhood depression, he observed his state as more a kind of incubatory brooding:

> It was not really that: rather, I was brooding on the secret. At times it was strangely reassuring and calming to sit on my stone. Somehow it would free me of all doubts. Whenever I thought that I was the stone, the conflict ceased. "The stone has no uncertainties, no urge to communicate, and is eternally the same for thousands of years," I would think, "while I am only a passing phenomenon which bursts into all kinds of emotions, like a flame that flares up quickly and then goes out." I was but the sum of my emotions, and the Other in me was the timeless, imperishable stone.[41]

Like the intrusion of nature as the *alchemical lapis* into the sphere of the spirit, the interlocutory stone here interrupts and disrupts the circle of self-identity, drawing it out of immediacy into a mediation through its *other*. The subject of self-representation becomes displaced, enigmatically located, destabilized. Ego-consciousness is subjugated to the reciprocity of a dialectic of identity and non-identity, which through the language of contradiction ("the stone that is not a stone"), lets the other break through into the innermost of self-identity, the fracture of the unitary ego-image. Jung's dialogue with the stone brings about a self-estrangement in which psychological naivety falls apart into self-division, begetting a complex of two. The anecdote of the stone bears a certain elementary weight as a founding experience in Jung's thought. It expresses a movement of consciousness that initially finds itself in a relationship of externality to the stone: the separate standing between Jung and the stone, independently spread out in time and space, in which Jung visits the stone, sits broodingly on it, then leaves it behind. "Inner" and "outer" stand over and against each other. Yet, Jung's account suggests something else by way of an internal relation. At a symbolic or imaginal level, what figures in Jung's saying is a sense of finitude, his human subjectivity, measured by the immensity of the stone's antiquity. The stone endures, whilst Jung recognizes himself as a "passing phenomenon." As a "passing phenomenon," Jung realizes his own dying return to the earth, the underlying whole that supports his living and dying as well as the enduringness of the stone: earth as the unspoken ground.

The stone then as the internal other, as a philosophical stone, represents an interiorization, not as Jung's own subjectivity, rather here one unlike his own. By affirming his finitude, embodied limitation, Jung's dialogue with the stone points towards an internal relation to the infinite: "The feeling for the infinite, however, can be attained only if we are bound to the utmost. The greatest limitation for man is… 'I am *only* that!'"[42] Such a notion of infinity draws a philosophy of nature into its circle. For it denotes nature's manifold life, in which the round-dance of finite beings arise and perish, in which infinite life, spirit, can only come into existence in this cycle of bodying forth, living and dying. This is where depth psychology touches on a philosophy of nature, for that is what the question of finitude raises, our embodiment. Jung's psychology does not overcome or heal the division between spirit and nature, rather, its task is to deepen our consciousness of it as a dialectical tension, a contradiction, realizing insightfully that tearing apart as the womb of its own conception: "the stone that is not a stone." It feels to me that in Jung's psychology—especially the alchemical psychology of the later years—nature is, and necessarily has to be, taken up in an *unnatural* way, in order to allow for the encompassing interiority which contains its own "outside" within, the soul's absolute interiority.[43]

NOTES

1. Charles H. Kahn, *The Art and Thought of Heraclitus: An edition of the fragments with translation and commentary* (Cambridge: Cambridge University Press, 1981), 33.

2. Wolfgang Giegerich, "Once More 'The Stone Which is Not a Stone:' Further Reflections on 'Not,'" in *Disturbances in the Field: Essays in Honor of David L. Miller*, ed. Christine Downing (New Orleans: Spring Journal Books, 2006).

3. Daniel C. Noel, "Beyond Projection—Jungian Psychology and the Recovery of the Mythic Perception of Nature," in *In A Wayward Mood: Selected Writings 1969-2002* (New York: iUniverse, Inc. 2004), 153.

4. I am ignoring the myth of Medusa and the too neglected work of R. D. Laing in his *The Divided Self,* which takes up the theme of "petrification" as an ontological state of terror.

5. C. G. Jung, *Man and His Symbols* (London: Aldus Books, 1964), 205.

6. *Ibid.*, 207.

7. *Ibid.*, 210.

8. *Ibid.*, 332-3.

9. *Ibid.*, 234.

10. Wolfgang Giegerich, "Jungian Psychology: A Baseless Enterprise: Reflections on our Identity as Jungians," in *Collected English Papers, Volume I, The Neurosis Of Psychology, Primary Papers towards a Critical Psychology* (New Orleans: Spring Journal Books, 2005); also in *Harvest 33, 1987-88, Journal for Jungian Studies* (London: Analytical Psychology Club, London), 91-103.

11. C. G. Jung, *Collected Works of C. G. Jung* (Princeton: Princeton University Press, 1960), Vol. 14, para. 643. [the *Collected Works* are hereinafter referenced as "*CW*," followed by the volume number and the paragraph number].

12. *Ibid.*

13. Jung, *CW* 11 § 759.

14. Schelling, quoted in John Sallis, *Delimitations: Phenomenology and the End of Metaphysics* (Bloomington: Indiana University Press, 1995), 225.

15. Jung, *CW* 11 § 261.

16. C. G. Jung, *Psychology of the Unconscious* (London: Routledge, 1916/1991), § 130.

17. Jung, *CW* 9i § 54; italics mine.

18. Jung, *CW* 10 § 135.

19. Jung, *CW* 8 § 681.

20. *Ibid.*

21. *Ibid.*, § 429.

22. *Ibid.*, § 682.

23. *Ibid.*

24. Peter Dews, "Lifeworlds, Metaphysics and the Ethics of Nature in Habermas," in *The Limits of Disenchantment: Essays on Contemporary European Philosophy* (London: Verso, 1995), 159.

25. Wolfgang Giegerich, *The Soul's Logical Life: Towards a Rigorous Notion of Psychology* (Frankfurt am Main: Peter Lang, 1998), 142.

26. William R. Newman, *Promethean Ambitions: Alchemy and the Quest to Perfect Nature* (Chicago: The University of Chicago Press, 2004).

27. Jung, *CW* 13 § 126.

28. Daniel C. Noel, "Veiled Kabir: Jung's Phallic Self-Image," *Spring 1974.*

29. C. G. Jung, *Memories, Dreams, Reflections*, recorded and edited by Aniela Jaffe (New York: Pantheon, 1963), 11-13.

30. *Ibid.*, 21.

31. *Ibid.*, 174.

32. *Ibid.*, 226-227.

33. *Ibid.*, 228.

34. Maud Oakes, *The Stone Speaks: The Memoir of a Personal Transformation* (Wilmette: Chiron Publications, 1987), 28; also quoted in David L. Miller, "'The Stone Which Is Not A Stone': C. G. Jung and the Post-Modern Meaning of "'Meaning,'" *Spring 1989.*

35. Jung, *CW* 9i § 197.

36. Oakes, *op. cit.*, 15.

37. John Sallis, *Stone* (Bloomington: Indiana University Press, 1994), 26.

38. James Hillman, "Concerning The Stone: Alchemical Images of the Goal," *Sphinx 5* (1993), 250.

39. Giegerich, *Soul's Logical Life*, 134.

40. Jung, *Memories, Dreams, Reflections*, 20.

41. *Ibid.*, 42.

42. *Ibid.*, 325.

43. Wolfgang Giegerich, "Is the Soul 'Deep?'" Entering and Following the Logical Movement of Heraclitus' 'Fragment 45,'" *Spring 1998.*

The Kingfisher

A bird of iridescent light;
of visionary blue; as painterly
as a sunflower, swift
as an arrow.

It longs for the milk of rivers,
kindling the rainbowed air
with feather-bright flame;
subtle-winged, the kingfisher
melting to water.

Unearthly jewelled that builds
its nest in the crux of worlds,
tunnelling the arcane earth;

like its wounded namesake,
sovereign of wastelands, whose chalice
pours its solvent of dreams.

Precision-tooled and cuts
like a blade cleaving the wind;
the sharp percussion of its dive,
plunged in its liquid essence.

—Michael Whan

THE EYES OF THE BACKGROUND NATURE, SPIRIT, AND FIRE-SIDE PSYCHOANALYSIS

GREG MOGENSON

TALKING BY THE FIRE

A younger and an older man sit by the fireplace in the older man's study. Muttering to himself, the older man remarks, "Fire-worship was by no means the most stupid invention." Falling into a reverie, in which he sees all manner of lively shapes in the glowing embers, the younger man readily appreciates the truth of what his mentor has said. He recalls that from childhood to the present he has enjoyed this sort of activity—the "observing [of] strange forms in nature"—"not so much [to] examine them [in the manner of a scientist] as [to] surrender ... to their magic, their oblique message."

> Long tree-roots, coloured veins in rock, patches of oil floating on water, flaws in glass—all such things had a certain fascination for

Greg Mogenson is a Jungian analyst practicing in London, Ontario, Canada. The author of many articles in the field of analytical psychology, his books include *A Most Accursed Religion: When a Trauma Becomes God*; *The Dove in the Consulting Room: Hysteria and the Anima in Bollas and Jung*; *Northern Gnosis: Thor, Baldr, and the Volsungs in the Thought of Freud and Jung*; *Greeting the Angels: An Imaginal View of the Mourning Process*; and (with Wolfgang Giegerich and David L. Miller) *Dialectics & Analytical Psychology: The El Capitan Canyon Seminar.*

me, above all, water and fire, smoke, clouds, dust and especially
the swirling specks of colour which swam before my closed eyes.

Waxing philosophical, the young man continues:

> The consideration of such images as I have mentioned, the
> surrender to odd, irrational forms in nature produces in us a sense
> of the harmony of our being with the will which has been
> responsible for these shapes. Soon we become aware of the
> temptation to think of them as being our own moods, our own
> creations; we see the boundaries between ourselves and nature
> quiver and dissolve and we become acquainted with the state of
> mind when we are unable to decide whether the lineaments of
> our body result from impressions received from outside or from
> within us. In no other practice is it so simple to discover how
> creative we are and to what extent our souls participate in the
> continuous creation of the world. To an even greater extent it is
> this same indivisible divinity which is active in us and in nature
> so that if the outer world were destroyed each one of us would
> be capable of building it up again. For mountain and stream,
> tree and leaf, root and blossom, every form in nature is echoed in
> us and originates in the soul whose being is eternity and is hidden
> from us but none the less gives itself to us for the most part in the
> power of love and creation.

Who is speaking? Some might think of Wordsworth in connection
to this question. In "The Prelude," the poet states:

> To every natural form, rock, fruit, or flower
> Even the loose stones that cover the highway,
> I gave a moral life: I saw them feel,
> Or linked them to some feeling: the great mass
> Lay bedded in a quickening soul, and all
> That I beheld respired with inward meaning.[1]

Or then, again, it might be Emerson. Speaking of the "analogies ...
that ... pervade nature," Emerson writes,

> These are not the dreams of a few poets, here and there, but man
> is an analogist, and studies relations in all objects. He is placed in
> the centre of beings, and a ray of relation passes from every other
> being to him. And neither can man be understood without these
> objects, nor can these objects be understood without man. All
> the facts in natural history taken by themselves, have no value,

> but are barren, like a single sex. But marry it to human history
> and it is full of life.[2]

Wordsworth and Emerson are certainly fellows of the same vision as
our speaker, but we have not yet established his particular identity. To
do this we must draw another comparison.

The comparison I have in mind is to psychoanalysis. The
conversation that the young man and his mentor are having as they
gaze into the fire may be likened to the conversations that occur in the
analyst's consulting room—the language of insight and change being
in large measure a language of image and metaphor. On the heels of
this assertion, however, an objection arises. Being devoid of the kind
of issues that today's therapies conceive themselves to be about, the
fire-side psychoanalysis of these two has more in common with the
poetics of mind explored by Coleridge, the actual originator of the term
"psycho-analysis" more than one hundred years before Freud,[3] than it
has with the science of mind that Freud inaugurated under the same
name. And, yet, Freud does make the very point that the younger man
and the aforementioned authors make, albeit more prosaically than they.
"In psychology," he writes,

> we can only describe things by the help of analogies. There is
> nothing peculiar in this; it is the case elsewhere as well. But we
> have constantly to keep changing these analogies, for none of
> them lasts us long enough.[4]

Sounding a little like our youthful speaker, Freud writes in an 1897
letter to Wilhelm Fliess, "In Aussee I know a wonderful wood full of
ferns and mushrooms where *you* must reveal to *me* the secrets of the
world of lower animals and the world of children."[5] Surely an "oblique
message" lurks in this passage. Just as the expression "the birds and
the bees" is a colloquialism referring to sex, so the "ferns and mushrooms"
in this line bring to mind the important discovery that Freud was
discussing with Fliess at that time: infantile sexuality.

A few years later, in *The Interpretation of Dreams*, the mushroom
analogy appears again:

> The dream-thoughts to which we are led by interpretation
> cannot, from the nature of things, have any definite endings;
> they are bound to branch out in every direction into the intricate
> network of our world of thought. It is at some point where this

> meshwork is particularly close that the dream wish grows up,
> like a mushroom out of its mycelium.[6]

And then there is this, from *Introductory Lectures on Psycho-Analysis*: "The mushroom is an undoubted penis-symbol: there are mushrooms [fungi] which owe their systematic name (*Phallus impudicus*) to their unmistakable resemblance to the male organ."[7] However questionable may be Freud's penchant for finding phallic symbolism everywhere, his finding it in the mushroom or by means of the mushroom is surely compelling.

Continuing to glean insights into the life of the psyche from the "ray of relation" which he half creates, half discovers in the phenomena of the natural world, Freud illuminates the compulsion to repeat, as this expresses itself in instinctual processes, in terms of an analogy to "... fishes ... [that] ... undertake laborious migrations at spawning-time in order to deposit their spawn in particular waters far removed from their customary haunts."[8] In a similar vein, he refers to "the migratory flights of birds of passage."[9] And then there are his comparisons of the psyche to a city built on ancient foundations, to political groupings, military actions, and the like. Something of the same use of analogies can be found in Freud's case studies as well. In this connection we may be put in mind of his dubbing one of his patients a "Wolf Man," another a "Rat Man," and of the fact that Little Hans, the five-year-old boy who so typified for Freud the conflicts associated with the Oedipus-complex, suffered from a horse-phobia and dreamt of twin giraffes.

Similia similibus percipiuntur. That Freud and his patients resorted to such figures in the fire as those we have just mentioned is entirely in accord with the nature of the unconscious, for "it is ... only as something conscious that we know [the unconscious] ... after [that is to say] it has undergone transformation or translation into something conscious."[10]

C. G. Jung concurs with his one-time mentor on the role that analogies play in the life of the psyche and the discourse of psychology. With the animating images that are constantly being thrown up by the psyche in mind, he adds his voice to the same discussion:

> The nature of the psyche reaches into obscurities far beyond the
> scope of our understanding. It contains as many riddles as the

universe with its galactic systems, before whose majestic
configurations only a mind lacking in imagination can fail to
admit its own insufficiency.[11]

In this passage Jung speaks in the broadest possible terms of how
resonant the diverse forms of this riddling universe are with the equally
diverse mysteries of our mental life—the unknown-ness or little known-
ness of the one realm shedding light upon what is unknown or little
known in the other. At other points in his writings, he is more specific,
highlighting now this and now that aspect of our psychic life-world
through the use of a wide variety of concrete analogies.

Examples are legion. In concert with Freud, Jung too draws analogies
between the life of the psyche and birds of passage as when, in a letter
to Freud, he refers to the "age-old animal power which drives the
migrating bird across the sea."[12] In an early paper, in which he discusses
the psychology of the transference, certain aspects of this phenomenon
are highlighted by speaking of them in relation to "the tendencies or
determinants that produce culture in man with the same logic as in
the bird they produce the artfully woven nest, and antlers in the stag."[13]
And then there is his likening of the morphogenesis of the archetype
"to the axial system of a crystal, which, as it were, preforms the crystalline
structure in the mother liquid, although it has no material existence
of its own."[14] Also noteworthy here is his comparing the psyche as "an
objective fact" to such weighty substantialities as "granite and ... lead"[15]
and his extensive amplifications of the tree as a symbol of the human
individuation process.

MULTIPLE LUMINOSITIES

A most important alchemical reference in relation to the
conversation of the young man and his mentor by the fire that we are
amplifying here is to the "scintillae," or sparks, which appeared to the
alchemist "as visual illusions in the 'arcane substance.'"[16] Variously
represented, both in alchemical texts and contemporary dreams, in
such imagery as that of a sea full of fish eyes, "star-strewn heavens,"
and "a regatta at night, with lanterns on the dark surface of the sea,"
the scintillae were interpreted by Jung as multiple centers of partial
consciousness in the unconscious.[17] Though not coinciding with the
ego, which Jung defines as the center of our consciousness, these sparks

of partial consciousness in the unconscious appear to us outwardly as the things of the world that attract our attention, compel our reveries, and stir imagination.

In this connection the reflection of a poet cited by Gaston Bachelard comes to mind: "[e]ach new object, well considered, opens a new organ within us." Commenting on this line, the great philosopher of poetic reverie and author, coincidentally enough, of the famed monograph, *The Psychoanalysis of Fire*, adds: "It is necessary to dream a great deal in front of an object for the object to bring about within us a sort of oneiric organ."[18] Is this what Jung had in mind when he spoke, with reference to the scintillae of the alchemists, of the multiple luminosities in the unconscious?

According to Jung "the unconscious always appears first in projected form,"[19] which is also to say as this, that, or some other thing. Applying this principle to the multiple luminosities in the unconscious, we may readily understand how it is that symbolical images present themselves so ubiquitously to us in and through the richness of the world's offerings. Stooping to pick up a stone from the beach or pausing to behold a bird or a flower: in each of these gestures we meet our infinity in the form at hand even as we raise each at the same time to what Bachelard has called "the rank of companion of man."[20]

Ferns and mushrooms, birds of passage, a stag in the woods that vanishes upon being sighted: like the long tree roots, flaws in glass, and patches of oil floating on water discussed by the young man in his mentor's study, each of these "sparks" or "rays of relation" is a luminous fish eye shining forth from dark depths, a star shining in the blackness of the night sky, a boat lantern on the dark sea.

But let us return to our pair by the fire. Given the references to psychoanalysis that we have just made, it should come as no surprise that the novel from which the conversation we are examining has been quoted—Hermann Hesse's *Demian*[21]— is based upon that author's experience in analysis with an early pupil of Jung's. The older man, identified in the novel as the church organist, Pistorius, is figurative of the analyst of Hesse's actual life, Dr. Bernard Lang, while the younger man in the novel, the youthful protagonist and narrator, Sinclair, is figurative of Hesse himself.[22]

Limiting ourselves for now to just one further excerpt from Hesse's novel, we can readily understand how what Jung meant by the unconscious, active imagination, and the individuation process had been absorbed by the novelist during the course of his work in analysis with Lang. "Look into the fire," declares Pistorius to the youthful Sinclair,

> gaze into the clouds and as soon as the presentiments come to you and the voices within you begin to speak, surrender to them, do not merely ask whether what you are doing suits your teacher or your father or this or that god![23]

GOD'S WORLD

In his great poem, "Ode: Intimations Of Immortality From Recollections Of Early Childhood," Wordsworth recalls "… a time when meadow, grove, and stream,/ The earth, and every common sight,/To me did seem/Apparelled in celestial light, /The Glory and the freshness of a dream."[24] In his memoirs, Jung recalls a similar period of his own childhood.

> … I had grown up … in the country, among rivers and woods, among men and animals in a small village bathed in sunlight, with the winds and the clouds moving over it, and encompassed by dark night in which uncertain things happened. It was no mere locality on the map, but "God's world," so ordered by Him and filled with secret meaning.[25]

Continuing to recall this time, Jung notes that it was apparent to him that "men did not know" that they dwelt in God's world. More sadly still, "even the animals had somehow lost the senses to perceive it."[26] In noting this, Jung again concurs with his poetic forebear. In his account of the wondrousness of a youth spent in the midst of nature, Wordsworth had also included an account of the fading of this "vision splendid" into "the light of common day."

> Earth fills her lap with pleasures of her own;
> Yearnings she hath in her own natural kind,
> And, even with something of a Mother's mind,
> And no unworthy aim,
> The homely Nurse doth all she can
> To make her foster child, her Inmate Man,
> Forget the glories he hath known,
> And the imperial palace whence he came.[27]

Like their owners and masters, the domestic animals that the youthful Jung encountered seemed to him to have suffered a loss of soul. This was evident "in the sorrowful, lost look of the cows, in the resigned eyes of horses, in the devotion of dogs, who clung so desperately to human beings, and even in the self-assured step of the cats who had chosen house and barn as their residence and hunting ground."[28] Perceiving a "ray of relation" between these animals and the men and women who owned and cared for them, it seemed to Jung that

> People were like the [domesticated] animals, and seemed as unconscious as they. They looked down upon the ground or up into the trees in order to see what could be put to use, and for what purpose; like animals they herded, paired, and fought, but did not see that they dwelt in a unified cosmos, in God's world, in an eternity where everything is already born and everything has already died.[29]

Jung's reflections here attest to the gulf he sensed between "God's world" and the world of others who had lost sight of this majesty or, as he also refers to this, the gulf between country life and city life.[30] Though he valued the science he had been introduced to at school, he also vaguely sensed, right from the start, that it led to "alienation and aberration from God's world" and to "a degeneration which [nature's] animals were not capable of."[31] Compared to people, who he was coming more and more to distrust, "animals were dear and faithful, unchanging and trustworthy."

> The earthly manifestations of "God's world" began with the realm of plants, as a kind of direct communication from it. It was as though one were peering over the shoulder of the Creator who, thinking Himself unobserved, was making toys and decorations. Man and the proper animals, on the other hand, were bits of God that had become independent. That was why they could move about on their own and choose their abodes. Plants were bound for good or ill to their places. They expressed not only the beauty but also the thoughts of God's world, with no intent of their own and without deviation. Trees in particular were mysterious and seemed to me direct embodiments of the incomprehensible meaning of life. For that reason the woods were the place where I felt closest to its deepest meaning and to its awe-inspiring workings.[32]

Brimming though it was with what Wordsworth identified as "natural piety,"[33] Jung's vision of "God's world" was not a sentimental vision, innocent of the darker things of life. When, in his later youth, the future psychoanalyst encountered the writings of Schopenhauer, he could readily assent to that philosopher's picture of an in-harmonious cosmos in which a blind, world-creating Will was ruthlessly at work. "This," Jung states,

> was confirmed ... by the early observations I had made of diseased and dying fishes, of mangy foxes, frozen or starved birds, of the pitiless tragedies concealed in a flowery meadow: earthworms tormented to death by ants, insects that tore each other apart piece by piece, and so on.[34]

Such recollections as these of a rural childhood amidst the "earthly manifestations of 'God's world'"[35] may remind us again of Freud's enthusiastic letter to Fliess about being initiated into "the secrets of the world of lower animals and the world of children" in the woods near Aussee. And amplifying these common sentiments of Freud's and Jung's with those of their poetic precursors, we may think as well of Wordsworth's adage identifying the child to be the "father of the Man"[36] and of Coleridge's characterization of the task of the poet as "carry[ing] on the feelings of childhood into the powers of manhood."[37] Arguably, the carrying on of what is here figured as childhood's feelings into manhood's powers, and the finding in the child (*or, rather, in that mode of perception that we figure as "child"*) the "father of the Man," is the task of the psychoanalyst as well.

Powerfully returning in the last years of his life to a consideration of the feelings of childhood that he had carried on into what became analytical psychology, Jung tells of his giving himself over to his unconscious impulses in the period of disorientation following the breaking off of his relationship with Freud, not knowing what else to do. The impulses that arose returned him to the building games of his boyhood. In his tenth and eleventh year, Jung had played passionately with building blocks. Somewhat later he had even "used ordinary stones, with mud for mortar" to build houses and castles. Recognizing, as he put it to himself at that time, that "there is still life in these things" and that "the small boy is still around, and possesses a creative life which I lack," Jung "began accumulating suitable stones ... and started building: cottages, a castle, a whole village."[38] It was through this giving himself over to the playful elaboration of the fantasies arising within him that he once again found himself in that majestic and uncanny mode of being-in-the world that he had known in his childhood as "God's world."

With the discovery of "the small boy" in himself who was "still around," Jung resumed, as an individuating self-relation, the mentoring conversation that had come to grief when it had been enacted as an interpersonal relation between himself and Freud. Misperceiving the boy of the soul as a budding Oedipus, whether he met it in a patient like Little Hans or in a younger colleague like Jung, Freud could not allow the child to be a father of the Man. An exponent of enlightenment consciousness and of the materialistic science of his day, Freud sought to bring these perspectives further to bear by focusing upon the vicissitudes of a child's "enlightenment," as he called it, regarding the facts of sexual life. The result of this was that the creative life of the psyche, such as Jung came to know it through the figure of the boy in himself, was devalued as something defensive, illusory, and perverse.

But the need for a mentor is irrepressible, archetypal. If there is no Pistorius to talk with about stones, tree roots, and the other "irrational forms ... [that] produce in us a sense of the harmony of our being with the will which has been responsible for these shapes," it still may happen that a stone, tree root, or irrational form of some other kind will be one's Pistorius for a time.

Mimetic to the motif of the child's being father of the man, Jung's midlife discovery of the boy in himself was soon followed by a series of encounters with an inner mentor figure that he likened to what in India is known as a "guru." The mentor or guru with whom he conversed, as he picked stones from the edge of the lake, and one day even the body of a dead kingfisher, was a figure with kingfisher wings whom he called Philemon. "Philemon," he writes,

> ... brought home to me the crucial insight that there are things in the psyche which I do not produce, but which produce themselves and have their own life. Philemon represented a force which was not myself. In my fantasies I held conversations with him, and he said things which I had not consciously thought. ... He said I treated thoughts as if I generated them myself, but in his view thoughts were like animals in the forest, or people in

a room, or birds in the air, and added, 'If you should see people in a room, you would not think that you had made those people, or that you were responsible for them.' It was he who taught me psychic objectivity, the reality of the psyche.[39]

Lumen Naturae

Besides the kingfisher he found, that was at the same time the Philemon of his dreams and fantasies, the middle-aged Jung had other mentors. These he came to know through wide reading in religion, mythology, and the history of culture that he had embarked upon as part of an effort to place the auguries of his boyhood and the insights of his fateful, midlife period in a wider historical and intellectual perspective. A most important figure in this regard was the Renaissance-period physician and alchemist, Paracelsus.[40] For Paracelsus (and other thinkers of that time), the analogies and rays of relation that man, in his essence, is both witness to and register of was known as the *lumen naturae,* or Light of Nature. An "invisible light" and "mentoring" consciousness ("the Light of Nature ... is man's mentor"[41]), the *lumen naturae* consisted of sympathetically felt and inwardly drawn comparisons of one thing to another and to another still, *ad infinitum.* Frequently personified as the *"filius philosophorum,"* or "son of the philosophers," for the very reasons we have already discussed with reference to Jung's and Wordsworth's recollections of childhood, the Light of Nature was "the central mystery of philosophical alchemy."[42] Issuing from the macrocosm of life and creation (the *anima mundi* or world soul), and known through the microcosmic vision of an imaginative eye that is marvelously fitted to it (Wordsworth's "vision splendid," Jung's "primordial image"), the Light of Nature was and remains a metaphorical light—the luminous and numinously emotive sheen of likeness itself.

Examples of this sapiential effulgence, which is at once both a "star in man"[43] and "the first and best treasure which the monarchy of nature hides within itself,"[44] are as plentiful as the plenty of this world and the plenty of the human soul. Limiting ourselves to a mere few that come immediately to mind, we may think of the fulsome sense in which snow is known by those who live in closest relation to it. To the Inuit hunter living off the land in the far North and to the Alpine skier as well, snow has as many names as there are analogies to be drawn to the various qualities or states of its being. And this is to say nothing of how the human soul, or "star in man," adds nuancings of its own to these names as it simultaneously out-pictures its qualities and states of being in snowy analogies.

Carrying on now from the Northern snow fields, ice floes, and wintry mountain slopes to the analyst's consulting room for our second example, it may be readily understood that the Light of Nature is a mainstay of the psychotherapist as well. Not only are analogies necessary for conceiving psychological theory, as we have already heard from Freud, they also well up in abundance from within the analyst during the course of his clinical work. Sitting with a patient, the analyst finds himself spontaneously associating to diverse scenes of life that often prove to be indicative of some aspect of the patient's plight or some dimension of the transference.

The imaginal impact of the analytic situation itself—with its fifty-minute hours, fundamental rule, abstinence, and August holidays—may also be read from the images that arise during the course of each hour. In this connection, it may be said that analysts have as many names for silence as Inuit hunters and alpine skiers have for snow. There are pregnant silences and sharp, hostile ones; forlorn silences and warmly shared ones. An especially fine specimen from this list is an expression of Freud's coinage that aptly conveys the resistant quality of the silence that is often present in the first session of an analytic week: "the 'Monday-crust.'"[45]

But let us hear a little more from Paracelsus. Writing with reference to "the auguries of the birds" ... "as when cocks foretell future weather and peacocks the death of their master and other such things with their crowing," Paracelsus writes,

> All this comes from ... the Light of Nature. [And] just as it is
> present in animals and is natural, so also it dwells within man
> ...[who] brought it into the world with himself. He who is chaste
> is a good prophet, natural as the birds, and the prophesies of
> birds are not contrary to nature but are of nature. Each, then,
> according to his own state. These things which the birds
> announce can also be foretold in sleep, for it is the astral spirit
> which is the invisible body of nature.[46]

THE EYES OF THE BACKGROUND

Consciousness, according to Jung, cannot exist "without the perception of differences."[47] The Light of Nature is no exception to this rule. The many names that the things of the world acquire when seen in the light of one another are so many discriminations or particularizations of difference. When tiny, these discriminations of difference, or *notitia* as they were once called,[48] kindle a soft glowing light of reflection within an event, situation, thing, animal, or person. Larger discriminations and greater differences, on the other hand, call the mind more brilliantly to the fore. Like a spark leaping the gap between energized poles, consciousness emerges to unite all manner of differences via spontaneous arcs of comparison.

"… I am like a dog," writes Jung, employing just such a comparison or arc of insight to describe himself.

> [A dog] can be tricked, but he always smells it out in the end.
> This 'insight' is based on instinct, or on a '*participation mystique*'
> with others. It is as if the 'eyes of the background' do the seeing
> in an impersonal act of perception.[49]

We have already met with these "eyes of the background." I refer to our discussion of "scintillae," the sparks or stars that appeared to the alchemist in the arcane substance. Jung's interpretation of these "multiple luminosities" as multiple centers of quasi- or partial consciousness in the unconscious is just as apt with respect to the expressions under consideration now—"impersonal act of perception" and "eyes of the background." As an impersonal act of perception, or a vast set of background eyes, psychological consciousness dawns in that twinkling of an eye (or reflexive turn of some other sense) through which the particular *contents* of one's consciousness—"tree-roots, coloured veins in rock, patches of oil floating on water," and the like—are interiorized to become the *style* or *form* of consciousness.

A poem of a patient in Jungian analysis, who later became an analyst himself, well conveys this reflexive turn from seeing in the mundane sense of empirical perception to seeing and being seen in an impersonal manner by the "eyes of the background."

> Water moistened
> Speak the stones
> The spirits of the stream
> Telling the current where to flow
> Remembering the sea.
> Pluck a dry one from the sand,
> Lick till its eye blinks open,
> And let it watch you run away
> Cross pastures to the ocean.[50]

Just as a stone, when wetted with a little spittle, reveals the beautiful hues that are as the iris of one of the stream-bed's many eyes, so a dog smells out the trail of its quarry, and patients and analysts make soul together, in the Aussee-like woods of the consulting room.

Carrying on from his tracking dog metaphor to explanatory concept, Jung attributes his capacity for impersonal perception and insight to "'instinct,' or ... a *participation mystique* with others." An important entry in the glossary of analytical psychology, the term *participation mystique* was originally an anthropological concept, first introduced into that field by Lévy-Bruhl. Freighted with Eurocentric, colonialistic bias, the term refers to states of animistic or psychic identity between "primitives" (so-called) and ensouled things—organic and inorganic—that make up their world. As adopted by Jung, however, *participation mystique* is not limited to archaic man or indigenous peoples. Though we more easily see it in others than in ourselves, we too are at some level always already enjoined together in a mode of consciousness or of being-in-the-world in which subject and object, self and other, are not unequivocally differentiated, as they supposedly are for the post-Cartesian mentality of modern enlightenment consciousness.

PARABLES, WISE SAWS, AND BARNYARD WISDOM

The Light of Nature is a spirit of knowing that has emerged out of life itself in the register of human witness. Call it what you will—*participation mystique*, natural piety, instinct, animism, or God's world—the gleams of this knowing are the effulgent product of what Jung, carrying something of this mode of knowing forward into our times, has called the "process of analogy-making."[51]

Poems, of course, are filled with analogies, as are proverbs and parables, adages and aphorisms, wise saws, barnyard wisdom, and dreams. Brimming with natural light, each of these forms corresponds to the "eyes of the background"—those luminous fish eyes, boat lanterns, sparks, and stars discussed above.

But how are these "intelligences or sparks of divinity in millions,"[52] as Keats called them, brought forth? Or to ask the same question another way, how are poems and parables, proverbs and the rest made? By wit of man—is that the answer? Much as we may agree with Blake that "where man is not, nature is barren,"[53] to answer with this adage merely begs the question.

In another of his letters, Keats writes that "if Poetry comes not as naturally as the Leaves to a tree it had better not come at all."[54] With this avowal we may heartily agree, but still our question remains. Indeed, far from its being answered another is raised. How, we may now ask, can such naturalness be squared with the movement against or beyond nature which the ladder of poetry so often climbs?

In "The Marriage of Heaven and Hell," Blake strings together a long list of proverbs that he had composed.[55] Though drawn from rural life and the natural world, many of these proverbs reach well beyond that life and world. This is particularly evident when they are quoted today, far from the dells in which Blake first coined them. Gazing at the bottom-line, a C. E. O. declares with Blake, "The cut worm forgives the plow." Advising the President in the Pentagon's war room, a salty old General drives home his position with respect to a foreign policy issue: "The fox condemns the trap, not himself." And, at a case conference a social worker who is attempting to convey the dynamics at play between a family and a school makes the Blakean aside: "The crow wish'd every thing was black, the owl that every thing was white."

Other proverbs from Blake's pen have already pushed off from their immediate origins toward wider meanings. We don't need to imagine them spoken in a different context to sense the transcendental acuity of their metaphors. Just as Blake wrote them, they carry across.

> As the caterpillar chooses the fairest leaves to lay her eggs on, so the priest lays his curse on the fairest joys.
>
> Prudence is a rich ugly old maid courted by Incapacity.

Prisons are built with the stones of Law, Brothels with the bricks
of Religion.

Returning to the questions we formulated above regarding the
emergence of mind and the making of poetry, suffice it to say that the
mind meets itself (and poems and adages are written) as the connections
that are its making coagulate. Or said another way, though drawn from
the plenty of world (the *prima materia*, according to alchemy, can be
found everywhere), the figures that analogy dialectically connects to
create the mind transcend, as mind, their worldly sources, even as the
proverbs we have just quoted transcend theirs. For as one thing is
brought into connection with another, the gravity of their naturalism
loosens its hold upon them. The *Aurora Consurgens*—metaphor—
dawns. And, with this dawning, reason discovers itself, even when it
has nothing to think with but ferns and mushrooms.

Clearly, the "green" philosophy of our woodsy philosophers, poets,
and analytic forebears is *not* the green of naturalism, pure and simple.
On the contrary, like the blue dog that lopes beside these authors as
they stride (the *filius canis coelici coloris* or "puppy of celestial hue"),[56]
it is the preternatural green of a transcendental idealist's palette.

Opus Contra Naturam

An old formula attributed to the alchemist Democritus states that
"Nature rejoices in nature. Nature conquers nature. Nature rules over
nature." Let us bring these reflections to a close by briefly touching
upon this movement as we find it in Emerson, Jung, and the pair by
the fireside in Hesse's novel, Pistorius and Sinclair.

For transcendentalists such as Emerson, nature is not only natural.
Far more than that, it is also "a great shadow pointing always to the
sun behind us,"[57] which is also to say to the intelligible world of insight
and idea, poem and proverb, spirit and God. While being deeply
appreciative of nature, rejoicing in it even, Emerson called those
moments of life the best in which nature, having awakened the higher
powers in man, reverentially withdrew before these as before its God.[58]
"Whole floras," exclaims Emerson,

> all Linnaeus' and Buffon's volumes, are dry catalogues of facts;
> but the most trivial of these facts, the habit of a plant, the organs,
> or work, or noise of an insect, applied to the illustration of a fact

> in intellectual philosophy, or in any way associated to human
> nature, affects us in the most lively and agreeable manner.[59]

Providing a ready example, the poet-philosopher refers to St. Paul's
having used the seed of a plant to speak of the spiritual fate of the human
soul at death — "It is sown in the natural body; it is raised in the
spiritual body."[60] Demurring only a little from this vision of nature
subdued, ruled over, and fully realized in the nature of its apex, man,
Emerson then asks, "Have mountains, and waves, and skies, no
significance but what we consciously give them when we employ them
as emblems of our thoughts?"[61]

If we extend Emerson's last comment to include the whole realm
of the unconscious, Jung, for all his difference in method and approach,
can readily be recognized as a fellow of a very similar conception of the
nature-spirit relation. Indeed, like Emerson, Jung pays an enormous
tribute to the auguries of nature in his writings. We have already
mentioned a few of the many analogies to nature that are drawn in his
works.[62] More compelling even than these are the dreams he amplifies
and interprets that contain animal images and other motifs from the
natural world. The unconscious itself Jung repeatedly describes as nature
in ourselves, as for instance when he writes of contemporary man's need
to "return, not to Nature in the manner of Rousseau, but to his own
nature."[63] As with Emerson, we find also with Jung that humankind
is regarded as the high point of nature, our metaphysical significance
residing in our capacity to make nature conscious of itself even as we
recognize its presence within us.[64]

Jung's vision, however, is far darker than that of the jubilant
Emerson. Where Emerson, finding metaphors everywhere, innocently
preaches his faith in the nature-spirit relation, Jung, in a more hard-
nosed fashion, speaks rather of the problem of their alienation. When
writing about "aphorisms and proverbs," for example, Jung, while being
as aware as were Emerson and Blake that "those sayings or ideals that
store up the richest experience of life and the deepest reflection
constitute what we call 'spirit' in the best sense of the word,"[65] is also
mindful of how such elementary forms of spirit can become abstracted
and totalized, such that their points of view, far from illuminating life
and nature from within, can harden into edicts and ideologies that place
us into opposition to these. And here we may think of how the spirit
that began with Christ as naturalistic parable eventually became the

colonizing civilization of Christianity. "There are all too many cases of men so possessed by the spirit," Jung cautions, "that the man does not live any more but only the spirit, and in a way that does not bring him a richer fuller life but only cripples him."[66] And again,

> Life is a touchstone of the truth of the spirit. Spirit that drags a man away from life, seeking fulfilment only in itself, is a false spirit—though man too is to blame, since he can choose whether he will give himself up to this spirit or not.[67]

Another contrast to the starry-eyed optimism of naturalists of Emerson's ilk (and to the Rousseau-like clamoring of the modern eco-psychologist to have an unmediated experience of nature) has to do with the nature-loving Jung's recognition that humankind's former relationship to nature has been irrevocably lost.

> Through scientific understanding, our world has become dehumanized. Man feels himself isolated in the cosmos. He is no longer involved in nature and has lost his emotional participation in natural events, which hitherto had a symbolic meaning for him. Thunder is no longer the voice of a god, nor is lightning his avenging missile. No river contains a spirit, no tree means a man's life, no snake is the embodiment of wisdom, and no mountain still harbours a great demon. Neither do things speak to him nor can he speak to things, like stones, springs, plants, and animals. He no longer has a bush-soul identifying him with a wild animal. His immediate communication with nature is gone for ever, and the emotional energy it generated has sunk into the unconscious.[68]

The last sentence of this passage is very important. Despite his love of nature, and the enjoyment he took in it at his country home at Bollingen, Jung recognizes that for modern man, "immediate communication with nature is gone for ever," our emotional rapport with it having sunken into the unconscious. The picture here is one of loss. The stones, springs, plants, and animals with which our ancestors lived in the most intimate of relations have fallen into a soul-less silence. We cannot speak to them any more, but only play at doing so. However, as Jung goes on to say, "This enormous loss is compensated by the symbols of our dreams," which "bring up our original nature, its instincts and peculiar thinking."[69]

> The symbol-producing function of our dreams is an attempt to
> bring our original mind back to consciousness, where it has never
> been before, and where it has never undergone critical self-
> reflection. We *have been* that mind, but we have never *known* it.[70]

There are, of course, many implications in this statement for our
stewardship of nature—hence the current interest in Jung among
certain environmentalists. In the essay from which this passage is
quoted, Jung draws a few himself, as, for instance, when he goes on to
suggest that the slogan regarding man's "conquest over nature" rings
hollow.[71] As a psychologist, however, Jung's interest is in nature's
becoming *conscious* in man. A passage from the chapter, "Late Thoughts,"
of his autobiography may be cited in support of this assertion.

> By virtue of his reflective faculties, man is raised out of the animal
> world, and by his mind he demonstrates that nature has put a
> high premium upon the development of consciousness. Through
> consciousness he takes possession of nature by recognizing the
> existence of the world and thus, as it were, confirming the Creator.
> The world becomes the phenomenal world, for without
> conscious reflection it would not be ....

A few lines later, he continues:

> Natural history tells us of a haphazard and casual transformation
> of species over hundreds of millions of years of devouring and
> being devoured. The biological and political history of man is an
> elaborate repetition of the same thing. But the history of the
> mind offers a different picture. Here the miracle of reflecting
> consciousness intervenes—the second cosmogony. The
> importance of consciousness is so great that one cannot help
> suspecting the element of *meaning* to be concealed somewhere
> within all the monstrous, apparently senseless biological turmoil,
> and that the road to its manifestation was ultimately found on
> the level of warm-blooded vertebrates possessed of a differentiated
> brain—found as if by chance, unintended and unforeseen, and
> yet somehow sensed, felt and groped for out of some dark urge.[72]

SINCLAIR'S DREAM

For our final reflection, let us return to Hesse's novel and to the
pair conversing by the fire, Sinclair and Pistorius. As in the Jungian
analysis that this novel is based upon, we are told that the two frequently

discussed their dreams with one another, Pistorius providing an interpretation.[73] One of Sinclair's dreams depicted him as able to fly, but only in such a manner as one who has been flung into the air and has no mastery of such airborne movement. Exhilaration changed to fear as the dream-ego obtained greater height. The dream ended, however, with "the comforting discovery that [he] could regulate [his] rise and fall by holding and releasing [his] breath."[74]

In his interpretation of his young friend's dream, Pistorius equates the dream-ego's capacity to fly with the ubiquitous, if often untapped, potential of humans to aspire to a life of the spirit. This, he explains, is based upon "the feeling of connection one has with every source of power."[75] This statement, I believe, is an allusion to the illuminating power of metaphor (Emerson's "ray of relation"), such as I have been describing in these pages.

Commenting on the lysis of the dream, the part at the end where the dream-ego learns to control his flight with his breathing, Pistorius celebrates this nascent sign of mastery. Being able to steer, both lifts the dreaming Sinclair above the mere man of the pavement and marks his difference from the madman who also knows flight, but only as a "whirl round in the abyss."[76]

Finally, Pistorius discusses the "new organ," the "breath-controller," which the dream has portrayed. This, he says, "shows you how impersonal your soul is down in its depths."

> ... it isn't new. It is a loan. It has existed for thousands of years. It is the fishes' sense of equilibrium, the air-bladder. And in point of fact there are a few strange and primeval genera of fish in which the air-bladder is a kind of lung and can function on occasion in that capacity. It closely resembles the lung you use for flying in your dreams![77]

As Jung himself is reported to have often done, Pistorius then brought Sinclair a volume of zoology to show him the ancient fish he had mentioned. Commenting on the stirring effect of this upon him, Sinclair notes that "with a peculiar shudder I felt conscious of a function that existed in me from earlier stages of evolution."[78]

In his account of Sinclair's dream, as well as in the interpretation that is given of it and the reference to Sinclair's shuddering response, Hesse well conveys the felt-experience of meaning that analysis often provides. In his feeling "conscious of a function that existed in [him] from earlier stages of evolution," the youthful dreamer feels linked back to nature or, as Jung would point out, to the nature in himself, i.e., *psychological* nature.

With further reflection, however, another very different insight is possible. The air-bladder of the fish that has been interiorized into the dreamer, who now uses its principle to fly with, has lifted him up and out of his fish-like immersion in the nature that preceded him. *Contra naturam*, he may now look back upon the former existence of man within or beneath nature in the manner, say, of an astronaut looking back upon the earth from a spaceship or space-station. The question arises: is this the gaze of Aquarius, the water bearer, who has emerged from the waters of nature, and now looks back at these as something that has been surpassed?[79] And Sinclair's flying: is this the sign that the transition from what tradition has called the Age of the Son into the Age of the Holy Ghost has come to pass in psychology's concept of the autonomous psyche?[80]

Remembering that Christianity's sign is the Piscean sign of the fishes, and that the resurrected Christ was himself a flying fish of sorts, let us note with Jung that "the gulf that Christianity opened out between nature and spirit, enabled the human mind to think not only beyond nature but in opposition to it, thus demonstrating its divine freedom, so to speak."[81] Of course, on the heels of quoting this passage it must immediately be added that we are no longer as certain as was Sinclair that "mountain and stream, tree and leaf, root and blossom and every form in nature is [so] echoed in us" that "if the outer world were destroyed each one of us would be capable of building it up again."[82] But without disparaging the hard-won consciousness and freedom that Christianity and the whole effort of Western metaphysics has brought (or turning against them as the modern eco-terrorist is wont to do), let us acknowledge that along with these comes an ever greater responsibility. As Jung expresses this, in words that are all the more prescient today in a world careening toward ecological disaster, "nature *must not* win, but she [also] *cannot* lose."[83]

NOTES

1. William Wordsworth, *The Prelude*, Bk. 3, lines 127-132.

2. Ralph W. Emerson, "Nature," in *Selected Essays*, ed. L. Ziff (New York/Harmondsworth, U.K.: Penguin Books, 1982), 50.

3. Samuel T. Coleridge, *The Notebooks of Samuel Taylor Coleridge*, ed. Kathleen Coburn (London: Routledge and Kegan Paul, 1957-), vol. 2: 2670.

4. Sigmund Freud, *The Question of Lay Analysis,* in *The Standard Edition of the Complete Psychological Works of Sigmund Freud* , ed. & trans. J. Strachey, *et. al.* (London: The Hogarth Press and The Institute of Psycho-Analysis, 1953-73), vol. 20, p. 195 (all subsequent references to Freud's *Standard Edition—SE—*will be by volume and page number).

5. Jeffrey Masson, ed., *The Complete Letters of Sigmund Freud to Wilhelm Fliess* (London: Belknap, 1985), 254.

6. Freud, *The Interpretation of Dreams*, SE 4-5: 525.

7. Freud, *Introductory Lectures on Psycho-Analysis*, SE 15: 164.

8. Freud, *Beyond the Pleasure Principle*, SE 18: 37.

9. *Ibid.*

10. Freud, "The Unconscious," *SE* 14: 166.

11. C. G. Jung, *Collected Works*, trans. R. F. C. Hull (Princeton: Princeton University Press, 1953), vol. 8, para. 815 (all subsequent references to Jung's *Collected Works*—hereinafter *"CW"* — will be by volume and paragraph number, unless otherwise noted).

12. William McGuire, ed., *The Freud/Jung Letters: The Correspondence between Sigmund Freud and C. G. Jung*, trans. R. Manheim and R. F. C. Hull (Princeton, NJ: Princeton University Press, 1974), 294.

13. Jung, *CW* 4 § 665.

14. Jung, *CW* 9i § 155.

15. Jung, *CW* 17 § 303.

16. Jung, *CW* 8 § 388.

17. Jung, *CW* 8 § 388-396.

18. Gaston Bachelard, *The Poetics of Reverie: Childhood, Language, and the Cosmos*, trans. D. Russell (Boston: Beacon Press, 1969), 166.

19. Jung, *CW* 8 § 584. See also *CW* 8 § 507, *CW* 13 § 285.

20. Bachelard, *Poetics of Reverie*, 154.

21. Hermann Hesse, *Demian*, trans. J. Strachan (London: Panther Books, 1969). The passages from this novel with which we began are from pages 97, 98-9, and 99, respectively.

22. For an account of Hesse's analysis with Bernard Lang and later with Jung himself, see Joseph Mileck, *Hermann Hesse: Life and Art* (Berkeley: University of California Press, 1978).

23. Hesse, *Demian*, 103.

24. William Wordsworth, "Ode: Intimations of Immortality From Recollections of Early Childhood," lines 1-5.

25. C. G. Jung & Aniella Jaffé, *Memories, Dreams, Reflections* [hereinafter *"MDR"*], trans. R. & C. Winston (New York: Random House, 1965), 66.

26. Jung, *MDR*, 66.

27. Wordsworth, *op. cit.*, lines 78-85.

28. Jung, *MDR*, 66-7.

29. *Ibid.*

30. *Ibid.*, 66.

31. *Ibid.*, 67.

32. *Ibid.*, 67-68.

33. *Ibid.*, 67.

34. *Ibid.*, 69.

35. *Ibid.*, 67.

36. Wordsworth, *My Heart Leaps Up*, line 7.

37. Samuel T. Coleridge, *Biographia Literaria*, ed. G. Watson (London: Dent, 1971), 49.

38. Jung, *MDR*, 173-4.

39. *Ibid.*, 183.

40. See Jung's long monograph, "Paracelsus as a Spiritual Phenomenon" (*CW* 13 § 145-238) and shorter essay, "Paracelsus the Physician" (*CW* 15 § 18-43).

41. Cited by Jung in *CW* 13, p. 114, note 6.

42. Jung, *CW* 13 § 162.

43. Jung, *CW* 13 § 163, 188.

44. Cited by Jung, *CW* 8 § 390.

45. Freud, "On Beginning the Treatment," *SE* 12: 127.

46. Cited by Jung, *CW* 13 § 148.

47. Jung, *CW* 14 § 603.

48. For a discussion of *notitia* as the "capacity to form true notions of things from attentive noticing," see James Hillman, "Anima Mundi: The Return of the Soul to the World," *Spring 1982*, 85.

49. Jung, *MDR*, 50.

50. The stone that blinks open as an eye when we lick it and which then watches us through the colored iris that is revealed in this manner, brings to mind a passage from Jung: "The organism confronts light with a new structure, the eye, and the psyche confronts the natural process with a symbolic image, which apprehends it in the same way the eye catches the light. And just as the eye bears witness to the peculiar and spontaneous creative activity in living matter, the primordial image [outwardly figured in the things of this world—GM] expresses the unique and unconditioned creative power of the psyche."(*CW* 6 § 748)

51. Jung, *CW* 5 § 203.

52. John Keats, *Selected Poems and Letters*, ed. D. Bush (Boston: Houghton Mifflin, 1959), 288.

53. William Blake, *Selected Poetry and Prose of Blake*, ed. N. Frye (New York: Random House, 1953), 127.

54. Keats, *Selected Poems and Letters*, 267.

55. William Blake, "The Marriage of Heaven and Hell," *Selected Poetry and Prose of Blake*. All proverbs of Blake's quoted in this essay are from this volume, 125-7.

56. Cf. Jung, *CW* 13, p. 232n.

57. Emerson, "Nature," in *Selected Essays*, 71.

58. Emerson, "Nature," in *Selected Essays*, 64: "If the Reason be stimulated to a more earnest vision, outlines and surfaces become transparent, and are no longer seen; causes and spirits are seen through them. The best moments of life are these delicious awakenings of the higher powers, and the reverential withdrawing of nature before its God."

59. *Ibid.*, 50.

60. *Ibid.*

61. *Ibid.*, 53.

62. For a comprehensive account of Jung's thought concerning nature and the psyche, see Meredith Sabini, *The Earth Has a Soul: The Nature Writings of C. G. Jung* (Berkeley: North Atlantic Books, 2002).

63. Jung, *CW* 11 § 868.

64. Cf. Jung, *MDR*, 255-56, 338-39.

65. Jung, *CW* 8 § 633.

66. Jung, *CW* 8 § 645.

67. Jung, *CW* 8 § 647.

68. Jung, *CW* 18 § 585.

69. Jung, *CW* 18 § 586.

70. Jung, *CW* 18 § 591.

71. Jung, *CW* 18 § 598.

72. Jung, *MDR*, 338-9.

73. Hesse, *Demian*, 101-2.

74. *Ibid.*, 101.

75. *Ibid.*, 101.

76. *Ibid.*, 102.

77. *Ibid.*, 102.

78. *Ibid.*, 102.

79. I allude here to Wolfgang Giegerich's analysis of the end of mankind's "in-ness" in nature and of the sublation of this into the *contra naturam* consciousness of Aquarian man. For an in-depth discussion of this, see his "The End of Meaning and the Birth of Man," *Journal of Jungian Theory and Practice*, vol. 6, no. 1, 2004, 1-23. See also Jung, *MDR*, 339-40.

80. For a discussion of the transition into the Age of the Holy Ghost and the aeon of Aquarius see the chapter, "The Sign of the Fishes" of Jung's *Aion*—*CW* 9ii § 127-49.

81. Jung, *CW* 11 § 261.

82. Hesse, *Demian*, 99.

83. Jung, *CW* 13 § 229.

THE SNOW WOLF

Over its skull, the snow wolf wears a crown
of winter, masking its lean existence
with white sleep, a timeless interval.
For eyes, a fallen truth,
keen as an owl. And where it looks,
far to the earth's rim, the surprise of space,
bright with the cold lantern
of the North Star. One of its kind
came visiting in a dream,
left its paw marks on the stairway;
signs of a vanishing kingdom,
a fragile zone. Across the years,
I can still see its fur beaded with frost,
it was so near, that veiled look of too much knowing,
the folds of its gentle hood.

—Michael Whan

OWL CRY

In the wind's echo,
I heard the owl cry,
as if all existence kept
in its taloned breath.
Stone, leaf, bird,
these are the wild keepers of the earth,
and we alone in the dark
like those answering owls,
the vast night cradling us,
while our restless dreams
invent the dawn.

—Michael Whan

Trans-Species Psychology: Theory and Praxis

G. A. BRADSHAW & MARY WATKINS

In the dream, the elder was joined by the animals of the forest and desert. One by one they came to sit around him: the stag, the bear, the mountain lion, the birds, the snakes, and others. As they gathered around, the animals spoke of their grief and broken hearts as they saw what human people were doing to the land and waters. The animals had come to the elder to tell him that their grief was so great that they were leaving the earth. The animals felt they had no place in a world without soul and one sculpted bare by humans absorbed in violence and destruction. As the tribal members listened to the elder's vision, they too were overwhelmed with sorrow. The elder exhorted the tribe to call the animals back before it was too late.

—Lakota Sioux Elder

G. A. Bradshaw, Ph.D., Ph.D., is a faculty member in the Depth Psychology Program, Pacifica Graduate Institute, and the Environmental Sciences Graduate Program, Oregon State University. Her research and teaching focus on trauma recovery, cultural conservation, and psychotherapy of elephants, parrots, and primates. She is completing a book on *Elephant Breakdown: The Psychological Study of Animal Cultures in Crisis*. Descriptions of current and past work and publications are found at her website www.kerulos.org. Her work on elephant trauma was recently featured in the *New York Times,* October 8, 2006.

Mary Watkins, Ph.D., is a core faculty member and the Coordinator of Community and Ecological Fieldwork and Research in the M.A./Ph.D. Depth Psychology Program at Pacifica Graduate Institute. She is the author of *Waking Dreams, Invisible Guests: The Development of Imaginal Dialogues*, the co-author of *Talking With Young Children About Adoption,* and a co-editor of *Psychology and the Promotion of Peace*. She has worked as a clinical psychologist with adults and children, and with small and large groups around issues of peace, envisioning the future, diversity, vocation, and social justice.

INTRODUCTION

P sychology is an all-encompassing discipline because it embodies how and why we each perceive and experience the world. Individual experiences inform our relationships and how we live. While *psych*ology lies at the heart of all of psychology schools, each defines "psyche" and "soul" uniquely. These definitions frame how psychological understanding and healing are approached. Conventionally, psyche has been restricted to humans and bounded by the paradigm of individualism. A range of new writers stress the need to release psyche from identification with solely human subjectivity. Archetypal psychologist James Hillman returned to Platonism to emphasize that each being—human, plant, animal, and man-made—has a soul spark.[1] Arne Naess offered the concept of an ecological self to emphasize how human subjectivity cannot be properly conceived of apart from animals.[2] Diverse cultural workers such as Vandana Shiva, Wangari Maathai, and Grace Lee Boggs from Kenya, India, and the United States have brought repeated attention to the interdependence of human psychological health and ecological renewal.[3]

These efforts are based on a well-being that re-envisions psyche existing across humans, animals, and nature. But while ecopsychology often reflects on environmental destruction—the devastation of forests, pollution of water and air, and degradation of soil—extinctions of individual animals and their communities are too often omitted. Rather than acknowledging the individuality and diversity of myriad species, psychological discourse maintains nature in generic anonymity: more like a scenic backdrop or an afterthought in the abstract. The construct of psyche decoupled from other species precludes interspecies' relationships with animals in ways other than as object or projection. Not only is human healing undermined, but the deep psychological suffering sustained by animals through such objectification is ignored.

Psychologies of liberation have been developed to help understand the psychical impact of oppression on humans in colonialism and in its present form as transnational capitalism. Such psychologies argue that individual liberation is not possible while simultaneously oppressing others. But they too have disregarded the similar oppression, marginalization, exploitation, forced migration, and genocide that animal communities experience. When Paolo Freire proposed his pedagogy of the oppressed in Brazil, he explicitly differentiated humans from animals, excluding them from the sphere of concern.[4] Ironically his descriptions of animals as lacking history and future, intention and reflection, are not unlike racist colonial descriptions of "natives" submerged in an endless present and merged with the natural world in a presymbolic manner: a "description" his work underscores and critiques. Similarly, when Ignatio Martín-Baró wrote that psychologists need to "make a contribution toward changing all those conditions that *dehumanize,*" he did not have in mind animals and our relations to them.[5] His discourse was limited to human conditions of poverty, violence, and injustice. Human concerns have placed animal suffering as unfortunate, but inevitable, collateral damage.

Congruent with depth and liberation psychologies' call to prioritize "what or who has been marginalized,"[6] we bring attention to the marginalization of animals and those aspects of psychology that exclude nonhuman species. The impetus to engage a liberation *eco*psychology derives from ethical and psychological considerations. *Psychology, by maintaining an agenda of speciesism, violates one of its central projects: individual development of moral consciousness.*[7]

Connecting the liberation work of Freire and Martín-Baró with ecology brings us to the question of the psychic toll endured by animals through human oppression, and, in its trans-species form, into the project of psychology. This expansion is consistent with historical analyses that show how liberation movements are always partial and require continued efforts to include the marginalized. Liberation movements are often themselves exclusionary, as for example, early American efforts to establish liberty left out both women and people of color (Native Americans, Africans, Chinese, and Mexicans). The animal rights movement calls attention to the exclusion of animals and their liberation.

We approach this imposed absence through the concept of a trans-species psyche and its praxis, which engages the principles of liberation and eco-psychologies together.[8] The model of the trans-species psyche explicitly names the interpenetration of human and animal domains in parity absent the assumption of ascendance.[9] Our intent is to articulate a trans-species psychology—a theory and praxis—in which the interdependence and well-being of humans and animals can be understood in parity, in the language, concepts, and practice of psychology.

We illustrate how a trans-species psychology might express as a multi-species praxis in the description of individuals working in African Elephant recovery. Like their neighboring human tribes, Elephants suffer deeply from the effects of violence that became systemic with European appropriation.[10] Borderland[11] people—individuals who psychologically and physically live across the species divide—such as evoked in animal rescue work illustrate alternative ways of being and knowing that are not bound by human privilege.

Much as liberation psychologists are asked to help change conditions that dehumanize, trans-species' psychologists are called to address conditions that de-nature humans by separating them through false species' distinctions. A trans-species psychology embeds humans in the continuum of nature through the disavowal of human privilege, thereby admitting to "the great principles of liberty, equality and fraternity over the lives of animals... [and letting] animal slavery join human slavery in the graveyard of the past."[12] Animal liberation is part of the critical step toward our own and other species' psycho-ecological health. By engaging in this liberatory work, there is a conscious embrace of psychological theory and praxis that is trans-species and understands animals as individuals deserving empathy, respect, and concern.

Psychology and Speciesism

For millennia, western views have held humans apart from all other species. But this is changing. Definitional boundaries are beginning to blur even in science where the human-animal divide has been strongly enforced. For example, stem cell researchers worry about mixing neuronal and psychological capacities of humans with other species in the creation of hybrid chimera. At the same time, new genome analyses bring human and chimpanzees almost to identity. Commenting on these recent findings, one Australian anthropologist reflected that "it could be possible for humans and chimps to have sex and produce offspring, although there would be ethical problems." Implicit in this almost casual statement is a profound observation. The remaining barrier separating chimpanzees from humans has begun to cease as a scientific issue and be understood in terms of ethical deliberation. However, this adjustment brings a certain sense of discomfort.

Three decades before the genome studies, when Jane Goodall reported on anomalous chimpanzee behavior, the news was received with startled interest mixed with reservations. Chimpanzees in Gombe, Tanzania, were gang-killing other chimps. Particularly disturbing were the accounts of the mother and daughter team killers, Passion and Pom, who killed and ate infants. Chimpanzees were behaving in very unpleasant, *human*like ways: exhibiting what appeared to be psychopathology. Today, nonhuman primate infanticide has been absorbed into scientific theory as normative behavior and has contributed to the expansion of evolutionary models to include psychology. But the concept of animal psyche is not entirely settled.

The use of the term psychopathology—not symptom—is important because psychopathology insists on attention to psyche, something that has been denied to all species except for humans. While animals play an important role in human myths and are used to symbolize aspects of human experience, they are relegated to psyche's periphery and excluded from psychological models except when used to assert human uniqueness and ascendancy. C. G. Jung's model of collectivity and psyche perhaps brings the clearest articulation:

> The various lines of psychic development start from one common stock whose roots reach back into the most distant past. Theoretically it should be possible to peel the collective unconscious, layer by layer, until we come to the psychology of the worm, and of even the amoeba. [13]

Jung's conceptualization connects psyche across species but does so by conforming to biomedical and cultural models of progressive evolution.[14] Psychological intersection between humans and other species in these models are permitted only in the common roots of instinct. Humans are related to animals only "from below [where] we trace back through our line of descent."[15]

The surprise from Gombe, therefore, was not chimpanzee aggression but the intentionality of violence—behavior that extended consideration of animal psychological experience beyond biological instinct. By definition, such behavior was un-natural because only humans are defined as lying outside nature; humans alone have been considered to possess the capacity to be un-natural. The fact that evolutionary theory was changed to accommodate nonhuman primate infanticide, thereby normalizing what was otherwise anomalous behavior for an animal, testifies to the resistance to acknowledging how close human and animal experiences may really be.

Even while maintaining human supremacy, C. G. Jung understood that the psychic loss of connection with nature had occurred by virtue of western worldviews.

> As scientific understanding has grown, so our world has become dehumanized. Man feels himself isolated in the cosmos, because he is no longer involved in nature, and has lost his emotional "unconscious identity" with natural phenomena… His contact with nature has gone, and with it has gone profound emotional energy that this symbolic connection supplied.[16]

Today, we no longer "seek animals' advice but, rather, require them to conform to our standards. We may 'love' them but domination is the strongest imperative in many of our interactions with them."[17]

Domination is a central theme in western understanding. The domination of nature is found throughout the archetypal images and fantasies of western human identity and *mythos*: the pioneer, the conquest of Nature through colonialization, and Nature as *terra nullis*—empty wilderness.[18] Symbol, myth, and cultural habits are deeply engrained in concepts of human and individual identities. Practices of speciesism begin early in childhood when "we begin a lifelong work of differentiating ourselves from [animals]."[19] Through a succession of collectively mediated disconnections, the human psyche becomes increasingly experienced as anthropocentric: a process that is defined by and demands the denial of animal agency and their reduction to the status of objects.

Psychology participates in speciesism by ignoring individual and personal animal psyche except in the form of colonized fragments as projections (e.g., anthropomorphism), symbol (e.g., mythic figures), or physical objects (e.g., laboratory animals) whose identities are shaped by human need. The pervasiveness of anthropocentrism is subtle. Margot McLean, in dialogue with James Hillman in their book *Dream Animals,* brings attention to the ways in which psychology translates animals from being perceived as psychological beings to beings in psychological service to humans:

> I wouldn't want to forget about the real fox. I think it is important to see the same respect given to the real animal wherever it appears. I think it is important to see the animal as you do in dreams, but dream animals must not be segregated from the animals living out back under your porch or in the bush...One must be careful when adopting an "inner" animal that the connection to the animal world is not reduced to a feel-good-about-me condition.[20]

In another example, a psychiatrist argues for "integrating animal images so that [we] can experience them as part of [ourselves]" and "to become the animal incarnate."[21] Even while seeking a restoration of *anima mundi*, such imaging can threaten psychological phagocytosis by imprisoning animals through definitions of and for the human psyche if animal agency and their psychological boundaries are not respected.

Consequently, bound in speciesism, individuation remains tethered to collective definitions of psyche, thereby violating a key project in depth psychology: individual development of moral consciousness. Locating ethical authority in collective mores "deprives the individual of the moral decision of *how to live his own life*" where "without [such] freedom there can be no morality."[22] By retaining animals as colonized fragments defined by human utility, psychology denies animal individuation and excludes animal agency from the creation of the ethics of everyday living.

New scientific evidence and political movements have begun to disable many epistemic arguments used to support psyche as a uniquely human possession. Science and society are converging on the idea of brain and psyche as trans-species.[23] Recognizing the trans-species nature of psyche removes presumptions that allow animal objectification and undermines rationales used to withhold animals' rights. This shift, however, raises several challenges. Dismantling human-animal psychological difference unravels a primary cultural organizing principle. Human-animal differencing comprises much of what defines western human collective identity and an ego construct based on what animals are presumed to lack. A theory of a trans-species psyche does not erase species differences—differentiation is how we decide what to eat, with whom to live, and how to live—but the epistemic logic informing core cultural and political agendas based on human privilege is significantly eroded.

LIBERATION PSYCHOLOGY AND THE ANIMAL RIGHTS MOVEMENT

Martín-Baró argued that liberation psychology begins by acknowledging that psychology itself must be liberated. Liberation is understood as actions and ways of thinking that do not require subjugation of an Other: a psychology whose theory and praxis is not contingent on exclusion or domination for its legitimization.[24] The transformation of how one perceives, thinks, deliberates, and acts necessarily engages both the oppressor and the oppressed. In this manner, liberation psychology engages the empowered and disempowered in mutual transformation. Echoing C. G. Jung's concept of individuation, Martín-Baró maintains that "[c]onsciousness is not simply the private, subjective knowledge and feelings of individuals" but relational.[25] However, historically, the relational basis of psychological transformation is often overlooked or represented in terms of individualism, not individuation.

The prevalent construct of individualism that forms the base of many psychological theories has tried to understand individuals with little cultural context and even less nature context. This decontextualization has meant that psychological theories and practices carried within them the seeds of the very pathologies from which its patients suffered.[26] This has been the case, for example, in the interpretation of black people in white people's dreams where often a similar lack of regard for the individuals symbolized has been carried.[27]

In contrast, psychologies of liberation have sought to work from an interdependent paradigm of the self. Rather than understand an individual solely in the light of their intrapsychic experience, their early family experiences, or even their biochemical dispositions, liberation psychologies assert that to understand individuals we must understand the historical and cultural context in which they live their daily lives. Further, it is necessary to decode prevalent ideologies that affect us or others psychically to fully grasp the roles they play. Psychology is urged not to limit individual change as a process in isolation, but rather facilitate the process as an ethical dynamic between an individual and their environment.

A liberation ecopsychology consciously expands the context of psyche to include consideration of conditions that oppress nonhuman species. Animal rights is "a liberation movement [that] demands an expansion of our moral horizons, so that practices that were previously regarded as natural and inevitable are now seen as intolerable."[28] By releasing psychology from collective assumptions of human privilege, we understand nature as peopled by psychological individuals of diverse specieshoods. Biological differences are re-conceptualized as extended definitions of cultural diversity. Psychologists are asked to refrain from the exploitation of other species as natural and inevitable and instead to ask for:

> a complete change in our attitudes to nonhumans [and] demand that we cease to regard the exploitation of other species as natural and inevitable, and that, instead, we see it as a continuing moral outrage.[29]

Linking ecopsychology with a liberation movement challenges the moral compromise implicit in psychological practices and theories based on speciesism. To uncouple psychology from the collective agenda of speciesism means to de-center from anthropocentrism and therefore compels a re-design of psychology so that the struggle, suffering, and aspirations of nonhuman individuals become integral to psychology's project.

AFRICAN ELEPHANT TRAUMA AND RECOVERY: TRANS-SPECIES RELATIONS

For over half a century, Daphne Sheldrick and the Elephant Keepers at the David Sheldrick Wildlife Trust have worked to rescue and rehabilitate orphaned Elephants.[30] Most Elephants arrive after experiencing severe trauma directly or indirectly caused by humans. Massive culls (systematic killing of Elephants to control population), translocation, altered habitat, hunting, and ivory and meat poaching have caused Elephant populations to drop in the last century from an estimated 10 million to less than half a million. Beyond statistics, it is difficult to deny that Elephant society is breaking down. As one African Elephant researcher sadly noted, outside a few parks, there are no normal Elephant herds left.

Similar to humans suffering genocide and war, Elephants are exhibiting symptoms related to social trauma.[31] Young male Elephants, orphaned by culls, killed over one hundred rhinoceroses in South Africa. Elsewhere, diminished mothering skills, infant neglect and rejection, and other asocial behavior have been observed. Elephant intra-species male-on-male mortality exceeds 70-90% compared with no to little mortality in relatively undisturbed landscapes. Some Asian Elephants raid villages for vats of alcohol, leading to alcohol causing uncharacteristic behavior such as "separations from [the]herd groupings and changes in ....behavior..[such as] decreased feeding, drinking, bathing and exploration for most animals [and increased] inappropriate behaviors such as lethargy and ataxia."[32] In India, "marauding Elephants" in Assam have killed 605 people over the past twelve years and over 300 people in Jharkhand in the past four years. Daily reports describe Elephants frantically storming villages and stalking lorries in search of food because of starvation.[33]

The relatively benign co-existence between human and Elephants of pre-colonial times has turned into civil war. Human on Elephant violence is considered so pervasive that a formal term has been coined to describe inter-species strife: Human-Elephant Conflict (HEC). Once revered as gods in Asia, Elephants are now regarded with hostility. The log book of one Indian veterinarian records scores of Elephant deaths that occurred after "torturing and shock induced by mahouts and other people, blood poisoning caused by torturing as well as arthritis, undernourishment and too strenuous work, shots from the police, constipation caused by wrong nutrition, electrocution, an explosive device in the Elephant's mouth."[34]

People at the Trust are working to redress the effects of this breakdown: indeed save Elephant culture from extinction. The Elephants who come to the Trust survive only because of human assistance. It is a time of both physical and emotional distress:

> The babies are always severely traumatized on arrival, often having witnessed the violent massacre of their Elephant family... [T]hey inevitably enter a period of deep grieving for their lost loved ones, something that can last for months. Not all calves can be persuaded to make the effort to try to live.[35]

One rescued orphan, Imenti, was literally born through trauma and into terror, born while tribesmen were hacking her mother to death and brought to the Trust Nursery still covered by foetal membranes.

The Trust is staffed by Elephant Keepers. These are Kenyan men who substitute for traditional Elephant allomothers—constellations of female Elephants comprising the natal herd responsible for the rearing and teaching of young wild Elephants. The Keepers are responsible not only for the infant's physical survival but for re-creating Elephant family life.

> It is very important that the young Elephants are psychologically stable, because if not, the wild herds will not want them. The key to this is the replacement family during infancy and 24 hour contact with their Keepers…. when the Elephants and their Keepers go as a group free ranging, but at night the Keeper will sleep with each Elephant in its stable.[36]

The Keeper-Elephant bond cannot be underestimated. In the event that a Keeper "has time off, or is sick, the Elephant will grieve and go into a decline" and behave like he or she is losing another family member.[37]

Rescue work at the Trust is distinguished from many other animal rehabilitation efforts because it recognizes the need for Elephant psychological care and healing. The Trust work describes conscious attention to psychological work with another species and thereby acknowledges psyche that is not bound to humans alone. Through relating to each other psychologically absent the agenda of human domination, Elephants and Humans suggest the beginnings of an interspecies culture where the power of mothering—irrespective of gender and species—is able to regenerate in the absence of traditional families. Humans have stepped in to help mend the holes in Elephant society created by Human violence.

Human mothering of Elephant infants relates to other cultural recoveries necessitated by similar experiences of community breakdown. For centuries, African people were also culled, had lost elder leadership, and were translocated as slaves to foreign lands. African traditions of non-nuclear family adult-child relations have provided some measure of resilience to traumatic attacks on the family by slavery, AIDS, famine, and separation of family by forced migration in these situations. These traditions call for children to be nurtured not only by their biological mothers but by "Othermothers," members of the extended community.[38] Where children have lost their mothers or where their mothers' attention is impaired by oppressive circumstances, Othermothers come to the fore. In the United States, Othermothers have provided a mothering constellation that is crucial in communities negatively impacted by the legacies of slavery. Othermothers rear their own and others' children and in the process, stitch together traditions with new world landscapes.

By combining western, tribal, and Elephant knowledge and experience, the Keepers cultivate social and ecological Elephant knowledge that is challenged by the human impacts on the environment. This knowledge is vital for the young Elephants so that they will know how to live, what to eat, how to be in healthy relationship again, and be an Elephant when they re-join wild herds. Like African-American Othermothers, the Keepers "provide road maps and patterns, a 'template'" which enables the Elephants "to create and define themselves as they moved from childhood through adolescence to adulthood."[39] Connection does not stop once the young Elephants re-join the wild herds. Traditionally, older Elephants bring younger herd members to visit the bones and skulls of family who have died.[40] In like fashion, many reintroduced Elephants return to the Trust with their young to meet their human relatives.

While some of the rescued orphans die, the Trust remarkably has saved over seventy Elephants and rhinoceroses. These survivors, as well as their human counterparts, live and raise families to pass on their experiences across successive generations.

TRANS-SPECIES PSYCHOLOGY: EPISTEMES, PRACTICES, AND CULTURAL CHANGE

It important to grasp the depth to which a trans-species psychology challenges practices in psychology, science, and culture at large. A trans-species psychology profoundly deconstructs foundational premises upon which globalized cultures, and much of psychology, are built in several ways. One of the most critical aspects of liberation ecopsychology is its charge to bring animal psychic well-being into the project of psychology. In so doing, it asks for a reconciliation of psychological theory and practice to serve human and animals equally.

In the main, animal well-being has been considered the territory of veterinary medicine and conservation science. These professions conventionally deny animal psyche and view collectively sanctioned methods such as culls, laboratory experimentation, and translocations as legitimate and necessary practices. Similar assumptions employed elsewhere in the history of slavery, labor abuses, and violence against women and children were also once part of cultural norms but later understood as profound abuses.

The trans-species psyche views both animal and human psyches as subjects of psychology's commitment to healing and care. It therefore disabuses the notion of psyche as uniquely human and throws into question the power differential that permits the sacrifice of animal objectification. Denying animals their full status as psychological beings is understood as a belief that abets animal exploitation. By recognizing a shared subjectivity, psychology ceases to be a solely a human enterprise and animals enter the sphere of psychological concern. This move prepares for what Martín-Baró's identifies as two requisite steps for deconstructing psychological and cultural privilege: the creation of a new episteme (a new way of seeking knowledge) and a new praxis. The task at hand is, given that so many of its methods are predicated on human cultural idiosyncrasies, how will psychology be able to serve animal psyches without their marginalization?

Much of psychology's methodology is tailored to meet not just human but Euro-American criteria[41] and thereby disallows animal cultures from participation. Science's epistemic model, to which much of psychology still adheres, "unfortunately, does not link knowledge and morality, but rather it connects knowledge and power and makes them equivalent."[42] Clearly an episteme and discipline, science and psychology, respectively, that have based much of their learning on animal experimentation is inappropriate. A trans-species psychology therefore compels the recreation of an epistemic basis alternative to the exclusionary aspects of science: one where the "fundamental horizon for psychology as a field of knowledge is *concientization.*[43]

Concientization "characterizes the process of personal and social transformation of the oppressed."[44] In terms of the trans-species model of psyche, this advocates for clarifying an ethical and practical re-orientation of western culture, episteme, and ontology that eschews the assumption of human ascendance and prioritization of human benefit. By understanding animals in psychological parity with humans and not as reduced, surrogate forms of human experience, psychology desists from such practices and models. Science and knowledge-making emerge as consciously relational processes that are accessible to both animals and humans. A multi-species science and *ethos* includes other species as partners in decision making, culture-making, and community meaning making. This brings us to another critical move in articulating praxis of trans-species psychology: the de-privileging of human language.

Trauma studies have underscored the importance of therapeutic relationships where psychological recovery can be supported without objectification of the injured (e.g., witnessing).[45] However, even such practices rely on the ability to hear, relate, and exchange experience symmetrically. Given the degree to which language plays a pivotal role in such relational exchange in psychology, how is interspecies dialogue to be comparably envisioned?

Euro-American cultures are heavily invested in spoken and written language. Indeed how human language is regarded has been used to define human superiority and animal oppression. Many channels with which humans have historically connected with nature have been lost through industrialization.

> Thunder is no longer the voice of an angry god, nor is lightening his avenging missile. No river contains a spirit, no tree is the life principle of a man, no snake the embodiment of wisdom, no mountain cave the home of a great demon. No voice now speaks to man from stones, plants and animals, nor does he speak to them believing they can hear.[46]

A liberation ecopsychology insists upon the de-privileging of human language and a renewed reconnection with all other beings. Michael Cohen writes that such:

> reconnecting with nature consists of bringing into your consciousness a sensory way of thinking and relating with which you are born. Moment by moment…nature produces consensual relationships at every level from microorganisms to natural people to weather systems. It is the process that nature uses to sustain its diversity peace and sanity.[47]

To be able to hear and speak across species bounds is to encourage modalities that permit such exchange. Most of these modalities—the wordless unconscious, smell, touch, sight, taste, other types of vocalizations (fifty-three by Cohen's count)—have atrophied in postmodern human culture but are increasingly acknowledged as core to human communication. Through the marginalization of other communication modalities, psychology has pathologized non-European peoples as well as animals.[48]

Many peoples have ways of communicating that facilitate exchange with other species. Aboriginal peoples of Australia practice *dajirri*: an "inner deep listening, a knowledge and consideration of *community* and the diversity and unique nature that each individual brings to *community*. It is communication for community benefit, not for lone individuals. The principles of reciprocity in *dajirri* are informed by the responsibilities that come with knowing and living *dajirri*.[49]

A liberation ecopsychology is informed through such listening and other modalities of communication engaged by individuals such as Elephant healer, Elke Riesterer. By shaping her therapeutic methods to the body and psyche of Elephants, Elke is able to translate human healing practices across species.[50] Elsewhere in the USA, the director of The Elephant Sanctuary in Tennessee, Carol Buckley, works in the recovery of severely traumatized, older captive Elephants rescued from zoos and circuses. She has created a process that supports Elephant individuation as they begin to process the decades' long layers of physical and psychological suffering. Key to these processes is her support of Elephant agency and concomitant deconstruction of any human-imposed power differential. She has changed her ways of being and listening from mainstream culture in order for Elephant healing to occur.[51]

These examples illustrate the creation of open, cross-species access to communication, mutual agency, and the emergence of a trans-species psychotherapy. Such practices, however, oppose a principle that is forcefully maintained by the mainstream culture: a human ego identity and ontology intact and apart from all else. Elephant trauma recovery at the Trust and the Sanctuary defy this position and the conventional myth that prolonged, intimate human contact is deleterious to wild animals.[52]

Conventional scientific models do not support intentional interspecies bonding nor do they legitimize interspecies communication that does not maintain a power differential. To engage in such is considered anthropomorphism, the practice of considering that animals share human experience and that is considered to be a serious breach of science. Affective and psychological aspects of interspecies transactions that blur species' boundaries, such as Keeper-Elephant bonding, have been a source of controversy for years.[53]

Orphan rehabilitation practices at the Trust, however, are consistent with psychobiological studies on infant development and care.[54] Human health workers consider these types of transactional rearing essential elements for supporting healthy psychological, behavioral, and neurobiological development.[55] The Keepers' attachment re-patterning with the traumatized infant Elephants transforms growth inhibiting (i.e., loss of Elephant family) into growth promotion (i.e., Keeper allo- and othermothering bonding) experience that characterizes relational healing. Through committed care and love, infant Elephants are encouraged to develop psychological agency and self-empowerment—factors that are considered key to human trauma recovery.[56] When applied through the conceptual lens of a trans-species psyche, psychobiological models[57] describe Elephant psychological recovery and brain-behavior development through the process of interacting Human and Elephant psyches. The Keepers emulate mother Elephants but their own scent, touch, customs, personality, ways of being, and ways of interacting are in dialogue with the developing Elephant self through socio-affective dialogue.

Psychology is moved beyond collective images that rigidly separate humans and other species to an ecological self.[58] Walls holding apart theory, practice, and professions of human and animal healthcare in the past begin to disintegrate at places like the Sanctuary and the Trust. These new approaches and models of interaction extend outside the therapeutic context to the conservation of Human and Elephant communities.

Most conservation models proposed to address Elephant and Human conflicts remain embedded in colonial agendas and values where humans and nature are positioned in opposition, or at minimum, in separation. Western epistemes separate cultural from ecological renewal in its deepest sense. Similarly, sustainability—the ability for people and nature to continue—retains an agenda that subordinates nature in service to humans. Western models contrast with ecological cycles and patterns that describe many local cultures whose historical identity has been intertwined in nature and was not defined by righteous speciesism.

Unfortunately, many Africans today have negative associations with wildlife conservation. Conservation is linked with colonial appropriation of tribal lands or seen as a way that threatens human survival by its disallowal of access to natural resources.[59] These are the themes that underlie the hostility characterizing Human-Elephant Conflict. However, little attention is given to the fundamental element that has impoverished tribal and animal lives: colonialization. Although Africans today are warring with Elephants, it has not always been this way. People killed Elephants and Elephants killed people before European occupation. These occasions were the exception relative to the recent past's systemic annihilation. Forced removal from tribal homelands and the concomitant loss of traditional livelihoods that integrated human culture into the matrix of nature have disabled the ability to survive in ways other than those dictated by colonial and neoliberal models. Colonial legacies are associated with efforts to conserve wildlife on lands that tribal peoples once shared with wildlife but from which they are now barred. Violence to nature is embedded in the historical experience of indigenous trauma.[60]

Trauma for Elephants and Africans is historical, ecological, and unresolved. Elephant ethologist Evelyn Lawino Abe speaks of how these disrupting legacies have propagated and affected both Elephants and her own tribe, the Acholi of northern Uganda. Her descriptions of the two species, like the histories themselves, are almost indistinguishable.

> Fate has the Acholi people and Elephant linked. The Elephant is the totem of the Acholi people. In the cultural beliefs of the Acholi people, the very existence of their lineage depends on the Elephant. These taxonomically divergent groups have both suffered massacres that graphically mirror each other. Both have suffered the annihilation of adult males and the eventual turning of guns onto older females leading to a destruction of both cultures.[61]

Similar to colonial situations where the effect of racism and enforced hardship turned oppressed groups against one another rather than mobilizing dissent, Elephant and tribal community interests have became pitted against each other in competition for lands made depauperate by colonial appetites.

For many aboriginals, colonialization has entailed the loss of "homeland, the moral sphere, the seat of life and emotion, and place of heart."[62] It has meant the loss of livelihood and meaning. Even when colonial rule has given over to nationals, the profound dismantling of the bonds between people, animals, and land caused by European social, economic, and psychological oppression has yet to be addressed.

Meaning making from the perspective of a trans-species psyche envisions human and animal restitution as mutually beneficial because it recognizes the necessary relational role of healing. By definition, the work of the Trust Keepers and Elephants engages in meaning making—the essential process that allows individuals to develop and live with a sense of intactness after the fabric of life is rent.[63] In creating new ways of being in relationship with the animals and land of their heritage, the tribal Keepers have an opportunity to engage in building a new ecological vision. The Keepers have a choice to relate to Elephants in a way alternative to exploitation or domination. For some, caring for the orphans is "not a job—it is a passion."

> [The Keeper] Amos feels that had he not worked here he would have never liked Elephants or any of the animals which pose a threat to his clan's livestock. Spending every day with these creatures enables you to learn so much about them and can even benefit from their knowledge so he now sees Elephants as a true asset to lands that the Samburu traditionally call their own.[64]

The Keepers provide the Elephants with what psychoanalyst Winnicott called a *facilitating environment* and simultaneously Elephant recovery also supports the Keepers by creating a dialogical space of security and creativity.[65] In such communities, individuals "create safety for each other as they re-build community, and what emerges is a deepening self-knowledge not just of the individual but of the group."[66] Practices lose their cultural identifiers becoming neither recognizably Elephant nor Human but merging elements of both with the land. Freya Matthews calls such re-connection through place a return to "nativism:"

> To be native is to have one's identity shaped by the place to which one belongs: one is a creature of its topography, its colours and textures, saps and juices, its moods, its ghosts and stories. As a native, one has one's taproot deep in a particular soil: one has

> grown in that soil, and continues to be informed and sustained
> by its essence. One is kin to all the other beings who arise out of
> and return to that patch of earth, and one draws one's substance
> and one's templates for meaning from it.[67]

Liberation ecopsychology's focus on animals does not entail the marginalization of humans: only human privilege. It is consistent with many indigenous philosophies and ways of beings where animal and human survival are considered one and the same. As Martín-Baró underscored, trauma recovery is not limited to the single victim but "extended to the roots of those traumas, and therefore to [the] social psychopathogenic situation."[68] Cross-species recovery opens to a new psychology—and culture.

CONCLUSIONS

The theory of a trans-species psyche and its praxis through engagement of a liberation ecopsychology extend depth psychology's project across species lines. People in multiple cultural settings are already participating in this model of psyche and ethos. Liberatory practices and principles of analytical psychology—the *vas,* the therapeutic alliance, transformative processes of counter-transference and transference—are expressed in multiple cross-species settings. Many live with their companion dog, cat, parrot, and lizard much as others live with their beloved human family. These are seeds of a dramatic shift to multi-species borderland communities where psychological and physical worlds are shared in parity.

In itself, the concept of a trans-species psyche does not require the dismissal of human privilege of Euro-American cultures. However, because the presumption of psyche as uniquely human has formed the foundation for legal and ethical justification of animal exploitation, its replacement by models of a trans-species psyche suggests a parallel reconfiguration. Globalized culture is literally built on the exclusion, and often extinction, of other species. In the United States, 100-190 million birds a year are killed through collision with plate glass windows —windows in houses built to keep out the elements but also other species. Many cultural and psychological identifiers—windows, roads, barbeques, fast food, rodeos, zoos, cars, fox hunting, Thanksgiving, cuisine, telephone wires—are simultaneously agents of animal death.

Unexamined, these cultural structures maintain human privilege inconsiderate of costs born by other species.

Adopting liberation psychology's call to include the dispossessed and decouple human identity from models of biological difference leads to a re-examination on how to live (or even if to live)[69] and at whose cost. Liberation ecopsychology beckons each individual to re-create an *ethos* in consideration of other species through examining our own ego identity and what is assumed to be requisite for survival. The intent of liberatory praxis is not to erase all difference but rather refrain from engaging in behavior and thought that can only exist by oppressing an Other. This brings us back to C. G. Jung's insistence on the purpose of individuation—the development of moral consciousness. In the articulation of liberation psychology, undoing cultural behaviors that impede survival and agency of others and their ability to participate in the creation of knowledge and meaning is required to create a praxis congruent with moral sensibilities.

Liberation ecopsychology places us at a radical edge of co-rights of animals and humans. It requires facing questions, as Peter Singer does, that move us beyond assumed species alignments.

> What, for instance, are we to do about genuine conflicts of interest like rats biting slum children? I am not sure of the answer, but the essential point is just that we do see this as a conflict of interests, that we recognize that rats have interests too. Then we may begin to think about other ways of resolving the conflict instead of killing [rats].[70]

Liberation ecospsychology asks each individual to undo the collective artefacts of colonialization and avoid oppression of another species in our thoughts and actions even when it may appear to threaten us, our children, and our species. We then:

> no longer distinguish sharply between our own interests and those of the beings with whom we are intermeshed—their interests are seen as implicated in ours; protecting them accordingly becomes a matter of 'self-defence.'[71]

Not only does the adoption of a trans-species psychology represent a "chance [for psychology] to restore its Otherness, its spiritual and religious element which was always the ground from which it sprang"[72] but a way to openly acknowledge the paralyzing grief and trauma in environmental destruction.[73] In seeking to deconstruct animal oppression, we are charged at the same time to engage in deep introspection and perhaps the reinvention of our own ontologies. To do so opens the possibility for regenerating ecological cultures and a way to call back the animals.

NOTES

1. James Hillman, *The Thought of the Heart and the Soul of the World* (Dallas: Spring Publications, 1992).

2. Arne Naess, "Self Realization: an Ecological Approach to Being in the World," in Alan Drengson and Yuichi Inoue (eds.), *The Deep Ecology Movement* (Berkeley: North Atlantic Books, 1995).

3. Vandana Shiva, *Earth Democracy: Justice, Sustainability, and Peace* (Boston: South End Press, 2005); Wangari Maathai, *The Green Belt Movement: Sharing the Approach and the Experience* (NY: Lantern Books, 2004); Grace Lee Boggs, *Living for Change* (Minneapolis: University of Minnesota Press, 1998).

4. Paolo Freire, *Pedagogy of the Oppressed* (Harmondsworth: Penguin, 1972).

5. Ignatio Martín-Baró, *Writings for a Liberation Psychology,* in A. Aron and S. Corne (eds.) (Cambridge, MA: Harvard University, 1884).

6. D. Hocoy, A. Kipnis, H. Lorenz, & M. Watkins, *Liberation psychologies: an invitation to dialogue,* (http://ww.online.pacifica.edu/watkins/liberationpsychologies, 2005)

7. C. G. Jung, Epilogue to "Essays on contemporary events," in trans. R. F. C. Hull, *The Collected Works of C. G. Jung* [hereinafter *"CW"*] (Vol. 10, pp. 227-244). Princeton, N.J.: Princeton University Press. 1947 (Original work published 1946).

8. G. A. Bradshaw, *Elephant Trauma and Recovery: Toward a Liberation Ecopsychology*, dissertation (Pacifica Graduate Institute, Santa Barbara, CA, 2005).

9. G. A. Bradshaw, A. N. Schore, J. L. Brown, J. H. Poole & C. J. Moss, "Elephant Breakdown," *Nature,* 2005, 433, 807.

10. *Ibid.*

11. Jerome Bernstein, *Living in the Borderland: The Pathological and the Sacred in Our Understanding of Consciousness* (Philadelphia: Brunner-Routledge, 2005).

12. Lionel Corbett, *The Religious Function of the Psyche* (New York: Brunner-Routledge, 2001), 89.

13. Jung, *CW* 8 § 322.

14. Henry Gee, "Aspirational thinking," *Nature*, 2002, 42, 611.

15. William James, *Essays on Faith and Morals* (Cleveland: Meridian, 1890), 64.

16. C. G. Jung, *Man and his Symbols* (London: Aldus Books, 1964), 95.

17. Elizabeth A. Lawrence, *Hunting the Wren: Transformation of Bird to Symbol* (Knoxville: University of Tennessee Press, 1997), 202.

18. Peter Cushman, *Constructing the Self, Constructing America: A Cultural History of Psychotherapy* (Menlo Park: Addison-Wesley Publishing, 2002); Carolyn Merchant, "Reinventing Eden: Western Culture as a Recovery Narrative," in W. Cronon (ed.), *Uncommon Ground: Rethinking the Human Place in Nature* (New York: W. W. Norton, 1996), 132-170.

19. Paul Shepard, *The Other: How Nonhuman Animals Made Us Human* (Washington D.C.: Shearwater, 1996), 187.

20. James Hillman and Margot McLean, *Dream Animals* (San Francisco: Chronicle Books, 1996), 5.

21. Neil Russack, *Animal Guides: in Life, Myth, and Dreams* (Toronto, Canada: Inner City, 2002), 43.

22. Jung, *CW* 10 § 460.

23. G. A. Bradshaw, "No longer a mind of our own," *Seed*, 2002, June/July, 43-45.

24. Mary Watkins, "Silenced Knowings, Forgotten Springs: Paths to Healing in the Wake of Colonialism," with Helene Lorenz, *Radical Psychology: A Journal of Psychology, Politics, and Radicalism* (online journal), http://www.radpsy.york.ca; Mary Watkins, "Seeding Liberation: A dialogue between Depth Psychology and Liberation Psychology," in D. Slattery & L. Corbett (eds.), *Depth Psychology: Meditations in the Field* (Einsiedeln, Switzerland: Daimon Verlag, 2000); Mary Watkins, "Depth Psychology and the Liberation of Being," in R. Brooke (ed.), *Pathways into the Jungian World: Phenomenology and Analytical Psychology* (London: Routledge, 2000); Mary Watkins,

"Depth Psychology and Colonialism: Individuation, Seeing-through, and Liberation," with Helene Lorenz, in D. Slattery & L. Corbett (eds.), *Psychology at the Threshold* (Einsiedeln, Switzerland: Daimon Verlag, 2002).

25. Ignatio Martín-Baró, *Writings for a Liberation Psychology,* in A. Aron and S. Corne (eds.) (Cambridge, MA: Harvard University, 1984), 25.

26. Mary Watkins, "From Individualism to the Interdependent Self: Changing Paradigms in Psychotherapy," *Psychological Perspectives,* 27, 1992, 52-69.

27. Michael Vannoy Adams, *The Multicultural Imagination: "Race," Colour, and the Unconscious* (London: Routledge, 1996), 34.

28. Peter Singer, *Animal Liberation: A New Ethics for our Treatment of Animals* (New York: Random House, 1973).

29. *Ibid.*

30. http://www.sheldrickwildlifetrust.org/

31. Bradshaw, et al., "Elephant Breakdown," *Nature,* 2005, 433, 807.

32. R. K. Siegel and M. Brodie, "Alcohol Self-Administration by Elephants," *Bulletin of the Psychonomic Society 22,* 1984, 1, 49-52.

33. Caroline Williams, "Elephants on Edge," *New Scientist, 2006.* 18 February 2006, 39-41.

34. Rhea Ghosh, *Gods in Chains* (Banglalore, India: WRRC [the Wildlife Rescue and Rehabilitation Center] Press, 2005), 159.

35. Daphne Sheldrick, "Elephant Emotion," retrieved February 15, 2005) from http://www. elephant.elehost.com/

36. Daphne Sheldrick, "The impact of elephants in Tsavo." Retrieved May 14, 2003) from www. elephant.elehost.com/ About_Elephants

37. http://www.sheldrickwildlifetrust.org/

38. P. Hill Collins, "The meaning of motherhood in Black culture and Black mother-daughter relationships," in P. Bell-Scott (ed.), *Double Stitch: Black Women Write about Mothers and Daughters* (Boston: Beacon Press, 1991), 42-61.

39. B. Guy-Sheftall, "Piecing Blocks Identities," in Bell-Scott (ed.), *Double Stitch,* 62.

40. G. A. Bradshaw, "Not by Bread Alone," *Society and Animal, 12(2),* 2004, 143-158, 58.

41. Lawrence Kirmayer, "Beyond the 'New Cross-cultural Psychiatry:' Cultural Biology, Discursive Psychology and the Ironies of Globalization," *Transcultural Psychiatry,* 43, 1, 2006, 126-144.

42. Vine Deloria, Jr., *God is Red* (Golden: Fulcrum Press, 1996), 223.

43. Martín-Baró, *Writings for a Liberation Psychology,* 39.

44. *Ibid.,* 42.

45. Judith Herman, *Trauma and Recovery* (New York: Basic Books. 1997); Kelly Oliver, *Witnessing: Beyond Recognition* (Minneapolis: University of Minnesota Press, 2001).

46. C. G. Jung, *Man and His Symbols* (London: Aldus Books, 1964), 95.

47. Michael J. Cohen, *Reconnecting With Nature: Finding Wellness Through Restoring Your Bond With the Earth* (Washington: Ecopress, 1997), 120.

48. Lawrence Kirmayer, "Beyond the 'New Cross-cultural Psychiatry': Cultural Biology, Discursive Psychology and the Ironies of Globalization," *Transcultural Psychiatry,* 43, 1, 2006, 126-144.

49. Judith Atkinson, *Trauma Trails: Recreating Song Lines*, (Spinifex Press, Melbourne, 2002), 16.

50. (www.listening_hands.org).

51. www.elephants.com; Carol Buckley pers. comm. May 2005.

52. Frans de Waal, *The Ape and the Sushi Master: Cultural Reflections of a Primatologist* (New York: Basic Books, 2002).

53. Still today, the work of George and Joy Adamson with the famed Elsa and other lions are rejected by most conservationists.

54. Bradshaw, et al.,"Elephant Breakdown," *Nature,* 2005, 433, 807; Michael J. Meaney, "Maternal care, gene expression, and the transmission of individual differences in stress reactivity across generations," *Annual Reviews of Neuroscience*, 24, 2001, 1161-1192.

55. A. N. Schore. "Attachment, Affect Regulation, and the Developing Right Brain: Linking Developmental Neuroscience to Pediatrics. *Pediatrics in Review*, 26 (6), 2005, 204-217.

56. Herman, *Trauma and Recovery.*

57. J. Bowlby, *Attachment, Volume I* (New York: Basic Books, 1969); Michael J. Meaney, "Maternal care, gene expression, and the transmission of individual differences in stress reactivity across generations," *Annual Reviews of Neuroscience*, 24, 2001, 1161-1192.

58. Arne Naess, "Self Realization: an Ecological Approach to Being in the World," in Alan Drengson and Yuichi Inoue (eds.), *The Deep Ecology Movement* (Berkeley: North Atlantic Books, 1995).

59. Thidalini Tschiguvho, personal communication, April, 2004.

60. M. Y. Brave Heart and L. M. DeBRuyn, "The American Indian holocaust: healing historical unresolved grief," *American Indian Alaskan Native Mental Health Research,* 8(2), 1998, 56-78; Jeffrey Alexander, C. Jeffrey, Ron Eyerman, Bernhard Giesen, Smelser, J. Neil, and Piotr Sztompka, *Cultural Trauma and Collective Identity* (Berkeley, CA: University of California Press, 2004).

61. Evelyn Lawino Abe, *My Elephants, My People,* manuscript submitted for publication.

62. Judith Atkinson, *Trauma Trails: Recreating Song Lines* (Melbourne: Spinifex Press, 2002), 28.

63. Viktor F. Frankl, *Man's Search for Meaning* (New York: Beacon Press, 1946); Henry Krystal, "Optimizing Affect Function in the Psychoanalytic Treatment of Trauma," in *Living with Terror, Working with Trauma*, D. Knafo (ed.) (Lanham, MD: Bowman and Littlefield, 2005).

64. http://www.sheldrickwildlifetrust.org/

65. D. Hocoy, A. Kipnis, H. Lorenz, & M. Watkins, Liberation Psychologies: An Invitation to Dialogue.(http://www.online.pacifica.edu/watkins/liberationpsychologies, 2005).

66. Judith Atkinson, *Trauma Trails: Recreating Song Lines*, (Spinifex Press, Melbourne, 2002), 213.

67. Freya Matthews, "Becoming Native: an Ethos of Countermoderni ty II, *Worldviews: Environment, Culture, Religion,* 3, 3, 1999, 243-272 (Cambridge, UK: White Horse Press, 1999).

68. Ignatio Martín-Baró, *Writings for a Liberation Psychology,* in A. Aron and S. Corne (eds.) (Cambridge, MA: Harvard University, 1984), 12.

69. Simone Weil, *L'Enracinement* (Paris: Gallimard, 1947).

70. Peter Singer, *Animal Liberation: A New Ethics for our Treatment of Animals* (New York: Random House, 1973), 24.

71. Freya Matthews, "Cultural Relativism and Environmental Ethics, IUCN EthicsWorking Group Report No. 5," August 1994.

72. Christopher Hauke, *Jung and the Postmodern:Interpretation of Realties* (London: Routledge, 2002), 209.

73. M. Y. Brave Heart and L. M. DeBruyn, "The American Indian Holocaust: Healing Historical Unresolved Grief," *American Indian Alaskan Native Mental Health Research.* 8(2), 1998, 56-78.

74. GB would like to give acknowledgments to Lorin Lindner and Debra Durham for comments on an earlier version. Special deepest gratitude to Ingeborg Ling Bradshaw, Fritzi Parnell Bradshaw, Panama Bradshaw, and Bob and Vine Deloria, Jr. who stood by me, kept me honest, and gave their testimony that makes up this work. In memory of Graham.

"My Daddy Was My Hero:" Steve Irwin, the Hero Archetype, and Australian Identity

FRANCES GRAY

Preamble

Two Australian heroes died within days of each other in September. On September 4th 2006, Steve Irwin died as a result of a sting-ray barb injury to his heart when he was swimming above a sting-ray while filming for a series that would feature his daughter, Bindi. On 8th September 2006, Peter Brock, an Australian rally-car driver was killed when his car hit a tree during a rally in Western Australia. The families of each of these men were offered the honor of State funerals: Steve Irwin's family declined and held, instead, a memorial service in Irwin's Crocoseum on the Gold Coast in Queensland. The service was televised to a worldwide audience. The Australian Prime Minister, John Howard, and well-known celebrities such as Cameron Diaz and Russell Crowe, and singer/composer John Williamson, attended. Peter Brock's family accepted the offer of a State funeral, and thousands of people flocked to St. Paul's Cathedral in Melbourne for the event, openly and very publicly weeping. Each occasion startled with its double figuring of tragedy and celebration,

Frances Gray is a philosopher who teaches at the University of New England, Armidale, NSW, Australia. Her forthcoming book, *Jung, Irigaray, Individuation,* will be published by Routledge in 2007.

and the enormous outpouring of grief evidenced in the behavior of many who were utter strangers to the dead men.

Both Irwin and Brock were media quasi-fictional characters created in the daily business of celebrity-making. They were sold to the Australian public, and in Irwin's case, to the rest of the interested world, by the media. And, as a nation we bought their quasi-fictionalization, as did many North Americans. Irwin appeared in advertisements for the Australian Quarantine Inspection Service (AQIS), on whose website he is described as "'Crocodile Hunter' Steve Irwin." His job for the Quarantine Service was to "warn Australian travellers of the dangers of breaching Quarantine laws when they return from overseas holidays over the northern hemisphere summer."[1] This apparent Government endorsement of Irwin simultaneously increased Irwin's exposure to the Australian public (and to anyone else who saw the advertisements) and implicitly legitimated his approach to the environment. The advertisements show him holding a crocodile in his "trademark" pose. He also appeared on American chat shows, hosted for example by Jay Leno, where he was lauded as a human marvel.

But it is not only their lives, but the drama of their deaths and their subsequent memorializing as dead heroes that is built into the quasi-fictionalizing of Irwin and Brock. The ongoing interest in Terri and Bindi Irwin, wife and daughter, respectively, of Irwin, transforms his death into a media feast focused on personal and collective loss. Terri's and Bindi's desires to emulate the work it is claimed he started (the saving of the environment) embroiders his hero status.[2] His catch phrase "wildlife warrior" captures some of the central features of Irwin's life and work: excitement, challenge, conquest. Irwin was on a salvific crusade for the environment and its creatures. Indeed, the philosophy of Irwin's "Australia Zoo" is "conservation through exciting education."[3] For Terri and Bindi to see themselves as inheritors of Irwin's crusade requires that they maintain this philosophy, a philosophy which I shall argue in this paper, is morally dubious.

Having said this, Irwin and Brock were more than media quasi-fictions: they were living breathing men with passion and perhaps extraordinary senses of adventure. Wrestling crocodiles and driving rally cars at high speed are not the characteristics of wooses. So apart from the media hype, the two men exemplify an apparent compulsiveness for risky activity, bravery even, that will, given their socio-cultural contexts and preoccupations, inevitably result in media attention. The confluence of intrinsic characteristic, cultural embeddedness, and media recognition is evidenced in the hero phenomenon constructed in and around them. Both Irwin and Brock are exemplary of the kind of man Australians count as national heroes. Even in their differences, the two men embodied the risk-taking, danger-courting, courageous individual who goes into combat against nature and wins. That each died doing what he loved and as a result of an unseen twist of nature is important. Courage, skill, and knowledge have limits and no matter how fully we embrace being, our deaths are always already inevitable. If we court Thanatos deliberately, wilfully, we give our lives an edgy meaningfulness that accentuates the grace of our living. If someone else can do it for us, then the vicarious pleasure we get from victory, but ultimately from a tragic albeit hero-enhancing end, reminds us that is not yet our turn. But it will come. Much weeping over these deaths is weeping for our own mortalities.

We can easily slip into sentimentalizing the dead; and it is not permissable to speak badly of them, even if what is said is a continuation of a conversation begun much earlier.[4] Stories told about the lives of the now-dead are often a mixture of their heroics and foibles, especially when celebrity is at stake, and frequently reflect the complexity of the deceased. Undoubtedly, Steve Irwin and Peter Brock were complex men. Complexity can be reduced to moral approbation or blame, with the result that ultimately the deceased is sanctified or demonized. I do not involve myself in such a conversation in this paper. So my purpose is not to discuss the desirable and undesirable aspects of either Irwin's or Brock's lives. Instead, this paper is an exploration of what I see as Steve Irwin's problematic relationship to animals and thus to the natural world. His crusade against the destruction of the environment and the attendant loss of biodiversity was admirable. But the relationship he appears to have had with animals, I will argue, founds his heroic status as he vicariously played out our, and his own, fear of the untamed, the wild, the uncontrollable. In that sense, Irwin's is an heroic crusade against the feminine. Our complicity with, and reinforcement of, his heroism can therefore be seen as symptomatic of our own crusade against the feminine.[5]

And my intent is to discuss Brock no further. His function in this paper, as we shall see, is to highlight the emphasis placed on a masculine heroism that both mediates and occludes the importance of other, less spectacular, encounters with the natural world. But Brock also functions to show the perversity of Australians in their choices of hero. Brock embodied much of what Irwin was opposed to. In reality, Brock was no conservationist: rally-car driving is paradigmatic of the kind of activity that disregards the sacredness of the environment, both in its execution and in the use of fossil fuels to drive the vehicles used. That he died in an encounter with a tree is thus highly significant. As contraries of, and within, the hero archetype then, Brock and Irwin symbolically capture the naiveté of the Australian unconscious. What brings them together is their deaths in action, in overcoming *physis*. But let us go back to the beginning and ask why we might, in the first place, think of Irwin as a hero.

Steve Irwin as a Manifestation of the Hero Archetype

Carl Jung's treatment of the psychological transformation of a subject includes a discussion of ritualistic identification with a god or hero. He argues that in Apuleius's *Metamorphosis,* the Osiris cult, and the Christian idea that each human has an immortal soul that participates in the Godhead, we find the notion of identification manifested in the transformation of individuals. This transformation is brought about through "participation in the fate of the god."[6] Jung says that in *Metamorphosis,*

> an ordinary human being is elected to be Helios; he is crowned
> with a crown of palms and clad in the mystic mantle, whereupon
> the assembled crowd pays homage to him. The suggestion of
> the crowd brings about his identity with the god.[7]

In Steve Irwin's case, there is no symbolic ritual, no obvious deity with whom he can be identified. Irwin's behavior is, however, emblematic of ritualized action in which he theatrically performs for an audience. Irwin is *de facto* made into a hero through the suggestion of a crowd, the most voluble voices of which are the media.

Irwin's internal drama demands an audience, acknowledgment, acclaim, reinforcement. The media is seduced by Irwin's charisma and he is seduced by the promise of the entertainment exposure it offers him. Irwin and the media mutually project their psychic needs onto each other, rather like two people in the early stages of romance. And we as participants/observers mediate their relationship as we consume the offerings they assemble in action and reporting and television programs. The quasi-fiction that Irwin becomes is consciously constructed by him and deliberately manipulated by the media in response to Irwin's own internal psychic necessities. The kind of necessities with which the media operates, structural artifacts as they are of Western capitalism, obscure any ongoing potential for critique. Irwin's intrusive presence in the home of penguins, humpback whales, and seals in 2004, and to which Germaine Greer refers in her September 6, 2006 article about his death in *The Guardian*, drew breath, but relatively constrained criticism from the media.[7a]

We, in turn, responded to Irwin's psychic necessities, although not always with approval. His appearance with his four-week-old son, Bob, tucked under his arm, as Greer also points out, to feed a dead chicken to a crocodile, was a ghastly display of sheer stupidity. Certainly, this action was met with shocked disbelief: but nothing *happened* to Irwin. No consent was possible for young Bob. And a crocodile would not stop to distinguish a baby from a dead chicken: it's all food to a crocodile. Nothing *bad* eventuated out of the incident, no harm was done to young Bob, so it does not actually matter? Are we all naïve consequentialists? Are badness (and goodness) only in consequences, only in what effects our actions have rather than in or perhaps together with intention? Is it morally appropriate to act as Irwin did? Unconsciously we could not tell our hero that what he did was morally reprehensible. And why, if we did not approve of his action, did we not disapprove more strongly? We should have stayed away from the Australia Zoo in droves, but it was business as usual. This is part of an overall "she'll-be-right-mate" attitude that crept through Irwin's crikeyeness and which we seemed willing to accept. And when approval is not forthcoming, those of us with dissident voices are marked as traitors to the Irwin cult. The *ad hominem* that adorns the Ageblog website which is directed at Germaine Greer for her negative comments about Irwin is testament to this.[8]

The hero archetype which Irwin exemplifies is turned towards the world. His was an extraverted psyche which needed endorsement in order to perform the understanding he had of his own crusading being. Like any entertainer, environmentalist or not, Irwin needed us, his audience. Furthermore, we believed, subliminally, in our own transformation, our own affirming change of heart and mind through his transformation: we participated in his heroics indirectly, by applauding and gasping, *but also by approving.* We saw our own selves as we would like them to be: triumphant over nature. Our wonderment at his astonishing control and pure strength of character as he bombastically insinuated himself (and continues to insinuate through the images left behind) into the lives of wild animals, saw us develop an imaginary self-understanding derived from seeing ourselves in his psychic processes. But what is going on in Irwin's psyche as he engages other animals and performs for us?

Robert Segal argues that the hero archetype is the opposite of the *puer* (*aeternus*). He says,

> The hero succeeds where the *puer* fails. In the first half of life an ego is heroic in managing to liberate itself from the unconscious and to establish itself in society. … Where a hero in the first half of life establishes himself in the conventions of society, a hero in the second half defies those conventions. But a hero is consciously defiant. A *puer* is only unconsciously so.[9]

One wonders where Steve Irwin sits in relation to this distinction and if an answer to the goings-on in Irwin's psyche can be found here.

To make this determination, it is useful to use Segal's analysis to compare Irwin to Timothy Treadwell, who studied bears in Alaska for many years and was killed by them in 2003. Treadwell's life and work are the subject of the 2006 Werner Herzog documentary *Grizzly Man.*[10] Based upon Segal's work, Timothy Treadwell could be seen as a *puer.* I say this, however, with reservation. Treadwell's tirade against the National Parks Service towards the end of *Grizzly Man* together with many of the comments made by him about his fellow humans suggests that Treadwell was a deeply disturbed man.[10] His passionate declarations of love for the bears *to* the bears, his trusting nature and innocent idealism about the bears' lives fascinatingly conveys the soul of someone who could not adapt to the norms and expectations of his own culture. His paranoia about their habitat, which he believed was threatened, as were the bears, was irrational according to some interviewees. Treadwell's preference for solitude and the company of the bears suggests, as one commentator points out, that Treadwell was more identified with the bears than he was with human animals. It is difficult to determine if Treadwell was consciously or unconsciously defiant of the conventions of his society. At times it seems, from the film, that he was deeply conscious of what he was doing; at others, it appears as if his unconscious takes over completely and this is the case with the tirade example.

Undeniably, Treadwell was a quite different person from the happy family-man and lover we found in Irwin. Yet Irwin seems at times to externalize an internal struggle in his unconscious or symbolic/imaginary world. This emerged in his need to "test himself" against crocodiles and tigers and snakes, the very place where his intrusive disregard for their integrity revealed itself. Irwin's assumption that it is acceptable to satisfy a crocodile's hunger by standing near it with a dead chicken which is then thrown to the animal as if the crocodile were actually one's pet, that patting a tiger and treating it as if it were the family cat, or that any other wild creature should be enfolded in a human embrace of one kind or another imitates, but parodies, the situation of domesticated animals. The fact that Irwin treated animals in this way, as entertainment, objectifies animals as entertaining spectacles bound to the human world in their ability to become sources of theatre. It is little more than disguised circus performance.

And we gullibly condoned Irwin as we urged him on, paying for the privilege to see him perform. Furthermore, we begin to see ourselves, through him, as performers too. Visit the Australia Zoo and, like Irwin, we can have our photos taken with tigers, as we reinforce the pretense that such creatures are really big pussy cats like our own. Such pretense is participation in *puer aeternus,* participation in the unrestraint of the unconscious, where we abandon caution and believe a story that is not only false but potentially lethal. In other words, we think we become heroes in our very own crikey stories, but we act out *puer.* What Irwin has legitimated, we, too, can do and be; we use Irwin to symbolically represent ourselves to ourselves: he stands for our unconscious projections. We allowed Irwin to play out for us, our collective *puer aeternus,* our immature, unconscious belief that we can conquer nature. We are the ones who legitimated Irwin's behavior in the first place: *we allowed the specularizing of animals to happen.* We allowed his son to be a potential dinner for the crocodile because we cannot control the limits we think we have set for the unconscious: he did it for us, sanctioned by our unconscious desires to court death and win. So Irwin is a hero in the same sense as Jesus, a kind of sacrificial lamb who offers himself for us to death, to Thanatos. In this story, there is, then, a god with whom we identify Irwin and in whom we consequently see ourselves. That god is death.

What is going on in Irwin's psyche? Irwin is playing the *puer aeternus* for us as he simultaneously is playing the hero. The two archetypes cohabit in his psyche and in ours. Irwin is a mirror for us, a means of abrogating our responsibilities to grow up. In this sense, he was our moral scapegoat. He raised money for conservation purposes, established a hospital for injured wildlife, even buying up land that could harbor wildlife populations. But he did no more than the Australian Conservation Foundation or the World Wildlife Fund or the NSW Wild Rescue Service (WIRES) in respect of animals and conservation. What Irwin did was not new in those terms. What *was* new was that Irwin revisited the spectacular and the thrilling and developed them as an aspect of pedagogy in what was, for him, an unproblematic manner. He taught us, or at least attempted to teach us, that wild animals are not worthy of respect, that we can tame them and feed them and keep them in zoos, encroach on their territory and integrity, and pretend that this is morally worthwhile.

In an article in *The Sydney Morning Herald* on September 8, 2006, Clive Hamilton compared Irwin's attitudes with those of David Attenborough "who approaches creatures with an attitude of respect verging on reverence." Hamilton argued that

> Irwin created a new genre of documentary called 'nature nasty' which rejects attempts to portray animals in their natural environment going about their usual activities. Instead it goes in search of the most dangerous, poisonous and bizarre and provokes animals into extreme behaviour.[11]

Hamilton's assessment of Irwin highlights not only the contrast between Irwin and Attenborough, but also brings into focus the impoverished expectations we have of our own wildlife warrior. Gung-ho and bravado are re-invested into the Australian psyche in the person of a white man, a recent, European-introduced exotic. It is of no small significance that Steve Irwin was a white man mediating the European experience of the Australian landscape, bush, and wildlife. We Europeans cannot, it seems, manage what the indigenous peoples have managed and coped with for forty thousand years or more; and we needed, we thought, a white hero to do this for us.

While this might seem like harsh judgment, our acceptance of his behavior as endearing and larrikinish serves to reinforce our own misunderstandings of our own relationships to the environment. Shifting crocodiles from human habitation, or killing sharks because they eat us when we surf, assumes that nature is ours to do with what we like. We create boundaries or lines across which animals are not permitted. But they are *our boundaries, not theirs.* Were the tigers to suddenly eat their keepers (or one of us), were a crocodile to lunge at the human and not the chicken, were a snake to bite, then they would be seen as rogue elements and destroyed. That is just what happened to the bear that killed Timothy Treadwell. Irwin reinforced our unconscious expectation to be treated by animals as if we are sacred beings, heroes, and gods. And we are not.

PROBLEMATICS OF THE HERO ARCHETYPE

Susan Rowland argues that "[t]he hero, with his final triumph over the territories of the [unconscious] other and his winning of the feminine as a prize, fuels the decay of modernity rather than healing it."[12] She notes Jung's ambivalence about the hero archetype as "a potent icon of masculine representation."[13] Irwin was just that potent icon; and he won the feminine as his prize. And we have applauded this win.

Bindi Irwin's appearance at her father's memorial service was her public initiation into the white Australian masculine symbolic. Her declaration that her daddy was her hero (and many little girls' daddies *are* their heroes) fulfilled our expectations of the daughter of a hero. Yet she also demonstrated our willingness to let little girls be appropriated by the masculine-paternal symbolic. Discussing Freud's death drive, Luce Irigaray argues that women are the source of specular duplication in which women mirror

> the construction of narcissistic moments [which] involves pulling the libido back from the object onto the self and desexualizing it so it can carry out more sublimated activities. Now if this ego is to be valuable, some 'mirror' is needed to reassure it and to re-

insure it of its value. Woman will be the foundation for this
specular re-duplication ...."[14]

Bindi is part of the prize that is the feminine and her job is to mirror
her father's value system, reassuring not him, but us, that this system
is valuable. She becomes the insurance, the guarantor, that his memory
and what it stands for will survive. We can see this in her youthful
comment that she wants to "help endangered wildlife like he did." "Just
like he did" evokes the antics Irwin engaged in to help wildlife. Why
"just like he did"? Was Irwin's life an extended narcissistic moment
that will see its continuation in the life of his daughter?

Bindi's and Terri's lives are shadowed by the specter of Irwin: of
course they are, for this is a recent bereavement. One wonders how
long that shadow will be. Terri Irwin is reported to have said that she
has a lot to live up to and that she will never marry again. Where is
Terri in these claims and where is Bindi when she says that she wants
to do just as her father did? Have Terri and Bindi become the re-
embodied anima projections of a dead Irwin, a dead hero? Do they
represent Irwin's final win over the territories (of the unconscious)? If
they are such a representation, we might reflect on why we so readily
accept the white, male iconic hero who has infiltrated our own psyches
and why we are so enamored of the speech of a little girl at her father's
funeral. And if we have been as responsible for the making of Irwin as
I have suggested, we might reflect on our own need to continue
reproducing in the other what we think we lack in ourselves.

Bindi's speech demonstrates a European-Australian preoccupation
with heroism, seen particularly in our alienation from the harshness of
this environment. Indigenous Australians have lived here for millennia;
we have let their lives and ways of being have little influence on our
understanding of the land and its creatures. We have needed to adapt
Eurocentric notions such as the hero to our perceptions of this land,
this people, and these creatures. What Steve Irwin models for us is our
own whiteness and our own anti-feminine sensitivities: the triumph
of the masculine over the feminine. The "Aussie bloke" should not be
given the place it is given in our symbolic/imaginary worlds. Nor should
we applaud the interiorizing of the values this bloke embodies if we
are to live harmoniously in and with this land. There are other ways.
And the hero is a worry.

POST-SCRIPT

Jill Bowling, an Australian conservationist who worked for the World Wildlife Fund as its director of conservation, was killed in a helicopter crash in Nepal on September 24, 2006. Bowling was doing what she loved when she died. She was involved in transferring "the Kanchenjunga Conservation Area to local community groups."[15] Bowling was a conservationist and a passionate advocate for the environment and its creatures.

NOTES

1. http://www.daff.gov.au/content/output.cfm?ObjectID=E9F70 814-0063-4C3B-84014834FBD59D04.

2. The website of the *Australia Zoo* says, "Australia Zoo Wildlife Warriors Worldwide (formerly Steve Irwin Conservation Foundation) is growing into a new era of local and global wildlife preservation. Our name has recently changed to better reflect the mobility and reach of our small but highly motivated organization. It is also indicative of the broad group of people, corporations and foundations who will be supporting the exciting conservation programs we are developing"— http://www.wildlifewarriors.org.au/steveterri/index.html (accessed October 4, 2006). We should note that Irwin's work is a recent addition to other long-established and successful but less aggressive conservation foundations such as the Australian Conservation Foundation and the World Wildlife Fund.

3. http://www.wildlifewarriors.org.au/azoo.

4. See Germaine Greer's article in *The Guardian*, Tuesday, September 6, 2006. Greer's assessment of Irwin has been less than appreciated by his loyal admirers. See for example the Ageblog at http://cracker.com.au/viewthread.aspx?threadid=137047&categoryid=11131 (accessed October 4, 2006).

5. The linking of woman/the feminine/the female with nature and nature with woman/the feminine/the female is widely discussed amongst feminists. See, for example, Simone de Beauvoir, *The Second Sex* (New York: Vintage Books, 1974); Iris Marion Young, *Throwing Like a Girl, and Other Essays in Feminist Philosophy and Social Theory* (Bloomington, IN: Indiana University Press, 1990); Karen J. Warren,

ed., *Ecological Feminism* (London: Routledge, 1994); Val Plumwood, *Feminism and the Mastery of Nature* (London: Routledge, 1993); Ynestra King, "The Ecology of Feminism and the Feminism of Ecology," in *Healing the Wounds*, ed. J. Plant (Philadelphia, PA: New Society Publishers, 1989), 18-28.

6. C. G. Jung, "Concerning Rebirth," in *Collected Works,* Vol. 9i (Princeton, NJ: Princeton University Press, 1969), 229.

7 *Ibid.*

7a. See note 4.

8. The kind of sentiment expressed on this site is appalling in its attack on Greer's character, marital status, and intellectual integrity. It shows that there is an incipient viciousness in the characters of some Australians.

9. Robert A. Segal, *Myth: A Very Short Introduction* (Oxford: Oxford University Press, 2004), 111.

10. In *Grizzly Man*, Herzog uses edited footage from Treadwell's thirteen trips to Katmai National Park in Alaska between 1991 and 2003 together with commentary by and interviews with friends and family of Treadwell, the pilot responsible for taking him on his trips to Alaska, and various wildlife (and other) experts. *Grizzly Man* is reviewed in this issue of *Spring* at pp. 311-316.

11. Clive Hamilton, "Death becomes an excuse to savage 'elites'— now that's nasty," in *The Sydney Morning Herald* Friday, September 8, 2006, 11.

12. Susan Rowland, *Jung as a Writer* (London and New York: Routledge, 2005), 174.

13. *Ibid.*

14. Luce Irigaray, *Speculum of the Other Woman,* trans. Gillian C. Gill (New York: Cornell University Press, 1985), 54.

15. *The Sydney Morning Herald*, September 26, 2006.

ART AND NATURE: THOUGHTS IN AND OUT OF THE STUDIO

MARGOT McLEAN

Being an artist whose work is directly related to the natural world, I find myself working "in" the outside world and working "in" the inside world of my studio, crisscrossing constantly between the two. While the physical act of producing an artwork does happen somewhere—studio, shed, living room, field, plaza—the making of an artwork is happening everywhere—walking down a busy city street, picking out tomatoes at the market, watching the night sky. Just as living in the world is not a contained activity, making art is not a contained activity. Things work on us all the time. Our senses are relentlessly engaged, and my job as an artist is to make something of these things that move us, disturb us, bore us, anger us. Like birds—thoughts, images, impressions, insights, voices, ideas, emotions, reactions are flying past all the time. As a bird watcher, I am always hoping for an image to land. Not to make sense of it, or to understand it, but just to let it in for its sake and to see what happens. When

Margot McLean is a visual artist who lives and works in New York and rural Connecticut. She received her BFA from Virginia Commonwealth University in Virginia and her MFA from Syracuse University in New York. "Catching light, migrations, water flow, extinctions," was her latest exhibition at La Specola Natural History Museum in Florence, Italy, 2005.

painting, you think your way through things by "doing" your way through things.

The Cut Field

> When I fail every theory I've constructed about myself and my life, when I grope about feeling wrong and blind, first inarticulate, then mute, I stumble closer to the origin of a bright success I know nothing of. I look out the window, no longer able to do anything else. I watch the gelding circle and circle in the cut field. He is protecting something, something that, I suddenly see with certainty, I will never be able to describe or know.

> —Mermer Blakeslee

PERCEPTION/IMAGINATION

I use the word nature, in these reflections to refer to plants, animals, and habitat given and built. Being a visual thinker, I find it essential to question preconceived notions about what we think nature means, and even more, what we think nature looks like, how it appears. Both nature and psyche present themselves in particular images. For a visual thinker, these images are primary. It all boils down to perception of the phenomenon, and imagining is in the perceiving.

> Thinking is more interesting than knowing, but less interesting than looking.

> —Goethe

ENVIRONMENTAL ACTIVISM

We humans have moved far away from our connection to the rest of the living world. This fact is far more frightening than anything else we hold to be frightening (terrorist attacks, illegal aliens, "other" religions). The distancing and nihilistic separation from what is fundamental for our very existence is not just striking (in the sense of logic) but suicidal (in the sense of survival). Perhaps this behavior is just part of the larger plan. Maybe we were never "connected" in the first place and our time here is limited. Maybe we are nothing but a virus that has gone terribly out of control.

Whatever the theory of the disconnection, today, we are smack-dab in the middle of a crisis, and if we cannot wake up to the world as participating members, we may as well congratulate ourselves, as we lie dying, for not having cared enough to do something when we had the chance.

Although I had been a longtime supporter of environmental issues, the time came when I felt the need to incorporate activism into my work. I embarked on an installation piece entitled *Portal of the Corporate Gods*, which became a major piece of research into the dumping of toxic waste into our rivers and streams. I sent for annual reports from corporations to contrast what they were touting as accomplishments with what I was finding in my research. For example, the annual report: "When industry takes water from rivers and streams, it has responsibility to return what is no longer needed in a way that won't harm the environment. This is a policy that guides all of Olin's manufacturing facilities and it gives the company a special insight into waste water management;" my research: "Ask Olin Corporation, which had to cough up 24 million in late Dec. 1982 for dumping DDT—837 tons of it—into the Indian Creek tributary of the Tennessee River. Ask the residents of Triana, Alabama, whose major source of food was poisoned by the Olin dumping, for their estimate of the cost. These were poor people. They depended on the fish from Indian Creek for their food supply. As a result of the dumping the residents had exceedingly high levels of DDT in their bodies." And so on …. We all know the slogans; Dupont: "Better Things for Better Living;" Sherwin-Williams: "We Cover the Earth" (an advertisement with a can dumping paint over an image of the earth). Love Canal, the James River, American Cyanamid—my list of offenders and atrocities was long.

Nearly half a century ago, Rachel Carson warned, in her pioneering book *Silent Spring*, about the consequences of human indifference regarding water. Only three months ago, I was attending a local town meeting regarding wetlands protection: whether to increase the 50-foot buffer zone to 100 feet. There was a large turnout and most of the citizens were belligerently enraged. The extension would *not* allow them to do what they wanted with their land. It was the same self-centered argument: the town is "taking away my rights as a citizen and jeopardizing the future of my children."

I was working on a series of birds at that time, many of which were wetland species. I knew how important this buffer zone was for their existence, not to mention the obvious need for the preservation of the community's drinking water. The room was silent (it was getting late) and no one spoke. *For all of those who cannot speak here tonight—stand up.* I stood up and with a shaky voice began to speak. I thought my heart would beat out of my body. "We no longer live in a time where we have the liberty to do whatever we want. We have an obligation to protect the wetlands not only for ourselves and the community we live in, but for the plants and animals that depend on this habitat for survival. Water tomorrow will be the oil of today." I sat down to a room full of stares. Why was it so difficult to express something that is so basic? What I had just said fell on disinterested ears. They were hearing the same old rhetoric full of shoulds and oughts. "Who are *you* to tell me what I can and cannot do with *my* land?" It was a desperate plea on my part, but the battle was already lost. Back in the studio, the American Bittern, Pied-billed Grebe, Common Moorhen, Great Egret were shifting. Their painted shapes, which had been floating and twisting and diving, were now slipping into places unknown.

Library

I sit down at a table and open a book of poems and move slowly into the shadows of tall trees. They are white pines I think. The ground is covered with soft brown needles and there are signs that animals have come here silently and vanished before I could catch sight of them. But here the trail edges into a cedar swamp; wet ground, deadfall and rotting leaves. I move carefully but rapidly, pleased with myself.

Someone else comes and sits down at the table, a serious looking young man with a large stack of books. He takes a book from the top of the stack and opens it. The book is called *How to Get a High Paying Job*. He flips through it and lays it down and picks up another and pages through it quickly. It is titled *Moving Ahead*.

We are moving ahead very rapidly now, through a second growth of popple and birch, our faces scratched and our clothes torn by the underbrush. We are moving even faster now, marking the trail, followed closely by bulldozer and crews with chain saws and representatives of the paper company.

—Louis Jenkins

Voices in Our Heads

Once, while working on a painting of a small monkey, I had pretty much figured out what I wanted to do. I would work laboriously on it for days and then in frustration and exhaustion put it aside for a rest. It would not let me rest, however. What the hell is wrong with this painting? It was as if some fierce outside force was resisting me. It took me a while to ask—could it be the monkey? Did it hate the dark, moody, depressing landscape I thought was perfect—what *I* wanted. Perhaps it wasn't perfect for the monkey. Something had intervened and had something to say. How do you listen when these voices come? And where are they coming from? Am I crazy in thinking the monkey hated the environment I had put him in? Do I dare admit this in public? What makes it so hard to listen? Why all this doubt? Our psyches are so overloaded with stuff that maybe the only way nature can get through is by stopping us in our tracks and making us so uncomfortable we have to pay attention.

> Someone asked me how to hear what nature is saying and I told him, "Just go out there, put your hand into a creek, and pull out a stone and listen. You'll hear something." The important thing is not to panic when you do start hearing something and don't know whether or not it's for real. Give yourself the benefit of the doubt. That is what most people fail to do. ... They come to me and say, "I think I heard something, but I would like to know for sure." I say, "What do you mean for sure? Let me tell you, that stone is for sure!"
>
> — Malidoma Somé

When I finally paid attention to the needs of the monkey something shifted radically. I cannot begin to explain it, but finally the painting opened up and moved to completion.

From Jung (1945):

> Primitives dread the sharply focused stare in the eye of the European, which seems to them like the evil eye. A Pueblo chieftain once confided to me that he thought all Americans (the only white men he knew) were crazy, and the reasons he gave for this view sounded exactly like a description of people who where possessed. Well, perhaps we are. For the first time since the dawn of history we have succeeded in swallowing the

whole of primitive animism into ourselves, and with it the spirit
that animated nature. Not only were the gods dragged down
from their planetary spheres and transformed into chthonic
demons, but, under the influence of scientific enlightenment,
even this band of demons, which at the time of Paracelsus still
frolicked happily in the mountains and woods, in rivers and
human dwelling-places, was reduced to a miserable remnant
and finally vanished altogether. From time immemorial, nature
was always filled with spirit. Now, for the first time, we are
living in a lifeless nature bereft of gods. ... Just when people
were congratulating themselves on having abolished all spooks,
it turned out that instead of haunting the attic or old ruins the
spooks were flitting about in the heads of apparently normal
Europeans (*CW* 10 § 431).

The Act of Painting

There is a hopeless gap between the making of art and the speaking
about the making of art. You can talk about exaltations or depressions
or surprises or insights or welcome mistakes or confusions or thick
brushes, thin paint, layering, line; still you are left with the inexplicable
act. We each have our style of putting on paint and taking it away, and
we develop our style in co-ordination with the idea. That's what makes
a painting work.

But—from one moment to the next, things creep in and intervene.
What matters is paying attention to the creeping. Why does my hand
go for the ultramarine when I'm thinking yellow? Who's the "who" who
has been in my studio when I walk in the next morning to a chaotic mess?

Animals

The animals are powerful, else why would we constantly use them
as images for advertising and promoting products that actually have
nothing to do with them? This displacement of the animal came to
me long ago when I kept noticing how many animal images were
arriving in my mailbox in the form of junk mail. Animals as metaphors
for "stronger," "compassionate," "nurturing," "sensitive" ways of doing
business. The image of the animal had become an important tool. Does
it not say something about the power of the animal itself? Does it not
demonstrate how much these creatures rule our psyches? How much
they penetrate our very being? So much so, the corporate world knows

exploiting them can bring great profits. The tragedy is that we fall for it hook, line, and sinker. Our connection to the world is through false and corrupted images that portend/pretend connectedness.

When these images of animals kept arriving in my mail, I wanted to do something with them. I thought, how can I "recycle" them—relocate them in a different context? A context more respectful. Maybe if I re-placed them in a painting, gave them somewhere else to be—removed from the advertisements they arrived in—they would regain some of their lost dignity. As Edward Casey writes about my work in his book *Earth Mapping*: "The re-inhabitation and the relocation are both *in the image*. Far from this latter being a mere refuge, it provides its own implacement, at once secure and precarious. Indeed, the image-place incurs new risks, for example, those of misappropriation and misinterpretation."

Years ago, after having given a presentation of these particular paintings, a question from the audience stayed with me: "If you are *really* concerned about the monkey, why don't you put it in a 'real' environment?" I asked her, "You mean paint it hanging from the trees in a jungle?" She said, "Yes!" I wondered: Why would that be more "real?" It is more conventional and romantic, but not more real. And why am I not concerned about the monkey if I have placed it in a wholly new environment? The desire to want the monkey hanging from trees in a jungle confirms exactly my point that we use these images to comfort and remove ourselves emotionally from the fact that the monkey has lost the trees because we have taken them for chopsticks.

If we see them all the time, on cereal boxes and detergent bottles, on beer cans and hood ornaments, they are still with us—somehow still around. The fact of their extinction becomes an abstraction. These products have registered in our psyches as close and familiar and even abundant. So, to confuse the image of the animal with the actual animal is a tragic mistake. The image is not a replacement. The real animal is always the issue; its habitat, always the issue. My paintings are a longing for, an homage to, a sadness about, a remembrance of all those things that are animal, including habitat and loss. And perhaps my subject here is as much the habitat of these animals as it is the animal itself.

Casey goes on to say: "In the wild, they are literally in their own place, living on their own terms and in their own way. They can also be located somewhere else (e.g., physically in a zoo or virtually on television), but in such cases their place is not their own. In the painted image, however, they gain a second place that belongs to them because it is fashioned for them; they are given a place of their own in the world of the image."

Imagine my surprise at my own naïveté and admitted stupidity in giving permission for someone to use these very animal paintings on a website. A side of me thought they would be respected for what they are—not that they would be cut up and destroyed into another design, which, ironically, was used as advertising. Back to the animals in the junk mail—except this time the animal had been wiped out. A friend remarked that it was as if I had allowed someone to come onto my property because he loved the beautiful animals that lived there, and then went hunting!

We have a lot to reckon with in terms of our obscene behavior towards animals. How does the psyche handle the knowledge that while we may always have the image of the tiger, we may no longer have the real tigers living on the planet, in the wild, on their own, in their own way?

Mark Jerome Walters writes in his article "Saying Goodbye:" "Each extinction is a unique voice silenced in a universal conversation of which we ourselves are only one participant. When the tiny wings of the last Xerces blue butterfly ceased to flutter, our world grew quieter by a whisper and duller by a hue. ... We have compiled the biological accounting of our spendthrift ways in lists of endangered and extinct species. What about our moral or spiritual accounting? Where is our mourning and remorse? ... Rarely ... do we pause to say goodbye. We may remember—but without true remembrance. ... Science alone cannot assess the diminished quality of a world without the ivorybill or the Xerces blue. Psychologists have not begun to ponder the emotional toll of the loss of fellow life. Nor have theologians reckoned the spiritual impoverishment that extinction brings. To forget what we had is to forget what we have lost. And to forget what we have lost means never knowing what we had to begin with. That would be among the greatest tragedies of all."

THE IMPORTANCE OF NATURAL HISTORY MUSEUMS

Walking through the halls of La Specola Natural History Museum in Florence, Italy, I was reminded of how many visits I had made to

Natural History museums in my lifetime. They called out to me because they housed pieces of worlds that I wanted to be close to. Worlds that I did not know but wanted to know. I could stand in front of the glass cases for hours if left to my own choice. The dioramas especially pulled at me. They sparked something in the imagination that was as interactive as any button-pushing, informationally "fun" kiosk in state-of-the-art displays. To stand with reverence and to observe: to stand motionless and yet feel so active and alive. The mysterious contents of these boxed-in spaces have a strange power to transport one to that far-off exotic place that the imagination understands.

Have you ever noticed how quiet these halls are? It is as if one has entered a sacred space like entering a mosque or a cathedral or a cemetery. Of course, this makes sense, since these cases are full of sacrifices, living creatures whose lives were taken for our benefit—to give us an opportunity to get as close to them as possible. Martyrs on the cross, sacrificial lambs, virgins. It is, for many of us, the only chance to have this moment. Sometimes I swear they are staring back at me with some kind of knowing intention in their eyes. I feel embarrassed. The exhilaration at being so close is coupled with the sadness that comes from knowing their fate was of our choosing and for our benefit and part of our knowledge-drive. We are their witnesses. We have a responsibility to look into their eyes (yes, the simulated glass ones) and make contact with their stares, which at one time followed the rhythms of life by opening and closing, as our eyes are doing now in their company.

> One does not meet oneself until one catches the reflection from
> an eye other than human.
>
> —Loren Eiseley

An Opinionated Gardener

I finally got around to pruning today. As I worked on the yew that the deer had pretty much eaten, I thought about all the unfortunate forsythia that had had their fate determined by a hand with an electric clipper, shaping them like yews. The bubble cut seemed so insulting, so not what they wanted to look like. Their freely arching branches say: "I am a forsythia." One of those spring yellows that moves lightly in the wind. Not so, when it has been reduced to a mushroom.

Each plant has its own growth pattern, just like our hair! We know what our hair wants to do, will do, and what it stubbornly will not do. Plants are the same way. I cringe at the crewcut of the forsythia, just as I would cringe if my own head of hair met the same fate. We trust professionals to handle our hair because they know what they are doing and they understand hair. When it comes to pruning, anyone can hack away, especially if he or she owns the pruner, not to mention the victim.

The control and ownership of nature in our own backyards gives us clues to our attitude towards the rest of the world. The prevalence of dyed-red mulch throughout suburbia is a perfect example. What is the fascination with it? Besides containing possible toxins (chromated copper arsenate), it is unsightly. It lacks any connection with the place, the actual color of the local earth. What is this dislike of the ground beneath us? Has it registered somewhere in our psyches that we have damaged to such a degree the fertile soil, once believed to be the giver of life, that we must cover up what we have done? Are we not actually administering the final deathblow—snatching away any breath left by suffocating it under a blanket of artificial decorative uniformity? The aesthetic insult is huge.

"The nation that destroys its soil destroys itself," said FDR.

"I Hate Dandelions!" said the woman on television advertising "weed" killer.

GATHERING VIRGINIA DIRT

Glass jars full of red Virginia clay sit with the other jars of earth on a shelf in my studio: Porto Ercole, Mohave Desert, Big Sur, Bloody Pond …. There is something inspirational (almost sacred) about them as they sit there. I ask myself: What more could I do? I have long intended for them to be used in some way or another, but there they sit, patiently, as if they are aware of their own importance. As time passes, it becomes ever more difficult to touch them as they grow stronger and more powerful.

The earth from the area of Virginia where I once lived found its way into many of my paintings. It's a beautiful burnt orange—full of clay. When working on a piece with this earth in New York, I realized I needed more. I called my father and asked if he wouldn't mind shipping me some. Not only did he agree, but he enlisted the help of a neighbor.

At my father's funeral, that neighbor told me about the "dirt collecting experience" and how it somehow changed the way he looked at that dirt. He told me how they shoveled the earth into cardboard boxes from various places in both his yard and my father's, making sure I would get a good assortment. "The colors were different depending on where we dug it from. In one place we had to pick out the rocks and in another it was all dried together in clumps." He added that any time I needed "*Virginia* dirt," he'd be more than happy to send me some. I was struck by how my desire for more of that specific earth affected another's perception of that earth. My father's neighbor used the word "dirt" for what I called "earth." We were talking about the same thing. Yet the word dirt has come to mean "dirty, something unclean," just as soil has become "soiled." The neighbor was using an old-time authentic and concrete description. I was using something that had become more abstract—Mother Earth, the whole planet. More and more, I've come to like the word dirt. Get down and dirty.

WATER

Precious, essential, crucial element of all living organisms. Critical for our very existence. My paintings of water emerged in the mid 1970s. The more I engaged with the idea of water and its qualities, my focus took a dramatic shift towards things other than human. It was as if the water was doing exactly what it is so good at doing—washing things away.

I want to interject here that my relationship with water had already begun earlier in a more literal way: fighting the prejudices against using acrylics (oil paint was the paint of "real" painters). I refused to succumb. It was not only a preference, but an ecological issue. I could not justify pouring turpentine and all the other solvents one uses with oils down the sink, as was the common practice. Nor did I enjoy breathing the fumes. Water-based pigments seemed less offensive. And this early decision has informed much of how I work today. I rely on water's intention to seep, saturate, blend, drip, soak, dissolve, stain, flood, clean, warp, run, soften, wash ….

A visit to the New England Aquarium in Boston back in that mid-70s period was the catalyst for this shift from human to water. There was something about the floating space and what it held that brought back my love and fascination with the sea. Having spent many childhood years in the company of the Atlantic Ocean and Chesapeake

Bay, I felt instantly reunited with all that I had so loved. "There is, one knows not what sweet mystery about this sea, where gently awful stirrings seem to speak of some hidden soul beneath," writes Melville in *Moby Dick*. All my canvases filled up with water and everything recognizably belonging to the human world floated, broke up, and eventually disappeared. I was submerged and swimming in Melville's "hidden soul beneath."

BIRDS

For the third time in a few months, a bird was flying around in my studio. Flew in when I left the door open, I guess. The bird always freaked out the moment I entered, but I was thrilled. I immediately took it as a good sign. An endorsement of what I was working on: birds.

It is easy to move in that direction—to think the birds are attracted to what I am doing. That they *like* "it." Makes *me* feel good after all. But what if they just flew in during a moment of confusion and, even more, couldn't care less that there were images of birds everywhere? And what about all the blobs of bird shit that were sitting on various surfaces—on the artwork itself? Was that their response? Their participation? Perhaps my initial response was a bit too fast. Before I had allowed myself to stop and "listen," I had already jumped to a satisfying interpretation.

The truth is, I don't know why these birds flew into my studio. There was nothing to eat there, and the weather wasn't cold. Maybe they were bored with the outside and just wanted to check out something new. In any case, our meeting startled them and provoked me into thinking again about painting birds in flight and watching birds fly. The migrating birds will soon be heading south.

FEELING SAD

In regard for nature the contemporary artist stands in much the same position as primitive man. He accepts nature, intuitively. He becomes part of nature. He is not the superman, the pseudo-scientist in nature. He accepts it for its own statement as existence. He marvels. Nature is beauty. Beauty becomes the point of departure—for celebration to produce the work of art.

—David Smith

The beauty of the phenomenon reveals at the same time a profound sadness. I am not referring here to an inherent sadness in the world, but rather to a specific sadness linked to loss and arising from realizing all that we have done to destroy this beauty. It is an angry sadness, and an appropriate feeling. The presentation of the world was once, and still is, a delight to the eyes, to all the senses, affirming our reason for being here, for being alive. To forget this could be our biggest mistake and one that we may never recover from.

Bill McKibben, in *The End of Nature*, said it so well: "For now, let's concentrate on what it feels like to live on a planet where nature is no longer nature. What is the sadness about? ... [M]erely the knowledge that we screwed up ... the sadness of losing something we've begun to fight for, and the added sadness, or shame, of realizing how much more we could have done. ... Our sadness is almost an aesthetic response— appropriate because we have marred a great, mad, profligate work of art, taken a hammer to the most perfectly proportioned of sculptures."

REFERENCES

Blakeslee, Mermer. "The Cut Field." Unpublished poem, used with permission of the author.

Casey, Edward S. "Memorial Mapping of the Land: Materiality in the Work of Margot McLean." In *Earth-Mapping: Artists Reshaping Landscape.* Minneapolis, MN: University of Minnesota Press, 2005.

Jenkins, Louis. "Library." *An Almost Human Gesture.* St. Paul, MN: Eighties Press and Ally Press, 1987.

Jung, C. G. *The Collected Works of C. G. Jung,* Vol. 10. Trans. R. F. C. Hull. Princeton, NJ: Princeton University Press, 1970.

McKibben, Bill. *The End of Nature.* New York: Anchor Books, Doubleday, 1989.

Smith, David. "Thoughts on Sculpture." *College Art Journal* (Winter 1954). In Barbara Rose, ed., *Readings in American Art since 1900: A Documentary Survey* (New York: Praeger Publishers, 1968).

Walters, Mark Jerome. "Saying Goodbye: Mourning the Loss of Extinct Species." *National Wildlife* 37.1 (Dec-Jan. 1998).

ESSENCE (AFTER HERACLITUS)

Dawn's cloudy pink hinted in the marble darkness
of the stream. The mountain night still inhabits the flow,

its presence ungraspable, nowhere and everywhere at once,
and slowly relents to its going, as we find ways to move

in the space of absence; for the earth offers no sanctuary
from itself; always we are nearest; and if it reveals

in this early light, even to our utmost touch of stone
and leaf, it withdraws from us, as if to keep what belongs

apart, since language must mourn all it names,
as water, all things relinquish, never twice the same.

—*Michael Whan*

THE SOUL OF THE SKY

NOEL COBB

Today I announce a new plan to extend a human presence across the solar system. ... It is time for America to take the next steps. Mankind is drawn to the heavens for the same reason we were once drawn into unknown lands and across the open sea. We choose to explore space because doing so improves our lives and lifts our national spirit.

> — George W. Bush, *January 2004 to the U.S. Space Agency,*
> *NASA Headquarters, Washington, D.C.*

We cannot fully exploit space until we can control it.

> — *2001 Commission to assess U. S. National Security,*
> *chaired by Donald Rumsfeld*

Juliet. It was the nightingale, and not the lark,
  What pierc'd the fearful hollow of thine ear;
  Nightly she sings on yon pomegranate tree:
  Believe me, love, it was the nightingale.

Romeo. It was the lark, the herald of the morn,
  No nightingale: look, love, what envious streaks

Noel Cobb practices and teaches archetypal psychology in London. In 1988 he founded the London Convivium for Archetypal Studies and *Sphinx: Journal for Archetypal Studies*. A website devoted to both these enterprises can be found at: www.ArchetypalSphinx.net. He is the author of *Archetypal Imagination—Glimpses of the Gods in Life and Art* (Lindesfarne Press, 1992).

Do lace the severing clouds of yonder east:
Night's candles are burnt out, and jocund day
Stands tiptoe on the misty mountain tops.
I must be gone and live, or stay and die.
— Shakespeare, *Romeo and Juliet*, III.5.1-11

What *is* the Sky? When does sky become space? Its everyday, everpresence could lead us to take it for granted and be, like the air, *simply there*. But the title of this conference* prompts us to reflect on the sky's actual and essential nature, and the more we do so, the more mysterious it appears.

It was there during the night when we slept; it was there in the day when we woke. We learn to know it in all weathers and seasons; and, even if we are imprisoned in a lightless cave, the memory of its existence consoles, inspires, or fills us with emotions as contrary as longing and dread. Goethe, it is said, spoke of holding one virtue before all others: Reverence. Reverence for what is above us, what is around us, and what is beneath us. Apart from the sky, if we were to give a name to "what is above us, around us, and beneath us" as well as in us, we could do no better than to call it the *Soul of the World* or, to give it its ancient Greek name, *Psyche tou kosmou*. Ancient alchemical wisdom says, "The greater part of the soul lies outside the body."

Heraclitus proclaimed: "No matter how far you may travel in any direction, you will never come to the edge of the soul."

In the *Enneads,* Plotinus quotes Sophocles' blind Oedipus at Colonus: "All the place is holy," adding, "and there is nothing without a share of soul." Plotinus is unambiguous on this: "For there never was a time when this universe did not have a soul, or when body existed in the absence of soul, or when matter was not set in order ...." Invoking another image, he says:

> It is as if a net immersed in the waters was alive, but unable to make its own that in which it is. The sea is already spread out and the net spreads with it, as far as it can; for no one of its parts can be anywhere else than where it lies ... wherever body extends there soul is. . . (IV.3.9)

*Editor's Note: This paper was presented at the "Psyche and Sky Conference," Sophia Centre, Bath Spa University, Bath, July 1-2, 2005.

Making absolutely sure we do not simply understand the intelligible world—which informs the soul—as being outside and above the world of the senses, Plotinus says that although "the sense-world is in one place, the intelligible world (the *Nous*) is everywhere." (V.9. [5] 13)

Now, Earth-and-Sky comprise a primordial, dyadic unity; something traditionally understood in most ancient cosmologies, where the two are personified as male and female, a couple. In any case, seeing Earth and Sky as *ensouled* means, first of all, apprehending their essential reality *as image.* Second, it means calling for that activity specific to soul: *personifying,* or "imagining things." This is basic to all questions of soul.

Robert Sardello speaks of "imaginal worlds, populated by the composing beings of the fabric of the physical planet," saying, "our imagination is the organ by which we know these composing beings … the psychic world is this world of the physical world and none other." There is a

> feeling we all have but never acknowledge, that everything is animated. Such feeling is not animism, for animism is a theory that says that soul life is projected onto an inanimate world from within the human psyche. On the contrary, soul inheres within the world and creates our psyches.[1]

For Martin Heidegger, Earth and Sky are part of a primal oneness that is four. Humans and divinities complete that fourfold oneness. "Human being," then,

> consists in dwelling and, indeed, dwelling in the sense of the stay of mortals on the earth. But, 'on the earth' already means 'under the sky.' Both of these also mean 'remaining before the divinities' and include a 'belonging to men's being with one another.' By a primal oneness, the four—earth and sky, divinities and mortals—belong together in one. Earth is the serving bearer, blossoming and fruiting, spreading out in rock and water, rising up into plant and animal.
>
> The sky is the vaulting path of the sun, the course of the changing moon, the wandering glitter of the stars, the year's seasons and their changes, the light and dusk of day; the gloom and glow of night, the clemency and inclemency of the weather, the drifting clouds and blue depths of the ether. When we say

sky, we are already thinking of the other three along with it, but
we give no thought to the simple oneness of the four.[1a]

The sky, like the rest, then, is ensouled. The soul of the sky is not
an element of the physical sky, to be found by chemical analyses of its
gases, molecular studies of stardust, or deepspace telescope-searches
for evidence of black holes or the Big Bang. Sky—Our Sky—is, since
Aristotle, not soul-less, placeless Space, an emptiness, but place, and
place as "the first of all things" which "has a power of its own to change
the course of events."[2] To see the sky as space is to empty it of place
and thereby soul.

First of all, the soul of the sky is to be found in its *"innerness."*
This *innerness* is not something *in* the sky at all, not in its atomic
structures or in the astronomical measurements of its immensely
complex, inter-related movements—as if it were one vast clock that
we could finally explain. The sky's *innerness* lies more in the natural
poetry of its self-display and in what it says to us mortals who are
under it, with one another, during our brief stay on earth. Take rain:
rain is one thing for the scientist, but another for the indigenous
rainmaker. Mohammed said that every raindrop that falls is
accompanied by an Angel—for even a raindrop is a manifestation of
Being. For ages, traditional wisdom has called rain "the elixir of life."

If the soul of the sky is given by images, "those images that yet,
fresh images beget" (W. B. Yeats), then we need not call a halt to the
soul's innate capacity to imagine itself. In the boundlessness of soul
there is room for everything. Heaven, says Plotinus, gains its value by
the *indwelling* of soul.

> As the rays of the sun light up a dark cloud, and make it shine and
> give it a golden look, so soul entering into the body of heaven
> gives it life and gives it immortality and wakes what lies inert.[3]

Many artists, like Constable, can arrive at only one conclusion: the
sky is "the source of light in nature" and governs everything.

The beautiful image Plotinus gives of the All[4]—as a "single living
being which encompasses all the living beings that are within it"—
does not exclude the existence of other images. It is not trying to prove
or explain anything—but to better imagine things as they are. "The
first idea was not to shape the clouds in imitation./The clouds preceded
us/There was a muddy centre before we breathed./There was a myth

before the myth began,/Venerable and articulate and complete./From this the poem springs ...."[5]

For Plotinus:

> This one universe is all bound together in shared experience and is like one living creature, and that which is far is really near ... and nothing is so distant in space that it is not close enough to the nature of the one living thing to share experience.[6]

"This All," at the same time, "is visibly not only one living creature, but many ...." He compares the "figures of the heavenly circuit," or constellations, to individual dancers, each moving in harmony with the whole "as if they were performing a single ballet in a rich variety of dance-movements"[7]— Plato's "choreography of the Gods." "In the All," Plotinus says, "there is an indescribably wonderful variety of powers, especially in the bodies which move through the heavens."[8] There is power both in the figures, or constellations, themselves as well as in the heavenly bodies, or stars, which compose them; as with dancers in whom each hand and limb displays distinctive powers as well as there being great power in the dancer herself.

For Plotinus, the truest and most satisfying image for the universe as a whole is an *aesthetic* one. The different movements of the Dancers of the All "serve the dance and help to make it perfect and complete ...."[9] Marsilio Ficino, who clearly based his famous study "On Obtaining Life from the Heavens"[10] on an inspired reading of this *Ennead,*[11] shares this aesthetic sense of the cosmos. As Eugenio Garin said, "The world as a work of art could be the title of all Ficino's philosophy ...."[12]

Ficino claims[13] that to receive the most from the very spirit of the life of the world, through the rays of the stars, our spirit must be properly prepared and purged. This *spiritus* is innate in everything from plants and trees, sea shells and stones, minerals, metals, and the elemental energies of the celestial bodies. It diffuses its rays, which are *not only visible but can also see,* through the stars which act as its *eyes.* The notion of the *stars as eyes* is a soul-image.

To see the stars as eyes we need to stop the habit of seeing as a subjective activity. It must give way to another kind of perception— no longer looking at a thing but being seen by it. The stars as watchers, witnesses. "When things look at us, they reveal, manifest themselves to the heart."[14]

In another essay, Ficino[15] reverses the idea of the "light of reason" to become "the reason of light;" light comes first, then "our reason." The *reason of light* is a gift of the divine, *not* a product of our making. The quality of this kind of reason is its connection to the deep psyche: the intelligence of "innerness," something far deeper than ego consciousness.[16] This intelligence, for Ficino, is *risus coeli,* "the Laughter of the Sky," and he imagines the sun as the eye of the heavens, an eye that conveys true spirit, as does the eye of the lover … or eyes in a smiling face. "Consider the difference," Tom Moore suggests,

> between a communication received from another person in words and the message conveyed through facial expression or even a twinkle in the eye. This latter is the analogy for the kind of spiritual insight Ficino would have us pick up in the world itself—an awareness of the twinkle in the eye of the cosmos.[17]

In the *Homeric Hymn to Demeter,* Earth grows a wonderfully bright narcissus to trick Persephone as a favor for Hades. This flower "astonished everyone who saw it, mortals and immortals alike. It pushed up a hundred heads, and the fragrance of it made the vast sky above, and all the earth and the sea, laugh," the poet says. A suspicion of collusion between world and underworld gives the classic abduction story a twist, and the laughter of sea, earth, and sky seems cruel when we consider Persephone's fate. Compare Plotinus:[18] "The life of the universe does not serve the purposes of each individual but of the whole" and "does not always give each individual what it wants."[19]

Heidegger reminds us that

> The nature of the image is to let something be seen. … Poetic images … are visible inclusions of the alien in the sight of the familiar. The poetic saying of images gathers the brightness and sound of the heavenly appearances into one with the darkness and silence of what is alien.[20]

"While psychology still locates imagination within the recesses of subjectivity, the word *imagination* belongs to the side of the world," says Sardello.

> The Indo-European root of the word imagination refers to anything changing or intermittent, capable of catching or fixing one's attention. The Sanscrit root of the word refers to the ever-

> changing, ensnaring play of appearances. Imagination also means
> something fleeting, like a cloud, or that which winks or signals.
> To approach the multiplicity of the things of the world requires
> imagination because they are imagination in action—things
> changeful, spellbinding, shuddering, arresting, magical, tricky,
> elusive, shimmering.[21]

The Egyptians personified the changing nature of the sky—the
arresting, magical, elusive, shimmering imagination of the world-soul—
in the image of Nut, the sky-goddess, seeing her as arched naked over
the earth, facing down with hands and feet touching the eastern and
western horizons. Sometimes represented as a suckling sow, she was
mistress of heavenly bodies; her children, the twinkling stars, entered
her mouth and emerged from her womb, giving an animal sense to
the sky as "the female pig who eats her piglets." As Mother of the Sun-
God, Re, Nut also swallowed him each evening and gave birth to him
the next morning. Nut was often engraved or painted on the underside
of a coffin lid, as if to say the deceased was now under her protection
and, like the sun, would one day be reborn after a passage through her
Kingdom of Heaven.

The theophany of Isis, Queen of Heaven, is pictured by Apuleius[22]
as the figure of a woman rising from the sea, garlanded with blossoms,
a crown of rearing snakes and waving ears of corn. The three colors of
her dress are radiant-white, saffron-yellow, and rosy-red. Leaving her
right shoulder uncovered—like images of the Buddha—a night-black
cloak envelopes her. Stars glitter over its surface, and a full moon blazes
among them. She wears sandals of palm leaves and her breath has all
the fragrances of Arabia. Could we find a more fitting way to personify
the soul of the world than this image of Isis?

These images speak of the life and soul of the cosmos around us.[23]
They are grand, yet at the same time intimate and near. Humans have
prayed to them for ages. Are they merely remnants of mankind's
superstitious childhood, to be let go of now that we are the "rulers" of
the universe?

Heidegger, deepening his thoughts on dwelling, says:

> Mortals dwell in that they receive the sky as sky. They leave to
> the sun and the moon their journey, to the stars their courses, to
> the seasons, their blessings and their inclemency; they do not
> turn night into day nor day into a harassed unrest.[24]

In *The Tempest*, Shakespeare expresses this humility in the words of Gonzalo, rebuking the courtiers who mock his care of the soul: "You are gentlemen of brave mettle; you would lift the moon out of her sphere, if she would continue in it five weeks without changing."[25] Or we could imagine the poet, Gerard de Nerval, saying to George Bush about his deadly, plutonium-fuelled "Prometheus Project"[26] for the exploitation and colonization of space:

> Free thinker! Do you think you are the only thinker/on this earth in which life blazes inside all things?/Your liberty does what it wishes with the powers it controls, but when you gather to plan, the universe is not there.[27]

NASA's loveless attitude for the earth is clearly mirrored in our unconsciously accepted belief in heliocentrism. Yet,

> the famous physicist, Ernst Mach, once contended that there are *no physical grounds* on which to argue that the earth is rotating around the sun, since the relativity of motion equally well allows us to say that the universe is rotating around the earth.[28]

A thoughtful woman's perspective on heliocentrism is given by Ginette Paris, who says:

> The cult of Hestia is linked to the geocentrism of the Greeks. If the archetype of the house, signifying a return to the center, is one of the important archetypes of our *psychological* life, it is understandable that the idea of our planet as the center of the universe is just as important in elaborating the *collective* values associated with 'our' planet. We could hypothesize that in losing geocentrism we have lost the feeling that this planet is our home; we have lost a bond with her. … We see two ideas reappearing simultaneously: the first is that the earth is not the center of the universe. The second is that of a departure: one day we shall leave this little planet and explore all other possible ones.[29]

The consequences of our drive to go further up and out has allowed our planet, our collective household, to deteriorate.

> It now takes ecology, 'domestic science,' to remind us to take care of our planet, as if once she ceased to be the center of our attention she became a peripheral fact, something we could leave after using it.[30]

For Hestian, geocentric consciousness, "our" sky is the sky of "our" Earth. "Our" sky is not a sky with six purple moons, nor a sky where fanged mushrooms fly through deadly methane outside a dome of controlled light and weather: "Our" sky enfolds "our" home, "our" Earth. The first house—said to be built by Hestia—echoes the vault of the sky in its roundness, a roundness perennially honored by the great Goddess-Domes: The Hagia Sophia, St. Mark's of Venice, St. Paul's of London, the Duomo of Florence, the blue mosque of Istanbul, and the Taj Mahal of Agra. Our sky is finite as well as infinite. At night it recalls Plotinus's great dancer, but the skies under which we live our little-life-of-everyday is rounded with a sleep and is also a particular life here-with-each-other. These skies are a deeply integral part of our griefs and joys. Our sky is, above all, an emotional sky.

Think of twilight, that time *"inter canem et lupem"*— between the dog and the wolf. Have you never felt the prickling at the back of your neck at its onset? Its luring, yet uncanny, ambiguity? By turns sensuous, playful, expectant, dangerous, deceitful, or ghostly, oracular, protean, and indefinable, twilight is a Crack between the Worlds, a mysterious, fluid, time-boundary—not-this, not-that; an archetypal arena beween the demands of the day and the enigmas of night; a dimming of blinding solar consciousness. Can you ever forget that moment at twilight in Bodhgaya—seat of Sakyamuni's awakening—when a huge red sun sank below one horizon, while a round ivory moon rose, opposite?

And, what is it about dawn? You sit cross-legged at the side of an inlet where the waves scarcely move. Light from the moon has brushed a path of liquid silver across the bay, as she slowly passed overhead to step behind the cliffs. Out of the darkness, hours later, a first gleam of light gives a faint blush to the sky in the east. The light brightens now, as if heralding the arrival of a king. The earth holds its breath, awaiting his appearance. Then on the lip of the horizon, the glimmer becomes the sheerest sliver of burnished gold. Like the head of a baby crowning its mother's vulva as it emerges from her womb, the sun pushes free and out of the night. Dawn brings with it such human joy, such fresh hope. As Sappho says: "Standing by my bed/In gold sandals./Dawn that very/Moment awoke me." And yet, dawn can, as for Romeo, also bring danger.

The moon also rises. But her light is colder, more hypnotic. Not so much human joy as a sense of ecstatic elation. The night air is chill and still. Father holds you in his arms, wrapped in soft wool. He has taken you out of the light of the house into the dark outside, and now he points overhead. Your eyes follow. There is nothing there but that bright, glowing ball. All around, the chill night waits. Does it wait? Father's breathing is the only sound. Then he says in a hushed voice: "Look! Look at the Moon!"

The miracle of imagination works its magic. Why does the moon play such a part in the psyche? It plays such a part because it reminds us of change. Empty to full. Full to empty. This change is different than the change from night to day. This change, like the Sun's, is about cycles of death and rebirth. As in breathing, but slower, deeper, as with the tides, the moon creates through its great attraction, as in lunar beings like women and the cat: "The cat went here and there/ And the moon spun round like a top/ And the nearest kin of the moon,/The creeping cat, looked up./Black Minnaloushe stared at the moon,/ For wander and wail as he would,/The pure cold light in the sky/Troubled his animal blood./Minnaloushe runs in the grass/Lifting his delicate feet./Do you dance, Minnaloushe, do you dance? ... Does Minnaloushe know that his pupils/Will pass from change to change,/ And that from round to crescent,/From crescent to round they range?/ Minnaloushe creeps through the grass/Alone, important and wise,/ And lifts to the changing moon/His changing eyes." [31]

When the moon is away, the nightsky is darker than indigo. And the desert air is crystal. I lie awake on one elbow in the Saharan sand-sea called The Grand Erg. Beside me, a star-map and a torch. I've turned the torch off and lain back, whispering the names of the stars I've learned to locate among the masses above. The sight is overwhelming. Here, infinity has an image, it isn't just mathematics. The spirit may long to calculate how many millions of stars there are, but the soul delights in their self-display. For me, it all started with Merak and Dubhe in The Great Bear, the first two my Dad showed me. Later, came the North Star, Polaris. Then, under the mediterranean sky, Cygnus, the swan, flying with wings wide and neck outstretched through the Milky Way. Further South, I found Orion with his sword and belt, resplendent with those incandescent eyes: Betelgeuze, Bellatrix, Rigel and Saiph. What wonder! And, all hail! Sirius, Dog star, brightest star in the sky! And the constellations: Castor and Pollux! Taurus the Bull, with its giant orange Eye, Aldebaran; Hercules, forever running the stellar Olympics; and the Pleiades, those lovely, veiled daughters of Atlas; Bootes, the herdsman, where the great daimon, Arcturus, lives; and, high in the spring night, Leo, guarding Regulus between his paws, five times bigger, they say, than the sun and 160 times as bright.

How many centuries have we looked up at the stars? The constellation of Leo, lion *couchant,* seems ageless. Who saw it first? And where? In the deserts of Sumer? On the rooftops of Babylon? At sea in the Indian ocean? The Oxford English Dictionary says flatly: "*constellation:* a number of fixed stars grouped together within the outline of an imaginary figure traced on the face of the sky." Yet, it lets slip a prime indication of Anima Mundi: "the *face* of the sky." Question: When we study the face of a friend do we see imaginary lines traced on it—or do we read the character of her soul?

Perhaps, as Plotinus taught, in this one universe, all bound together in shared experience, that which is far is really near. That night so many years ago I hadn't read Plotinus. Nor had I yet heard Sir Laurens van der Post say the Kalahari bushmen felt "known by the stars." But in that great desert night, the sense that our planet is *known* by the stars was suddenly very real. Our heliocentric culture had taught me our Earth was "insignificant." I couldn't really believe this. Yet, who were we? And could we hold up to the stars something worthy of their attention? The question seemed unanswerable. Then the thought came: music! I had a small tape recorder on which, lonely for familiar sounds, I would sometimes play recordings. But since arriving in the desert, mortal compositions seemed out of place. I'd tried many favorites: classical/modern. Nothing could stand before that sky. At last, I remembered a recording of Verdi's *Requiem,* conducted by Barbaroli. These sounds, these voices, might be beautiful enough to reach the heart of a listening star … if "Mozart is sunshine," as Dvorak said, then we must add that "Verdi's *Requiem* is starlight!" Yes, this music was worthy of the stars!

Daily climbing higher in the Nepalese Himalayas, we had reached the last outpost of civilization: Tangboche Monastery. My companion and I paused to regain our strength and adjust to the thin air. On a grassy slope surrounded by blossoming rhododendrons, we rested in contemplation. Meditation texts speak of one's "innate Buddha nature" as the clear, open sky. That day, the sky was the deepest ultramarine I had ever known. Mt. Ama Dablan soared above us, nearly as tall as Everest, with her necklace of dazzling glaciers gleaming in the sunshine. Gazing into the depths of this azure vault, my eyes gradually made out tiny golden sparks which formed into shapes. At first, I couldn't believe it. Then, it became impossible to doubt! The entire sky a lattice-work of tiny, golden buddhas! In wonder, I sat with this blessed vision, until distracted, I lost my concentration. When I looked again, I saw only the intensest blue of the sky—except now the thinnest wisp of vapor was caressing the mountain's cheek. As I watched, the white wisps thickened, became cloud. I was watching the actual formation of cloud out of clear sky. Ancient meditation texts say this is the way thoughts form in the mind. We can watch them, but we do not create them. The clear blue sky is like our "original mind."

The circumscribed fears and passions of mortals shrink in humble lowliness beside the sky's, and yet we strain to reach its dignity and grandeur. If the sky's emotions show in its moods, then any sky can never be one ideal, pure, stainless blue. Not for long. Its moods are ever-changing. To yearn for permanent blue skies, where all is spiritually pure and heavenly blissful, is to dream of a sky that is not of this Earth. It is to fall prey to a monotheistic fallacy, a life-negating fantasy of ultimate paradise.

Seated on a meditation platform built by hermits in the Saharan Hoggar—on the edge of a steep precipice—I became aware of the changing light on the mountains in the distance. By late afternoon, what seemed to have been black, opaque rock-scapes began imperceptibly glowing with pigment: long rays of liquid sun brushed dark ravines with powders of all the spectrum: rust tinged with verdigris, saffron, scarlet, and vermillion: as if a rainbow had melted into earth. The air was motionless; nothing breathed. Miles away a Touareg and his camel slowly merged into deep mountain shadow. The whole day had been a reverie on that 3rd century text: *Celestial Hierarchies*—the distinctions between "orders" of invisibles. Without warning, a loud crack of wind exploded behind me, nearly toppling me over the edge. The fear I felt then was not of falling, but of experiencing Wind-at-its Source, the entry of spirit into the world. *Pneuma*. The Breath of the Sky.

The sky speaks with many voices. One bright August morning in Norway's Rondane range, the sky grew black and utterly quiet before one deafening thunderclap—and that was all. The Greeks would have said Zeus had spoken.

A different experience was that of the skies over the ancient kingdom of Swat where no rain had fallen for six months. One midsummer night, far to the west over the Hindu Kush, growing rumblings warned of stormclouds moving closer. For hours, lightning played like the charged crackling of a dragon's transparent nervous system as it twisted and coiled over the hills. The parched earth waited. If rains came, the parched Earth would be charged with the glory and grandeur of Sky, the maize could be planted, and the harvest would be assured. At midnight, standing on the flat roof of my Gujur house, I felt the Dragon's furious presence overhead—the sky-rolling roars and flashes of his eyes—and, with this, the heavens opened.

From the Makabeng in northern Transvaal to the New Mexican deserts of the Hopi, from the Taoists of old China to the last San bushmen of the Kalahari, rain has been drawn down to earth by chants, cries, dances, and drums—ritual prayers made in the hope of quenching earth's thirst with the life-giving water in the sky. "Who doesn't weep when the stars throw down their spears/ and water heaven with their tears?" What better metaphor for blessings? "The quality of mercy is not strain'd,/It droppeth as the gentle rain from heaven/ Upon the place beneath."[32]

How different the uncanny panic that led to Edvard Munch's painting "The Scream"! "I stopped," he said,

> and leaned against the railing, half-dead with fatigue. Over the grey-blue fjord, the clouds hung, red as blood and tongues of flame. My friends drew away. Alone and trembling with fear, I experienced Nature's great scream.[33]

And, let us not forget van Gogh's skies: from ominously oppressive to watchful and shining with stars; ecstatic blue spirals over twisted cypresses; hot and blazing, or doom-laden and threatening, filled with flapping flocks of crows.

The sky can deepen our dread and mirror premonitions of disaster: fine flakes of ash dropping out of brown, overcast skies telling of large-scale forest fires; sinister sky-silhouettes over burning London; cliched pictures of the FIRST ATOMIC MUSHROOM filling the sky; U.S. helicopters napalming Vietnamese straw-huts from the sky.

Closer to home, RAF jets ripping through the sky overhead as we walk among the newborn lambs. In the last century, humanity has learned to fear the sky in altogether new ways: death-gas sprayed from the sky over families of fleeing Kurds, as thoughtlessly as over cornfields and apple orchards. Pests? Get rid of them! Untold millions of birds—those ecstatic celebrants of flight and song—extinguished! Whole species gone forever—because men believe they can dispense death without consequences—stubbornly ignorant of how all things are connected.

Is there a more glorious embodiment of the soul of the sky? Those "free-flying/leaves,/champions of the air,/petals of smoke,/free,/happy/ flyers and songsters,/... navigators of the wind," Pablo Neruda calls them. Birds! whose tiny, feathered skulls contain, it seems, entire maps of constellations to guide them on their migrating way over seas and continents at night. As Blake says, "How do you know but ev'ry Bird that cuts the airy way,/Is an immense world of delight, clos'd by your senses five?"

And further, do birds not respond to our emotions? What? You've never heard birds join in with an opera broadcast or imitate human noises? Songbirds—original purveyors of melody, the soul's evocation of inspiration and mood. Surely nothing in the world is more expressive of joy than the pure music of the nightingale's bright song, that kind of

> brilliant calling and interweaving of glittering exclamation such as must have been heard on the first day of creation, when the angels suddenly found themselves created, and shouting aloud before they knew it.[34]

And who has not felt an ancient melancholy tug at his breast with the mournful honking of geese, passing by overhead on their long distance wings?

Who notices the soul of the sky? In times past, it was the sailor, the farmer, the star-gazer, and the auger. Speaking of the Etruscan augers, D. H. Lawrence mused:

> To them, hot-blooded birds flew through the living universe as feelings and premonitions fly through the breast of a man, or as thoughts fly through the mind. . . And since all things corresponded in the ancient world, and man's bosom mirrored itself in the bosom of the sky . . . the birds were flying to a

portentous goal, in the man's breast as he watched, as well as
flying their own way in the bosom of the sky. If the auger could
see the birds flying in his heart, then he would know which way
destiny too was flying for him.[35]

Imprisoned by sky-scrapers and filthy skies, who even sees the
constellations or the morning star, the Moon, or the sunrises and
sunsets? Yes, we can also befoul the sky with our unconsciousness.
While the Victorian poor of London coughed out their lungs in smog,
even great artists, like Whistler and Monet, who saw beauty in those
polluted skies while rooming at the Savoy, never protested outside
Parliament against the outpouring of 200, 000 tons of soot into those
same skies each year.

The sky dwarfs our most extreme despairs, with its natural rages—
hurricanes and tornadoes—demolishing all that lays before them. Yet,
is there any greater measure of human grief than Lear, at the death of
Cordelia? "Howl, howl, howl, howl! O, you are men of stones:/Had I
your tongues and eyes, I'd use them so/That heaven's vault should
crack. She's gone for ever!"

I have been talking of the soul of the sky as a face of *anima mundi,*
and how we apprehend it. I spoke of the Sky's "innerness" in images of
sky, of the soul's innate capacity for personifying itself, of learning to
feel perceived by the sky, to sense its emotions and how intimately
our emotions—whether or not we are aware of it—continually respond
and correspond to it. I propose we place "the emotional sky" at the
heart of this collective gathering. This is no sentimental projection. It
is an essential countermeasure to the Puer-Prometheus-Mars-Apollo
drive to soar away from "our" world and "our" sky into abstract space—
"somewhere over the rainbow"—whether literally or in the deadly
glamorization of science and the hubris of its belief in a scientifically
objective world.

James Hillman has indicated what should be obvious to everyone
here: that emotion is a two-way bridge between us and the world,
that "our own emotions … are continually interacting with the world
of nature," and that

> every 'cut' between subject and object is arbitrary. Man and
> world are fundamentally inseparable because the same energy
> constitutes man and world. This is evident on the physical level,

> i. e., we are composed of the same elements as the world about
> us. But on the psychological level we experience the cut because
> we neglect our emotions and thus miss the emotional aspect of
> things. We have such little and such primitive emotional
> awareness that the world about us is either dead and without
> value or falsely overcharged. ... We have left undeveloped the
> faculty of apprehending the world as emotional.[36]

John Keats feared that a scientific gaze would "unweave a rainbow" and "empty the haunted air" by "conquering all mysteries by line and rule." The rainbow is the only phenomenon in nature depending for its appearance not only on the sun but also on us, moving with the observer.[37] Thus, says Sardello, we are face to face with, or directly perceiving, the soul of the world. The soul of the world, in other words, is not perceived unless we give it emotional attention, and turning that attention away from it to "line and rule" is one way of destroying the bridge which unites above and below and whose magical outcome is the world's enchantment.

The sky—"our" sky—with its "greater and lesser lights," its moods, its stars and planets, its mists and clouds and rainbows is our best teacher and image of Awakening.

In Sanscrit, "the one who came awake," fully awake, was known as Buddha, who described himself as awakening to the delusion of all independently existing things. At the end of the "Diamond Sutra," we read: "Thus shall you think of all this fleeting world: a star at dawn, a bubble in a stream; a flash of lightning in a summer cloud. A flickering lamp, a phantom and a dream."

But there is something else those say, who have gazed long and lovingly at "the world as a work of art:" that whatever else it may be, the world is beautiful. To see this is to love it. So, although Shakespeare and the Buddha teach that we are such stuff as dreams are made of and even the great globe itself and all that it inherit shall dissolve into thin air, they may not have been altogether against the kind of attachment to the beauty of the world that comes from love and not from acquisitiveness and the wish to exploit that breeds envy, hatred, and strife.

The sky teaches something else, then, besides awakening. Love! —"the love," as Dante says, "which moves the Sun and the other stars." And Jalal 'uddin, our Mevlana, says: "The soul within the soul lives in a lover./Consider this metaphor: how you love is/ the open sky."

NOTES

1. Robert Sardello, *Facing the World with Soul* (Hudson, New York: Lindisfarne Press, 1992), 22.

1a. Martin Heidegger, "Building, Dwelling, Thinking," in *Poetry, Language and Thought* (New York: Harper & Row, 1971), 149.

2. Edward Casey, *Spirit and Soul* (Dallas, TX: Spring Publications, 1991), 293.

3. Plotinus, *The Enneads,* trans. A. H. Armstrong, Loew ed. V.i.2.

4. The All, in Plotinian terms, is equivalent to everything existing in the universe "after" the One. The quotes in this section are from Plotinus, *Enneads* IV.4.32, trans. A. H. Armstrong.

5. Wallace Stevens, "Notes Toward a Supreme Fiction," IV.

6. Plotinus, *Enneads.* The whole quote is as follows: "This All is visibly not only one living creature, but many; so that in so far as it is one, each individual part is preserved by the whole, but in so far as it is many, when the many encounter each other they often injure each other because they are different; and one injures another to supply its own need, and even makes a meal of another which is at the same time related to and different from it; and each one, naturally striving to do the best for itself, takes to itself that part of the other which is akin to it, and makes away with all that is alien to itself because of its self love."

7. *Ibid.*

8. *Ibid.,* IV.4.36.

9. *Ibid.*, IV.4.33.

10. Marsilio Ficino, *Liber de Vita*, Book Three, *De Vita Coelitus Comparanda.*

11. Plotinus.

12. Eugenio Garin, *Astrology in the Renaissance* (London: Routledge and Kegan Paul, 1983)(Arkana ed. 1990), 76.

13. Ficino, in chapter eleven of book three of *De Vita.*

14. Sardello, *Facing the World with Soul,* 127.

15. *De Lumine.*

16. "The qualities of this light of the heavens, are: the fruitfulness of life, the perspicacity of our senses, the certitude of our intelligence, and the bountifulness of grace." Thomas Moore, *The Planets Within,* 91.

17. *Ibid.*, 92.

18. For these ideas, see *Ennead* IV.4.38-39.

19. *Ibid.* Plotinus says the difficulties about "the gift of evils coming from the gods" would be solved by considering that it is not their deliberate (single) choices which are evil, but the resultant mixture of actions as a consequence of the life of the one universe.

20. Heidegger, ". . . *Poetically Man Dwells*. . .", in *Poetry, Language and Thought*, 226.

21. Sardello, *Facing the World with Soul*, 129-30.

22. In Apuleius, *The Golden Ass*.

23. "The divinities are the beckoning messengers of the godhead. Out of the holy sway of the godhead, the god appears in his presence or withdraws into his concealment. When we speak of the divinities, we are already thinking of the other three along with them, but we give no thought to the simple oneness of the four." Heidegger, "Building, Dwelling, Thinking," in *Poetry, Language, Thought*, 149.

24. *Ibid.*

25. *The Tempest*: II.i.177-9.

26. The actual name given to the project at NASA.

27. Gerard de Nerval, "Golden Lines," trans. Robert Bly, in *News of the Universe* (San Francisco: Sierra Club Books, 1980), 38.

28. Quoted in Robert Svoboda, *The Greatness of Saturn* (Sadhana Publications, 1997), 16.

29. Ginette Paris: *Pagan Meditations* (Dallas, TX: Spring Publications, 1986), 175-7.

30. *Ibid.*

31. W. B. Yeats, *The Cat and the Moon*.

32. *The Merchant of Venice*, IV.i.184-86.

33. Edvard Munch, as quoted in Noel Cobb, "The Morbid and the Beautiful," *Sphinx 1: The London Convivium for Archetypal Studies*, (1988), 46.

34. D. H. Lawrence, *Sketches of Etruscan Places and Other Italian Essays* (London: Penguin, 1999), "The Nightingale," 212.

35. *Ibid.*, "The Painted Tombs of Tarquinia," 6l.

36. James Hillman, *Emotion* (Evanston: Northwestern University Press, 1992), 265.

37. Sardello, *Facing the World with Soul*, 24.

TEMPLE TO GRAVITY

MEREDITH SABINI

Where shall we build temples to the nature gods? So many places need them today. A water temple for New Orleans, where the levees broke; another in Sri Lanka, where the tsunami came. The Gulf Coast and Caribbean Islands, regularly blown by hurricanes, are surely places for temples to the gods of air and wind. For the village of La Conchita, carried by mudslide downhill and across Pacific Coast Highway, an earth shrine. And temples to fire could be built in the Oakland Hills, where three thousand homes were lost, or Malibu, or Berryessa Ridge, where a huge wildfire consumed my house and barn and moonscaped the land.

Nature temples, remember, were not only places to give thanks for the bounty of plants and animals that provide our food and shelter. They were also places where humans prayed and made sacrifices in hopes of propitiating nature deities out of fear of and respect for their potency. The hope was of maintaining balance between the human and nonhuman worlds.

Meredith Sabini, Ph.D., is the editor of *The Earth Has a Soul: The Nature Writings of C. G. Jung*. A licensed psychologist in the field since 1972, she specializes in Dream Consultation and directs The Dream Institute of Northern California. She lives off the e-grid.

Ironically, on my land that burned, we had planned to build adobe shrines—by hand with clay, straw, and water—to the four nature gods.We were restoring an old mineral spring as a nature sanctuary and retreat for healers, much like an Asklepion. The gods obviously had something else in mind. This was shown to a relative of mine in a dream two weeks after the devastation: *My four grandparents were seated in a fire circle and said, "Tell Meredith that this was done with a purpose." They then showed her how all the buildings on the land had been marked so that fire would come and take them. They also showed the old spirits departing the land and the future verdancy it would enjoy.*

Of the seven thousand acres of wilderness burned in that fire, only my parcel lost dwellings. A visitor from the local nature conservancy remarked upon seeing the pattern of the fire, "Why, it looks as if the fire came over the ridge *just* to get your place!" What deity had done the marking that called fire to come? With neighbors, I was taken by helicopter to observe the expanse of the fire, which burned steadily for more than four days. I was stunned at the sight, and wept. The fire burning below was an awesome spectacle—very clearly an autonomous entity or force.

I had sold my urban house and come to this wilderness land as part of a quest to restore my own heritage along with the dilapidated buildings. I come from a lineage of those whose religious practices are community-oriented and earth-based. The diaspora that carried previous generations from country to country, state to state, over the centuries left me not knowing what to call home. I harbored the typical Western illusion that "home" could be found, bought, or built. Fire consumed that fantasy as well. How many of us today are in a similar position—more or less homeless, just under the surface—and faced with paying increasingly exorbitant prices in a desperate effort to feel settled.

In 1909 on a trip to America, Jung had an important dream of a multi-storied house, which he came to understand as representing the ancestral home of our species, built up of successive layers of history. In its lowest level were bones and shards from our phylogenetic past. Jung realized that this level was no dead relic, but alive in the psyche in each and every person, whatever culture they are born into—urban, rural, tribal, peasant, indigenous. "In the cave . . . I discovered the world of the primitive man within myself—a world which can scarcely be reached or illuminated by consciousness . . . bordering on the life of the animal soul."[1]

I too have found my way down through the floors of our "species' house" to that primordial cave at the bottom. This journey has taken place with the help of hints Jung left behind, the guidance of my own dreams, and the experience of living on that wilderness land where I could expose myself to the elements, to wild animals, and to the spirits inhabiting it. A mysterious "pull of gravity" seemed to take my individuation process in that downward direction toward "endarkenment."

One hot afternoon while making swales for the kitchen garden below the house so the natural flow of spring water could keep the spiral rows of plantings moist, I took a break from hoeing and stood quietly in the scorching sun. Suddenly I felt my legs extend downward into the earth to a length twice that of my body. Rarely do I have "physical visions," but on this land they came frequently, as if the primordial world was alive and eager to include me.

"Gravity" has two meanings: it is the force of nature that binds us to earth; and it means seriousness, as in "the gravity of the situation." "Temple" also has two meanings: a place of worship or shrine; and that section of our forehead where we place a finger when contemplating serious matters, grave matters. Our situation today is grave. We need to put our heads together at the temples. Both meanings apply.

Psyche is homeless, banished from nature, extruded from matter centuries ago when a new scientific worldview claimed that plants, rocks, and trees no longer contained nature spirits with which humans could communicate. Matter became lifeless and thus could be moved around in whatever way humans pleased, for any reason. Minerals are extracted from the earth's body without so much as a "Thank you." Forests are clearcut for toilet paper, cardboard boxes, greeting cards. An ecopsychologist I know purchased redwood for a new deck—"only a little bit," she said. Matter doesn't matter. I regularly contribute my share of pollution and damage to the air, water, and soil through the car I drive, wood I burn, rayon clothes I wear, incandescent bulbs I buy. But there is also a position of holding the opposites that I try to maintain: I am bicultural in a new sense. Not because of the Amish nation to which I belong, which has its own laws, mores, and practices, but because I am both modern and primordial, a bicultural classification not yet recognized.

We've had one hundred years of psychotherapy and the world is in no better shape because the healing professions have not ventured far from the upper floor of our species' house. If Jung's discovery of the phylogenetic foundation of the human psyche could be linked with the newly emerging field known as evolutionary psychology, perhaps greater possibilities for healing would open. I feel it is crucial that those of us who have made this journey from the modern to the primordial speak about it, much as explorers of the outer physical world came back with tales of their experiences. In the limited space of an essay, I would like to highlight the stages of this journey.

My title was inspired by a religious structure that appeared in a recent dream: *"I am walking outdoors, slightly uphill, and come to a striking scene: the doors of a church are open and the vista inside is vast. It seems as if a pool, or perhaps a lake, is inside, with trees in the distance. I go up to the door of the church and realize that this scene is inside the church. Or perhaps the church opens out onto the nature scene. A woman minister is there; I ask her what the occasion is. She says they are about to celebrate the long marriage. I see each of them, a black couple, and go over to talk."* Upon waking, I realized it was not clear if nature was inside the church or the church was inside nature, and puzzled over this.

But to distinguish nature and religion, as I was trying to do, is to force an old paradigm template over a new paradigm experience. In the dream, religion and nature are brought together in a new way. Joseph Henderson said that the cure for our present-day neurosis, our cultural neurosis, has to awaken both spirit and matter "to a new life." He believes we are still trying to solve this problem "on too personal, too psychological a level, without fully realizing that at bottom it is a religious problem."[2]

How does the celebration of a long-term marriage connect with this theme? For thirty years, I have been committed to healing the rupture in my relationship with nature by inviting and discovering spirit in the materiality of my body, home, environs, world. The dream felt like a culmination or celebration of this commitment. Why would it be symbolized by a black couple? Because it has involved working with "nigredo"—aspects of our humanness banished into the shadows, marginalized, prejudiced, in myself and the culture. During this process, lengthy in terms of one life span but miniscule in terms of evolution, I have repositioned myself so that I stand at the borderland of civilization where the timeless, universal ways of hunter-gatherers and outcasts can be my guides. Just as the position of ego consciousness shifts as it comes into relation to the Self, so it shifts as our modern selves come into relation with the primordial.

In practical terms, it has meant asking myself, "Is this something anyone, anywhere, anytime, might do?" as a way of evaluating my actions and decisions to bring them into harmony with the survival strategies of our species. It has meant sacrificing privileges of Western entitlement: I gave up medical insurance and cast a vote in favor of our natural healing potential; gave up a clothes dryer and hang laundry out to dry; gave up consuming more than my portion of the world's resources by using what is already in circulation in thrift shops. It has meant learning about nature's wild garden—which "weeds" and "toadstools" are suitable for food, medicine, dyes, fiber. These daily acts allow me to keep one leg anchored in the primordial world while the other remains alert to the modern and its constraints.

It is not clear whether Jung himself really ventured into archaic territory or merely discovered that it exists. Michael Vannoy Adams, in *The Multicultural Imagination,* suggests that Jung came up to that door while in Africa but would not go through, for fear of "going black." Perhaps Jung was only an explorer who came upon a new land but did not spend much time there. It is not important. He did leave a map, whether he intended to or not. It is sketchy, but adequate to find our way there. It is not the esoteric description of the marriage of spirit and matter found in his alchemical writings but a more pragmatic guide from Jung the peasant, the country doctor, and the medicine man who knew the sickness of his tribe and how to heal it.

Activated by this return of psyche to its home in nature are "imaginal fields," or mythic motifs. I have organized my description of the stages of the journey around poetic quotations from Jung that characterize them. These are like cairn, small piles of stones left atop boulders along a trail to indicate to others that they are not lost, but are on a path where others have trod. Psyche does know its way home.

> *Consciousness has somehow slipped from its foundation and no longer knows how to get along on nature's timing.*[3a]

For those who live in earthquake country, this image of a house slipping from its foundation is no abstract metaphor. Houses do slip.

When shaken by tremors, the house may go in one direction while the foundation stays in place. In this quote, Jung was referring to the overvaluation of consciousness, which assumes it can move about the world as it pleases, without consulting the two-million-year-old foundation upon which it rests. He distinguishes between the timing of these acts and nature's timing. We wake up with an "alarm" clock, drink tea or coffee to perk up, work through the afternoon slump in our circadian rhythm. Men override nature's clock by continuing to father children in old age; women now can override nature's timing by artificially inseminating their womb, even after menopause. Resetting my own internal clock took years of analytic work; dreams had to tell me in plain words that I would feel better if I went to bed when first tired rather than overriding that signal and staying up as late as I'd come to believe adults had to. My sleep cycle now functions well, provided I honor its wish to retire at sunset and get up at sunrise.

This motif of our house having slipped from its foundation shows up in dreams exactly this way: houses that have cracks in the foundation, are unbolted, lack foundations, or are built far above the ground. And so it was with the initial dream I had upon beginning analysis in 1972: *"I am several stories up in a high rise, looking down at the ground, where I could see my analyst. I shout to him excitedly, 'I can see the ground! I can see the ground!' Next, he gave me the diagnosis of my condition: 'You have a cultural neurosis'."*

This phrase became a koan for the ensuing years. I came to understand that my neurosis was as much from the culture as from my personal family and that my neurosis paralleled the culture's. As a child, I used to look up at the night sky and wonder why people didn't float off into the vast expanse of open space that seemed to be so close. Thanks to the split between science and religion, I got an answer from the former but not the latter: gravity. Only now can I see in that youthful query the symptom of rootlessness from which I was suffering. My family moved fourteen times during my childhood, chasing the American dream of success and unconsciously repeating the migration pattern that preceding generations had enacted.

The healing movement downward is already present in that dream: I am looking down and shouting down to someone on the ground; whether referring to my analyst objectively or to the subjective healing potential he symbolized, this image points the way. That the ground is visible is a good portent; that I am excited to see it shows the availability of psychic energy to begin the journey. Gravity is doing its work.

People walk in shoes too small for them. That quality of eternity so characteristic of primitive people is entirely lacking.[3b]

The next signpost along the way brings us down to earth, to a specific motif that describes our connection with the ground of reality: shoes. This image frequently appears in dreams of those searching out a new relationship with nature: women's heels are too high, men's wingtips too stiff. Outer evidence of this tendency is that women, especially, tend to purchase shoes one-half to a full size smaller than their feet are; look around as you walk downtown one day and you will notice this trend. As women mature and come into their own, shedding cultural pressures and anima definitions of beauty, they begin to select shoes that are more comfortable to walk in and less showy: soft moccasins, Oriental tabis, handmade loafers—shoes that buffer the rawness of nature but have less of the highly polished persona of "civilized versions."

What intuitive leap takes Jung from this motif of shoes to a reference to eternity? How are the two linked in primitive people? Shoes symbolize our standpoint in life, the philosophy that supports and contains us. Jung envied the philosophy of the Pueblo Indians, which he learned of when visiting Taos Chief Biano in 1925. Their religious practice was to greet the sun every morning: "With our religion we help Father Sun go across the sky. We do this not only for ourselves but for the whole world. If we were to cease practicing our religion, the sun would no longer rise." Jung saw that the dignity and tranquil composure of the Indian "springs from being son of the sun (whose) life is cosmologically meaningful, for he helps the father and preserver of all life in its daily rise and descent."[4] A philosophy like this provides large "shoes" to wear, so that one's stance and standpoint are in alignment with a cosmology of eternity. Anchoring oneself in the two-million-year ancestry of *Homo sapien* has a similar effect whereby one stands within the ongoing life of our species.

> *Most of our difficulties come from losing contact with our instincts,*
> *the age-old unforgotten wisdom stored up in us . . . Loss of instinct is*
> *primarily responsible for the pathological condition of contemporary*
> *culture.*[5]

Instinct was the word Jung frequently used to identify the biological, behavioral, and infrared aspect of the archetypal spectrum; he considered instinct central to the health of a society. "Age-old unforgotten wisdom" is the poetic way Jung described the evolved survival function of instincts. They are often portrayed in dreams by animals throughout the phylogenetic range, and their loss appears in images of those that are injured, underfed, ill, mistreated, or otherwise neglected.

Cats seem to have a special place in the psychology of women. At one point when I had a private practice, a majority of my women clients were having cat dreams. The healing process seemed to follow a particular sequence. Initially, the cats that appeared in dreams were injured, ill, or suffering in ways that symbolized the specific treatment the woman's bodily instincts had received when she was a girl. The next phase, corresponding to the emergence of primary narcissism, showed the cats being groomed, given food and water, and let out to play. The behavioral manifestation of this phase was that women began to tend more carefully to their needs for eating, bathing, resting, socializing. Once instincts began to function more organically, the cats in dreams often took on more spiritualized roles of speaking words of wisdom, guiding the dreamer or accompanying them on challenging tasks.

In a 1960 letter, Jung said that the collective unconscious is identical with Nature. It is the "preconscious aspect of things on the 'animal' or instinctive level."[6] He described archetypes as the

> roots psyche has sunk in the earth . . . the most effective means
> conceivable of instinctive adaptation . . . The chthonic portion
> of the psyche . . . in which its link with the earth and the world
> appears at its most tangible.[7]

In charming and often humorous passages in *The Vision Seminars,* Jung claimed that animals are more pious than humans and the assimilation of our animal nature could have a profound healing effect on ourselves and the world around us. He was deeply worried about "the dangerous atrophy of instinct" and repeatedly and insistently referred to this central symptom of modern life.[8]

> *Every civilized person is still archaic at a deeper level . . . When a*
> *person is fifty, only one part of their being has existed for half a*
> *century; the other part, equally alive, may be millions of years old.*[9]

These statements capture the essence of what Jung discovered at the foundational level of our species' house: that the two-million-year-old aspect of the psyche is still alive. Contemporary studies in evolutionary psychology give empirical validation for this discovery. In the words of Paul Shepard, the first professor of human ecology, it is not that we *were* Pleistocene, but that we still *are* Pleistocene.[10] The way of life our species has lived for ninety-nine percent of its history still shapes our personal, familial, and societal behaviors. Obviously this level of psyche is more dormant and less easily accessible for those of us born and raised in techno-industrial civilizations, and thus the psychological distances we have to go to contact it are likely to be greater.

What sort of dream motifs appear as we descend the stairs of our "house" and approach its phylogenetic foundation? As with Jung, they may at first be only "dusty remains" of earlier cultures, imaged in dreams as pictures of cave paintings or prehistoric scenes in a museum diaorama. The primordial, at this juncture, is still remote, distant, and not yet vitalized. As an approach is made, more vitality appears. A woman at one of my lectures reported dreaming that she was out hunting and crossed a road where, suddenly, a full-fledged Neanderthal stood, holding a spear. This parallels the experience Jung had when setting out for Mombassa: he saw a slim African man leaning on a long spear, observing the train Jung was on:

> I was enchanted by this sight . . . and had the feeling I had
> always known this world . . . as if this dark-skinned man had
> been waiting for me five thousand years.[11]

Von Franz told a similar anecdote about a dream that took place when she moved to Bollingen: monkeys were "romping blissfully" in tall trees adjacent to her house. "You can imagine how much my 'monkey soul' was enjoying life in nature while my urban ego consciousness was reacting rather fearfully," she commented; for her psyche had gone beyond the pagan level to that of "animal ancestral spirits."[12]

In each of these accounts, the primordial is experienced as "other" and is thus still several degrees removed from oneself. As the primordial becomes more accessible to assimilation, it may appear as part of oneself. In *Pregnant Darkness,* analyst Monika Wikman tells of an experience she had while traveling in the Dordogne: stepping out of a shower, she looked down and saw her feet

> blurred into a subtle-body interplay with a primordial woman's feet . . . primitive, rough, hairy, ancient, knowing, sensitive . . . larger than my own but distinctly female, they emanated a felt sense of the original source of being.[13]

Analyst Marea Claassen, who did her Zürich thesis on the "Call of the Primal Ancestors," tells of being an ancient aboriginal woman in a dream, walking on red earth: looking down at her feet, she says, "I am very old, I am ninety thousand years old, I have to walk very slowly."[14] I too had a striking dream experience of looking down at my hand and seeing that it was simian. Earlier in the dream, I was pondering humanity's evolution, wondering whether its stages could be recalled; the image of my own hand as simian seemed to be psyche's response to this question.

The primordial, archaic, or two-million-year-old being in us wants to be known, but often lacks language. It may appear as dream references to aboriginal peoples, ritual body markings, or extinct animals coming back to life. Jung's recognition of the archaic level of the psyche provides a fresh way of interpreting "dark" figures in dreams. Like that black couple in the nature-church, these may not signify aspects of our personal shadows (though that should be considered) but rather are echoes of our evolved African ancestry, our original "home."

A beautifully realized account of an individuation process that led to Africa-as-mother can be found in analyst Rose Emily Rothenberg's book, *The Jewel in the Wound.* Wounds appeared on her body as keloid scars at significant developmental points in her early life. Amplifying the symptoms led her to discover that scarification is intentionally done on women's bodies in some tribal initiations. To see this, she made a pilgrimage to Burkina Faso in West Africa.

> The scars had been made deep within me, and going to Africa to study them was my fate, my odyssey in search of wholeness . . . Returning the keloids to their source would return me to mine.[15]

She too experienced this commitment in terms of a marriage between spirit and matter:

> If I belong to the keloid, it is like a marriage that I gladly participate in. It is . . . connecting to the continuum—going back in time to Africa and forward in time for the sake of the life process.[16]

As with any initiation ritual, linking the primal with the modern involves the basic stages outlined by Van Gennep: separation from one's previous stance in life; a period of liminality in which one is betwixt and between, neither tribal nor modern; and a return to society with the capacity to contain the new pair of opposites.[17] The descent takes us down the stairs of our species' house, away from civilization, and into the "Outback." In the liminal phase, we may experiment in living without some of the cultural artifacts and edifices that keep us above the ground of reality—doing without a car, without insurance, without clocks, without cosmetics, or perhaps in a quasi-tribal arrangement such as co-housing or off-grid. What happens when we make the return journey? This phase too is identified for us by a cairn Jung placed on the road:

> Should it appear in the form of a conflict, then we should keep it in our consciousness and test the two possibilities against each other—the life we live and the one we have forgotten.[18]

If we attempt to bridge the modern and the primal, we will eventually be in an intense conflict. The natural self does not need medication to sleep or gyms for exercise, does not like communicating in soundless, sensory-free blips, or socializing merely because a date is affixed to a calendar. The primal or natural self is not intrinsically rebellious or obstinate, but it may be forced into that stance due to its having been severely repressed:

> The tempo of the development of consciousness through science and technology was too rapid, and left the unconscious, which could no longer keep up with it, far behind, thus forcing it into a defensive position which expresses itself in a universal will to destruction.[19]

Our fantasied notion of progress has dragged our primal self into increasingly mechanized ways of living that are antithetical to our survival patterns.

Just as there are many steps toward restoring one's instincts, so too there are many phases in tolerating and resolving this conflict between the archaic and the modern, which will unfold according to one's personality and typology. I can offer only a few examples, for I have not encountered many who are interested in maintaining the daily tension of these opposites. (The temptation to settle for concretistic or simplistic compromises—such as my own wish to stay on wilderness land—is great.) Dreams may show cave dwellings inside city limits, prehistoric and domesticated animals together in a field, aboriginal and modern people dancing and singing, or houses that face both wilderness and city. Rothenberg cites her own dream of African animals trying to get into her small urban home.

CONCLUSIONS

Jung was a culture shaman to whom intimations of the fate of Western civilization were given. As time went on, the statements he made about our situation grew increasingly urgent: "The cultural order has suppressed primitive disorderliness too long and violently."[20] In 1959, he said, "What is needed is to call a halt to the fatal dissociation that exists between man's higher and lower being; instead, we must unite the conscious man with primitive man."[21] In the many years I have been involved in analytical psychology via seminars, conferences, editing, and publishing, I have rarely heard references to the seminal concerns Jung had about "atrophy of instinct," "age-old phylogenetic experience," or the fate of our "primate nature." Analytical psychology has been more oriented toward and differentiated along the ultraviolet or image end of the archetypal spectrum, to the neglect of the infrared or instinctual.[22]

In the 1990s, I began giving presentations on Jung's evolutionary psychology, often quoting passages from *The Two-Million-Year-Old Self* where Anthony Stevens makes the bold statement that

> the natural world of our planet now depends for its whole future survival on what it can achieve through its intrapsychic representative—the primordial survivor in ourselves.[23]

Just prior to doing a public program in which I planned to explicitly refer to our being at risk as a species, among other endangered species, I had the following dream:

I am giving my talk in Los Angeles. Men remark/complain about how busy they are. I make the interpretation that that is the cultural symptom I'm referring to—busyness is symptomatic of being in the grip of a cultural neurosis, and this is putting us in danger of extinction. But with this comment, I intervened too soon and did not let them talk about why they are so busy; so I ask. Then I complete my presentation by saying that those of us who are healers have to model how to come to terms with this symptom so others can; if we can't, no one can.

I realized I needed to be more empathic to the fears people have about our situation. People sense the death threat unconsciously, but keep busy 24/7 via all the new information and communication gadgetry in order to avoid experiencing the gravitational pull of its seriousness. The dream emphasizes the special role those of us in the healing professions have in terms of curing ourselves of the culture's neurosis, especially its addiction to speed, which overrides the slow pace at which matter and evolution proceed.

A Roman senator's daughter had a dream in which a goddess appeared to her, demanding that her neglected temple be repaired. The girl took her dream to the Senate, which voted funds for the temple's restoration.[24] We have no temples to nature gods and can hardly obtain funds for basic maintenance on roads, schools, or highways, much less restore contaminated soil, air, or waterways. Jung warned that

> the facts of nature cannot in the long run be violated. Penetrating and seeping through everything like water, they will undermine any system that fails to take account of them, and sooner or later they will bring about its downfall.[25]

The facts of nature not being taken into account are now bringing about the downfall of hotels built too close to seacliffs, homes constructed on overly steep hillsides, levees that block the flow of water.

We have come to know the gods as diseases: heart disease, chronic fatigue syndrome, AIDS, and other autoimmune conditions that typify the self disorder of modern society. Now we are seeing the repressed gods return as natural disasters on a global scale. They, indeed, are registering complaints about their neglected temples on the material body we all call home. Psyche knows the situation is grave, and is trying hard to restore balance between primal and modern, spirit and matter.

Walking on that wilderness land one hot summer day before the fire, I glanced over at a boulder at the edge of a trail and saw looking up at me a primordial face that was neither young nor old, male nor female, but universal. I was deeply impacted by its presence. I have spoken here of how the two-million-year-old self may affect us subjectively. The healing process also presents material not meant to be personally assimilated but related to objectively. In dreams or waking experience, there suddenly may be a lion, wooly rhino, panther, or elephant or another larger-than-human creature in one's house, in one's path, whose presence evokes a response from our own equivalent but not-yet-experienced primordialness.

I now live on a modest piece of land that is neither wilderness nor city but between the two. In the small circle of trees that I have made into a chapel are objects of rough beauty reclaimed from the debris of modern life: a mandala-shaped tractor clutch, the blade of an old tree saw, the rusted but elegant disk of a harrow, some sprung bedsprings. I arrange them, paint them, inviting spirit to return to dense matter. This is my temple to gravity. I hold the daily prayer that we remain fastened to this earth for at least as long into the future as we have been here in the past. Perhaps an unworthy species, we are apparently the most current experiment and ought to try to become as fully human as we can. To paraphrase Rothenberg's words about Africa, "Can we be the eyes through which God sees the world?" I have decided I am willing to return again and again to participate in this unfolding. Will you join me?

NOTES

1. C. G. Jung, *Memories, Dreams, Reflections* [hereinafter "*MDR*"] (Princeton, NJ: Princeton University Press, 1961), 160.

2. Joseph Henderson, *Shadow and Self* (Wilmette, IL: Chiron Publications, 1990), 279.

3a. C. G. Jung, *Collected Works* [hereinafter "*CW*"] 8 (Princeton, NJ: Princeton University Press, 1960), para. 802.

3b. Jung, *CW* 8 § 739.

4. Jung, *MDR*, 252.

5. William McGuire, *Jung Speaking: Interviews* (Princeton, NJ: Princeton University Press, 1997), 89; Jung, *CW* 18 § 1494.

6. *C. G. Jung Letters, Volume II*, G. Adler (ed.) (Princeton, NJ: Princeton University Press, 1975), 540.

7. Jung, *CW* 10 § 53.

8. Jung, *CW* 12 § 74, 174; *CW* 13 § 15; *CW* 18 § 1494-95.

9. Jung, *CW* 10 § 105; and McGuire, *Jung Speaking: Interviews,* 57.

10. Paul Shepard, *Coming Home to the Pleistocene* (Washington, DC: Island Press, 1998).

11. Jung, *MDR*, 254.

12. Marie-Louise von Franz, *Archetypal Dimensions of the Psyche* (Boston: Shambhala Publications, 1999), 3-4.

13. Monika Wikman, *Pregnant Darkness* (Berwick, ME: Nicholas-Hays, 2004), 194.

14. Marea Claassen, "The Call of the Primal Ancestors," unpublished diploma thesis (Zurich: C. G. Jung Institute, 1997), 190.

15. Rose Emily Rothenberg, *The Jewel in the Wound* (Wilmette, IL: Chiron Publications, 2001), 140.

16. *Ibid.*

17. Arnold Van Gennep, *The Rites of Passage* (Chicago: University of Chicago Press, 1960).

18. Jung, *CW* 17 § 336.

19. Jung, *CW* 9i § 617.

20. *C. G. Jung Letters, Volume II,* Adler (ed.), 81.

21. McGuire, *Jung Speaking: Interviews*, 397.

22. Meredith Sabini, "Phylogenetic Foundations of Analytical Psychology," *Journal of Jungian Theory and Practice* (Fall 2000), No. 2.

23. Anthony Stevens, *The Two-Million-Year-Old Self* (College Station, TX: Texas A&M Press, 1993), 120.

24. Jung, *CW* 18 § 250.

25. Jung, *CW* 16 § 227.

Deep Time*

Immeasurable, this finger-span,
this sight of an ancient sea.

It heaves within and around us,
a constant motion holding
the gulls momentarily;

like the white flakes
of a snowboat
beginning to dissolve
in the dark waters;

as we too descend
into deeper time, blown
by the strange weather
of our lives.

—*Michael Whan*

---

*First published in *Link* #8, Autumn 2000.

Hurricanes, Lightning Bugs, and Individuation

This article is dedicated to Battle Bell, III, a fellow New Orleans analyst, my Jungian brother, colleague, and dearest friend, who died June 26, 2006 from cancer and the aftermath of Hurricane Katrina. —Battle-R.I.P.

DAVID SCHOEN

> The common background of micro-physics and depth-psychology is as much physical as psychic and therefore neither, but rather a third thing, a neutral nature which can at most be grasped in hints since in essence it is transcendental.
>
> — C. G. Jung[1]

It was evening and an unusually cool, quiet stillness clung to the air for a late August day in south Louisiana, north of Lake Ponchartrain. After six hours of howling, screeching, horrifyingly fierce and devastating winds and continuous torrential rain, it was strange to

David Schoen, L.C.S.W., M.S.S.W., is a Jungian analyst and clinical social worker in private practice in Covington, Louisiana. He is a senior analyst with the Inter-Regional Society of Jungian Analysts, a member of the teaching faculty of the New Orleans Jungian Training Seminar, and advisor to the C. G. Jung Society of Baton Rouge. The author of *Divine Tempest: The Hurricane as a Psychic Phenomenon* (Inner City, 1998), he is presently working on a new book, *The War of the Gods of Addiction*, about the psychodynamics of addiction viewed through the Twelve Steps of Alcoholics Anonymous and Jungian psychology.

encounter the stillness when they stopped as everyone paused, exhaling a little from breaths held longer than imaginable, hiding in hallways under mattresses terrified, fearing that the next tornado-like gust would signal the end of their world.

Once the winds ceased, slowly, gradually, humans stirred and came out from their various burrows, tiptoeing cautiously outside onto the tree-debried streets, surveying the damage to people, houses, and property. Pine trees had crushed through homes and businesses from the roof to the ground like giant blunt-edged knives slicing through butter; cars were smashed; one-hundred-year-old pine trees fallen, snapped in two or twisted unrecognizably; giant oak trees uprooted as if a Titan had been weeding a garden. It was miraculous that we were still alive. It was amazing more people hadn't been killed directly in the storm. The destruction was incomprehensible. Words cannot describe it, and pictures cannot capture the vast scope and depth of the devastation.

Everyone was numb, stunned, in a trance. It was as if we were zombies walking outside into a living nightmare from which we could never escape, no matter how hard we tried. The sun was setting slowly as we attempted to figure out what to do now. The electricity was out, and any form of telecommunication was impossible. We were completely isolated and shut off from the rest of the world.

I was standing outside on my front porch when I was suddenly and surprisingly distracted from my focus on the decimated environment by little lights twinkling off and on in the debris and tangle of the twisted and fallen trees. I wasn't sure at first what it was; then I realized it was what we in Louisiana call lightning bugs (fireflies), flicking their taillights off and on, hundreds, thousands of them all over, more than I had ever witnessed before. It was the most amazingly beautiful spectacle of dancing lights I had ever seen. I then began to notice one, two, then dozens of humming birds, flying, zipping around, standing still in mid-air, looking for the sweet nectar of the flowers in the devastation. Then, as if orchestrated by Walt Disney, brightly colored butterflies emerged, came swarming out of nowhere, flitting all over the fallen landscape followed by a chorus of birds and squirrels running all around. I swear I didn't make this up, it was not an hallucination, and I did not imagine it, it actually happened. It was so unbelievable at the time that I went inside and got my wife, Peggy, to witness it with her own eyes.

As I observed with delight this spectacle of nature, I had two thoughts (or more like questions of wonder!). One, how could these tiny, fragile, oh-so-vulnerable creatures have survived this devastating hurricane, in which winds snapped massive pine trees like mere toothpicks and stripped clean every green leaf from hundreds of thousands of trees? And, two, where did they hide until it was safe to come out? I had no answers, only marvelous appreciation for nature and the tenacity, ingenuity, and creativity of these little creatures. I also realized that it was this same thing I called "nature" which had sent Hurricane Katrina to forever shatter and change the lives of millions of people in New Orleans and on the Gulf Coast of Louisiana, Mississippi, and Alabama—a land mass the size of the United Kingdom. I was experiencing first-hand the incredible duality, splitting, and ambivalence I had written so much about in my 1998 book on the psychological significance of hurricanes, called *Divine Tempest: The Hurricane as a Psychic Phenomenon*.

My personal story is nothing compared to those of neighbors, friends, family, and colleagues who lost literally everything on the Gulf Coast, when the tidal waves—some ninety-two feet high—scoured clean the earth for miles inland like an atmospheric bulldozer, and when levees topped and broke in New Orleans and adjacent parishes, flooding and destroying lives and homes for generations.

The theme of this *Spring Journal* is "Psyche and Nature." My particular contribution to this topic will be about psyche and nature as it manifests in the unique relationship between hurricanes and human beings, especially how we are changed, transformed, and moved psychically by the great storms.

I. Some Facts and Figures

Hurricanes are the greatest and most destructive storms on the face of the Earth. They kill more people each year than all other storms combined. The power of a hurricane is mind boggling. If the heat energy expended by one average hurricane in one day could be converted into electricity, it could supply the electrical needs of the entire United States for six months. The life span of an average hurricane is eight to twelve days. That would be enough power to light up the United States for four to six years—incredible! The energy equivalent of this same average hurricane in one day would equal eighty earthquakes, each the magnitude of the Great San Francisco earthquake of 1906, which completely destroyed the city. The heat energy released by an average hurricane in one day would equal the blast from the simultaneous explosion of four hundred hydrogen bombs of a twenty megaton size.[2] This is more fire power than the nuclear arsenals of the United States and the former Soviet Union combined. Remember that one hydrogen bomb is hundreds of times more powerful than the atomic bombs that destroyed Hiroshima and Nagasaki in 1945.

Some people, impressed by the power of the gigantic mushroom cloud of the atomic bomb, have suggested it might be possible to drop an atomic bomb into the eye of a hurricane to break it up. However, as one commentator put it, trying to stop a hurricane with an atomic bomb would be about as effective as trying to stop an elephant stampede with a B.B. gun.[3]

The deadliest hurricane (typhoon, cyclone) in history hit the mouth of the Ganges River in November 1970, slamming into the coast from the Indian Ocean. More than a million people were killed. The devastation was so terrible that the region rebelled against the government of Pakistan and established the independent nation of Bangladesh. The deadliest storms in U. S. history to date are the Galveston, Texas hurricane of 1900, which killed around 8,000 people; the Southeast Florida hurricane of 1928, which killed 2,500 people; and Hurricane Katrina of 2005, which has killed 1,600 people and counting (more bodies are still being found and more deaths being attributed to the storm as of this writing). The costliest hurricane in history is Hurricane Katrina at $75 billion. Katrina is also being touted as the costliest natural disaster of any kind in U. S. history. Hurricane Andrew in 1992 cost $26.5 billion, and Hurricane Charlie in 2004 cost $15 billion.

The 2005 Atlantic hurricane season set many records: most named storms (27); most costly hurricane (Katrina, $75 billion); lowest barometric pressure (Wilma, 888 millibars); highest storm surge in the U. S. (Katrina, 35 feet; Camille, 25 feet, in 1969); and, most retired names of storms in one season (Dennis, Katrina, Rita, Stan, and Wilma).

Between Hurricanes Katrina and Rita in 2005, 58 recorded tornadoes were spawned. Hurricane Beulah in 1967 holds the record for most tornadoes at 155.

The 2005 hurricane season is the first time the World Meteorological Organization, which names the storms now, has had to go to the Greek alphabet to name six storms after the regular 21-name list was exhausted.

In general, storms are getting bigger, more frequent, and more intense, which certainly raises the very serious question and concern about the effects of global warming, which heats up the oceans and increases the energy available for hurricanes to give them life and keep them running. Cold water and land are the deadly enemies of the hurricane.

It is interesting to note that the hurricane in one way or another creates, contains, or contributes to all other types of storms and natural disasters. Hurricanes incorporate torrential rains, thunderstorms, and lightning. They also involve tidal waves and gale force winds. They cause flooding, mud and landslides. Tornadoes are a primary spin-off phenomenon of hurricanes. There is evidence that hurricanes contribute to blizzards too as excessive moisture moves north or south into the colder regions and results in driving snowstorms. The secondary spin-off winds from hurricanes can fan inland forest fires hundreds or thousands of miles away. A great earthquake in Japan in 1923 is believed by some scientists to have been caused partially by a typhoon that resulted in a significant enough imbalance of barometric pressure on the fault line to trigger the quake.[4] The Great New England hurricane of 1938, which killed 600 people on Long Island registered shock waves on seismographs over 3,000 miles away.[5]

Hurricanes also contribute to volcanic eruptions as the driving torrential rains seep down, deepening the cracks in the volcanoes. This is how most of the Caribbean Islands were created—through volcanic lava flow.

Hurricanes also have a prominent place in history, sending Columbus more swiftly to the Americas where he first heard the word "Hurakan," used by the Mayans to describe their almighty, all-powerful god of the great storms. Columbus brought the term back to Western Europe as the word "hurricane."[6] Hurricanes were involved in helping to sink the famous Spanish Armada by the English in 1588. Shakespeare refers in his works to the hurricane: "Rage, blow you cataracts and Hyrricanos spout." ("King Lear")[7] Hurricanes and stories about them told by sailors are believed to have been major influences and inspirations for Shakespeare's writing of both "The Tempest" and "King Lear."

The hurricane is unique in many ways. It is the only type of natural disaster which we anthropomorphize by giving it an individual, personal, human name and relate to it through written signs and vocalizations as if it has a consciousness which can hear, see, be communicated with, and be influenced in some way.

When a hurricane approaches a community, there is created a relativization of time, space, and activity around its coming, arrival, and leaving. All human endeavors not related to the hurricane and survival cease to be of importance. All commercial, social, educational, and religious activities and events are canceled. Everything stops, stands still; there is a kind of collective and literal holding of the breath until the great storm passes. Civilization is literally suspended, as if to acknowledge and bow to a power greater than itself.

II. The Hurricane Splits Us

In my research on the hurricane, I found over and over the theme motifs of ambivalence, duality, and splitting swirling around in and through and about the great storms. The hurricane spins counterclockwise in the Northern Hemisphere, which is associated symbolically with Medusa's eye, evil, the Satanic Mass, and the negative destructive aspects of Mother Nature. It spins clockwise in the Southern Hemisphere, which is associated symbolically with the eye of the Great Mother, who is good and nourishing and reflects creative transformation. Counterclockwise movement symbolizes stagnation, dismemberment, death, and unconsciousness. Clockwise movement symbolizes growth, integration, life, and conscious development. The hurricane incorporates both of these seemingly oppositional and incompatible aspects.

In researching symbols and myths, I found just as many masculine as feminine references to the hurricane: Masculine—Hurakan, Poseidon, Set/Typhon, Indra, Wotan, Aeolus, wizards, etc. Feminine— Guabancex, Hera, Tiamat, Harpies, Chimaera, witches, etc. Hurricane names are now equally divided between males and females. The hurricane flag is red and black. Alchemically, red is most often associated with the active masculine principle; black is primarily associated with the receptive, dark feminine principle. The hurricane is made up of air and water. Air is associated with the masculine spirit principle. Water is associated with the feminine soul principle, etc., etc. The duality of the hurricane as both masculine and feminine echoes throughout its many images and associations.

Though most people are quite aware of the negative, destructive, and harmful aspects of hurricanes, few seem to be conscious of their positive, helpful, constructive, and creative ones. To start with, hurricanes are essential to maintaining and keeping the world's heat thermostat system in balance. Hurricanes annually move and distribute tremendous amounts of heat energy, which builds up in the tropics from the equator to cooler areas near the poles, thus helping to maintain an equilibrium of temperatures around the world.[8] Hurricanes are also essential in bringing precipitation to drought-stricken areas, deserts, and to normally dry tropical islands as well as to restoring wetlands with needed moisture and nutrients. They help in distributing water to many places on earth which would not get any otherwise.

Hurricanes also prune and clear away old, decaying structures , sometimes wiping them completely clean, allowing new possibilities for life and growth. New Orleans and the Gulf Coast have a chance to renew and rebuild in ways that were never possible before Hurricane Katrina. Many individuals and families have started new and better lives in other places, which would have never been considered before the storm. Businesses have the opportunity to retool and restructure in more efficient, profitable, and competitive ways. Government has a new mandate to organize and more consciously serve the good of the community. People, in general, have the opportunity to reprioritize and decide what is truly most important, essential, and meaningful in their lives and then to act on those choices and decisions.

Hurricanes are essential in the distribution of plant life, animals, fish, and birds to new areas of the world. Species diversity relies upon hurricanes to move different species out of their normal habitats and environments to new regions and give them new opportunities to thrive. Some species, carried by the wind and waves and in the eyes of the storms, have been found transplanted thousands of miles to new homes. Hurricanes are great biodiversity mixers for our planet.

Some scientists believe that hurricanes were a necessary and essential ingredient in the very creation of life itself. Three to four billion years ago, the earth had cooled to a seething boil—an all-encompassing envelope of raging storms. Hurricanes dominated the planet. Over time, these storms interacted with inert elements and chemicals. Somehow, the elements and chemicals were energized by the great the storms, perhaps by the electricity of the lightning. Thus complex organic compounds were created, and this is believed to be the beginning of life itself. These compounds gradually evolved over millions of years into living organisms, which began their long evolutionary trek, eventually populating the planet with a vast variety of species of every kind, including human beings.[9]

When people ignorantly talk of the benefit of getting rid of hurricanes, they are being short-sighted, not realizing that this could have potentially devastating consequences for the environment and perhaps even contribute to the destruction of our planet. So it's important to see the whole picture of the hurricane, both its positive and negative qualities, how it both creates and destroys, adds and subtracts, how as a part of nature it both kills and gives life.

Another example of this duality and split around the hurricane appears in society's strong ambivalent reaction to hurricanes, an approach-avoidance phenomenon which has us at the same time wanting the storm to come and for it to go away. People are both attracted and repelled. This duality of response creates a tension-of-opposites field of powerful excitement, fascination, anticipation, fear, and dread. We want to get close to the awesome power and energy of the storm, to be touched, but not to be hurt or destroyed by it. So when the storm hits somewhere else, we are both relieved and disappointed. We want to be safe and protected, but we also want to be close to the whirling wind and fire of the gods.

III. AFTER THE STORM: POST-TRAUMATIC STRESS DISORDER (PTSD)

After a major hurricane hits a region or a community, the physical and psychological implications are profound. My own experience after Hurricane Katrina, as well as that of my clients, has enhanced and deepened my understanding and appreciation for how powerful, nuanced, and complex this whole process is for so many people.

When one person or one family loses their home, it is tragic and traumatic, but the rest of the community is still intact, still functioning and available as a resource and to provide help and support. But when the whole community is traumatized and a majority of people lose their homes, it's as if everyone is raped, impoverished, and homeless, all at the same time. The normal resources and networks of support and help are not available, or are greatly diminished because everyone is trying to find a way to cope and survive.

Hurricanes can bring out the best and the worst in human nature. The crises created by the hurricane and desperate human need activate the most generous, heroic, compassionate, and selfless acts by many people toward perfect strangers. This can be attested to by the numerous images and stories of heart-warming care and heroic rescues exhibited during and after Hurricane Katrina. But the hurricane can also call forth the worst, darkest, most selfish, greedy, abusive, and degenerate parts of human nature: looting, rape, murder, fraud, profiteering, price gouging, abandonment, and sadistic cruelty. You hear many of these stories after the storm, too. The hurricane seems to bring out the extremes in us of love and hate, good and evil, hope and despair.

When a community is hit by a major hurricane, we see many of the classic symptoms of Post-Traumatic Stress Disorder (PTSD): easy to startle and become frightened, high agitation and irritability, emotions on the edge—angry outbursts, crying at the drop of a hat, free-floating anxiety—depression, fear, worry, difficulty sleeping, nightmares, overeating, overdrinking, panic attacks, restlessness, distractibility, mental confusion, trouble concentrating and focusing, forgetfulness and memory difficulties, flashbacks, excitability, overreacting, low energy and physical exhaustion, motivation problems, lethargy, and difficulty investing in normal goals, activities, and relationships.

After Hurricane Katrina and other devastating storms, like Andrew and Camille, the psychological reaction to the devastation and destruction is often people in shock, whose only comparative analogy is that it looks and feels like they are in a bombed-out war zone. Interestingly, military personnel, who recently served in the Iraq war and then came to help with Hurricane Katrina relief, reported that the aftermath of Katrina was much worse in scope and level of destruction than anything they had experienced in Iraq. Remember how powerful a hurricane is—the simultaneous explosion of 400 hydrogen bombs.

The suicide rate after a major hurricane goes up 31% in the general population and stays elevated for two years. After Hurricane Katrina the National Suicide Prevention hotline reported their average monthly calls had jumped from 3,000 to 6,000 a month with most of the increase coming from the Gulf Coast region hit by the storms. Reports indicated that PTSD symptoms were epidemic in New Orleans ten months after Hurricane Katrina, affecting three-fourths of the population, and that the suicide rate has tripled even though less than one third of the pre-storm population has returned to the city. Hopelessness and despair, whether to keep on trying or not, to keep on fighting to live through many stages of the recovery process are very real concerns when you've lost so much, sometimes everything. Your future is uncertain, and perhaps all you have left is your life. The hurricane pushes many people to that existential breaking point, to be or not to be, to choose life or death.

Alcohol and drug abuse both increase significantly after a major storm; divorce rates rise 30% over normal times; child abuse reports multiply; domestic violence increases. The stresses on family systems are tremendous—where to find food, shelter, clothing, work, medical services, etc.

Over 70% of the deaths attributed to Hurricane Katrina during and after the storm were elderly people sixty-five years of age or older. The multiple stresses of evacuation and the aftermath of a storm, the disruptions in routines and in medical and care services for the elderly, sick, and the very young, put them at the greatest risk of death. They are the most vulnerable segments of the population, whether they live in a more developed nation or not. Recent statistics indicate there were Katrina-related deaths outside of Louisiana in thirty-one other states, and the count continues. The stresses after a major storm create both physical and mental exhaustion and burn-out. Three to six months after Hurricane Katrina many previously healthy individuals have been suddenly diagnosed with cancer, heart problems, and other life threatening, stress-related illnesses. A significant number of my colleagues, neighbors, and friends have died within less than a year of the storm. Many others are now battling for their lives. It seems one of the aftermaths of a severe hurricane is that stress and exhaustion not only compromise us mentally, but physically and biologically, as our immune systems and defense mechanisms weaken, making us more vulnerable and less able to ward off and resist disease and major illness.

A number of my clients who are medical professionals practicing in south Louisiana have told me that since the storm they are seeing many more sick people, more often, with more severe forms of illness. A greater percentage of their patients are dying, and the hospital beds are overflowing.

When I'm asked what to expect psychologically for the next hurricane season after terrible storms like Katrina, Andrew, and Camille have hit, it is much like telling a person who has been raped last year that there is a possibility that the rapist may be in their neighborhood anytime in the next six months, but we can't say for sure exactly when or where. The high level of anxiety, anticipation, fear, and panic attacks becomes normative, and even reasonable, in the general population.

My mantra to everyone affected by Hurricane Katrina is to try and breath, relax, slow down, meditate, take care of yourself, smell the roses, exercise, eat healthy, escape, take vacations, give yourself a break, pray, take naps, find a way to reduce tension and stress—if you don't, it could very well cost you your life. Recovery is a marathon, not a sprint, we must pace ourselves for the long haul. Operating on adrenaline indefinitely will only result in burn-out, and we will ultimately crash and burn.

IV. The Hurricane as Archetype

I make the case in my book, *Divine Tempest: The Hurricane as a Psychic Phenomenon*, that the hurricane is a universal symbol reflecting an archetypal image of the Self in perhaps its most primordial, pre-human, pre-organic form. Our instinctual response to the hurricane very much follows the description of "The Idea of the Holy" in Rudolph Otto's classic book on the subject. He talks about qualities such as the "*mysterium tremendum*" (the tremendous mystery), the "daemonic" fascination, the "absolute overpoweringness" of getting close to the divine, to the holy, of having a "numinous experience" of the transcendent. The hurricane evokes and activates all of these responses and experiences in human beings. We are moved by the hurricane in exactly the same visceral way that human beings throughout human history always have been moved when they encounter the divine.

Mythologically, the hurricane shares the most symbolically with Mercurius, the Uroboros, and, of course, Hurakan and Guabancex from Central American myth, who are the all-powerful gods associated with the hurricane. In Indian myth, there are aspects of Siva and Indra reflecting the hurricane. Elements of Oceanus, Hera, Aeolus, Typhon, and Poseidon mirror aspects of the great storms in Greek myth. From Egyptian myth, Set and Typhon make their claim. From Assyro-Babylonian myth, Enlil, Adad, Lord Marduk, and Tiamat enact the drama around storms and hurricanes. In Teutonic/Germanic myth, Wotan/Woden/Odin is the lord of the hurricane. Jung even refers to the collective seizure of the German people by Hitler through the powerful archetype of Wotan, the god of war, as a "hurricane" breaking loose in Germany.[10] Chinese myth posits a yin-yang dynamic which creates and incorporates the hurricane. There is a similar tradition in Tibetan myth; and, in Japanese myth, there is a whirlwind god, Haya-ji. Other myths break up the different attributes of the hurricane among a number of lesser deities.

I have also found that synchronicity and ESP phenomena occur frequently around hurricanes (such things as clocks stopping, presence of ghosts, physical sensations, and precognitive dreams) which Jung says most often happen when an archetype has been activated. In addition, a number of people I interviewed reported that the most significant transformative experiences of their lives were connected to either an actual hurricane or to a hurricane which the psyche conjured up inwardly.

The hurricane has many mandalas, spiraling, circumambulating, and centering eye features of the Self. One is Edinger's idea of "circulatio" in alchemy, the recycling of substances by heating— ascending, condensing, and descending repeatedly. Another is Neumann's "centroversion" principle, the synthesizing of introversion and extroversion into a third unifying process of all parts. Both of these operate in the Uroboros and in the human psyche as well. An abundance of the anthropological, mythological, alchemical, scientific, and psychological data confirms and reenforces the hurricane as an archetypal image of the Self.

In my research on hurricane dreams, I found what I call "symbolic hurricane dreams," which are neither anticipatory dreams of actual hurricanes nor PTSD post-hurricane nightmares. They are instead dreams where the psyche appropriates the image of the hurricane and uses it for its own symbolic purposes. In these dreams, which occur much less frequently than do tornado, earthquake, thunderstorm, volcano, or tsunami dreams, the psyche seems to use the image of the hurricane selectively to up the ante from some personal fear complex of the dreamer (such as fear of growing up, getting a divorce, having a baby, riding horses, doing creative writing, or disappointing other people) to what I call "archetypal fear," imaged by the powerful, chaotic, swirling, destructive/creative energies of the hurricane. Dreaming of a hurricane can signal the opportunity for the most creative, transforming experience of our lives, or it can toll the bell for the most overwhelming destruction we will ever know—all in the name of individuation.

All of the evidence points to the psyche using the hurricane image of the Self on a very undeveloped, primordial level, indicating huge amounts of raw psychic energy potentially available to consciousness for integration if the correct conscious ego attitude and actions can be adopted. If the alignment of the ego-Self axis can occur successfully, great things are possible: growth, integration, healing, and transformation. If the individual is unsuccessful, remains in the old or wrong conscious ego attitude, or fails to take the appropriate actions called for as happens in so many fairy tales, then all of that incredible, raw, potential psychic energy can turn upon the individual and swamp him or her with overwhelmingly destructive consequences, physically and psychically. If we don't respond to the call of the Self, we can cut ourselves off from the great divine flow of life and energy.

In the scriptures in the Old Testament it says that "the beginning of wisdom is the fear of the Lord." (Proverbs 9: 10) This "fear of the Lord" is the "archetypal fear" that I am talking about, which is imaged in "symbolic hurricane dreams." The "beginning of wisdom" translates in Jungian terms to mean the beginning of individuation.

It seems the psyche wants us to become more conscious, to develop a relationship with the Self; and it uses the hurricane image with its inherently powerful, awesome, transcendent, and primitive components of archetypal fear to get our attention in a way that few other things do. People don't often appreciate enough how important and essential the experience of fear is for both our personal survival and for our individuation journey. Without fear and the humbling of our inflated egos, we live in dangerous grandiose delusion and illusion and cannot enter into the appropriate cooperative relationship with the divine, the Self, the will of God in our lives.

Nothing moves us, stirs us up, turns us around, grabs our attention, gets us out of ourselves, or scares us to death more than our relationship to the hurricane. Walker Percy, the great existentialist Southern novelist from Louisiana, would say that the hurricane and other such disasters are the impetus that shakes us up, that wakes us up to leave the malaise of our routine, boring, everyday, robotic lives—what he often referred to as the Wednesday afternoons of life—and to begin to live, drinking every drop of our lives, every moment, with as much fullness, aliveness, awareness, and appreciation as possible. What we Jungians, less poetically, would call becoming conscious!

The hurricane is eternal, as far as humans are concerned. It comes every year, it existed before us throughout our human history, and probably will still be around when we are gone as a species. It is nature's consummate emissary from the Self, calling to us every hurricane season to find the Self, to live the symbolic life, to cooperate with our uniqueness, our individuation, and the most authentic meaning of our lives. This truth is even more real to me after Hurricane Katrina than ever before.

Finally we need to remember that in the midst of the devastation, destruction, chaos, loss, and death of the hurricane, miracles are happening: lightning bugs, great selfless acts of heroism and compassion, generosity overflowing from strangers, species redistribution, water to the thirsty, transformative renewal, new opportunities, new life, new creation, new chances for change and ultimately for individuation itself to occur.

> There are indications that physical and psychic energy may be but two aspects of one and the same underlying reality. If this turns out to be the case, then the world of matter will appear as, so to speak, a mirror-image of the world of spirit or of the psyche, and vice versa.[11] — Marie-Louise von Franz

NOTES

1. C. G. Jung, *The Collected Works* (Bollingen Series XCVII), ed. William McGuire and R. F. C. Hull (Princeton: Princeton University Press, 1977), vol. 14, par. 768.

2. Gary Jennings, *The Killer Storms: Hurricanes, Typhoons and Tornadoes* (New York: J. B. Lippicott Co., 1970), 59.

3. *Ibid.*, 181.

4. *Ibid.*, 93.

5. *Ibid.*, 97.

6. Marjory Stoneman Douglas, *Hurricane* (New York: Rinehart and Company, 1958), 42.

7. Act 3, scene 2, lines 2-3.

8. Sally Lee, *Hurricanes* (New York: Franklin Watts, 1993), 9.

9. Jennings, *Killer Storms*, 49.

10. Jung, *CW* 10 § 389.

11. Marie-Louise von Franz, *C. G. Jung: His Myth in Our Time,* trans. William H. Kennedy (New York: C. G. Jung Foundation, 1975), 236.

Ovid's Praise to a Crow on Going into Exile

This wintry day, crow huddled and black, sat on a stone wall. What does he contemplate in the bleak nightfall of his eye; 'enviroment,' bare horizons, arctic conditions? Or, does he simply stare into the vacancies? His mind toughened like bitter steel, riveted, tensile, gleaming in the rough winds, until it conceives a wilderness of dense forests and granite air, one where crow can fly economically for years and years.

Crow has acumen, blessings, and his flight takes the path to nowhere, glacial, fusing feathers and elements. But he is always clever in this province of disaster with its refined torments and butchered heart. To him just meat, carrion. Indeed, he has a mindful tolerance for winter and life's zero. Its lens of nothingness grants him relentless insight, since without memory and desire, he can sit on a wall, huddled and black, all this wintry day; needless in a world of fragments, without Platonic access to wholes and universals; a bird of particulars and a harsh cry. One of nature's iron installations, showing for an entire season in the earth's out-of-doors galleries, here and there. Unlike owl who proclaims the 'woo-woo stuff,' mysterian of midnight theorems, 'post-' everything in the stoic cowl of a warrior-monk, a posthumous veteran of the wastelands.

Oh, let the world ever shield the dark figment of your grace; in your wildness its preservation. Holy naturalist of the uplands, share with me the loving secret of your dawns, how you begin the rosy-fingered day. Teach me the passion of your unfathomable formula, your elixir of rugged survival, your courage to live; the diamond hardness of your refusal, the tender concealment of your compassion for your young. Tell me how nature manufactures such creaturely negation, combining in cold fusion your wing and prayer, wherein extremes touch indefinitely. Lend me the mask of your austere existence, that I may metamorphose to endure, before tomorrow's exile, to winter out the coming years.

—*Michael Whan*

Cyborgian Drift: Resistance is not Futile

GLEN SLATER

As we enter the 2030s there won't be clear distinctions between human and machine, between real and virtual reality, or between work and play.
  —Ray Kurzweil[1]

If we are downloaded into our technology, what are the chances that we will thereafter be ourselves or even human? . . . on this path our humanity may well be lost.
  —Bill Joy[2]

The facts of nature cannot in the long run be violated. Penetrating and seeping through everything like water, they will undermine any system that fails to take account of them, and sooner or later they will bring about its downfall.
  —C. G. Jung[3]

If certain trends in technology, psychology, and society at large maintain their present direction, thirty to forty years from now a new species of human being will stand before us. Stepping straight from the pages of science fiction, the cyborg,[4] the human-machine

Glen Slater, Ph.D., is a core faculty member at Pacifica Graduate Institute where he teaches in the departments of Mythological Studies and Depth Psychology. He is the Film Review Editor of *Spring Journal*, and has written articles for various psychology publications.

hybrid, will be realized. The nature of being human, human nature, will be forever altered. In the wake of physiological and functional changes that will begin with artificial organs and move to the neural implanting of computer chips and nano-sized robots, the psyche as we know it will cease to exist. The instinctual and archetypal roots of existence will be detached. The ability to perceive and experience life in a manner that reflects the evolution of the earth and our adaptation to its environment will fade away. Leaving behind these ties to nature, we will enter a cycle of development governed by values of efficiency, longevity, rational intelligence, and adaptation to technological surrounds. The dawn of a second creation, a remaking of ourselves in our own industrialized and egocentric image, will be upon us.

Natural contexts, within and without, psychological and ecological, are already altered by psychotropic drugs, virtual interfaces between mind and world, and fabricated simulations of social and communal life. What it means to be human is being redefined within these artificial and manipulated contexts. Whereas history has always been determined in part by technological innovations, until now these innovations have largely remained tools outside of our essentially human form. Technology has changed our interactions with the world, but not essential human physiology or the psyche that brings the universal patterns of primordial life into the present. Body, mind, psyche, though exposed to technology and partially adapted to it, have also remained substantially apart from it. This is about to change. Within decades the human body and mind will be redefined as they merge with developments in robotics and computing. As cyborgologist Donna Haraway writes, "the mercurial Terminator is also an image on the seed package of a possible future."[5] *Homosapien* meet *Homo Cybernicus*.[6]

It is naïve to think that technological innovation will not continue largely unabated, and it is untenable to participate in society as a Luddite and run in the opposite direction. However, *altering* course remains an option. Such an option will depend on our capacity to digest and respond to the psychological and humanistic implications of the prospective changes. Altering course will also depend upon cultivating sensibilities that ensure technology serves the ground of being, challenging notions that aim to remake that ground in service of technology. As I intend to show, at the heart of the issue is the capacity to preserve psychic nature and the qualitative state we refer to as soul.

To turn this corner and remain human, a deepened sense of soul and a fidelity to the imagination may be the makeweights.

Psychology is the estranged twin of technology. "Why do we have psychology?" asks Jung. "Because we are already strangled by our rational devices."[7] As we move into this new millennium, the psychological implications of a cyborgian life, the first phase in the so-called "posthuman" phase of evolution, must be explored. In what follows I will use the term "cyborgian" to connote a psycho-cultural orientation to human-machine hybridization, in contrast to the adjective "cybernetic," which describes the artificial enhancement of an organism's capacity to process information, though not the mindset that pursues this state. "Drift" suggests being caught in a movement without being conscious of its direction. Although compelled to look at possible futures to perceive the direction of this movement, the concern comes to rest in the actual present. Cyborgian drift is well underway, and its implications are upon us: We have already lost an awareness of ourselves as animals, as a species belonging to an ecosystem, and we are fast developing psychologies that reduce our experience to robotic and computational processes, conceiving of ourselves as analogues of complex machines. Mechanical metaphors now dominate medicine, psychiatry, and mainstream psychology. An examination of these themes reveals that it is today's mindset that will extinguish tomorrow's psyche.

BEYOND HUMAN NATURE

In 1965 Gordon Moore, the inventor of integrated circuits and the former chairman of Intel, made a prediction: every year the surface area of the transistors that are the basis of computer chips would be reduced by half. In 1975 he reportedly updated the prediction to every two years. Essentially, this meant that the power of computer chips would double every two years.[8] "Moore's Law" has proven to be remarkably accurate. This exponential growth in computing power forms the backbone of a cybernetic future: Once computer chips gain enough power to roughly parallel human thought, and interfaces between human brains and silicon based technology are developed, the divide between human and artificial intelligence will collapse. At this point, computers housed in robotic form will develop the capacity to think and behave like humans, and humans will turn their minds over to the seemingly infinite enhancement in mental function that computer augmentation of brain function would provide. Direct neural connection to cyberspace will occur somewhere along the way.

At the same time the mind is wedding the computer chip, genetic engineering and nanotechnology will be entering vast new terrain. The meeting of these fields is referred to as "GNR" technology—genetics, nanotechnology, and robotics. Couples will be given the opportunity to choose among a hundred fertilized eggs for the most genetically sound; rudimentary forms of the designer baby scenario will follow. Later in the life of these genetically select or redesigned individuals, nano-sized robots will be injected into the bloodstream to repair tissue damage, fight viruses, and otherwise fill the gaps between larger scale artificial replacement parts. At some point nanotechnology will enter the brain and begin to alter the speed and patterns of neural connections.[9] The ever-expanding range of psychotropic medications, designed to tune our moods and iron out personality quirks, will seem antiquated by the time the nano spiced brain arrives. By this stage human nature will be a thing of the past. These scenarios are predicted to be one generation away.

An expansive literature exists detailing such changes on the horizon, mostly written by technologists eager to bring forth the human-robot synergy. Rodney Brooks,[10] Hans Moravec,[11] and Ray Kurzweil are some of the leading advocates of this movement. Of the group, Kurzwiel is the most prominent voice. His works, *The Age of Intelligent Machines*,[12] *The Age of Spiritual Machines,* and, most recently, *The Singularity is Near*, paint a vivid picture of the cyborgian age to come.

Kurweil suggests "it is reasonable to estimate that a $1000 personal computer will match the computing speed and capacity of the human brain by around the year 2020."[13] From this point on, the merger of human and silicon forms of intelligence is portrayed as inevitable. The stepping-stones are easy to follow and laid out by Kurzweil in ten-year increments. 2009 will see the multiplying of chip-based gadgetry on and around our bodies. We already have palm-sized computers, phones that attach to the ear, and running shoes with microprocessors. The smaller these chips become, the more ubiquitous they will be, and the more likely they will enter our bodies. Using molecular electronics, "where individual atoms and molecules replace lithographically drawn transistors,"[14] IBM scientists have already built logic circuits that are less than a trillionth of a square inch in size.[15] By 2019 virtual reality will surround us, from glasses with various visual enhancements to holographic phones that display those we call in three dimensions. By this point, "People are beginning to have relationships with automated personalities as companions, teachers, caretakers, and lovers."[16] By 2029 various kinds of neural implants will be available "to enhance visual and auditory perception and interpretation, memory and reasoning." Further, implants will "provide auditory communication in both directions between the human user and the worldwide computing network."[17] Machines will claim consciousness and issues concerned with their ethical treatment will be widely debated.[18] There will no longer be a firm line between human and machine. Kurzweil's description of bodily change at mid century sums up these unparalleled shifts:

> I envision human body 3.0—in the 2030's and 2040's—as a more fundamental redesign. Rather than reformulating each subsystem, we (both biological and nonbiological portions of our thinking, working together) will have the opportunity to revamp our bodies based on our experiences with version 2.0. . . . One attribute I envision for version 3.0 is the ability to change our bodies. . . . so we'll be able to rapidly alter our physical manifestation at will.[19]

A largely synthetic body that could be altered at will is no body we would currently relate to. Whereas such a fabricated existence seems impossibly alien to our current condition, when each link in the chain is examined, slipping from one stage to the next is not hard to imagine. It is the *unexamined* adaptation to technological innovation at each successive stage that constitutes cyborgian drift.

In April, 2000, Bill Joy, cofounder and then Chief Scientist at Sun Microsystems, wrote an article for *Wired Magazine* expressing serious reservations about Kurzweil's predictions. Entitled "Why the Future Doesn't Need Us," Joy's piece originated from a bar conversation with Kurzweil and Berkeley philosopher John Searle following a panel discussion at a conference. As an insider in technology circles, Joy's cautionary musings have made quite an impact and forced writers like Kurzweil to admit that the "promise and peril of GNR" technologies are "deeply intertwined."[20] Joy gets the (cyborgian) drift, writing: "with each of these technologies, a sequence of small, individually sensible advances leads to an accumulation of great power and, concomitantly, great danger." He expands:

> Perhaps it is always hard to see the bigger impact while you are in the vortex of a change. Failing to understand the consequences of our inventions while we are in the rapture of discovery and innovation seems to be a common fault of scientists and technologists; we have long been driven by the overarching desire to know that is the nature of science's quest, not stopping to notice that the progress to newer and more powerful technologies can take on a life of its own.[21]

The zenith of these trends is envisioned as the end of bodily-based existence. Two scenarios are often described. In one scenario, silicon-based intelligence will assert itself as the superior "species" and simply displace human beings. Human consciousness in any form we might imagine it then disappears. Some see this inheritance of the earth by robots as not only inevitable, but part of natural evolution.[22] The other scenario maintains a pretense of preserving some vestige of the human mind, but abandons the form of human life in all other ways. If we can imagine the gradual replacement of worn out body parts with manufactured ones, and the parallel processing of brain and computer function, we have to imagine a point at which the remaining threads of human life are given up for a machine-based existence. Having a body, even a mechanical one, will seem pointless, so our minds are "downloaded" into cyberspace and live an immortal "life" among the ones and zeros of computer code.

As David Noble has indicated, these visions of a bodiless existence have religious overtones. In his work *The Religion of Technology*,[23] he assembles an array of voices to back up the point: Moravec writes enthusiastically of minds being "rescued from the limitations of a mortal body," and "personal immortality by mind transplant."[24] A researcher of human interface technology: "Cyberspace will feel like Paradise . . . a space for collective restoration [of the] habit of perfection."[25] A computer-industry consultant: "What better way to emulate God's knowledge . . . Over such a cyber world human beings could enjoy a god-like instant access."[26] A software engineer: In cyberspace "floats the image of a Heavenly City, the New Jerusalem of the Book of Revelation . . . a place where we might enter God's graces . . . laid out like a beautiful equation."[27] Noble's thesis is that the trajectory of technology is an extension of the Christian mythos, indicating the "true inspiration" of technologists lies "in an enduring, other-worldly quest for transcendence and salvation."[28] Wolfgang Giegerich has also addressed the technology-Christianity relationship. In a paper entitled "The Burial of Soul in Technological Civilization," he argues:

> The Incarnation, seen ontologically, is the grandiose outline of the idea that nature can be replaced by *a second, no longer natural nature*. It is the program designed to substitute a technological world for the natural world.[29]

I will consider some of Giegerich's ideas on technology towards the end.

These renditions of a possible future express *in extremis* the spirit-soul split that Hillman has argued dominates Christianized culture and nullifies "that intermediate realm of psyche."[30] Put simply, the departure from the body and being in the world is also a departure from soul. Without a bodily existence in the world there is no soul. As Jung puts it, "Without any body, there is no mind and therefore no individuation."[31]

Although the end points of these developments seem entirely alien and contrary to everything many of us regard as the essence of existence—a soul-centered reality that is intrinsically tied to an embodied life in a mostly natural world—we must face the many ways in which we are already today moving toward a mechanical makeover. There are already artificial organs; there are already rudimentary neural implants that provide electrical stimulus of brain function to counteract the symptoms of Parkinson's disease; there are already devices that restore eyesight and hearing through computer circuitry; there are already technophiles at MIT walking the streets with specially equipped glasses that constantly project an on-line world into their field of vision. Some of these innovations return normal functioning to the disabled; some prolong life that would otherwise end prematurely. However, the benefits are increasingly difficult to differentiate from a broader dissociation from the course of nature, which has receded behind more dominant strands of thought.

As we look ahead, the issue is not the end point of these innovations, or what may or may not be possible, the issue is that we have already stepped on to this ride, the bar will shortly come down, and we're about to leave the platform. As a friend of Bill Joy's commented: "I'm as fond of my body as anyone, but if I can be 200 with a body of silicon, I'll take it." Many of us will be tempted in this direction.

Psychological Perspective

A triad of motivations underlies cyborgian drift: The denial of death; the search for perfection; and the need to believe that scientific discoveries and their application are synonymous with human progress. Each of these motivations may be examined separately and have been discussed elsewhere at length.[32] Here we can consider how they weave together behind the movement toward the robotic human.

As Ziegler reminds us, nature "operates in polarities of life and death" and is invested in our illness just as much as our health.[33] The life-death pairing is the very ground of the psyche. When "health" is unaccompanied by a sense of limitation and dissolution, somewhere a monster results, as if death will not be denied, even if it must haunt life. We see this dynamic appearing whenever artificial life forms leave the laboratory and enter the imagination. Prolonged health and well-being are often cited as motivations for cybernetic research, but cyborgs often appear in the imagination as monsters, returning the face of death in living form. Referring to the Frankenstein saga, Romanyshyn writes: "The animation of lifeless matter . . . is motivated by a wish to conquer death."[34] Fittingly, Kurzweil has explicitly stated his intention of prolonging his own life until GNR technology would allow one to "live forever."[35] His rhetoric is also full of references to "the severe limitations of biological form."[36] Once the idea of prolonging life really kicks in, the body appears more like a death trap, something we need to overcome. Cyborgian drift flows freely through the gap that opens when the meaningful bond between life and death is broken.

Similarly alienated from a sense of human limitation, the drive for perfection creates a constant need for "newness"— products, sensations, surroundings—as the spark of the new always offers the possibility of the perfect. Perfectionism tends to avoid the here and now, engendering an endless grasping for the future or a romantic nostalgia for a non-existent past. It thus removes us from the body and the soil we stand on. Tomorrow's promise of a body that can be tailored to a desired aesthetic and a mind that may be shaped at will reflect today's increasing unease and discontent. The problem is perfection never arrives. Wisdom traditions have long recognized that perfection belongs only to God. So the Persian rug maker always leaves one loose knot, just as sacred artists of all kinds leave small imperfections in their work. When this spiritual, non-human background to perfection goes unrecognized, when the religious impulse remains unconscious, we attempt to perfect body and matter, which are inherently imperfect. Still, it is addictive, and it fuels the fantasies of an ultimate facelift.

It's easy to see how the promise of science and the magic of technology collude with these other motivations, offering technological solutions to issues that are really existential and psychological in origin. Aside from keeping deeper motivations unconscious, putting all of our eggs in the techno-solution basket forces the imagination into a one-sided focus on problem solving, obscuring the need to live with open questions and deeper understandings. The age of quick fixes is also the age of declining empathy, lacking reflection, lost wonder, and absent mystery. The pursuit of new knowledge and its applications is an authentic expression of the human spirit, but the unquestioned faith in this pursuit is a maintenance plan for a collective neurosis. It's a vicious circle, with science and technology acting as a defense against the anxiety of facing death in an imperfect world.

In concert with these motivations, the path to a cyborg existence hangs upon two kinds of reductive thinking. The first has to do with the use of computer and machine-derived imagery to describe and comprehend biological and life. Stated simply by one writer, "our brains themselves are machines."[37] Kurzweil refers to molecules and enzymes as "special machines" and uses terms like "the machinery of life" to describe biological processes.[38] He summarizes this snapshot of the DNA base of life—"nature's own nanoengineered computer"[39]—by saying: "This is our understanding of the *hardware* of the computational engine driving life on Earth. We are just the beginning, however, to unravel the *software*."[40] Kurzweil ignores anything that does not reinforce this analogy; he sees life and evolutionary processes *merely* as complex machines being run by a kind of computer code. Once human nature is regarded this way, "hardware" can be replaced by more reliable and functional versions, and once the brain is reverse engineered, its "software" can be rewritten. Further, he sees nature's process as flawed and slow, so he seeks to learn "the information-processing basis of disease, maturation and aging" so as to gain "the means to correct and refine evolution's unfinished invention."[41] Such thinking is what makes way for creating the human-machine. Contrasting the possibilities inherent in this prospect, Kurzweil says of the natural process: "It has one deficiency—evolution is too slow."[42] Common to all advocates of a cyborg future is worship at the altar of speed.

Boiling down psychological life to brain function and seeing brain function in computer terms is made possible by another form of blinkered vision: the privileging of the intellect over other aspects of being—animal sensation, instinct, aesthetic response, intuition. All mental activity can then be understood in terms of an I.Q. oriented functionalism. In simple terms, the psyche becomes the rational intellect—just the kind of intelligence that is most analogous to computer-based intelligence. Challenged with this issue, principally in terms of the role of emotional intelligence, Kurzweil suggests that the process of reverse engineering the brain will allow us to keep some of the emotional base of our experience, but:"The ability to control our feelings will be just another one of those twenty-first century slippery slopes."[43] The mindset to engage in this kind of rewiring of emotion is already present in the overuse of psychotropic medications, which have gone from treating acute and chronic symptoms to maintaining socially defined goals of efficiency and elevated mood.

For those driving full speed towards a cyborg future, there is little awareness of the values governing their perspectives. These values place the kind of intelligence that seems most germane to technological innovation and its acceleration not just at the top of the psychological stack, but often as the only aspect of mental life worth preserving. Alongside an absent awareness of values lies a similar unconsciousness of operating within particular paradigms—materialist, Cartesian, quantitative, positivist, atomistic. This lack of consciousness morphs the scientific method as a rigorous path of inquiry into science as an ideology, which wants to read every aspect of existence in scientific terms.

It is tempting to dismiss a future based upon such a narrow mindedness if not for one thing: These are the minds that shape our age, the information age. Increasingly, we experience ourselves through the mediums they create—computers, cell phones, advertising, and digitized reality. The effect of these mediums is increasingly hard to differentiate from everyday perceptions of what's real. IBM, Intel, Microsoft, and Google are reshaping our sense of reality, in a sense already rewriting our psychological "software." So while it is tempting to dismiss the selective, reductive views behind imaging ourselves as robots, we can't afford to do so—not with Bill Gates writing a blurb for the back of Kurzweil's book.[44] We are immersed in a stream of consciousness that is carrying us toward a cyborg existence. The concern, in its essence, is that to the degree we imagine ourselves in robotic terms, we will, as our mastery of nature increases, turn ourselves into the very thing we imagine. What is actually possible fifty years from now is not the problem. The problem is our contemporary perspective on human life. One commentator has suggested we are already "fyborgs"—functional cyborgs.[45] Another asks the question: "Is Google God?"[46]

As technology has provided us with a desirable buffer from the unpredictable and sometimes destructive whims of nature, it has also opened Pandora's box of psychopathology. If we cast our minds back over 150 years of Western history, we can see that depth psychology has always been gearing up to battle a disembodied creature, detached from its instinctual roots. "In the last analysis, most of our difficulties come from losing contact with our instincts."[47] Psychopathology as we have come to know it was birthed at the height of the industrial revolution, at the same moment workers entered the production line, tuning themselves to the rhythms of automation—in the eyes of one early nineteenth century observer, already becoming "animal machines."[48] Neurasthenia was imagined by Beard as a result of progress, the "fast pace of life," railway travel and a scientific mindset.[49] (in 1869!) Hysteria was understood in terms of the repression of instinctual, animal impulses in an age of reason. Neurosis in general was defined at the end of the nineteenth century as the failure of the rational mind. Psychopathology has functioned as the canary in the mineshaft of technology. But as more effective means of isolating and medicating psychological symptoms are assembled and our social fabric adapts to psychopathologies like borderline and narcissistic personality styles, sensitivity to this subterranean canary is declining.

Science, technology, neurosis, and the robotic future come full circle when we consider the strange life of René Descartes. Romanyshyn has pointed out that hysterics may be considered the bastard daughters of Descartes.[50] The hysterical dissociation from the body and the quest

to transfer human consciousness into computer driven robots share a
Cartesian background. Descartes is said to have created his own
automata—a living doll, an android—made in the likeness of his
daughter, Francine, who died of scarlet fever at age five. The story persists
that sailors discovered the mechanical figure while Descartes was sailing
to Sweden, where he spent his last six months of life. More evidence
exists for Descartes' earlier attempts to build robotic humans and
animals.[51] So at the very philosophical beginnings of modern science,
we also find the impulse to build artificial humans. Beyond mere
coincidence, Descartes posthumously published work, *Treatise on Man*,
is focused on the idea of humans as elaborate machines. In describing
human anatomy, he writes:

> these functions follow in this machine simply from the disposition
> of the organs as wholly naturally as the movements in a clock or
> other automaton follow from the disposition of its counterweights
> and wheels.[52]

The second part of the work considered how the soul coexisted with
this human machine, but the manuscript was lost.

CULTURAL WARNING DREAMS

Archetypal patterns exist beyond brain structure. They are not
confined to the psychic realm but also reside in the earth and in the
nature of the cosmos. However, our capacity to experience these patterns
comes through the body and through bodily participation in the
phenomenal world. Without this experience of archetypal forms and
the imaginal life they generate, what remains of the psyche will go
unregulated and these universals will degenerate into their rawest, most
compulsive form. When archetypal patterns go unreflected, the Gods
are slighted. And whereas ignored Gods may return as symptoms, when
the voice of symptom is also extinguished, the Gods give up their
ground to their primitive ancestors, the Titans. Without psyche,
Titanism reigns and life reverts to unmitigated power and chaos. Such
is the scenario that appears on the horizon, impressed upon us by
recurrent themes appearing in imagined futures.

The boundaries of space and time break down in the depths of
the psyche. It is not only the past but also the future that exists in the
unconscious. Precognitive dreams and synchronicities demonstrate this

understanding. This awareness gives rise to the phenomenon of the warning dream, the dream that assesses the direction of the psyche, detects a problem, and sends a signal to change course. Very often, if the signal is ignored, the dream image will intensify—a car hitting and injuring a dog becomes a Mack truck running down a group of school children. When the notion of the warning dream is combined with reading contemporary images of science fiction—as if these expressions are dreams[53]—a disturbing picture results: The collective unconscious projects a future that features a range of nightmarish states, from pervasive psychopathy to planetary apocalypse. Cinematic imagery in particular indicates a future where human nature is either severely compromised or completely overtaken by autonomous technology.

At one end of this devastating spectrum lies what I've come to call the "Tin-man syndrome"—humanoid figures of various types in search of a heart. Created to look and behave like humans, these figures lack the capacity to feel emotion, relate like humans, or engage the world with any sense of creative play. Like the Tin-man, these figures are acutely aware of their lacking human essence and often demonstrate a longing to acquire what can only be called "soul." At the other end of the spectrum are stories of enantiodromic reversal of human exploitation via industry and technology—situations where the machines turn on their human creators. Sometimes these motifs are combined, as if to say that it is the lack of soul sense that precipitates a world ruled by machines.

Just as Frankenstein's monster demands a partner after falling into a vortex of absent eros, the cyborg, the genetically engineered "replicant,"[54] and the robotic human tell us in their most reflective moments of empty interiors. *Star Trek* characters Data and Seven of Nine show this characteristic in different ways. Data undertakes a self-development project to engage in feeling-oriented human discourse, often referring to his "emotion chip." Seven of Nine, who was once fully human but underwent a partial "assimilation" by The Borg—a race of destructive cyborg automatons—barely hangs on to a capacity to relate in human terms, her humanness is more a dim light in a cloud of logic and utility. Other examples include the artificial boy of *A. I.*, who longs for a mother and family, the robot "Andrew" in *Bicentennial Man*, who gradually humanizes, hungers for love, and faces the need for mortality, the helpful cyborg in *Terminator II: Judgment Day*, who wants to understand why people cry, and the replicants of *Bladerunner*, in search of life and love. All these characters tell us the same thing: To be a non-human, human is inhuman.

Self-reflective humanoid figures grappling with matters of the heart offer enough sense of caution. However, other heartless figures have also entered the picture, displaying what can only be described as a psychopathic bearing. The first cyborg to appear in mainstream awareness was the cold-blooded killing machine in *The Terminator*, played by Arnold Schwarzenegger. The hero and savior figure of the film declares: "Cyborgs don't feel pain . . . (the terminator) can't be bargained with, it can't be reasoned with, it doesn't feel pity or remorse or fear." We had already seen the single red-eyed computer, Hal 9000, in *2001: A Space Odyssey* display psychopathic traits.

Describing the psychopath, Guggenbühl-Craig uses the term "invalidism of eros,"[55] a notion that distills the lacking capacity for empathy, guilt, remorse and inability to mourn that typically accompanies the psychopath. Although this description captures the psychopath's manipulative exploitation of others, the wider context of Guggenbühl-Craig's understanding is central to the present discussion: Eros is the one quality that determines whether the archetypes appear in creative or destructive form. In mythic terms, he puts it this way:

> Without him (Eros) there would be no movement among the gods: in fact there would be no gods at all. It is Eros who makes the gods—the archetypes—loving, creative and involved.[56]

Furthermore, we must remember it is Eros that makes Psyche, psyche (soul)—Eros makes soul. Without eros there is no soul, which is the sense aroused when looking into the eyes of a psychopath.

The voices that speak to us as we dream of a possible future describe an emptying soul and a path to psychopathy. At first glance they seem remote from our present day concerns. Yet social commentators with an eye on collective psychology, like Robert W. Rieber, are already describing a growing cultural adaptation to psychopathic traits, a normative adjustment to "the violation of social norms and bonds, mechanism of dissociation, an antisocial pursuit of power, and pathological thrill-seeking."[57] Rieber employs phrases like "failure to experience emotional conflict,"[58] "successful evasions of the moral code,"[59] "skilled in evasion and rationalization,"[60] and the ability to wear "the 'mask of sanity.'"[61] His thesis is that widespread practices, like achieving success through the manipulation and exploitation of others as well as the tendency to embrace this behavior at an institutional level, are now embedded in the social fabric. He writes of "the startling phenomenon of normalized psychopathy in high places"[62] and argues, "it is the phenomenon of widespread social distress in contemporary American social life that, in my view, is to a great extent responsible for the rise of normalized psychopathy in high places."[63] In other words, patterns of psychopathic behavior appear as a strategy of adaptation to changing social conditions, especially conditions that evidence little natural restraint. Psychopathy may be the default position in an evolutionary adaptation to a fabricated world.

The Corporation, a recent documentary film, convincingly demonstrated how large organizations that put profits ahead of all other values fit the diagnostic criteria of psychopathy. In imagined future worlds, it is often the techno-industrial backdrop to the cyborgs that carries the psychopathic characteristics, manipulating the masses toward its own inhuman aims. In *Bladerunner* the replicants are master-minded by the cold and calculating Tyrell of Tyrell Corporation. Despite the corporation motto —"more human than human"—Tyrell's creations finally turn on him like Frankenstein's monster. In *Alien*, the ship's crew is caught between an unstoppable predator and a mining corporation interested in preserving this creature for military purposes: "crew expendable." As Janice Hocker Rushing and Thomas S. Fentz have pointed out, the motif of an autonomous technology turning on its maker is a reversal of the primal hunting impulse. When the hunt and its tools are not tethered to a sense of the sacred and turn instead to exploitation, the hunter soon becomes the hunted. Their persuasive analysis of films like *The Terminator* and *Bladerunner* shows how this dynamic arises. Reading these situations through a mythic template, they write:

> Tasting great success in conquering the wilderness, the frontier hero desires to maintain and extend his control over the earth. Because he is so good at making machines, he now uses brains more than brawn, and he prefers to minimize his contact with nature, which can be uncomfortable and menacing. Thus he creates ever more complex tools to do his killing and other work for him. Having banished God as irrelevant to the task at hand,

the hero decides he is God, and, like that now obsolete power, creates beings "in his own image;" this time, however, they are more perfect versions of himself—rational, strategic, and efficient. He may fashion his tools either by remaking a human being into a perfected machine or by making an artificial "human" from scratch. Unfortunately, however, these new creations have designs of their own that the hero fails to foresee. At first, they demand to be cared for, to be given a legitimate and valued place in human society. Afraid and repulsed at what he has done, the creator refuses his offspring's requests. Like their human creator, these technological beings develop a desire for complete freedom, and so they declare themselves to be God and set out to hunt and ultimately to eliminate their maker.

The key themes mentioned here—control over then distance from nature, dismissal then identification with God, the usurping of god-like creativity and the drive for perfection, the autonomy and then the antagonism of the new creations—are increasingly recurrent in science fiction films, showing an apocalyptic enantiodromia involving human displacement by artificial intelligence. This same scenario is the basis of *The Matrix* series, where machines breed and store humans to produce bio-fuel. Oblivious to their actual state, humans are wired into a fully fabricated virtual reality where—in their disembodied minds—they live, work, and die. Similarly nightmarish, *Star Trek's* Borg are an insidious race of hybridized beings, whose goal is to capture, mechanize, and "assimilate" biological beings into their "collective." The Borg have a collective mind; their assimilated members literally plug into a massive computerized network, ruled over in bee-like fashion by the Borg queen. The Borg mantra: "Resistance is futile." These images extend the motif of the hunter becoming the hunted by returning us to the most basic levels of existence. The highest becomes the lowest and individual consciousness is overtaken by collective unconsciousness—a hypertrophy of the dynamic Jung described as a dangerous tendency of modern consciousness when it displaces the religious instinct onto secularized systems and ideologies. The Borg epitomize the mass-mindedness Jung perceived as the antithesis of a psyche-centered life.

These images of psychopathy and apocalyptic displacement of humans by machines, when regarded as collective warning dreams, may be read as attempts to thwart the blind course of certain technologies and wake us from our unconscious slavery to machines. The cyborg, the android, the replicant send a message back from the future, a longing for lost soul, a plea to preserve fragile bonds with nature. In the final moments of the film *Bladerunner*, replicant Roy Batty says it best: "All those moments will be lost in time, like tears in rain." If digested at this juncture in history, such images help question current trends and prompt an altered course. Although technology is imbedded in the fabric of contemporary life, and is driven by both psychological and socio-economic forces, there's nothing inevitable about the direction it will take. However, other factors will have to come into play.

FINDING A WAY THROUGH

Cyborgian drift may be countered from two sides. From one side, the underlying motivations and reductive styles of thinking that foster blind technological advance may be challenged, and, from the other, nature may be apprehended as the ultimately indispensable taproot of existence. As a world dominated by machines ultimately threatens the whole of earthly existence, this prospect must be met with a declaration of ultimate values—humanity and soul. These values suggest the need to preserve certain qualitative states—sensual awareness, erotic bonds, embodied thought, beauty, wisdom, limitation, imagination, empathy, reflection, artistic expression, and playfulness. The list is long, but nothing on it is possible outside of the evolved instinctual and archetypally patterned basis of consciousness. The end of nature also means the end of these experiences.

The challenge for psychology is to become aware of its increasing deference to computerized and robotic metaphors. The two streams of thought currently dominating the field—psychopharmacology and cognitive behavioral therapy—both show success in treating psychological symptoms. They also reflect a collective demand for a symptom-free existence. Although psychotherapists of all persuasions are likely to utilize one or the other of these modalities at some point, this is not the issue. The issue is the way mechanistic theories become ways of understanding the psyche in general. How many people have been told that their depression is just a "chemical imbalance"? Despite the fact that psychotropic medication rarely provides a permanent solution, despite drug reactions varying widely between individuals, despite so-called serotonin "balance" having never been measured, despite the expanding use of anti-depressants to treat all manner of other disorders, despite the epidemiology indicating social factors, we still come away with the idea that depression is explainable as a neurological mechanism gone awry. Neurological theories of depression are worked backwards from drug effects. Rather than the vicissitudes of experience, it is the mind-as-machine metaphor that determines the facts to acknowledge and the facts to ignore. Similarly, when you open any cognitive-behavioral textbook you find flow charts that are essentially no different from those used in computer programming. "Cognition," "mood," and "behavior" are put in boxes with various arrows drawn between them. As effective as tinkering with "automatic thoughts" and behaviors can be at times, when the theory displaces a sense of inner realities, you arrive at the idea the psyche can be placed in a Skinner box and regulated with inputs of outer stimulus and rewriting software. When understandings of psychic depth, complexity, and history are displaced by these materialist and mechanistic theories, it lends impetus to the idea we can rewire our brains and create humanoid robots, turning ourselves into that which we already imagine.

A far more intricate challenge to standing on the side of nature is presented by Wolfgang Giegerich, who has argued that psychology must catch up to the contemporary state of technological thinking[64] and accept that mythos, the Gods, and even nature are dead.[65] In taking this position, he deliberately goes against the whole grain of the depth psychological world, particularly Jung's insistence that the facts of nature cannot in the end be violated. He writes:

> . . . now we live on a totally different, abstract *level* of reality. Even though the forces of nature are still there, nevertheless the level on which we live has superseded the level of natural things and processes, the level of what can be perceived and imagined in terms of perception and sensory intuition.[66]

> The conventional way of looking at things in terms of human desires, efforts and mistakes or crimes, on the one hand, and of natural forces on the other, *simply does not apply any more* on this new level of life. . . . Consciousness has to advance beyond pictorial thinking and move on to the abstract level of thought proper.[67]

Taking psychology beyond nature and reorienting our notion of soul in the direction of *abstract thought* rather than in the direction of symbol, image, and emotion, Giegerich argues that soul has, at bottom, a logical life. Recognizing this would, he suggests, place us in better stead with the times in which we live.

Giegerich proposes that:

> science, unbeknownst to itself, is a true religion in the double sense of careful observation (*relegere*) and of the archetypal dominants binding (*religare*) our perceptions, thinking, and behavior. The scientific instinct is the same religious instinct . . .[68]

The problem is the "unbeknownst," which indicates an unconsciousness that makes a great deal of difference, as we have seen, and indicates the exact location our work must enter. Science pursued with religious zeal is not the same thing as science and religion sharing an instinctual basis. Science is not a "true" religion; it has merely usurped the religious instinct and therefore falls prey to the plethora of grandiose fantasies I've recounted. In taking this stance Giegerich collapses a qualitative differentiation that courses through the whole of Jungian thought, obfuscating the difference between relating to an archetypal impulse and being swept up by one.

In carrying through the argument he contends that soul is simply where our psychic energy resides and God is simply that which functions in our lives in a god-like fashion. Science and technology may well be where the psychic center of gravity resides, but as it functions as a god in an *unconscious* fashion it becomes subject to the illusion of manageability in egocentric terms.[69] Giegerich's soul is not ensoulment in the sense of consciously integrating archetypal forms, nor is it soul-making that requires a seeing-through to the Gods and a personifying sense of their presence. His recent writings imply that the time for this form of soul is over, a perspective that may be read in conjunction with his rather fatalistic view of the entwinement of technology with the Christianized movement of history quoted above, where the transcending of nature appears inevitable.

A generous reading of Giegerich's argument would suggest he is applying shock therapy to the Jungian world and wanting to ensure psychology remains relevant in a technological age. But in declaring that there's no way back to an instinctual basis of mind, his approach becomes difficult to recognize as depth psychology, particularly as Jungian or archetypal psychology. There's little room here for Jung's view of archetypes as "the chthonic portion of the psyche . . . that portion through which the psyche is attached to nature, or in which its link with the earth and the world appears at its most tangible."[70]

Aside from declaring the Gods, nature, and myth dead, Giegerich appears to dismiss the psychic distress evident alongside technological advance as well as the psyche's own counteracting response to these trends of collectivity—some of which I've detailed here. He may be right in asserting the need for a more rigorous psychology that can articulate the "logic" of soul within a stronger philosophical frame. Yet a turn to philosophy at the expense of phenomenology seems only to encourage more dissociation. Considered against the backdrop of cyborgian drift, the idea of moving "beyond the imaginal"[71] into abstract thought invites a distancing from emotion and instinct that ultimately props open the door to a robotic existence. Jung's description of abstract thought as "ruthless" and "dangerous" underscores the problem.[72]

There's nothing inevitable about the direction of technology. We don't need to unconsciously drift along and passively adapt to its innovations. However, simply unplugging won't work either. Machines are here to stay and artificial intelligence is on the horizon. To change the direction of technology may mean responding *now* to the humanoid voices of the future in search of a heart, and forging a different kind of relationship with our machines, one that includes eros, aesthetics, and the rhythms of nature. Sometimes, when you live with technology for a time, you discover this kind of relationship—naming cars, coaxing computers into cooperation, caring for equipment in a hands-on way, choosing craftsmanship over utility. Machines behave differently when we invest consciousness in them. Sensitivity to such things would keep technology within the bounds of human concern, and perhaps even open a soul space for engaging our gadgets. Moreover, cultivating these kinds of connections would sensitize us to technologies that bring a monstrous, autonomous, and inhuman quality. We might grow more wary, for example, of the obsession with speed, newness, and disposability. In other words, instinct would remain present to invention.

There's a recurring motif in science fiction stories that speaks to this notion of a more humanized technology. Stories that pit the underdog against an oppressive, dark, more advanced collection of machines pivot on the presence of what I call "funky technology." In *Star Wars*, Han Solo's Millennium Falcon—a space jalopy with lots of "add-ons" and needs to be hit with a wrench to start-up—saves the rebel force from Darth Vader and the Death Star. In *Terminator II: Judgment Day*, the savior figure, John Conner ("J.C."), hot wires cars, rigs computers to milk cash machines, and finagles his way through a myriad of techno challenges. In *E. T.: The Extraterrestrial*, the space visitor "calls home" by rigging up a device from an assortment of electronic toys and uses wind power to keep it working. His gadget vividly contrasts the oppressive technology of the grown-ups trying to keep him on earth. What is apparent in these images is a psychic proclivity for a more Hermetic style of technology—a hands-on inventiveness that uses odds and ends (like Hermes' lyre) to solve a problem. It is the very opposite of the monolithic technology that eviscerates body and soul in these stories.

Whether or not we end up as cyborgs will depend on recognizing what drives us forward and finding ways to reimagine our relationship with technology as it unfolds. It is vital that we maintain an awareness of undercurrents and archetypal contents that arise in the form of compensating images. Insights derived from the imagination function as antibodies in the collective psyche, preventing certain viruses from completely overtaking the system. If there are enough antibodies, enough instinctual, gut-level reactions, if there's a small critical mass of awareness in different disciplines and the culture at large, it may be enough to alter an otherwise blind course.

NOTES

1. Ray Kurzweil, *The Singularity is Near* (New York: Viking, 2005), 341-342.

2. Bill Joy, "Why the Future Doesn't Need Us," *Wired Magazine*, April 2000. Online: http://www.wired.com/wired/archive/8.04/joy.html

3. C. G. Jung, *The Nature Writings of C. G. Jung*, ed. Meredith Sabini (Berkeley CA: North Atlantic Books, 2002), 128.

4. The term "cyborg,"coined by Manfred E. Clynes and Nathan S. Kline in 1960, is a shortened term for *cybernetic organism.*

5. Donna Haraway, "Cyborgs and Symbionts: Living Together in the New World Order," in Chris Hables Gray, ed., *The Cyborg Handbook* (New York: Routledge, 1995), xv.

6. This term was used by Ian Pearson, employed by British Telecom to track future developments in information technology. Quoted in Bill McKibben, *Enough: Staying Human in an Engineered Age* (New York: Henry Holt, 2003), 87.

7. Jung, *Nature Writings*, 149.

8. Ray Kurzweil, *The Age of Spiritual Machines* (New York: Viking, 1999), 20.

9. Kurzweil, *Singularity*, 316.

10. Rodney Brookes, *Flesh and Machines: How Robots will Change Us* (New York: Pantheon Books, 2002).

11. Hans Moravec, *Robot: Mere Machine to Transcendent Mind* (New York: Oxford University Press, 1999).

12. Ray Kurzweil, *The Age of Intelligent Machines* (Cambridge, MA: MIT Press, 1990).

13. Kurzweil, *Spiritual Machines*, 105.

14. Joy, *Why the Future*.

15. McKibben, *Enough*, 67.

16. Kurzweil, *Spiritual Machines*, 206.

17. *Ibid.*, 221.

18. *Ibid.*, 224.

19. Kurzweil, *Singularity*, 310.

20. *Ibid.*, Chapter 8.

21. Joy, *Why the Future*.

22. Moravec, *Robot*.

23. David F. Noble, *The Religion of Technology: The Divinity of Man and the Spirit of Invention* (New York: Penguin Books, 1999).

24. *Ibid.*, 162.

25. *Ibid.*, 159.

26. *Ibid.*, 159.

27. *Ibid.*, 160.

28. *Ibid.*, 3.

29. Roberts Avens, "Reflections on Wolfgang Giegerich's 'The Burial of Soul in Technological Civilization.'" *Sulphur* 20, Fall 1987, 40. Online: http://esquipulas.homeunix.com/giegerich.html. [*Editor's Note*: Translated in its entirety for the first time into English for this volume, "The Burial of the Soul in Technological Civilization," provides crucial background to understanding Giegerich's views on the nature\psyche relation which has ignited controversy in recent years.

This paper was originally presented by Giegerich at the 1983 Eranos conference in Ascona, Switzerland and was published in German as "Das Begräbnis der Seele in die technische Zivilisation," in the Eranos Yearbooks, *Eranos* 52-1983, pp. 221-276.]

30. James Hillman, "Peaks and Vales," in *Senex and Puer,* ed. Glen Slater (Putnam, CT: Spring Publications, 2005), 71.

31. Jung, *Nature Writings*, 155.

32. For example: Ernest Becker, *The Denial of Death* (New York: Simon and Schuster, 1973); Marion Woodman, *Addiction to Perfection* (Toronto: Inner City Books, 1982); Lewis Mumford, *The Myth of the Machine: The Pentagon of Power* (New York: Harcourt Brace Jovanovich, 1964).

33. Alfred Ziegler, *Archetypal Medicine* (Woodstock, CT: Spring Publications, 1983), ii, 13.

34. Robert Romanyshyn, *Technology as Symptom and Dream* (London: Routledge, 1989), 160.

35. Kurzweil, *Singularity*, 323.

36. *Ibid.*, 389.

37. Marvin Minsky, quoted in Noble, *Religion of Technology*, 157.

38. Kurzweil, *Spiritual Machines*, 40-41.

39. *Ibid.*, 107.

40. *Ibid.*, 41 (italics added).

41 *Ibid.*

42. *Ibid.*, 44.

43. *Ibid.*, 150.

44. Kurzweil, *Singularity.* Gates writes: "Ray Kurzweil is the best person I know at predicting the future of artificial intelligence. His intriguing new book envisions a future in which information technologies have advanced so far and fast that they enable humanity to transcend its biological limitations—transforming our lives in ways we can't yet imagine." (Back cover). Bill Joy also contributes a back cover blurb, though he indicates his disagreement with Kurzweil over "the balance of promise and peril" inherent in the new technologies.

45. Cited in Michael Chorost, *Rebuilt: How Becoming Part Computer Made Me More Human* (New York: Houghton Mifflin, 2005), 42.

46. Thomas Friedman, *The New York Times*, June 29, 2003.

47. Jung, *Nature Writings*, 98.

48. Quoted in John and Paula Zerzan, "Industrialism and Domestication," in John Zerzan and Alice Carnes, eds., *Questioning Technology: A Critical Anthology* (London: The Freedom Press, 1988), 204.

49. George Frederick Drinka, *The Birth of Neurosis* (New York: Touchstone, 1984), 192.

50. Robert Romanyshyn, "'Anyway why did it have to be the death of the poet?' The Orphic Roots of Jung's Psychology," *Spring* 72, 55-87. For further reflections on Descartes' role in the background of depth psychology and phenomenology, see Romanyshyn, *Technology*, 138-144.

51. Gaby Wood, *Edison's Eve: A Magical History of the Quest for Mechanical Life* (New York: Anchor Books, 2002), 4-5.

52 *Ibid.*, 10.

53. Robert W. Rieber suggests the role of literature and film as "social dreams." *Manufacturing Social Distress: Psychopathy in Everyday Life* (New York: Plenum Press, 1997), 114-115.

54. Gaby Wood notes that "a 'replicant' . . . is a combination of a replica and a revenant—as if they had returned from the grave in order to mimic humanity; as if death were inherent in the simulacrum." Wood, *Edison's Eve*, xviii.

55. Adolf Guggenbühl-Craig, *The Emptied Soul: On the Nature of the Psychopath*, trans. Gary V. Hartman (Woodstock, CT: Spring Publications, 1980), 29.

56. *Ibid.,* 26.

57. Rieber, *Social Distress*, 7.

58. *Ibid.,* 14.

59. *Ibid.,* 23.

60. *Ibid.,* 47.

61. *Ibid.,* 39.

62. *Ibid.,* 17.

63. *Ibid.,* 22.

64. Wolfgang Giegerich, *The Soul's Logical Life* (Frankfurt: Peter Lang, 1998).

65. Wolfgang Giegerich, "The End of Meaning and the Birth of Man: An Essay about the State Reached in the History of Consciousness and an Analysis of C. G. Jung's psychology project," *The Journal of Jungian Theory and Practice*, 6.1 (2004), 1-65; "The Burial of the Soul,"49.

66. Giegerich, *Logical Life*, 27.

67. *Ibid.*, 28-29 (italics added).

68. Giegerich/Avens, "The Burial of Soul," 42-43. Avens uses the term "Christianism" to describe the presence of Christianity in technology as Giegerich relates this overlap. The difference between Christianism and Christianity reflects the difference between relating to the archetype and unconsciously identifying with it. (See Jung on the psychology of "isms," *CW* 10 § 103; also 488-548). Giegerich suggests at one point, "The task which science and technology unconsciously try to accomplish is to build, manufacture, and simulate God in actuality (in flesh)." "The Burial of Soul," 43. Yet he also argues at length why we should not regard this as inflation or hubris. "Burial of Soul," 44-48. See also "The End of Meaning," 24-25.

69. For Giegerich's argument on these points see "End of Meaning," 22-23; "Burial of Soul," 47-48.

70. Jung, *Nature Writings*, 199.

71. Giegerich, *Logical Life*, 11.

72. Jung, *Nature Writings*, 143.

A DYING HARE

On its brown flank,
a red stain, and in its eyes
exhaustion, as if already too much
had drained from its weary body.
Letting go of the mad hare,
the leaping hare, the hare
of the moon and March frosts;
all slipping away, leaving
only a hare of the sorrows;
the gap of melancholy
entering its eyes, filling them
with the dark ages;
scratching its heart
with a stone knowledge
as old as the runes.

No answering this sovereign wound
its unanswerable question.
The red trickle now from its mouth,
its ordeal nearly over;
a stillness growing into death.

—*Michael Whan*

THE BURIAL OF THE SOUL IN TECHNOLOGICAL CIVILIZATION

WOLFGANG GIEGERICH

In 1803 Friedrich Hölderlin prepared the following poem for print.

Hälfte des Lebens	Half of Life
Mit gelben Birnen hänget	*With yellow pears*
Und voll mit wilden Rosen	*And full of wild roses*
Das Land in den See,	*The land extends into the lake,*
Ihr holden Schwäne,	*You lovely swans,*
Und trunken von Küssen	*And drunk with kisses*
Tunkt ihr das Haupt	*You dip your heads*
Ins heilignüchterne Wasser.	*Into the holy-sober water.*

Wolfgang Giegerich, Ph.D., is a Jungian psychoanalyst in private practice in Wörthsee, Germany, who has lectured and published widely. His books in English include *The Soul's Logical Life: Towards a Rigorous Notion of Psychology*, Frankfurt/Main *et al.* (Peter Lang), 3rd ed. 2001; *Dialectics & Analytical Psychology: The El Capitan Canyon Seminar* (with David L. Miller and Greg Mogenson), New Orleans: Spring Journal Books, 2005; and, most recently, *The Neurosis of Psychology: Primary Papers Towards a Critical Psychology*, Volume One, Collected English Papers of Wolfgang Giegerich, New Orleans: Spring Journal Books, 2006.

Translated for the first time into English for this volume, "The Burial of the Soul in Technological Civilization," provides crucial background to understanding Giegerich's views on the nature\psyche relation which has ignited controversy in recent years. This paper was originally presented at the 1983 Eranos conference in Ascona, Switzerland and was published in German as "Das Begräbnis der Seele in die technische Zivilisation," in the Eranos Yearbooks, *Eranos* 52-1983, pp. 221-276.

Weh mir, wo nehm' ich, wenn	*Woe is me, where will I get, when*
Es Winter ist, die Blumen, und wo	*Winter has come, flowers, and where*
Den Sonnenschein,	*The sunshine*
Und Schatten der Erde?	*And the shadow of the earth?*
Die Mauern stehn	*The walls stand*
Sprachlos und kalt, im Winde	*Mute and cold; in the wind*
Klirren die Fahnen.[1]	*The weather vanes are clanking.*

The poet's standpoint is summer in its pleromatic fullness. Standing in the middle of this summer within an intact nature, the alarming thought of winter emerges in him, a winter not simply of ice and snow, but of mute ("speech-less") walls of stone and clanking weather vanes of iron. Summer and winter are here not seasons of nature, but refer to an upheaval from a natural world of yellow pears, wild roses, and lovely swans, a world which certainly has its own natural winter too, to a world of technology with its mute, cold, soulless things.

And this at a time when at bottom such unpoetic things were not even known. The walls at Hölderlin's time were still built up with hand-hewn natural stones; and do not such walls, as we at times still find them around old cemeteries, precisely *speak* to us today? And weather vanes and other wrought iron implements from those days have a high nostalgic value and are traded at corresponding prices in antiques market, which shows that they do speak to the soul. Only we, with our walls of concrete, know what a really mute wall is, and of course we also already have a simple answer to Hölderlin's desperate question, "Woe is me, where will I get, when winter has come, flowers?" We simply spray paint the missing flowers, just like that, with loud colors on the intolerably mute concrete wall, or stick them as a bumper sticker on that cold metal conveyer belt product, the automobile, thus imposing on this technical object a voice that is not its own. The soul that is in this way painted or pasted on no doubt drowns out the speechlessness of the things, but on the other hand, it can *ipso facto* also make us aware of it in an all the more uncanny way.

Hölderlin's summer and winter are not the changing phases in the year of *nature*, but refer to the revolutionary shift from nature to a technological reality. But if this upheaval is seen as a change from summer to winter, as a change of the seasons in a *historical* world year, then the question arises why the poet, and we along with him, try desperately to hold on to summer as our yardstick, and with a "woe is me" balk at the movement of time. Perhaps flowers and sunshine and shadow of the earth do not have to be around all the time. And maybe winter is mute only when we comprehend the speaking of summer as the only speech there is. Could it not be that winter has its own yardstick and is speaking its own speech, and could it not be our task to accompany the course of the year and to follow without reserve the movement of being immersed in the holy-sober water, in such a way that we are inside it with our hearts and view the world from its standpoint, with its measure?

This would mean that we would no longer resist the winter that has been the condition we have been in for a long time already, resist it by continuing to hold on, over and against our reality, to the familiar summer speech of flowers and either nostalgically leave our hearts in the good old days of nature, myth, symbols or anticipate, in utopian style, a fictitious future summer of true humanness. In both cases winter is only skipped, and the now prevailing technological civilization is disparaged from a cultural-critical standpoint high above it and external to it. To be immersed in the holy-sober water would mean through patient listening to learn from the cold and mute things of technology themselves a new language with its own rules and its own idioms, a language that is not our mother-tongue, but the foreign language of concrete walls, airplanes, moon rockets, television sets, computers, nuclear bombs, and also the language of advertizing, statistics, and the economy governed by multinational concerns.

It is not truly so that between the yellow pears of the beginning and the clanking weather vanes of the end there is an unavoidable rupture. In the reality of the image there is a continuous movement from summer to winter, which in the first stanza announces its coming through the fact that the lovely swans dip their heads drunk with kisses into the holy-sober water. This movement appears as a *rupture* solely because the poet himself within his poem breaks out of his own poem: Suddenly an I stands up and in its desires and timidity wants to assert itself against the guileless objective self-unfolding of an image.[2] We do not learn what happens when the swans dip their heads into the water and what they see there. The image is artificially disrupted. Instead, we are forced to suddenly circle around another center, around an I with its subjective fears of this movement.

The real rupture is not between summer and winter, but between the innocence and objectivity of a self-moving image and the uprising of a subjectivity that ruthlessly pushes its way into the delicate self-contained image and talks about itself instead of listening to the image. Woe is *me*, where will *I* get, when winter has come, flowers? But maybe this uprising and breakout on the part of the I is, in a deeper sense, itself after all a part of that guileless going-under into the holy soberness of the water that brings up winter. And maybe it is our task to acquire this deeper understanding, an understanding capable of seeing that even the ruthlessness of this poetic I is still encompassed within the innocence of being.

Of course, in giving my talk the title "The Burial of the Soul in(to) Technological Civilization" it could seem that I, too, play the same familiar tune as the discontented and wish to bemoan the soullessness of technology, bemoan "civilization and its discontents." But the implications of the expression "burial of the soul" are not quite that simple. It does not simply have a negative, derogatory meaning, as we moderns are inclined to think, because we have no relation to grave and burial. This was, for the ancient Egyptians for example, very different. They created the products of their entire cultural activities for the most part for the sole purpose of burying them and letting them disappear for good in graves. Just as we today invest billions in tanks and rockets and disk drives, which, after a few years, are only fit for scrap, so the Egyptians, if I may use such an inappropriate, grotesque comparison, invested their most precious treasures into the world of graves, not only gold and jewels of inestimable material value, but also the creations of their artist-craftsmen, sculptors, painters and poets.

We, by contrast, are a culture which exactly the other way around excavates that which formerly had been buried and displays it in bright light, just the same as all our present-day productions. Starting with archeological digs via the philological and historical unearthing of sources, the dissection of corpses in medicine, investigative journalism, and in general the publication of information through the media, the display of nudity in magazines, up to psychoanalytic uncovering of repressed truths, it seems to be a basic need of our culture to bring the hidden to light and thereby disprove the realness of the grave.

Even something like the anatomical dissecting of the body by no means arises merely from practical necessities, as we might perhaps be inclined to think, but from a specific idea of what is absolutely important, from an "archetypal" need of modern man. For as Ludwig Edelstein[3] shows, anatomical dissection appeared to the Greeks as superfluous for purposes of *medicine*; it only served the intellectual curiosity of the philosophers. Greek medicine obviously could get along quite well with the hiddenness and darkness of the body, without feeling it to be a regrettable evil. For us, however, it is considered as self-evident and absolutely imperative that the unknown be wrested from its hiddenness.

Between the sinking of the highest value and central symbol of the Egyptians, the dead Pharaoh, into the mummy, into the several sarcophagi and into the richly adorned world of the grave on the one hand, and our archeological excavating, our museum exhibitions, and scientific explanations on the other hand, there is that event that we call in an essential sense occidental history, one single event. This event of Western fate found its highest articulation as Christian religion, above all in the idea of Incarnation. There are of course quite a few symbols constitutive for Christianity, such as Crucifixion, Resurrection, and the effusion of the Holy Ghost, and Incarnation is but one of them. The question with which of these events Christianity begins and which symbol is thus the most central must not be answered here. Maybe this question is even mistaken from the outset, inasmuch as all essential symbols of a religion are probably all equally primary (*gleichursprünglich*) and interlocked so that each one comprises within itself all the others and no single one can be understood in isolation. There is not the one central symbol from which the others could be derived or to which they could be subordinated. The structure of a hermeneutic whole, such as a living religion, is of such a nature that it is there in its entirety all at once—not in a historical sense, but in essence. If I nevertheless focus on the Incarnation alone, then I do this not to the exclusion of Crucifixion, Resurrection, etc., but for the sole reason that it is the significant aspect of Christianity in the context of my topic. For the Incarnation seems to mean in my view nothing else but the burial of the soul in technology.

To comprehend the idea of Incarnation as the truth of technology and technology as the fulfillment and completion of Christian Incarnation contradicts all our usual ideas. Modern technological civilization after all originates from the great counter-movement to the

Church and Christianity, the Enlightenment. With the latter, modern man liberated himself from Christian religion and perhaps even from any religious outlook altogether and attempted to establish a wholly secular, maybe even antidivine world. I do not want here, prior to my taking up our actual topic, to deal with these important objections, because it is the very task of the following discussion to demonstrate in detail the inner connection between seemingly secular technology and the idea of Incarnation. But at the beginning a reference to one obvious fact is in place: that technological civilization came into existence only in the West. This fact is so obvious and familiar that the statement contained in it can hardly be heard. For it states that technology must be rooted in the highest and deepest concerns of Western culture and must be understood accordingly.

We can of course not say that technology flourished in the Western world for the simple reason that only in it were people intelligent enough, or that only here the scientific preconditions for inventions existed. Rather, it is the other way around; Western man had to apply his intelligence almost exclusively to technological development and to creating the scientific preconditions because his consciousness was informed by specific archetypal dominants whose nature it was to lead in that direction. For example, besides many other technical inventions, gunpowder was invented much earlier in China than in Europe. But what was it used for? It was "squandered" by way of fireworks, effused into the air, for the purpose of the ritual celebration of the New Year festival, whereas in Europe the invention of gunpowder set a development in motion which lead via cannons and bombs up to nuclear missiles and served the purpose of an ever more intensive access to reality.[4] It is unthinkable that the Far Eastern world could have produced, on the basis of its own tradition, something like the atom bomb or more generally a mechanized world. On the basis of Chinese culture, technical inventions were no doubt possible, but their use, their status, and function was fundamentally different because the position of man towards Being was a different one. Man's position towards Being finds its expression in the central motifs of his religion, just as conversely the latter's motifs inform his consciousness and give it a specific orientation. That, however, which sets the religion of the West most apart from all the other religions is Incarnation, the idea that in the empirical-historical man Jesus of Nazareth God himself has entered the world. It is this historical basis on which in the last analysis Christian religion's claim to absolute truth, most clearly elaborated by Hegel,[5] is based, the Christian awareness, not existing without some justification, of the incomparability of Christianity. If Western culture is distinguished from all other cultures by two incomparabilities, by the development of a technological civilization on the one hand and by having an "absolute religion" (which is absolute because of its historical basis) on the other hand, the idea is not completely out of place that both could be connected or perhaps even identical.

I am speaking here as depth-psychologist and psychotherapist and not from a theological standpoint. But precisely a *depth*-psychological examination of technology cannot do without religious and theological aspects. In the depth, theology is decisive, which is why already Freud and Jung were inevitably induced, in the course of their psychological studies, to deal with religious or theological questions. This is not really a border violation because the concern behind this interest in religion is and remains the therapy of the soul. By concerning myself with Incarnation in connection with technology, I do not desert the psychological, imaginal standpoint in favor of a historical or theological one. I am not trying to put the blame for the predicaments of the technological age on any earlier age, movement, or individual person; I do not attempt to find a "culprit," neither Christianity, nor the ancient Greeks, nor the Old Testament Hebrews. Although my glance seemingly turns backwards, I nevertheless remain in our present[6] and ask what are the efficacious images and living ideas under whose dominion we live today and that we suffer from. C. G. Jung already saw it similarly. He said,

> My problem is to wrestle with the big monster of the historical
> past, the great snake of the centuries, the burden of the human
> mind, the problem of Christianity. ... Other people are not
> worried by such problems, they do not care about the historical
> burdens Christianity has heaped upon us.[7]

Precisely in view of our ever more alarming situation—death of the forest due to pollution, stocking up on nuclear arms, overpopulation of the earth, etc.—I do not want to try to find ways out that would allow us to shake off this historical burden. There are enough ways out. Rousseau, Hegel, Hölderlin, Marx, even Heidegger, to mention only a few, sought for and recommended ways out. By contrast, I would like to merely listen to our plight, without partiality, in order for us to finally get truly into our Christian mode and our technology and so that it might perhaps become more likely that one time we might, for the first time in Western history, become able to *truly carry* our historical burden.

It is very hard for us to grasp and accept that the Christian tenets could also be a burden. Because it preaches charity and redemption, for a long time we have been wont to see in Christianity only something that redeems and to blind ourselves about the shadow that precisely a religion of redemption must bring along with it. Ordinary theology knows nothing of the *burden* of Christianity. It shook it off. However, if it makes out the contents of the Christian doctrine as mere truths of *faith*, is this not a playing down, a minimization, through which the doctrine is kept out of objective reality and immunized against it? Since the age of the Reformation at the latest, theology and the Church have left the real course of events, the real intellectual and social development, to its own fate and if anything at most offered, as bystander and onlooker from outside and above, moral exhortations. And correspondingly they also no longer derived their own truth from out of the plight of each age, forgetful of the fact that the divine never comes to us only from out of a written-down history, but always only as one's "future" (*Zukunft*: literally "that which is coming toward us") from out of each present that we are in, and its reality. If, however, the truths of theology and the Church have lost touch with the real world (technology, industry, natural sciences) to such an extent and have ceased to be *the simple articulation of the active forces operative in reality*, can they then still be considered the authoritative interpreters of the *living* Christian truth? If they understand the Christian truth as what formerly, 2000 years ago, had in fact been intended by the historical Jesus or the Apostles or the early Church and if this is the truth they want to study, preserve, and restore, is what they do then not merely something like an archeology of their own truth and a preservation of their own historic monuments? And when they reserve their truth for faith in the interior of man and keep it *opposed* to objective reality, do they in this way not also systematically keep themselves in the impotence of unreality?

By the way, if I speak here of the Christian truth, or of truth in general, what is meant is not truth in a theological or metaphysical sense, some "absolute, eternal truth," the "true per se"—I have no knowledge about that—but truth in a psychological sense: an idea or fantasy is *psychologically true* if it is active, effective.[8]

In view of the alarming situation of the world it seems to me very urgent no longer to follow the undervaluation and derealization, promulgated by the Churches, of the Christian truths, but to take these truths more seriously and think them more rigorously than is typically the case on the part of theology and the Church. The Christian truths must not be conceived as a matter of mere personal faith and inner experience. It is precisely the real development of the Christian West which we have to regard as authoritative for the Christian truth. Our external public reality including technology, advertizing, exploitation, etc. is not opposite to the Christian truth, but rather belongs to it, is essentially an integral part of it. Christian truth does not only have its upper mental and "conviction" ("faith") aspect, but, like every religion, also its own physical reality and earthly weight (and as the religion of the Incarnation naturally a different type and a much more massive physical reality than other religions).

Only by allowing the Christian truth to have its essential life precisely in reality (and I mean the way reality really is and not how it ideally "is supposed to be") will we also do justice to the deep psychotherapeutic concern that C. G. Jung could not get out of his mind: the integration and redemption of the fourth. "Ever since the *Timaeus* the 'fourth' has signified 'realization,' i.e., entry into an essentially different condition, that of worldly materiality ..."[9] What is needed is to

> see in matter itself the equivalent of spirit, but this 'spirit' will appear divested of all, or at any rate most, of its known qualities, just as earthly matter [in the image of the Mother of God] was stripped of its specific characteristics when it staged its entry into heaven.[10]

If we split off the fourth (the earth, the shadow, the material reality) by refusing to acknowledge reality as the locus of the Christian truth—which direction would then be open to us? Only that of a kind of Manichaeism and the allocation of the reality of the world to Fallen man, with the psychologically disastrous consequence that the real development would continue not to be connected to consciousness and thus could take its course in blind obedience to archaic instinctual patterns.

If we want to acquire a real inner connection to our factual world (technological civilization), then it is decisive for our success to recognize in the Incarnation a psychological *reality*, that is, not a mere reality of faith, but a real factor of our intellectual life, an objective might with determining force that has to be reckoned with in reality because we all are in it and exposed to its workings in our ordinary practical reality. It is not a mere claim, an idea that we may or may not entertain. It is not (a representation) *in us*, but we are *in it*. It is the world in which we live, the scope of our existence. And thus it is absolutely irrelevant whether we believe in it, have inwardly experienced it and accept it or not. It is the unrelenting fate of all of us. The Incarnation must not be reduced to a Church-internal matter, it must be a public concern, and not a matter of faith and personal feeling, but of general, "official," and binding knowledge.

In what follows I want to look into the Incarnation from five points of view: 1. The interment of Heaven, 2. The artificiality of the flesh, 3. The fabrication of God, 4. The inflation of things, and 5. Divestiture.

1. THE INTERMENT OF HEAVEN

In the mythical world, it is nothing uncommon that gods take human guise and appear to mortals. To illustrate it with a familiar example, in the Odyssey Telemachus believes to have hosted a friend of Odysseus's, a friend bound by a tie of hospitality to the latter, namely Mentes, the king of the Taphians—while in reality it was the goddess Athene who had appeared to him in this guise.[11] In the Christian myth it is said that God had become man. In Jesus of Nazareth, who is a veritable human being, God has come close to man. And faith is capable of beholding the glory of God in the man Jesus, quite similarly as Telemachos all of a sudden recognizes in the departing Mentes the godhead. However, as analogous as the two conceptions seem to be, they are diametrically opposed to each other. The Christian "myth"[12] of the Incarnation breaks out of the mythical constitution of the world and is that "myth" that founded a nonmythical or antimythical existence.

Through severe controversies the Old Church struggled to grasp the specific nature of Christ and to ward off all sorts of reductions and one-sided views. Christ is neither simply a God who so to speak for appearance's sake took on human shape, nor, conversely, a man who became equal to God, and also not a semi-divine cross between both natures, but at one and the same time, as Luther worded it, true God, born of the Father in eternity, as well as true man, born of Virgin Mary.[13] For Christianity it is of highest importance that the divine and human natures of Christ are both acknowledged in full purity and intensity and that this contradiction is in no way weakened or mediated. Rather the task is to see to it that the two oppositional natures come together in one and the same person *without* their difference being blurred or, conversely, being construed so starkly that the two natures would practically fall apart into two separate essences, which had only accidentally found a lodging in one and the same person. The psychological content that in Christianity pushed its way forward into consciousness and was the driving force behind the passionate struggles of the early Church obviously demanded such a precarious tightrope walk, this extremely difficult balancing act, in order to arrive at an appropriate wording for it. It was a matter of conceiving of the idea of a reality in which the divine and the human-earthly were *at once* identical and different.

In the mythical situation in which Telemachus found himself, everything was very different, if not inverse. His father's guest-friend only appeared to be a human, while in reality being a goddess. But inasmuch as we are not allowed to see in Telemachus a superstitious supernaturalist, it is just as true that after the godhead had become disclosed, also the human-earthly reality of his conversation partner was not obliterated. As a matter of course it had been and remained to be Mentes, king of Taphians, who had spoken to him. Rather the god relativizes the human and the human the God, and what factually remains behind all this is solely what in fact had happened and obviously iridesces in two directions. It has an ordinary-human face and a divine face, and neither one is "the absolutely true one." We could here neither speak of a "true man" nor of a "true goddess," let alone, as in the case of Christ, of "a true man *and* a true god"—because here such a radicalized true being, i.e., a reality in the literal or positivized sense, does not exist.

Already here the radical novelty of the Christian situation becomes apparent. But in order to be able to appreciate the enormous event that in the Christian Incarnation found its most emphatic articulation, we must still go back a bit more. There is a significant, widespread mythologem referred to by Erich Neumann[14] as the separation of the primordial parents and by Heino Gehrts[15] as the myth of the distancing of Heaven and Earth. In the beginning Heaven and Earth were lying on top of each other in cohabitation, and everything was darkness. There had never been a separation of them, so their children, the sons of Heaven and Earth, had to live in eternal night—until one day one of the sons of the primordial parents heaved Heaven up and separated them from out of his position in between them. Thereby the open, light space that we perhaps can call "the World" in the emphatic sense, was created for the first time. In Greek mythology this motif lives on in the figure of Atlas, whose task it is to carry the vault of heaven. Frequently it is a world tree that keeps Heaven and Earth or the upper world and the underworld apart, so that the open clearance of the human World arises.

As the figure of Atlas demonstrates, the one-time act of heaving up Heaven was not enough. The distancing had to be constantly maintained. Human existence was overshadowed by the fundamentally existing possibility that Heaven crashed back upon the Earth. Man was called upon to re-establish and affirm the separateness. This happened partly through special rituals, partly also simply through the mythical-ritualistic mode of existence. As Heino Gehrts[16] in his profound essay on the nature of the spear showed, through the ritual of the erection of the spear the distancing of Heaven and Earth was ever again renewed and along with it archaic mankind's dwelling in the open clearance each time newly acquired.

What, by contrast, does the Christian Incarnation mean? The moving force behind the Christian vision aimed for what is called *perichoresis*, that is, the mutual interpenetration of the divine and the human nature. What was to be achieved was that God and Man, *logos* and *sarx*, word and flesh come in fact together *in one point*. This is the meaning of "Jesus the Christ" and it is what makes this figure so unheard of and exciting. Jesus the Christ or the Incarnation means nothing less than the systematic undoing of the Heaven-Earth-distancing. The mission and the achievement of Christianity was to knock over the erect spear, to make Atlas collapse and to cut down the World Ash. Heaven and Earth have by no means lost their difference, but they have now been collapsed *into* one and *as* one identity. They are superimposed without interstice, nay, they even interpenetrate each other. Heavenly Logos has now been interred in earthly flesh. The World as the in-between, as the separateness providing an open clearance, is gone.

From out of the collapse of the world, understood as described, something fundamentally new, something that had not been there ever before, emerges: the *one* point given in empirical-historical reality in which Heaven and Earth are intricately intertwined in such an indissoluble and inexpressible way that they appear to be a homogenous whole. This point becomes real as the self-enclosed thing of physical reality, the body as empirical-literal reality. The Incarnation means the installation of a new constitution of being, of being in the sense of empirical-physical reality, the inauguration of the somatization of being. Only through the Incarnation did our concept of factuality and of sensible-objective physicality obtain a sound mythic foundation. Only the Christian vision renders the much older saying, *sôma sêma psychês*[17] (the body the grave of the soul), really true.

Is it astonishing that Greek medicine did not see any necessity for anatomical dissection, whereas our entire medicine both in a substantial sense rests on anatomical investigations and in a temporal sense began with them? For the man of the Christian West the body has apparently become an impenetrably enclosed physical thing that one needs to cut open if its nature is to be brought to light. For the Greek physicians, by contrast, the body was apparently not closed *from the outset*, rather it opened up an entire world with its own Heaven and its own Earth, a world extending to the very stars. For this reason a literal dissection of the body from outside, with which the anatomist on his part would remain outside, would not have provided access to its reality. The access to the body was only gained by the physician's *own* entering that world; and in order for him to be able to do that it had to be *a priori* open: the physicality of the body had to be an imaginal one.

Is it astonishing that the Egyptians buried their most precious treasures, while we take to excavating and exhibiting? The Egyptian burying meant, as a renunciation of the treasures, a distancing, through which a clearance, an open space was acquired, not all that different from forcing Heaven and Earth apart from out of the position in-between them, or different from the ritualistic erection of a spear. To *absence* was given a real presence in life. The Egyptian buried the precious *things* and thereby opened up the grave as a *World*. We conversely feel the urge to dig things up from the graves and to pull out of their hiddenness the farthest stars by means of radio telescopes, and the minutest particles of matter by means of electron microscopes, and to zoom in on them, to exhibit and stare at them, because we are under the dominion of the Incarnation, the *perichoresis*. For us the thing has become the purpose of our spiritual existence because in it Logos and *sarx* have to come together. Spellbound we have to search for the ultimate point of matter. The smaller that point, all the better, inasmuch as then the mutual interpenetration of Logos and flesh takes place in an even narrower area and still more of the world-constituting openness is destroyed.

The Egyptian surrendered the fleshly (physical things) to the *sarko-phágos* (the flesh-eater) and through this sacrificial ritual achieved an *extractio spiritus*. Our doings, too, are a ritual, a ritual of continual knocking over the erected spear, the ritual of an ever deeper interment of heaven. The Word has become flesh. Here it is not the flesh that is eaten (as in the case of the sarcophagus) for the purpose of setting the wide world of the imaginal free, but the flesh conversely absorbs the Logos into itself. This has consequences even for the psyche of the individual person in modernity. For C. G. Jung neurotic symptoms are, as it were, the gods that have been buried in the empirical personality. He stated, "The gods have become diseases; Zeus no longer rules Olympus but rather the solar plexus, and produces curious specimens for the doctor's consulting room ..."[18]

Is it astonishing that nowadays "the world has become small"? This is by no means due to our airplanes and means of communication, but, conversely, these could only be invented because the world had already become small, indeed nonexistent. How narrow (in a literal empirical sense) were in former times the dimensions of an Egyptian royal tomb or the geographic horizon of people in ancient days compared with the vast global distances into which our vacation or business trips take us or which are daily brought to us via television into our livingrooms. But the tomb opened up a world of cosmic dimension, whereas our airplanes connect individual thing-like (positive) points within an empty space devoid of "world."

Kant still thought that he was able to look up in admiration and awe to the starry heaven above himself.[19] For him heaven obviously was still something qualitatively different from the earth and ontologically distinct from it. We have in the meantime lost the possibility for good to look up to something (although subjectively it is of course still possible). An upward-looking presupposes an open distance and also establishes it. For us there is only *one* homogenous space, one homogenous *uni-versum* (that which is merged into one), no longer an in-itself-contentious cosmos. The starry heaven has merely still the *name* heaven, but in reality it has become a just as earthly a reality as our earth itself. This is also the only reason why mortal man can penetrate into outer space: the earth is thereby not really left at all. As long as one could look up to the real heaven above us in veneration, not even the most ingenious mind could have invented airplanes or rockets. For through this upward-looking, the distance of heaven, i.e., its absolute, namely qualitative, ontological, unreachability from the earth was established and acknowledged. Only after heaven has become interred in the earth, and *ipso facto* had become earthly itself ("sky"), did it turn into a freely accessible space for technological inventiveness.

I pointed out that the distance that in mythological times had to be reproduced ever anew was not only reconfirmed through certain rituals such as that of the erection of a spear, but also through the mythological-ritualistic mode of existence itself. If we recall for example Telemachus, we can say that the mode of existence described by Homer consists in, and is mythological for the reason that, figuratively speaking, within a quite ordinary occurrence, the visit from a guest-friend, a spear is erected. The spear erected in the event keeps *the Heaven and the Earth of (within) this very occurrence* apart and at bottom for the first time sets up, through this type of distancing, the mortal man *as* mortal man and the goddess *as* goddess from out of an otherwise anonymous, clotted event.[20]

It is my thesis that this is what every myth, every symbol does. A thing is a symbol then and only then if it within itself opens up a whole world and illumines reality as a whole in the light of this "world." Not participation, *pars pro toto*, not analogy or correspondence, not representation of something irrepresentable in or by means of something sensible, not an assigning of a higher figurative meaning is what constitutes a symbol, but the Heaven-Earth-distancing *within* the one concrete thing or event in question. The real thing is not transcended by the symbolic-mythological meaning, but itself *is*, exactly the way it comes, the symbol. The real concrete object contains everything it needs within itself to be a symbol, to be an image, to be mythological. It is self-sufficient. Nothing must be added or done to it. The only thing indispensable is that within itself its own Heaven and its own Earth separate and it thereby opens up into a World.

The Incarnation is for that reason indeed the myth of the unmythological, because it instructs our consciousness to construe *everything* as the one positive-factual point in which Logos and *sarx* come together, in which they are clotted; for as a mythical idea it does not want, in the manner of what is reported in our history books, to talk about long-bygone facts of the past, but essentially appears with the claim to be a living presence for every present and to transform the ontological constitution of the whole world. In this way it produces in the last analysis not only the mute concrete wall, the mute atom, or the stifled occludedness of the sexual organs in today's pornography. It also lays the foundation for our faith, for example, in hormones and vitamins or brings about many a failure of marriages, because it forces us to demand that our marriage partner as this ordinary human being be at the same time divine. A separation of the earthly and the heavenly marriage is not permitted any longer.

Nowadays the idea of a development of mankind from unconsciousness to consciousness is widespread. In the light of the picture drawn here this theory seems to me untenable. The popular distinction of the matriarchal from our allegedly patriarchal orientation does not get us any further, but rather obscures the subject-matter. The—in fact ascertainable—changes in the mode of human existence should not be seen as a rise from unconsciousness to consciousness, but as a reversal in the essential meaning of conscious and unconscious. In the mythical world, consciousness means to have erected a spear and in this way to keep apart a World. In order to achieve and maintain this awareness, archaic man had of course to leave in darkness not only the dead Pharaoh and many a precious object, but also a wealth of scientific and historical facts or even to actively bury them. We achieve our type of consciousness by excavating and exhibiting all these things. Our exhibition of things and facts in the light of day is, however, in itself the burial of Heaven, of Logos, and of soul precisely in those exhibited things.

By giving over the fleshly to the *sarko-phágos*, mythological man also sacrificed a possible consciousness about ontic things for the benefit of a consciousness in the sense of the ontological opening up of a World. But we are compelled to press back together the ontological distance into the worldless occludedness of the ontic things that results from this action, so that the ontic, the flesh aspect of things, can be brought into the limelight. The unconsciousness of mythological man was based on a conscious sacrifice; our unconsciousness, by contrast, is the obfuscation and occlusion of things and facts in the light—the "consciousness's becoming unconscious," as Jung called it,[21] or, with the image of the Christian myth, the Logos's becoming flesh.

2. THE ARTIFICIALITY OF THE FLESH

When in conversations the topic of God comes up, the first question immediately suggesting itself is, is there a God in the first place? From this it is apparent that the most obvious perspective from which the topic of God is viewed is the question about his existence. This is not only the case in the modern ages and not only among the sceptics, but is characteristic for the Christian West at large. Already during the Scholastic Middle Ages, at a time when the belief in God was an undisputed common property rooted in the whole experience of life and when doubt was no more than a playful intellectual exercise, already then the need was felt to prove the existence of God. And that on the part of learned, pious monks who certainly could not be suspected of having had secret doubts that they needed to soothe. The question about the proof of the existence of God in the one or the other form occupied the entire Western thinking also later, not only up to Kant, who had demonstrated once and for all the impossibility of proving the existence of God, but also much later, be it, as with Hegel, in the sense of a renewed rescue of the proofs, or in the various atheistic, materialistic movements of the 19th century that precisely tried to prove the nonexistence of God. The question is alive to such an extent that it was possible as recently as a few years ago that a theological book by

Hans Küng appeared with the probably provocatively chosen title, *Does God Exist?*

The question, Is there a God? has been raised so often, on a high philosophical level just as in pseudoscientific pamphlets and in everyday conversation and is thus so familiar to us that we no longer notice that it is by no means an obvious question, indeed, how unnatural it is. God and existence, God and an "Is there in reality...?"—this combination of terms or ideas is not simply inherent in the nature of the human mind, but only arises on a very specific historical ground, just as does the other typically Western-modern question whether I as I demonstrably exist or whether my existence is maybe not merely an idle dream. As we can see in Descartes, questions about the existence of God and of the I are intricately connected or perhaps only two different versions of one and the same question. The Western fixation upon the existence of God and the I expands into the general necessity on the part of the natural and historical sciences to insist on the proof of factuality.

In order to be able to understand that these questions are by no means obvious ones, we must again make the mythological situation clear. In that situation, the question about existence could simply not be asked. Here one could neither say that, for example, Zeus exists nor that he does not exist. The notion of existence simply passes over the reality of the mythic gods. How should one be able to ask: Is there Helios? One obviously lived in his light day after day and felt the effects of his rays on one's own body. We, too, do not ask: Are there dogs? Is there such a thing as wind? Do earthquakes exist? Natural phenomena have always already overtaken the question about their existence. Our doubts and questions come too late because the *answers* have always already been given to us by nature herself. How should it be feasible to ask: Is there Zeus? Quite apart from thunderbolts and other natural phenomena—had one not been to Olympia and seen the great statue of Zeus, and was it there not as plain as can be that it was god?

The fact that in the real sun or in a statue made by humans the god could in fact be seen is not due to gullibility or superstition, but is to be explained from the mythic meaning of the word god, which can be demonstrated most easily using the example of the Greek *theós*. This word does not signify a personal agent, nor an existing being; it was originally not a possible subject of a sentence, but, as Kerényi[22] has shown, a word that could only be used as a predicate. This is why one could not form a vocative case of *theós* in the ancient language, and nothing could be predicated of it (in other words, one could not say: god, *theós*, is this or that). The word much rather had the function of predicating something of real events. Functionally *theós* is therefore similar to words like "unheard of," "extraordinary," "marvelous" (although it is not an adjective but a noun, and the particular words mentioned here do of course not give an idea of the *specific* meaning of *theós*). For example, the Greeks could say: "If one person helps another, this is god." The event, the phenomenon, is god.

This fact is of greatest significance. For what it means is that if the Greeks saw god in the sun or in a statue or in an occurrence, they did not read something mysterious into what they saw. It did not imply a claim of something hidden behind or inside it, it was not a matter of faith and therefore could not be a matter of doubt either and obviously could not be proven. It would have been absurd to wish to prove anything here, as absurd as if I thought to have to prove that I am happy or sad. C. G. Jung, whose psychological understanding of the God-concept coincides in this regard exactly with the mythological one, states it is

> just as stupid to try to prove the existence of God as to deny him. If a person feels happy, he needs neither proof nor counterproof. Also, there is no reason to suppose that 'happiness' or 'sadness' cannot be experienced.[23]

For the Greeks and correspondingly for mythological man in general the thoroughly natural phenomenon, as it was perceived with the senses, was itself *theós*. "God" signified a quality of real events themselves, an effect they had on man.

The gods of mythology, which were the qualities of natural reality vividly portrayed as figures, therefore were natural gods. This is of course a truism. But what it means to say that the mythic gods were natural gods and what inferences have to be drawn from it remains to be gauged. Even if theoretically we perhaps already know better, the conception about myth still operative in the depth is that it is something like the world interpretation, world view, or world explanation of early man. In view of nature, so this thinking goes, the primitive, too, had to somehow form a notion of it, and the result of his attempts is myth.

This understanding of myth misses the mark of what myth in essence is and retrojects a Christian-modern situation into the time of archaic man.

If we really want to go through with the insight that the mythic gods are natural gods, then we have to realize much rather that myth is not the interpretation of the world, but nature itself. The mythological images do not come subsequently after the fact, secondarily, but they are the heart and soul of real nature. Nature owes its essential character and being to mythological images, and not the other way around. The god images do not represent an imaginal equivalent for a theory, they are rather the natural itself, natural instinct and natural world. Myth does not have a *relation* to instinct and to external reality; rather, what *we* now see as the opposition of inner instinct and external reality, and furthermore distinguish from mythic image, is precisely contained in myth, encompassed by it. Myth has nothing outside of itself. There is not first a nature or an instinct and then in addition a mythic image.

Rather, myth *is* the very reality of the life of man. Mythological man did not live in the environment and not in his body and also not in his inner world, but he lived *in myth*. This, the myth itself, is mythological man's instinct, drive, his inner and his real world, and the real world is for him conversely his myths. This is of course due to the fact that in each concrete phenomenon Heaven and Earth are kept apart so that man sees things from inside, because as spear-bearer he has his place in the open clearance between the heaven and the earth of the respective event. The fact that myth is the really lived life itself and not an image of it, this precisely is the essence of myth just as much as of nature. For "natural" or "instinctive" means "to be there of its own accord," always already being there, *prior* to all opinions, all human willing and acting, guilelessly, innocently, self-contained and self-certain. Nature is what in an emphatic sense is "a matter of course," that which is taken for granted because it is really *self*-apparent. That is to say, it is something that is in no need of being, and cannot be, understood by us, but *it* conversely speaks of its own accord, thereby bestowing *itself* and its meaning on us. According to an adage of Heraclitus, nature is something whose character it is to be evasive or to cease to exist if one tries to get to the bottom of it, to explain or prove it: *phýsis krýptesthai phileî.*[24] It is the nature of nature that *myth is* the real environment and the inner world of man all in one, the real house of man's existence. Nature means that the immediate, instinctive image itself has a full and all-comprehensive reality character.

Because the mythic gods were natural gods, it was impossible to believe in them or to have doubts about them. One could never have asked whether they exist. They were after all, in the sense indicated, self-apparent and would have withdrawn the moment one inquired about them. However, if in the Christian world the question "Is there a God?" keeps the minds occupied, then this shows that the Christian God is not a self-apparent, natural God any more, but a God whose innermost nature it is to be somehow imposed from above, a God who does no longer manifest itself *phýsei*, simply as an instinct-experience and without question. Now he is, to be sure, substantial, a personal agent, an existing hypostasis and a possible sentence subject, but this is not an acquisition, but a loss. For his having become a subject he payed dearly with an ontological deficiency. The idea of the Incarnation expresses both aspects of this transformation of the essence of the divine in one and the same image. God has become flesh. What does this mean? Inherent in the idea of becoming flesh is, first of all, that the nature of God ceases to be "only" imaginal, mythic, and instead wants a positive, substantial existence, an existence in the flesh. God wants to be Something or Somebody, a real entity, the *summum ens*. This gives the impression as if it was God's wish precisely to enter nature. But, and this is the second aspect, the fact that this God had to *become* flesh shows that by nature he is somehow incorporeal, without substance, unreal. The natural gods did not ever need to *become* flesh because they bore their physical reality always already in their image-nature and, being image, could effortlessly and without much ado appear in this or that shape.

From this follows a third and most significant point. Flesh gives at first the impression of being a word that signifies most decisively natural existence. But in the context of the Incarnation and through it, a fundamental transformation of the essence of flesh and, along with it, of nature ensues. The Logos becomes flesh. Here we must really hear *what* is stated with the idea of the Logos turned flesh and must not content ourselves with what is *meant*. Not what is intended is crucial, but what has really been said and what is the historically active force. If a mythic idea such as that of the Incarnation is a life-transforming reality, then the competent commentary to the Bible is written by history and not by the exegetes.

We must not screen the idea of the Incarnation off from reality as a free-floating idea in empty space, which is believed in (or maybe not believed in) by individuals in their interior. No, we have to comprehend that it decides about *the constitution of reality as a whole*. The Word becomes flesh. Here something *happens*. And not only to the Logos that descends from above, but also to the flesh (i.e., to earthly reality) into which the Logos enters. The concepts of flesh and Logos are, of course, not assembled together into the dictum of the Incarnation as static entities like building bricks, with fixed dictionary meanings, but they are themselves exposed to the living process of the thought expressed in that sentence and are seized and transformed by it. What we are concerned with here is the incredible occurrence that the flesh (together with the Logos) receives a radically different nature. The concept, the notion of flesh, of earth, of reality is transformed. The flesh now has no longer its ground in nature, but it is flesh from above, and actually not really flesh at all, but *Logos* having become flesh.

The things of nature had their own Logos, too, but this was of course the natural Logos, the Logos of *nature*, the Logos expressed in *mythos*. Now, however, an inversion or pole changing has taken place: the Logos heretofore contained in nature escaped from it, made itself independent as something in its own right and of its own origin, and thus turned into the primary, the fundamental and comprehensive reality. The Incarnation amounts to an ontological revolution. The reality character is moving from the natural, from the sensual-mythical, to what comes from the Logos above. From now on the quality of 'being real' is no longer to be assigned to what exists by nature. Realness, this is from now on supposed to mean: the Logos-quality (in the completely novel sense, established by the Incarnation, of the pure Logos, the Logos isolated from nature). Here the new reality concept that the natural sciences will later take as their basis is conceived and the mythic foundation for it is laid. The Incarnation therefore is ontologically speaking the grandiose blueprint, reaching out far ahead into the future, of the idea of the substitution of nature by a second, no longer natural nature, the program of the translation of the natural world into a technological one. In the Incarnation the Christian "myth" of the supernatural God lays the foundation, as is done by every myth in its own way, for *its own* type of "corporeality," "earthy substantiality," and "reality." The theological name for the new type of corporeality is "flesh," today's philosophical name: "positive, technological reality."

What else could one expect technological reality to be but the Logos become flesh? And how else could one conversely imagine a Logos become flesh than in the style of technological reality? (At least if the Incarnation is not a lofty idea with no roots in the ground, but one that *does* something to reality.) Technology is Logos because it is what has its origin in reason, a product of the mind, idea. It is flesh because it is material reality and does not simply remain idea. And it is the result of a becoming because it is not what grew by itself (*physis*), but something artificially made, the realization of the idea into a tangible practical reality. This is not only true for the technical apparatuses, but also for the explanation of the world by the sciences. This explanation, too, is technology in the sense of a conversion of Logos into flesh, inasmuch as it is the substitution of the natural world (myth) by the positivistically conceived reality. Thus we see that flesh *after* the Incarnation does no longer mean the same as before, and it is precisely the purpose of the Incarnation to express or bring about this transformation of the essence of flesh, i.e., reality. Flesh, as Logos become flesh, is realized, transformed Idea, not natural flesh, neither literally as animal or human body, nor in the figurative sense as the already-existing earthly reality. Natural flesh would be, as we have seen, precisely mythic image, and mythic image God would never have still needed to become.[25] This he would have originally been from the outset, without this, however, already having qualified him for being given the name flesh in this emphatic sense.

Through God's having the urge to become flesh, i.e., the urge for a positivistically conceived existence, the mythic image is split into two extreme directions and thus destroyed. Its reality / nature / corporeality aspect is separated as "flesh," as the total novelty of a factual existence in empirical-historical reality. And along with it its Logos aspect conversely breaks out of natural reality and ascends into the unattainable otherworldly height of the pre-existent Logos. The Old Testament God had to some extent still been a mythic, intramundane, natural god, and the creation story, too, still has a largely mythic character within the context of the Old Testament. Only through the Incarnation does God really cease being a mythic image and turns into a completely extramundane, absolute God, i.e., a God detached from nature. Only through the pre-existent Logos does God truly turn into the creator God, and only through the Word's becoming flesh does the creation through God's word become fully realized. Because God is now no longer the most natural thing in the world, no longer mythic image, but as the wholly Other without *immediate* accessibility he is opposite to the natural world of man, he is for man somehow imposed from above, only asserted, and for this reason God must be intensely concerned for his real existence and demand faith. We must realize that the godhead was not pre-existent and infinitely distant from time immemorial and only through the Incarnation finally came close to man. Rather, God's embodiment in the flesh and his separation from nature arise simultaneously; they are one and the same, although

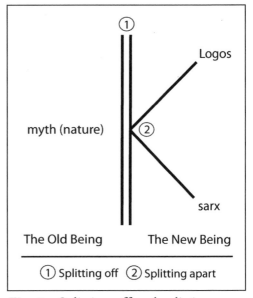

Fig. 1. Splitting off and splitting apart

conflicting, process. Logos and sarx are the decomposition products of myth, the fission product of nature. Today they are for example called, infinitely faded, theory and reality.

Whereas in the previous section we saw that the Incarnation undoes the Heaven-Earth-distancing, we now must note that this undoing is only the other side of a carrying the Heaven-Earth-distancing to an extreme. As pre-existent Logos and positivistic flesh, Heaven and Earth are no longer distanced, but dissociated, split off from each other. The distancing has, so to speak, been taken literally, as an absolute separation. In contrast to the distancing (the tension between the two separated poles of the world), their dissociation means that now the world occurs twice (in two separate complete versions), once for example as theory and secondly as reality, or once as Beyond and once as this world, and man is correspondingly doubled too, having as the one person two parallel existences (split-off personalities): he is at once *wholly* the fallen man of the flesh and *wholly* the redeemed man according to the spirit (Luther: *simul iustus et peccator*). The literal way of conceiving things then also results in *the* literal, in positivistic reality along with the abstract way of thinking, the fixation on tangible, demonstrable existence. The radical tearing apart of Heaven and Earth (dissociation) and the factual collapsing of Heaven and Earth in one point (Incarnation) apparently are the same. The moment that God breaks out of the simplicity and sheer self-apparency of the mythic image or, which is the same thing, out of nature, the situation gets complicated, paradoxical, conflicting.

The event that found its articulation in the Incarnation also means, as a transformation of the essence of God from mythic, natural Being to extranatural Being, a transformation of the constitution of reality; and it means the task of consistently realizing or executing this transformation. Being is translated from one language into another, from the language of nature into the language of physics or technology. To be sure, we call our chemistry, physics, physiology, etc. *natural* sciences, but this is much like we still speak of 'heaven' after heaven's having ceased to exist centuries ago. That which is explored by the natural sciences is not nature. The essence of nature is only accessible in myth, only in image—simply because the natural is by definition that which exists of its own accord, that which is self-apparent.

What the natural sciences are concerned with is, like everything *literally* (*positivistically*) existing, nothing self-apparent, but a reasoned-out artifice—only accessible through one's abstracting from the natural as it presents itself of its own accord in sensuous-imaginal form; only accessible through the invention and use of highly artificial apparatuses and cleverly devised methods. Natural sciences serve the Incarnation: the instillation of the Logos, from above and outside, into what formerly was the natural and thereby the production of positive reality. The natural sciences are not a way of cognition, but of translation, the translation of Being from the constitution of nature into that of technology, from the mythological reality's mode of being into the mode of being of Createdness (having been made). The things of the natural, mythical world are psychologically or ontologically speaking essentially uncreated, because as that which is or comes into being of its own

accord, it is their nature to be that which "always already is there" and
to be the unquestionably, instinctively certain. Only through the work
of the natural sciences is the constitution of the whole world truly
brought into the status of createdness. This is because the perspective
into which the natural sciences coercively transpose the world in its
entirety is the question how the things are "made," constructed (and
constructible).

Technology is not simply the sum-total of the apparatuses and
machines, but *one* way the world as a whole can be constituted. And
nature is correspondingly not simply the entirety of trees, mountains,
animals, and lakes, but one whole constitution of being. It is true, there
have already been technical inventions and apparatuses in prehistoric
ages and in antiquity, too. But this was not technology in the sense
employed here, but it was really nature, inasmuch as the inventive spirit
is part of the nature of man. Every technical invention was embedded
in a myth. Gods, Prometheus, heroes were the inventors or founders,
the *prôtoi heuretaí*. Every technical activity followed a ritualistic *nomos*
(law) and initiated into a mystery, into a world (quite clearly for example
in the case of the blacksmith's craft).[26] Today technology is something
qualitatively different: technical *civilization*. Now it is the horizon by
which human existence is contained. It is total, absolute, foundation.
Our whole being and understanding of being are technified and
oriented towards technification. The technical has become an end in
itself in whose service we are, which is why the interpretation of
technology as an instrument, from the point of view of practical benefit,
is obsolete and naive. Technology in the strict, ontological sense has
existed only since Being had turned into the Creation, and this means
into the Logos having become flesh. True, in nature, too, there is a Logos
at work. One just needs to have a look at a spider web. But this the
natural Logos, is not the pre-existent, extramundane Logos of
technology, which *is* not, but has to *become* flesh.

True, we still have poets and painters and also forests and rivers,
but we no longer have any nature; and art, too, as already Hegel[27] stated,
has, *as far as its highest determination is concerned*, become a thing of
the past for us. Just as myth, so also art can objectively be there only
on the ground of nature and nature only on the ground of art and myth.
The great lyric poetry of nature of, say, Goethe is no evidence to the
contrary. It is not only since the *waldsterben* that nature is dying. It

has long been dead in its essence, at least since, in the saying transmitted by Plutarch "The Great Pan is dead," the going under of the nature gods has been negatively stated, and since Christianity with its Incarnation positively sealed this statement by installing a new, wholly other God. Goethe's and the Romantics' nature poetry, as beautiful as it is, has been wrung and wrested from a reality that had already become unnatural—to express it crassly: it had been deviously usurped through the tour de force of the subjectively feeling I. The vacant position of the genies in the natural things has without more ado been taken by "the genius," the I as the magician who in the Storm and Stress of *his* feelings was able to evoke the impression of an animatedness of *nature*. From "*Wanderers Sturmlied*," e.g., one can immediately see how much effort it cost young man Goethe to force an animatedness from the world, contrary to the reality of the world,[28] just as it cost old man Goethe an enormous struggle to maintain his "theory of colors" against the real physics of his age, and to maintain his symbolic view of the world against the general spirit of his time[29]—until he, with unreserved honesty, admitted the irrevocable past of the symbolic and gave voice to the new truth in his *Faust, Part II.*[30] Nature poetry, which was produced even long after Goethe, had no objective truth. How should it have had, how should there still objectively be nature, when the natural gods are gone? Objective art existed when the things themselves were still poetic and the poet did not give expression to his feeling-experience, but only listened to and reproduced the voice of nature. The death of the natural gods means that the anima, and along with it poetry, emigrated from nature and that now only the human being has a soul. After the death of the gods, nature is, and I say this in view of the beautiful lake before us,[31] either only the ghost of itself or, where it is in its new *truth*, it is the organization of forces, cells, molecules, and particles and thus in its essence technological. "God's beautiful nature"—this is a contradiction in terms. Beautiful nature is the guileless, uncreated nature of the mythic gods, not the nature of the Christian God.

To be sure, there are still nature, art, symbols, but they have no *being* anymore. They exist only as non-realities, *mê onta*. They belong under the heading of leisure pursuits, subjective feeling experience, antiquities—things of the past in other words, which as atavisms still extend into the present and have a noncommittal life alongside the real life. *A rose* was *a rose,* was *a rose* ... It *is* no longer a rose. And chickens and pigs are no longer natural animals, in the sense of the real animal that James Hillman last year helped us to appreciate.[32] Rather, they are egg-laying machines and meat-production apparatuses. This is not wrong and immoral, it is not an abuse, but it is not right and good either, not any more than rain or sunshine are false or right. For nobody made it this way. It is simply the new *truth* of being, the truth of the fact that the moment when reality becomes the incarnated Logos, the flesh has become technological, even including literal pork, a truth, however, that we have been trying to get around for 2000 years because we do not want it to be true.

3. THE FABRICATION OF GOD

Most of the time the question of the proof of the existence of God is seen as a matter of a disconnected, purely intellectual interest that has nothing whatsoever to do with real piety. However, if one takes into account that the Christian God himself is primarily concerned about his existence, his factual being-there and that he for that reason is dependent on faith, then one cannot simply brush the efforts to prove God's existence aside as merely intellectual pursuits and oppose them to piety. Rather, these efforts are precisely a form of genuine piety, even though they do not present themselves as prayer or edifying emotion, but are clothed in the garment of logical arguments. For here, man opens himself to a decisive aspect of the nature of this God. We must not comprehend the proofs of the existence of God from out of an intellectual desire for certainty, but conversely we have to understand this desire for certainty as the expression of the fact that God presses for a real, objective presence, for his "There *is* ...," for his concrete being. God did not want to remain Logos (mere idea), but to incarnate.

We must see through the logical-argumentative character and sense the immense dynamism behind that question of proof of the existence of God, the elementary force that compelled already the people of the Middle Ages to ask it, contrary to their obvious practical needs. This question quite evidently does not have its basis in a human need, for not one of the medieval monks had any doubts concerning the existence of God, neither intellectually, nor in his heart. Medieval man still had an almost mythical relation to God, so that it was precisely the question of the proof of the existence of God through which the new special nature of the Christian, no longer mythic, God fully came home to people. In this question, the Christian God himself makes himself felt; *he* presses into consciousness. The question has drive character. But of course, the drive that was stirring here, is not sexuality or one of the other "natural" drives, but it is the Logos that wants to become flesh, and because it is the Logos, it first of all makes itself felt in the style of logical argumentation.

We must get clear in our minds that the Christian Middle Ages were the age of Scholasticism: the age of the school. The Early Middle Ages, converted from pagan religions to Christianity, had, to be sure, taken over the Christian contents, but had absorbed them with a still more or less mythic consciousness, which in no way corresponded to the nature of Christianity. During those early times, Christianity was still a quasi "nature religion" in character, a mythological religion, the only difference being that in its particular *content* it already dealt with a post-mythological absolute God. And thus it had been the task of the High and Late Middle Ages "to go to school" (*schola*) in order to conquer for itself, through century-long efforts, the basics of the specific *spirit* of Christianity for the first time. That was the achievement of Scholasticism, especially with the aid of Aristotelianism. Here Christianity was for the first time comprehended as a task and taken over as question, exactly as it corresponded to its post-mythological, no longer naturally self-apparent Logos nature.

In all respects and in ever new attempts, Scholasticism questioned the contents of the Christian doctrine in order to acquire a thorough comprehension of it with all its implications, up to such questions, hardly understandable for us any longer, as the one about how many angels can stand on the point of a needle. It is as if Scholasticism acted according to the adage, "What you inherited from your fathers, acquire it in order for it to truly become your own." Myth, with its natural gods, was sufficient unto itself. Not so Christianity with its supranatural and unnatural creator God. As everything artificial, it required a special acquisition and the strenuous effort of the Notion, simply because it cannot be taken for granted as natural.

Through a diligent "working through" penetrating down to every fibre of his being, man had to be ejected from his natural basic position in and toward the world into the unnatural one, until the latter would have become his second nature. Because we have long had our firm place in this second "nature" and it therefore has become such that it is simply taken for granted, we can hardly still understand what degree of strenuous effort and unending repetitions was needed during the Middle Ages to extricate human existence from out of its imaginal constitution and to instill the Christian stance into man in such a way that it would be truly his own.

To be sure, in accordance with the word "Scholasticism" this acquisition occurred in a "schoolboyish" style. One still clung to the dogma and the wording of the doctrine and had to cover oneself by always quoting Biblical passages and referring to ancient authorities. What makes the pupil a pupil is that he does not dare to say anything that is not in the books; he does not venture beyond the literally understood teachings of his teacher, whom he regards as an unreachable authority above himself. The mature, come-of-age mind, by contrast, precisely leaves the literal wording of his teacher behind, but has in return taken over as his *own* task the living spirit of the real concern that was hidden behind the material explicitly taught; it expresses this concern in its own way and independently develops it forward. The mature mind no longer looks up to the teaching of his teacher. He has it no longer outside and above himself. The concern that gave rise to it lives and seethes in him and pushes him forward, often even into having to contradict his teacher, in such a way, however, that with his contradicting he precisely stays faithful to him in a deeper sense.

The conventional view about the Modern Age (*Neuzeit*)[33] with its natural sciences is that it more and more broke away and distanced itself from Christianity. I believe the opposite is the case. With the end of the Middle Ages Western man had, as it were, learned his Christian lesson so that he had mastered and comprehended the deeper living concern at work in Christianity and was now (unconsciously) moved and captivated by it. It was not that he had to make the Christian teachings as the object of his studies his own—this he had done ages ago—but they had meanwhile awakened in him to a life of their own and had thus become the actual subject performing his research. If one identifies Christianity with the pupil-like clinging to the literal wording of the doctrine, then the Modern Age no doubt had deserted Christianity. But if we understand by "Christianity" a specific living concern, a quest on the part of the spirit, a real mystery that can take hold of a culture (in this case: Western humanity) and propel it onwards, then we can say that with the emergence of the natural sciences Christianity had finally come home to itself and learned to stand on its own for the first time.

When surveying the development of the natural sciences and technology, one is struck by its immense, historically unprecedented dynamism, even unrest. We are wont to class the sciences, because they are rational and use mathematics, with consciousness and the calculating mind. But despite the fact that the world explanation performed by natural sciences is in formal regards rational, the phenomenon of the natural sciences itself is by no means rational. They are irrational to the highest degree, they are drive, possession, passion. I am here not referring to a personal passion on the part of the individual scientist, but to Western humanity's possession by a powerful question and search that it could not break free from. But this means nothing else but that the natural sciences as a whole are, although unbeknownst to themselves, genuine *religio*. This assertion creates only difficulties for those who already decided beforehand how a religion must look, instead of conversely allowing themselves to be taught by reality which guises the devotion to the divine can take. We can learn from C. G. Jung that it makes no difference whether one calls a given phenomenon either an addiction, phobia, compulsion, a mere instinct—or whether one calls it God.[34] The real phenomenon does not change through the label assigned to it. It remains in either case one's being driven by a force that one cannot escape.

The religious drive that propelled the natural sciences forward with elementary force, thereby recklessly overriding even the human need for a world speaking to the imagination and the heart, this drive is the unconscious urge, taken over from Scholasticism, to prove the existence of God. Not of just any god, but of him whose very essence it is to demand this proof, so that to furnish this proof is the true form of devotion to this God. The concern of Scholasticism and of the natural sciences is identical. Only the form that it takes has changed decisively. It is not the natural scientists who have deserted Christianity. It is the Church that has abandoned the scientists and disowned the lively further-developing and vigorously-instinctually progressing Christian truth. Instead it raised the medieval-scholastic (pupil-like) form of the Christian truth to the rank of the actual truth and froze it in this status.

Christianity was supposed to remain pure Logos (dogma, metaphysical doctrine, subjective faith, inner experience) and not have a material reality. God was supposed to be reserved for the beyond and thus to be defused.

By believing it had to burn the early progressive-scientific minds and their books at the stake, the Church itself involuntarily expressed her acknowledgment of the fact that her own living fire of the truth did no longer burn in the Church and theology, but now at the place where the natural sciences are. The lighting of the fire for the progressive minds and their books is not only repression (which it is, too). It is also a sign for her own fire having gone out and for her need to get heat from an alien fuel, a fuel that of course could and should really have been her own. If the latter had been the case, this fuel would not have had to be *literally* burned at all, but could have been the creative fire of the spirit consuming her adherents themselves from within.

As we have seen, the natural sciences had taken over the inherited Christian concern. Only the form that this concern took had become a different one over against Scholasticism. Science no longer searches, pupil-like and literally, for the proof of the existence of God, because it has comprehended that a literal understanding precisely fails to achieve the task. For if the proof is furnished only as a logical (intellectual) one, it remains itself still a matter of thought and does not get to fleshly reality. The Logos would remain to be only Logos (noetic) and as such could of course possibly also be nothing but a figment of the imagination.

Natural science had, as it were, comprehended (without however having a consciousness of this, because it had been pushed into the corner of irreligion) that there was only one single possible way of proving the existence of God. An absolute God, a God, in other words, who was no longer to be taken for granted because he was apparent from nature, but, as an extramundane one, was so to speak imposed from above, can only be proven by being manufactured. The Logos becomes flesh only through its fabrication, just as the idea of a house becomes only real if I build this house. The unconscious, but in fact accomplished task of science and technology therefore had been the building or fabrication or simulation of God in actual reality, as the continued work upon his incarnation. This is the empirical proof of the existence of God through his *produced* physical existence. God had to become positivistically demonstrable. The extent to which the natural sciences and technology have mastered this task I want to demonstrate at least sketchily by means of a few examples in the next section.

But first it is necessary to clear a few obstacles out of the way. If God has been manufactured, so we might perhaps argue, then he has, to be sure, been empirically proven, but then he is *ipso facto* no longer a God. Because a manufactured god is not a god, let alone a transcendent, other-worldly God, a creator of the world. He would under these circumstances be himself a creature. And furthermore, how could there still be a faith that does not see and yet believes (cf. John 20:29)?

Concerning the first point we must realize that the manufacturing of gods is actually nothing unusual. Gods were always fabricated in art, as statues, masks, etc., just as in general, according to C. G. Jung, "every spiritual truth is gradually reified and turns into a substance or tool in the hand of man."[35] Why should therefore, for example, an atom bomb not be a just as legitimate modern equivalent for an archaic statue of a god, all the more so since in our case we are dealing with a God whose nature it is to realize himself, to become, *as* Logos, flesh? The difference is only that the legitimate way of manufacturing the natural gods is art, the *presentation* in an *image*, an image that *releases* and opens itself into a whole "world." In the image, the God is only present as an absent one, that is to say he is "buried." But precisely this is what makes his ontological nature (his godship) manifest. Under the conditions of technology, *fabrication* (in contrast to presentation) means that the God, or his attributes, must be given a literal (physical) existence as positive fact: simulation. In the full visibility and ontic (i.e., positive-factual) givenness of the divine predicates in the guise of things entrenching themselves within themselves, the ontological divinity or godship of these predicates is precisely concealed. The technical things make a completely ungodlike and soulless impression.[36]

It is true, the fabricated God must remain a transcendent God. The question is only how to understand "transcendent," "absolute," "extramundane," "not visible with the eyes (non-sensual)," and "creator." If transcendent, absolute and supernatural would indicate that God has nothing whatsoever to do with empirical reality, then he would be of no concern to us and we could not have any knowledge of him. Such a notion would be totally nonsensical. The transcendent God, too, must as a matter of course be immanent to the world, if God is not supposed to be a naught, of absolutely no relevance for us.

The task therefore is to think transcendence not literally and metaphysically, but as one quality within reality, an *ontological* quality, another "*style*" of the real. In other words, we have to conceive of an empirical absolute, an immanent transcendence, an intramundane extramundane or supernatural, a sensibly given non-sensible and a created world resulting from uncreated nature. All this holds true for technological reality. As something artificial, unnatural, man-made within the natural world it is what has left the natural world and transcends it. It is that which in the course of scientific and technological progress more and more "absolutizes" itself, i.e., which *cuts itself loose from the naturally given* and even pushes beyond itself, permanently overtaking itself. It is never finished. This is transcendence as an ontological quality of real things. And if physics teaches us that a piece of wood, in total contrast to it natural-sensible appearance, is in actuality empty space interspersed with a few tiny particles in comparatively cosmic distance from each other, then this is the empirical non-sensible, and the knowledge of the sciences is realized faith, faith that does not see and yet believes. In style and spirit, the natural sciences are sheer "*super*naturalism."

4. THE INFLATION OF THE THINGS

Paul Tillich's well-known definition of religion is: our ultimate concern. This definition is not implausible, but has two disadvantages. First of all, it still (covertly) posits, in a metaphysical manner, something Absolute, even if it does not hypostatize it as *the* Absolute, but transposes it, as "our unconditional and total involvement," into the human subject. Secondly, it understands religion from the position of man and makes God (as the symbol of the absolute) circle around man: "*our* concern," *our* involvement in the "wholeness of our being."[37] I therefore prefer other expressions, for example C. G. Jung's concept of the "symbolic life."[38] Jung understands by this a life in which we, beyond our banal, ordinary, or irrational existence, partake in the ritual of life and rather than satisfying our subjective needs and desires, respond to an objective being-needed. Needed for what? Here one could, following Hegel's wording (which however is already committed to the Christian view), say: for the representation of the Absolute, for the purpose that the Eternal may have a real existence in the human world. To be sure, the "Absolute" is no concept for Jung, not a concept for the psychologist. But there is for him, in addition to personal life, also an objective-psychic "spiritual life" which makes the demand on us to be allowed to partake in our life and that engages us for the purpose that *it* may *be*.

In this sense the symbolic life, although it cannot be without our activities, is nevertheless actually by no means *our* life, but an autonomous life of the mind, that needs and uses us, much like the drama uses the actor, for its own needs, whereas what is our "interest," our concern, is irrelevant for it. Jung mentions the example of the Pueblo Indians who saw in the sun their Father and had the obligation to help him, their Father, to move across the sky—not for their own personal practical gain, but for the purpose that the sun might *be*. As one can see, this is through and through a matter-of-fact, ontological concept—in sharpest contrast to any definition of religion that circles around subjective emotional experience. If Jung says about our present age: "there is no symbolic existence in which I am something else, in which I am fulfilling my role, my role as one of the actors in the divine drama of life,"[39] then everything here revolves around *it*, the divine drama of life itself, for which man has been put into service. Of the primitives of Australia, Jung stated that they sacrifice two thirds of their disposable time to the symbolic life of the ancestors. And how enormous the role must have been that the symbolic life played for example among the Egyptians can be gauged from a single glance at the funerary worlds they left behind. The life of the Egyptians must to a large extent have been in the service of the purpose that the world of the dead *be*, that it may receive a real existence.

There is today no symbolic life in this sense anymore. Or is there perhaps one after all? Is it not possible that we, too, sacrifice two thirds of our disposable time to the symbolic life, with the only difference that we do not acknowledge it as such because we think that a symbolic life would have to be similar in content to that which we find among the Australian Aborigines, the ancient Egyptians, or in the Middle Ages?

Millions of people are sitting night after night for hours in front of their television sets. We think, and they themselves probably think so too, that they do this for their pleasure. But as correct as this is in a superficial sense, in a deeper sense it is nevertheless only an egoic, subjectivist cover explanation that serves to camouflage the objective process. Both the existence of the phenomenon called television in general and the extent of the daily practiced cult of watching television do not have their origin and cause in our natural-human desires, which can be seen quite simply from the fact that such inventions first met with rejection and depreciation. Man's natural desire is by no means directed towards entertainment. Around the year 1700, there were no daily newspapers, no magazines, no cinemas, etc., and the only books that were to be found in an ordinary household were the Bible, a hymnal, and at best also a book of country lore. These books were read again and again. From our point of view an unending monotony. And the time after the day's labor was not called *Freizeit* (spare time), but *Feierabend,* a word that evokes the notion of the solemnity of the evening. A fundamental difference. And this is how it had been one way or another from time immemorial. It in turn required an ingenious technology pursued with an immense energy, namely advertizing, in order to "arouse" (i.e., create) in people the desire for television and all sorts of other new inventions.

No, the fact that television exists today does not come from out of man. Behind it, there is an objective necessity, a compulsion to produce and spread it. It does not serve the purpose of *our* entertainment, but we serve it. What is television in its objective essence? It is show, show as *theatrum mundi,* the mixed bag of an attempted assassination of the Pope, a new world record, an earthquake catastrophe, a western movie, an Oscar award ceremony, a quiz program, and a summit meeting. It is the theater of life with its ups and downs, with its spectacular events and its banality. It is "Formation, transformation, / Eternal Mind's eternal recreation." We are used for the purpose of playing in this drama (the divine drama of the eternal Mind's eternal recreation) the ritual role of the eternal Mind, that is, of the Christian God. Man as consumer is needed and used so that the position of the absolute God as the indifferent spectator can be in fact filled, in other words, so that God can be visibly represented as incarnated. Television must exist so that the *Divina Comedia* is not merely idea and poetic work, but has a real existence in the flesh. Television has so little to do with personal pleasure or gain that it is not uncommon that it remains turned on even when nobody watches it. Its sole, secret meaning is apparently that the show *be.*

We have a low opinion of advertizing and even ridicule it. But in this way we misjudge its serious nature. Just as mythic poetry was the joyful praise of uncreated nature and its many gods, so advertizing, as the 'singing the praise' of commercial products, is—in its deepest meaning—the hymnic praise of production: of the creation and the one Creator God.

If we look at the computer only from the point of view of the saving of labor we cannot either explain the driving force behind this invention and its immense dynamic further development. The motivation behind the computer is, first, the powerful vision of making God as the *noêsis noêseôs*, the thought thinking itself, real and true in the flesh, that is, as a thinking that runs completely automatically and contained within itself and is completely self-sufficient. It has no referent outside of itself, no object, without which the thinking of finite man cannot possibly be. And secondly it is the vision of the real fabrication of God as the *intuitus originarius*. Our finite thinking is discursive. We can only think one thought after the other, whereas God's thinking can encompass and comprehend the whole at once. This is what the computer is supposed to simulate, as well as it is possible under the conditions of temporality. The driving force behind the computer is furthermore the vision of the real fabrication of God as the All-Knowing. Because the goal is the total storage of all information. The point is not *our* omniscience—we rather become still more ignorant through computer technology—but simply that omniscience *be*.

The technology of telecommunication and the computer, on the one hand, cars and airplanes on the other hand have the purpose of simulating the overcoming of the limits of space and time.

In our satellites and with space travel, God's transcendent, supernatural standpoint or the supernatural as such obtains its empirical existence. And every day when television presents to us the new satellite weather map, we celebrate this supernatural standpoint.

Spy planes that can recognize items as little as a golf ball on the earth from the height of many miles, are the real fabrication, under the conditions of empirical life, of the all-seeing eye of God. The whole reconnaissance technology and the whole interest in reconnaissance is driven by the necessity to supply the All-Seeing and Inescapable One (e.g., Psalm 139)[40] with a real existence. What is demanded of Christian humanity is to totally record that which is, the real fabrication of an overall view—not for a practical human gain, but for the sake of blessedness. And not only because of new machine-readable identity cards and passports and through a census do we turn into mere numbers. We *are*, have already been, numbers for a long time; more than that, the very hairs of our head are all numbered.[41]

The development leading to the systematic breeding of new animal and plant species and to the manipulation of genes arises from the necessity to realize God as the Creator. Natural animals are uncreated beings produced by nature and as such represent a constant living "counterevidence" against the idea of the Creation. The Being of living organisms, too, must be given the constitution of being technological, of being made.

But above all it is the atom bomb[42] that serves the purpose of guaranteeing a real presence to the absolute Lord over the world. There had to be something that really and totally had the existence of the world in its grip. Otherwise, the Absolute would have remained a mere idea and not have become flesh.

These few examples must suffice here. They indicate that technology has the task of literally (physically) manufacturing the predicates of God in actual reality. These predicates were no longer supposed to be *nomina*, a *flatus vocis*, but *realia*. In my opinion it would be misguided to seek in each individual technical invention a different god. A manifold of different divine figures is to be found in the things of nature. But technology as a whole is the work on the edifice of the one absolute God, the God of technology, as we have seen. This is what distinguishes the no longer natural God: that he has to be a single one and for that reason a total, all-embracing God. In order to be truly the Creator, he must subdue everything that manifests of its own accord under his domination. As long as there still are natural things, things that can be taken for granted as self-apparent, he has not yet worked himself up to his full being. It is inherent in his nature that he must permeate and conquer, extensively as well as intensively, one people, one culture, one realm of reality after the other. In his lack of being (his un-natural nature) lies his power (his dynamic force: his pressing for his realization). The natural, the mythic is (even as a world of concrete physical things) guileless and tender, because it is by nature instinctual image; and this is also why it is defenseless against massive seizure by the artificial. The innocence of simple being has no weapons;

that it does not have any weapons and does not want anything from anything outside of itself, this precisely constitutes its nature. It is only the artificial that has an "object" vis-à-vis and outside itself, that always already finds the world as given to it, so that its very character consists in having to assert itself against the natural that it finds by overcoming it. And technological civilization is capable of this overcoming because for it the things have become positive-fleshly. Each thing is here the contraction of Heaven and Earth in one point and carries the concentrated force of a collapsed world in itself. Not only what the artificial does and brings about, but already its ontological nature, its very being, is force and doing violence.

The explanation of technology from the hubris of man seems to me to miss the facts. It is likely to be an assertion serving a particular purpose, namely the purpose of camouflaging the "symbolic life" that in fact drives and steers us, but obviously must not become conscious. Technology is our burden, an obligation demanded of us, whether we want it or not. It is our fate, which is why it is reasonable to avoid any moralistic value judgment. The true hubris of consciousness seems to me to be precisely this personalistic-moralistic interpretation of technology, because it makes something out as the achievement of man that is certainly not his doing. Fundamentally other categories must be employed to grasp this amazing, outrageous, incredible phenomenon that we call technology. The purer it unfolds its true nature, the more baffled and helpless we get towards it.

When we have a good look at the objective behavior of 20th century man, then the opposite of hubris stands out, an exceptional modesty, even shame (*aidôs*). We no longer afford the luxury of kings so that they would represent for us our self in its highest form. We do no longer afford servants, who would give us the feeling of being superior. We identify with the socially weak and oppressed; it is therefore in them that we have our self, our identity. We feel compelled to present ourselves in a deliberately casual, if not sloppy way and to dress in tennis shoes, blue jeans, and T-shirts. We like best to have our picture taken in the form of a snapshot and avoid poses and ostentation. It is impossible for us to use pompous language, and the sublime we can, if at all, only tolerate in one of three forms: either in the style of parody, satire, persiflage, irony; or in the wrapping of a scientific report about past forms of life; or in the form of a reductive unmasking (which, however, is also just *one* possible style of presenting the sublime). Does all this not precisely betray an unconscious knowledge on the part of modern man about the special danger of inflation today, because God is so uncannily close and real in technology as never before, namely in the flesh? Does it not show an urge to make himself small? An awe of man (although hidden from himself and denied) before the sacred, which makes him cover up his face—in his own way?

No, it is not man who is inflated, but the technical things. Not only is more and more Logos, are more and more predicates of God stuffed into them; they also receive ever more weight of their own and ever more autonomy. The things are becoming the *fascinosum*—the camera, the car, the stereo system. The soul has been invested into them. From here the often completely senseless buying compulsion and consumption of commodities can be understood: it is an act of unacknowledged devotion. Already Marx spoke of the "fetishism of commodities," albeit with almost the opposite intent from mine, namely an unmasking and ironic one. Nevertheless, the phenomenon had been seen and adequately named by him.

The throwing away of things in our throw-away society is another aspect of the situation under discussion. It is as if the things only wanted to be bought by us (so that we pay our tribute to them), but did not want to be permanently available for *our* consumption and use. They become worthless, that is to say, they withdraw themselves and their value from us and remain autonomous. The same is the case with tourist attractions. Each tourist feels impelled to photograph for the millionth time this castle or that Greek temple. The things demand by themselves to have their picture taken again and again, in order that in this way respectful deference is shown to them. The photos thereafter usually gather dust in some drawer. They are not really for us, for our enjoyment. A similar case in point is the electric candles on Christmas trees. They are lit and twinkle "automatically" and all by themselves, no matter if someone is present and sees them or not. Music, too, ceases to be human music-making and is being somatized in the form of the independently existing, reified records. And even the music engraved into its grooves is one that has *never* been played by real people, but is a sophisticated artificial product of sound engineers. School children no longer have to calculate in their heads; the process of calculation takes place, literally "objectively," in their pocket calculator.

The life of the mind moves out of the human world and settles in the world of things. The things become the masters and man slowly becomes of secondary importance, turning into the *Bediener* (servant, operator) of the apparatuses (or under certain circumstances even to their slaves or victims). The place where the action is, the place where the essential decisions happen has passed from man (reason, way of thinking, morality, instinct) to technology. Most blatantly this becomes visible in the atom bomb, where the decision about its actual use is more and more taken out of the hands of man and is taken over by the automatic mechanism of computers, in other words, machines. The time window for subjective-human decision-making is being reduced to few minutes or even seconds. The world of things obtains spontaneity, numinous-irrational power and a dynamism of its own. In sharp contrast to the illusion of consciousness that still today believes in humanitarianism, freedom, the individual, and subjective experience, the factual development moves ever more into the direction of a sober, objective existence governed by necessities. We speak derogatorily of *Sachzwänge*, factual constraints. However, this conflict between consciousness and what is really happening is something that already belongs to the next chapter.

5. DIVESTITURE

C. G. Jung reports that during his expedition in Kenya they once had taken a local black African along in their jeep who had never before sat in a car. After a while, the African asked that the car be halted and he then laid down on the ground. When asked what he was doing, he responded that he was waiting for his soul, which due to the fast ride had not been able to follow.[43]

We confound the situation of this African with ours. We still believe that it is we who, through the rational and technological development of our civilization, have rushed on ahead of the soul and that therefore the soul was still in that which *was* and lies behind us: in nature, in instinctual life and sexuality, in our body, in the earth, in the myths, or in traditional religion. But our soul has long emigrated from all that. It is *she* who is driving off at breakneck speed in the jeep, *she* who is at the helm of technological progress, whereas we have gotten out of the jeep and are waiting on the ground for the soul to finally catch up with us from the very point back there from which it set off moving ahead of us long ago. Or, strictly speaking, we have not gotten out because there is no getting out of the jeep of history. We are merely intellectual and psychological escapists and thus are and have been riding, now already for centuries, *with our backs to the direction of travel.* And then we complain about being alienated!

Asked if he thought that God is dead, Jung answered, not God, not the gods are dead, but we are merely removed from the place of such happenings.[44] We are indeed removed. It is all there, but we don't see it. The things conceal and withhold their meaning from us; the soul is truly buried in them for us. What Jung, however, did not say with the same clearness is that the place of such happenings has become a different one,[45] new wine in *truly new* bottles, and that our removal consists in our having stayed put at the old, meanwhile deserted and empty place. Nature, myth, the ancient gods are truly dead. And it is not prohibited, but impossible to awaken ones who have died.[46] We have had ample time—2000 years—to get used to the notion that nature is that which is over, or actually 3000 years, if one keeps in mind that already for Homer the gods were a thing of the past.[47]

We only believe that we are still living on the earth. In truth, our anima has already for some time been orbiting around the earth on our satellites out there, in empty, icy outer space. Every satellite weather map on television evidently demonstrates to us that at bottom we look down on our earth from above and outside. Our psyche has long left behind the standpoint earth. We simply do no longer look *up* from the earth to Heaven. But we obdurate our hearts against this truth; we deny our soul and our *real* religion—in favor of vain convictions that require preaching or demonstrations on the streets or force of arms to get a semblance of power, or that as subjective feeling experiences or clever theories have only the status of a private hobby.

Seen from the one side, our deep love of nature and our interest in and feeling for the cultural treasures of the past as well as for myths and symbols are valuable human impulses. But from another side, they are sentimental nature romanticism and myth nostalgia lulling us into a dangerous sleep. They hold us in the delusion that what was formerly true was an *eternal* truth, that Mother Earth was indestructible, the old values unalterable. But the air and the oceans will not become clean again, and the tropical rain forest, once destroyed, will not grow again. More than that, independently of this ontic destruction, nature is, and has been for a long time, destroyed in its ontological essence. There are a number of fundamental real changes that have radically altered man's stance to the world, and factually so, that is to say, no matter what his subjective attitude may be and whether he himself is aware of it or not: these are first the literal, physical possibility to leave the earth and to fly to the moon, secondly the possibility to literally, physically annihilate life on earth, indeed perhaps the entire globe. With this having become possible for and available to us, we have irrevocably fallen out of nature and now are psychologically standing outside and above it. We have *de facto*, whether we want it or not, a "higher" standpoint and are "superordinate" to it. We have encompassed the whole globe with our networks and in this way pocketed it, as it were (road network, electricity grid, installation of cables for telecommunications, etc.). This is our objective-psychic reality, our ontological situation. Unless we fool ourselves and walk into the trap of our sentimental feelings, there cannot any longer be a real in-ness in an intact world (nature, myth, faith), but only the remembrance of what is long gone.

Our consciousness, however, clings obstinately to the medieval soul condition against the truth of the age; we are concerned with our self-realization (the salvation of our individual soul), the truly humanitarian society (Christian love of the neighbor), an intact nature (God's world), the meaning of life (the true faith), and our moral responsibility (our innocence of mind, purity from sins, our good conscience). Nowadays billions are invested in industrialization, in armaments, in the development of computers, in outer space research, etc.; but all this is only done, so we try to persuade ourselves, by repressive rulers, exploitative captains of industry, and deluded technocrats full of hubris. It is completely neurotic. The right hand does not want to know what the left hand is doing. They are *our* captains of industry, our dictators and technocrats, who in our place, so that our ego-consciousness can feel innocent, perform the exploitation, repression, and hubris. They carry our shadow for us, and this is why we belong to them, precisely to them whom we so much despise.

There is a sure sign for the true locus of the soul: "For where your treasure is, there will your heart be also" (Matth. 6:21). The place where our money flows, there the soul has its place, not our private, non-committal psyche, but the real soul, the collective unconscious in Jung's sense, today's realm of archetypal images. The rationalistic character of technology must not deceive us. It is not the opposite of instinct and unconscious psyche, but another style or mode of the unconscious. It is not that our ego-consciousness has become rationalistic—it is precisely idealistic, nostalgic, sentimental. Rather, our psychic instinctual life has changed its language and medium, away from the mythic to rationalism. The objective-psychic, this is today technology (to be understood as a mode of being). *It* is *our* nature, our new earth, our drive, our body, our spiritual, symbolic life.[48] It is the place where the real action is. Here a real wind is blowing, a powerful *pneuma* of unparalleled dynamism. Technological reality is not in the wrong toward us, no, our consciousness conversely owes something to it: Our conscious thought and feeling since the Middle Ages withheld psychology and theology from it. And thereby they withheld the acknowledgment from it that *it* is *our* locus of "soul-making," *our* form of the alchemical opus and *our* place of theophany. This is what caused technology to be split off. It lost the connection to consciousness, to the conscious development, and consciousness lost the connection to what was actually going on in the depth. Technology was totally banished into the unconscious, and to such an extent that we do not even have an inkling that it is our true unconscious; and the scientists were condemned into the mindless narrowness of a split-off experts' mentality. They had no chance to know about *what* dimensions their work has: that they are in truth the advocates and trustees of incarnation and that it was they (together with captains of industry and the advertising experts) to whom the administration of the Christian truth had passed. Because the title "religion" or "theology" was already occupied by the frozen dogmatics or by the inner feeling experience, they therefore represented for the scientists, too, the authoritative notion of theology and religion, so that the religious dimension of their own work had to escape their notice.

Our ego-consciousness denies the natural sciences and technology their being psychological and theological and then is amazed that they are soulless and godless. Conversely it awards the titles "religious," "in close touch with nature," "concerned about meaning" to the backwards orientation—whereas the latter is after all the deliberate break with religion, nature, and the meaning[49] of real life. So we are twice removed: once from myth and nature, because the objective psyche has left them and has settled in technology, and secondly from technology as our present-day nature and mythology, because we cling to and are stuck in nature.

Mythic man lived without a pluralism of opinions by virtue of the authority that his sensual-mythic instinctual nature possessed. How was he capable of living this way? It was made possible by the fact that he acknowledged his real deeds and not his opinions and wishes as the actual truth about himself and about Being. For us, too, there would not have to be a pluralism of opinions and no opining at all—*if* we allowed ourselves to be *given* by *our* instinctual nature, by *our* real work (technical development) the ways we have to think about that which is the true, and if we saw in our actual direction of travel the real sense and meaning of life, the only meaning that deserves the predicate "meaning of life." Instead, we insist that our familiar thinking and wishing be allowed to prescribe to psychic reality how and where it ought to be. The big question is: does in such a conflict between an idea of religion, nature, and instinctive soul that is familiar to us, on the one hand, and the current reality of religion, nature, soul on the other hand, does in such a conflict the truth lie with the idea or with reality? Must we say: "All the worse for reality!"—or: "All the worse for our idea!", because *it* has shown to be null and void?

However, the very conflict between consciousness and reality is itself essentially part of Christian Incarnation. The latter is the divestiture or surrender, the *kenôsis* (Phil. 2:7, "emptying"), through which the divine Logos lowered himself, taking on the humble position of a slave. This is how it appears from within the Christian myth. If, however, we reflect on the happening of the Christian myth on its part, the divestiture is to be comprehended in a somewhat more complex way, no longer, first, as God's stepping out of his natural-mythic form of being and, simultaneously with that splitting *off*, secondly as the splitting *up* of the divine itself into two: in the pre-existent Logos and the flesh, the exalted triumphant victor and the humble form of a slave. This splitting up continues in the opposition of *saeculum* and *civitas dei*, of Sunday and work-day, of leisure time and labor. Because the Christian truth is split in itself, there are also two modes how the Incarnation itself can be seen, from the Sunday or Logos point of view, on the one hand, and from the work-a-day or the flesh point of view, on the other.

The Sunday truth about the Incarnation, however, on its part has not yet fully humbled itself to its own slave form, that is, to the workday truth. The Sunday truth is the religious truth of the Middle Ages and of present-day Churches as well. Its structure is ambivalent. It has clearly drawn a dividing line between myth and itself as no-longer-mythic; it maintains, however, over against the natural sciences, the position of the former myth. This in-between position is that of "metaphysics." Incarnation here means that a (somehow metaphysically imagined) God has become flesh in the historical human Jesus. One immediately sees that this is not a humbling, but the rise from nature to Logos, in other words, only the first half of the Christian truth. Because previously, the divine resided in tree and mountain, bull and eagle, sea and sun. If the anima emigrated from there, from pre-logical nature, and now man, the "rational animal," the *zôon logon echôn*, turned into the singular seat of the soul, then this mythical happening means the first-time establishment of that Logos for whom the true humbling to the form of a slave and the acquisition of a bodily reality appropriate to it (namely as "flesh") is still in store. Thus it was consistent that gradually the preliminary or improper truth of Christianity (the truth of ego-consciousness, the Sunday truth) was superseded by its actual truth, the objective-psychic work-day truth, whereby technological reality turned into the seat of the soul.

From the point of view of the Sunday religious truth, religion means: faith in the historical Jesus as the Christ and as "my personal" savior. Here everything revolves around man as person, his interior, his moral attitude, his faith. Through the Incarnation understood in this way, the idea of "the human" becomes psychologically the topmost value. Thereby our humanism and humanitarianism receives its mythic backing, as does at the same time the introspective inwardness and the individualism of modernity, in short, the entire hubris of consciousness that is based on an inflation through the incarnated Logos misunderstood as literal man. When "man" is the authoritative shape of God, then the truth about Being receives the form of the mental and of what corresponds to human reason: concept, doctrine, theory, ideology, metaphysics.

The thinking and experiencing of the Christian West dwells within the Sunday truth and from this height looks contemptuously down upon the work-day truth, a truth, which, however, determines what is done and the real process. We afford the luxury of freedom of thought, that is in the last analysis, the freedom of giving over our world view and religion to one's subjective and arbitrary choice, because our thinking no longer feels bound and obliged by our work-day and its ritual reality (*religio* in the sense of *religare*). We act as if everything depended on *our* thinking, whereas the only thing that really counts is what our real behavior thinks. Our consciousness is no longer willing to be taught by *factual deeds* (mechanization, armament, industrialization, etc.) about what it must take for its truth and how it must think, but from a preconceived idea about the true and the good denies our factual action as our having gone off on the wrong track, and thus as an untruth.

We lead a double-track life. We spend immense sums for "culture" (theater, museums, restorations, concerts, antiquities). And at no time before ours was it possible, as it is today, for such a broad public to see *ad libitum* the works of art and culture of millennia in the original or in true-color reproductions and to participate in the immensely rich treasures of knowledge about religions, symbols, and rituals. But all this passes through us, to say it with the words of Lichtenberg, "like the magnetic matter goes through gold, namely without giving us a direction" and changing our reality. All this obviously has its place in the compartment of "leisure time," which as "free," disconnected time runs in a noncommittal way parallel to the compartment "work-time" or "real world." The whole striving for freedom of modernity in its manifold political, social, intellectual, and individual-psychological forms is also driven forward by the need to convert human existence into the ab-soluteness and abstractness of "Sunday" (the decision-free realm of ego-consciousness). Behind the political idea of freedom, too, there is in the last analysis the metaphysical urge for freedom from the real, from the earth and its weight.

It is urgent for us to know and acknowledge that "man" (humanism), freedom, the individual, and our interiority are the untruth of the West. We are not Indians who in fact find their truth in their Self (Atman) and for whom it is a perfectly legitimate striving to attempt to rise above matter and material reality. What is India's truth is for the West a settlement in the lie—neurosis. The Western truth is the opposite of the Indian one: it is Incarnation, the movement into external reality as *the* manifestation of the objective psyche. The culture

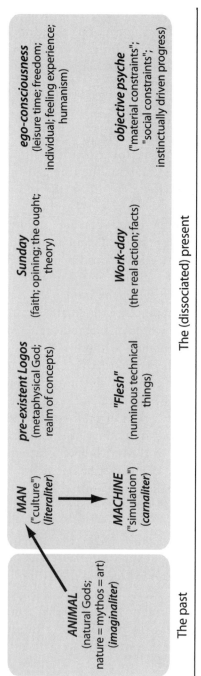

ANIMAL
(natural Gods;
nature = mythos = art)
(*imaginaliter*)

MAN
("culture")
(*literaliter*)

MACHINE
("simulation")
(*carnaliter*)

pre-existent Logos
(metaphysical God;
realm of concepts)

"Flesh"
(numinous technical
things)

Sunday
(faith; opining; the ought;
theory)

Work-day
(the real action; facts)

ego-consciousness
(leisure time; freedom;
individual; feeling experience;
humanism)

objective psyche
("material constraints",
"social constraints";
instinctually driven progress)

The past

The (dissociated) present

Fig. 2. The historical movement of the anima and the metamorphosis of the Gods

"Man" is apparently only a detour, an in-between station between the two real forms of the divine (ANIMAL and MACHINE): "*Middle Ages*" (which, however, in the sense here employed had already announced its coming in the human shape of the Greek gods and in the gradual substitution of the gods through philosophical concepts). "Man," "the human," had been the "means" or the fulcrum through which Being could be lifted from the one side (nature) to the other side (technology), but which on its own part was *not an authentic form*. Jung saw clearly (*GW* 12 § 41, my trans.) that the purpose of Christianity was "the lifting [of existence] out of the embeddedness in nature" and that the separation or redemption from the embeddedness in nature could succeed only "through a connection with the historical figure of the Redeemer." Through the idea of the historical Redeemer "man," (the human) was raised to the status of a "metaphysical" principle and inaugurated as the fulcrum. That "man" as this "metaphysical" pivot nevertheless remains inauthentic and enthroned only for the time of the obfuscated "Middle" Ages that are now coming to a close is not merely a contingency, but follows from the essence of the "human": Only the ANIMAL and the MACHINE are capable of giving an authentic expression to the autonomous, fundamentally different reality of the gods, whereas with the human shape the divine is far too much brought into line with the human subject and thus becomes subjectivized and derealized as a mere matter of faith. What is lacking is the expression of the objective vis-a-vis.

of the Occident as a whole precisely did not produce convincing individual inner truths, but its major movement is the powerful shift to ever larger collective, objectively real, autonomous, and anonymous structures: physics, technology, industry, multinational concerns, commodities and consumption and advertizing, bureaucracy, statistics. This is the direction of Western libido, and there is *our* truth, our meaning, our anima.

But to what degree do we not, for example, feel superior to the phenomenon of advertizing, although it is one of the pillars of our economic existence and we all contribute to its funding. We ridicule advertizing slogans as if they were nothing and nonsense. But the institution of advertizing as a whole simply expresses quite innocently what *is*, the true being of the things today. It is not that advertizing deceives us (by and large), but we deceive ourselves by conceitedly looking down on it, which is, after all, our reality. When a cigarette commercial speaking of the "taste of freedom and adventure" is effective and "works," so that it becomes noticeable in the sales figures, then this shows that the cigarette in truth *is* the taste of freedom and adventure and we are in the wrong when we think that it is merely a rolled piece of paper filled with tobacco and that the slogan only serves the purpose of manipulation. By thinking so we deny our psychic reality.

By holding on to humanism and introspective interiority the divestiture is literally realized as self-alienation alias neurosis. Incarnation is two different things. The *Word's* becoming flesh on the one hand apparently *posits* the *Wörtlichnehmen* (literalizing) of the Logos in the sense of "Christian faith," of free, disconnected thinking and leisure time. For it is after all the *Word*, the Logos, that is supposed to become real (flesh). But on the other hand, Incarnation at the same time demands the *sublation* of the Word through the Logos's complete going under in(to) the flesh. For Incarnation has precisely also the meaning of the Logos becoming *flesh*. However, the Logos refuses to go *completely* under into its form of a slave; it rather wants to maintain itself, in addition to and above the latter, as literal Logos in the height and the light of our free believing and opining. It wants to remain identified with the literal empirical human being (the ego) and for this reason, by way of an underpinning of the ego, seeks to hold on to the metaphysical God outside and above the real as a whole. This, however, has the effect of getting human existence into the condition of inner conflict or dissociation. Man now has two identities at once, but in such a way that the one does not know of the other. He is *totally* a free lord over all things and subject to nobody ("Sunday," freedom of thought, leisure time, free citizen) and *totally* a dutiful servant of all things and subject to everyone[50] (assembly-line worker, manipulated, exploited, threatened by factual constraints and nuclear armament, oppressed by military dictatorships). The more freedom the Logos wants to achieve, the more oppressed must the fleshly form of a slave become. As long as this duplicity remains in effect, Christianity will remain fundamentally unredeemed. And yet, the divestiture, if it were followed through *all the way*, would in itself be its own salvation.

The Incarnation only finds it fulfillment when the divestiture is total: in the crucifixion. The crucifixion is itself the Incarnation, the complete immersion in, indeed under, earthly reality. Through it the God up high including the pre-existing Logos ceases to exist, also in the sense of Hegel's "speculative Good Friday," ("My God, my God, why hast thou forsaken me"), because now he has fully entered the flesh and exists exclusively in it, without reserve, without leaving himself a way out through which the metaphysical God up there could once more be restored after all. For this purpose of the restoration of the "former" metaphysical condition of God the Resurrection has constantly been misused. The Resurrection, however, is not the return of the old, but the Resurrection of the *Crucified* and God-less! The Resurrection does not undo the divestiture, but seals it. It states that the divestiture must not be understood in an abstract, literal way, as if the Crucifixion meant the absolute end of God. No, he lives on; with the Incarnation/ Crucifixion he merely changed his shape or locus. He is now once more a non-metaphysical, innerworldly God, just as the mythic Gods had been, too. The only difference is that he has his place not, like they did, in nature, but in the artificial world of technological civilization. As this technological civilization he is the Risen.

Actually it is a glaring injustice to speak, with reference to our technological civilization, of secularization. Technology is not *saeculum*, but precisely the realized *civitas dei*, merely unacknowledged as such. Carl Améry spoke with respect to the dangers of technology of the *"gnadenlosen Folgen des Christentums"* ("merciless consequences of Christianity").[51] But one can do this only if one has lost the knowledge of what *Gnade* (grace, mercy) is. If we do not confuse grace with banal personal well-being, but rather understand it as the presence of God, then we must recognize that Christianity brought the fullness of grace—not despite technological civilization with its dangers, including the nuclear bomb, but precisely through it, in it. For the technical things are the empirical presence of the absolute God. And our age is the most Christian of all, because in it the fulfillment and completion of the Christian truth is in the offing, God's real "becoming flesh." Seen from the point of view of the work-day, the Occident lives extremely piously, almost faithful unto death, if one considers the atom bomb and the destruction of the environment. It is almost as if the motto of technological development had been: *fiat deus et pereat mundus* (may God *be*, even if the world perishes).

But perhaps the change from the natural gods to the absolute God, that is, the substitution of nature by the artificial world of technology, would not have needed to take on such *literally* devastating forms, if it had not only been the pre-existent Logos that has lowered itself to the shape of the workday slave, but if the human Logos, too—the soul, the heart, consciousness—would have followed this movement, instead of resisting it, saying, "Woe is me, where will I get, when winter has come, flowers?" For then the ritualistic form of human existence would have been restored all by itself. Not in the sense of a repristination of nature, but in the sense of a first-time progressing to a complete burial of the soul in the flesh. Through such a completed immersion, Occidental humanity's relation to reality would no longer be one of being neurotically split-off. It would not look down upon it from outside and above as onto the *saeculum*. It rather would have its position again in the heart of earthly reality, analogously to how it was for archaic man. This means to be human could mean once more: to be the carrier of the spear that keeps apart the Heaven and the chthonic Earth of his world, the Earth, which, however, has meanwhile turned into the new, technological world. The Crucifixion would not only be followed by the Resurrection, but also by the *descensus ad inferos* and by Ascension. The new, artificial "earth" promised and brought by Christianity, would itself be image again, mythical, in itself the underworld and "heaven" on earth. And our religion would no longer have to be imposed on us through preaching, because it would be our external reality, in which we live to begin with. Christianity and technological civilization would have become psychological: because we would have acknowledged that we are surrounded by them on all sides as by our objective psyche—which would amount, so to speak, to a return of "*animism*," albeit not as a repristination of what was the truth of bygone ages, but in the completely new form of technological reality.

In view of technology, it is not sufficient to abstain from it or to make scanty use of it and apart from that to appeal to the moral conscience of others. We cannot get away so simply. The truth of the age does not want to be avoided, it wants to be acknowledged, owned up to. And in order to take the step from Sunday to work-day, it is not sufficient to practice the Christian love of one's neighbor at the workplace and in one's neighborhood, and in this way to put Christian doctrine into practice. For with such a method the Logos would merely ennoble the work-day from above in a Sunday style, while keeping itself pure and free and innocent. It would deny the *reality* of the shadow (the work-day sphere) and its *autonomous* psychic power. This had precisely been the reason why the Christian doctrine, as we initially lamented, had to be given out as a mere matter of faith and be immunized against reality. Reality can never be reached and changed by moral exhortations, but only through ritual. If God is truly incarnated, then he demands as his authentic tribute that the Logos performs the "becoming flesh" all the way down to "Good Friday" in *us*, too, in our consciousness. This means that the Logos humbly takes its place beneath matter, beneath the technical things: that it acknowledges *them* as the locus of its own truth, own meaning, own soul, and of its God; that it therefore also abandons the faith in an extramundane God and "my personal redeemer," just as well as the hubris to feel personally responsible for technology. With this complete burial of the soul into technology the rehabilitation of the Fourth (Jung) would have been realized at the same time. If, however, this tribute is not consciously paid, then it will be forced out of us, and with interest, against our will and from behind our backs.

We cannot pick out our gods. We find them as givens. Whether we willingly agree or not, we have to deal with the absolute monotheistic God of Christianity and his post-natural, artificial reality. All our re-imagination from the point of view of the many natural gods of mythology has no chance over against it. It is this God and this reality that demand the tribute of our owning up to them.

On July 2, 1796, after having read the manuscript of Goethe's

Wilhelm Meister, Friedrich Schiller wrote to Goethe: "How vividly I experienced during this reading ... that over against the superb there can be no freedom except by loving it."[52] Maybe we can apply this moving statement to our situation, characterized by television, computers, and atom bombs, in the following modified way: Over against reality there is no freedom except by worshiping it.[53] To this we would only have to add the following (adapted from Thomas Mann[54]): If we can do it, we will do it. If we can not, it will be done to us.

NOTES

1. Fr. Hölderlin, *Sämtliche Werke*, Große Stuttgarter Ausgabe, vol. 2,1, p. 117. For the complicated history of the creation of this poem see vol. 2, 2 (commentary). For the interpretation of this poem see Ludwig Strauss, "Friedrich Hölderlin: 'Hälfte des Lebens,'" in L. S., *Dichtungen und Schriften*, ed. by W. Kraft, München (Kösel) 1963, p. 478–512.

2. Norbert von Hellingrath (Propyläen-Ausgabe von Hölderlins sämtlichen Werken IV, 301) already emphasized that *only* in the second stanza "the poet's own I speaks up."

3. L. Edelstein, "The Relation of Ancient Philosophy to Medicine," in *Ancient Medicine*, Baltimore (John Hopkins) 1968, p. 349.

4. J. Lohmann ("Der Sophismus des Kung-Sun-Lung," in *Lexis* II, 1 (1949) p. 4) pointed out that compass, paper, letterpress printing, gunpowder and dialectics were used in China only in a playful way, whereas with us they led to a revolution in all areas of life. – A parallel observation of Jung's about the Romans, i.e., the Western pre-Christian antiquity, is interesting in this connection. It is, however, embedded in reflections of his about the origin of psychology: "... It was therefore quite logical that the discovery of psychology falls entirely within the last decades [Jung said this in 1928], although long before that earlier centuries possessed enough introspection and intelligence to be able to recognize psychological facts. In this regard it is the same as with technology. The Romans, e.g., were familiar with all the mechanical principles and physical facts which would have enabled them to construct a steam engine, but all that came of it was the toy made by

Hero of Alexandria. The reason for this is that there was no compelling necessity to go further. This necessity arose only with the enormous division of labour and the growth of specialization in the last century. It needed the *pressing psychological need [or predicament]* of our age to push us into the discovery of psychology. ..." (*CW* 10 § 159, transl. modified).

5. G. W. F. Hegel, *Vorlesungen über die Philosophie der Religion. Dritter Teil. Die absolute Religion* (Theorie-Werkausgabe, vol. 17, Frankfurt/ Main (Suhrkamp), 1969). – If Hegel states that in Christian religion "the universal and the individual spirit are inseparable ...; its absolute identity is this religion and the content of the latter" (p. 189, my translation), then he is justified to think so on account of the idea of God's Incarnation in Jesus of Nazareth. – On the absoluteness of Christianity cf. Ulrich Mann, *Das Christentum als absolute Religion*, Darmstadt (Wissenschaftliche Buchgesellschaft) 1970.

6. Cf. W. Giegerich, "The Present as Dimension of the Soul: 'Actual Conflict' and Archetypal Psychology," now chapter 5 of *The Neurosis of Psychology* (= Collected English Papers, vol. 1), New Orleans (Spring Journal Books) 2006, pp. 103–117. The original German version ("Die Gegenwart als Dimension der Seele: Aktualkonflikt und archetypische Psychotherapie") appeared in *Analyt. Psychol. 9* (1978), pp. 99–110.

7. C. G. Jung, *CW* 18 § 279.

8. Concerning the idea of psychological truth see C. G. Jung, *CW* 11 § 4 f.

9. C. G. Jung, *CW* 11 § 251.

10. C. G. Jung, *CW* 9i § 195.

11. *The Odyssey*, Book 1.

12. Here I must emphasize that I do not mean by Christianity the doctrine of the early Christian community, a small Jewish sect 2000 years ago, a doctrine that can only be accessed through hypothetical reconstruction, but a Western historical force into which just as much Greek mind as Israelite heritage entered.

13. Martin Luther, Explanation of the 2nd article of faith in his *Kleiner Katechismus*.

14. Erich Neumann, *Ursprungsgeschichte des Bewußtseins*, Zürich 1949, chapter "Die Trennung der Ureltern oder das Gegensatzprinzip."

15. Heino Gehrts, "Vom Wesen des Speeres," in *Hestia* 1984/85, pp. 71–103.

16. *op. cit.*

17. Plato, Gorgias 493a; cf. Kratylos 400c.

18. C. G. Jung, *CW* 13 § 54.

19. Kant's *Gesammelte Schriften* (Akademieausgabe 1910 ff.), vol. V, p. 161 (Kritik der praktischen Vernunft).

20. On this whole topic see Martin Heidegger, "Der Ursprung des Kunstwerks," in *Holzwege*, Frankfurt/Main (Klostermann) ⁵1972, pp. 7–68.

21. C. G. Jung, *CW* 12 § 563, translation modified.

22. Karl Kerényi, "Theos: 'Gott' – auf Griechisch," in *Antike Religion*, München (Langen Müller) 1971, pp. 207–217.

23. C. G. Jung, *Letters 2*, p. 4, to Heinrich Boltze, 13 February 1951.

24. Heraclitus, fragment B 123 (Diels-Kranz).

25. As one can see here, the term "natural" in such a sentence, and frequently in my parlance in general, is not used in an *essentialist* sense. It does not refer to "literal" nature as something primary that exists outside and independently of the relevant discourse. What "natural" means is in each case to be understood from what it is opposed to within each context. Therefore the word can mean one thing when the difference between animal and human is discussed and something very different when it is a question of the difference between the gods of pagan mythology and the Christian God (or the corresponding statuses of human consciousness). Inasmuch as I do not refer to an ontological given, I can say that in each context it is the one Concept that happens to be under discussion that within itself *establishes its own* difference between "the natural" and "the unnatural." It bifurcates into these opposites as its internal moments, which mutually define and limit each other.

26. Mircea Eliade, *The Forge and the Crucible* (New York: Harper Torchbooks, 1971).

27. Hegel, *Vorlesungen über die Ästhetik*, Theorie Werkausgabe, vol. 13, pp. 25, 141.

28. Emil Staiger, *Goethe* vol. I, Zürich (Atlantis) 1964, pp. 68 ff.

29. Andrew O. Jászi, *Entzweiung und Vereinigung. Goethes symbolische Weltanschauung*. Heidelberg (Stiehm) 1973.

30. On the acknowledgment of the *past* of the symbolic in *Faust II* see my "Hospitality toward the Gods in an Ungodly Age" (1984), now in W. G., *The Neurosis of Psychology: Primary Papers towards a Critical*

Psychology (Collected English Papers, vol. 1), New Orleans (Spring Journal Books) 2006, pp. 197–217.

31. The Casa Eranos, in which this lecture was presented, is situated at the shore of Lago Maggiore.

32. J. Hillman, "The Animal Kingdom in the Human Dream," *Eranos 51-1982*, pp. 279–334.

33. When I speak of modernity in other texts I usually mean the time (philosophically speaking) after the closure of metaphysics, (economically) the time beginning with the Industrial Revolution, in other words, roughly since 1800. But here I mean the period beginning with the Renaissance. In German we can distinguish between the two periods terminologically, as *Neuzeit* on the one hand and *Moderne* on the other. But when this paper was written, I still used *Neuzeit* or "modern age" in an inclusive sense, for everything that came after the Middle Ages up to the present. I had not become aware as yet of the fundamental hiatus separating the two ages. However, this hiatus is not relevant for the present theme.

34. See, e.g., C. G. Jung, *CW* 13 § 55; *Letters 2*, pp. 487f., to Tanner, 12 February 1959.

35. *CW* 13 § 302, translation modified.

36. I distinguish in this paper between the "ontological" and the "ontic." As indicated, the "ontic" is synonymous with the positive-factual or the empirical or also the literal, referring to demonstrable realities, whereas the term "ontological" refers to the Being or the modes of Being that realities may be in. One and the same entity can be one thing in ontic regards and a very different thing in ontological respects. An example I often use is nature. Ontically nature is very much alive if one considers the devastation that is caused, e.g., by tsunamis and tornados. But ontologically, nature has been dead for a long time inasmuch as it has ceased being the dwelling place of gods and nature spirits and, as far as its real logical status in our world-relation is concerned, been reduced to dead objects, mere raw material for human production. From the point of view of my later writings I could say that the ontological refers to what I later call the logic or soul of the realities in question, in contrast to their empirical-factual aspects. This distinction is similar to the "psychological difference," the difference between man and soul, between, e.g., literal behavior and the inner logic or psychological (soul) meaning of this behavior.

37. Paul Tillich, *Systematische Theologie*, vol. I, Stuttgart (Evangelisches Verlagswerk) 1956, pp. 19–22. Tillich states, of course, that it was a question of "the object of 'infinite interest' (Kierkegaard), that makes us to *its* object if we try to turn it into our object" (p. 19). But even this wording only confirms that from which it wants to move away: the subjectivity of the ego as the decisive factor. It does not make any difference if the one is called the object of the other or vice versa: the ego-centeredness is inherent in the *perspective* of the here prevailing relation to an ego ("involvement," "interest," object).

38. C. G. Jung, "The Symbolic Life," *CW* 18, pp. 267–290 (§§ 608–696).

39. *CW* 18 § 628.

40. "Whither shall I go from thy spirit? or whither shall I flee from thy presence? If I ascend up into heaven, thou art there: if I make my bed in hell, behold, thou art there..." Ps. 139:7f.

41. Matth. 10:30, Lk. 12:7.

42. W. Giegerich, "Wildnis und Geborgenheit," in *Analytische Psychologie* 14, pp. 108–125 (1983), especially pp. 117 ff., "Saving the Nuclear Bomb," in *Facing Apocalypse*, eds. V. Andrews, R. Bosnak, and K. W. Goodwin (Dallas: Spring Publications, 1987), pp. 96–108.

43. See, e.g., C. G. Jung, *Letters 2*, p. 622, to Roger Lass, 11 February 1961.

44. This is a contraction of passages from three letters, *Letters 2*, p. 594 (to Miguel Serrano, 14 September 1960), p. 612 (to von Koenig-Flachsfeld, 30 November 1960), p. 630 (to John A. Sanford, 10 March 1961).

45. Jung knew well enough about the "metamorphosis of the gods" (see, e.g., *CW* 10 § 585, *Letters 2*, p. 250, to Walter Robert Corti, 2 May 1955), but he saw it mostly in the distant past, for example in antiquity in the "decay of Olympus and the transformation of the gods into philosophical and theology ideas" (*Letters 2*, p. 337, to Père Bruno de Jésus-Marie, 20 November 1956). The metamorphosis of the gods from out of these ideas into machines and technological objects and structures he for the most part did not take note of. See, however, his essay "Flying Saucers: A Modern Myth of Things Seen in the Skies" (*CW* 10, pp. 307–433). The following passage, too, is quite plain (*Letters 2*, p. xlvi, to Christian Stamm, 23 April 1949): "Nowadays animals, dragons, and other living creatures are readily replaced in dreams by railways,

locomotives, motorcycles, aeroplanes, and suchlike artificial products (just as the starry sky in the southern hemisphere, discovered relatively late by European navigators, contains many nautical images). This expresses the remoteness of the modern mind from nature; animals have lost their numinosity; they have become apparently harmless; instead we people the world with hooting, booming, clattering monsters that cause infinitely more damage to life and limb than bears and wolves ever did in the past." *Animals have lost their numinosity!* This means nothing else but: nature is dead. Numinosity (i.e., the absolute reality character) has gone over to technology.

46. Hölderlin, "Germanien" verse 15 f.: "... ich fürcht' es, tödtlich ists, / Und kaum erlaubt, Gestorbene zu wecken" (... I fear it, it is deadly and hardly permitted to awaken ones who have died). *Op. cit.*, p. 149.

47. This has been pointed out most decisively by Walter Bröcker, *Theologie der Ilias*, Frankfurt/Main (Klostermann) 1975.

48. "Technology is cursed by our mechanical idea of it. It is the great repressed, the unconscious... Technical things ... are concrete images of animation, locations of the hylic anima..." James Hillman, "The Imagination of Air and the Collapse of Alchemy," in *Eranos 50– 1981*, p. 327. This whole essay is of fundamental importance for our topic.

49. "Meaning" in German is *Sinn*, and *Sinn* ("sense") originally meant direction. So the meaning of life could also mean the real direction in which life is moving.

50. Martin Luther, "Ein Sendbrief an den Papst Leo X. Von der Freiheit eines Christenmenschen" [1520, "A Letter to Pope Leo X. On the Freedom of a Christian Man"] Eyn Christen mensch ist eyn freyer herr / über alle ding / und niemandt unterthan. Eyn Christen mensch ist eyn dienstpar knecht aller ding und yederman unterthan" ["A Christian man is a free lord of all things, and subject to none; a Christian man is a most dutiful servant of all things, and subject to everyone."] Luthers *Werke in Auswahl*, ed. O. Clemen, vol. 2, Berlin (de Gruyter) 1959, p. 11.

51. Subtitle of Carl Améry, *Das Ende der Vorsehung*, Reinbek (Rowohlt) 1980.

52."Wie lebhaft habe ich bei dieser Gelegenheit erfahren, ... daß es dem Vortrefflichen gegenüber keine Freiheit gibt als die Liebe," in: *Briefe an Goethe*, Hamburger Ausgabe vol. 1, Hamburg (Wegner) 1965,

p. 232. Goethe was so impressed by this avowal on the part of Schiller that he included this sentence in his *Wahlverwandtschaften* (1809, "Kindred by Choice") in a modified form: "Over against great merits of another person, there is no other rescue but love." (Goethe's *Werke*, Hamburger Ausgabe, vol. 6, (Wegner) 1968, p. 398.

53. We could also follow Goethe's wording and say: Over against the menace of the superior force of reality there is no rescue but worship (nota bene: the worship of this very reality!)

54. See Thomas Mann, *Joseph und seine Brüder*, no place, S. Fischer Verlag, 1976, p. 682.

Pollen*

Inside the flower-head, another earth
is hatching from the radiant dark.
I listen to the knowing wind, having
never thought of flowers as eggs;
of the pollen-dusted bee trying
to realise itself, hovering like a humming-bird
at the point of iridescence,
the confluence of lonely grace
between seed and bloom.
I dip my mind's ache in its petalled cup,
moistening the self's element, its stung flesh,
the wind blowing through me
like a language returned.

—*Michael Whan*

*First published in *The Umbrella Newsletter*, Summer, 2001—in-house Jungian journal.

ON THE DEATH OF NATURE:
A PSYCHOLOGICAL REFLECTION

MARCO HELENO BARRETO

In this article I develop my argument taking as reference the theoretical framework present in Wolfgang Giegerich's psychological thought, though I have not situated myself wholly within it. As a matter of fact, I believe that Giegerich would probably object not only to some points of my exposition, but to the argument itself.*

****

In the fourth act of *Faust*, Goethe's restless hero looks to the vast ocean in its untamed power and is caught by the desire to wrestle with nature, conquering it, and channeling its power for human purposes. A great change has taken place in Faust's relation to nature: from the initial desperate magical evocation of the Earth-Spirit in the beginning (*Night*), going through the passive contemplation of the *physis venerabilis* in the opening of the first act in the second part, until now, when Faust does not recognize nature's grandeur anymore. The earth— or nature—has no spirit to be invoked, but is only a realm of the

Marco Heleno Barreto is a Jungian psychotherapist in Belo Horizonte, Brazil and teaches philosophy at the Jesuit Faculty of Philosophy. He has recently finished his doctoral thesis in philosophy, entitled "Symbol and Practical Wisdom: C. G. Jung and the Malaise of Modernity."

*Editor's Note: For Dr. Giegerich's indeed very different views regarding the death of nature (in the logical, not literal sense), see his "The Burial of the Soul in Technological Civilization," published in this volume on pp. 197-256.

indifferent and useless display of elemental fury which can be dominated by man's genius. Faust no more recognizes himself as a son of nature: he has reached the position of its master.

This transformation may be read as a parable of the historical evolution of modern consciousness, from the pre-modern containment in a living and responsive nature to the attitude of domination of nature, now seen as *res extensa*, fundamentally alien to humanity. The specific notion of "death of nature," intrinsic to the modern form of being-in-the-world, makes its explicit debut. It means that nature is now seen and dealt with by means of the psychological image of the *machine*, which is the operative root metaphor underlying the metaphysical stance of modern scientific mechanism. This image determines a particular kind of relation between man and nature: namely one of technological domination, in which consciousness assumes the position of *master of nature*.

Historically, the first modern form taken by this relation implies a radical alienation between man and nature. It rests upon a simple form of negation in which nature is taken only as *raw material* that is subjected to man's will and interests. No form of reciprocity is recognized, and thus the extension of man's drive to dominate and exploit nature finds no limits. And here lies the fundamental flaw in this first modern form of domination and what is false in it: the unlimited human desire for domination is projected onto nature's limited (but not recognized as such) potentiality of being exploited. In other words, the Faustian drive for domination is ruled by the "bad infinity" of desire and clashes against the concrete finitude of nature. The increasing diversity of ecological catastrophes in our time is a sign of that flaw and that falsehood. It bespeaks the logical insufficiency of *this* form of domination.

What is at stake here? Let's return for a moment to Faust. In the last moment just before his death, the old and blind Faust has a final vision of a prosperous and free state of humankind, reached through the extension of technological domination of nature. Like Moses contemplating from the distance the Promised Land into which his entry is denied, Faust dies nurturing a happy dream: he believes that the sounds he hears are produced by workers actively bringing his project to completion, but the truth is that what he hears are the lemurs digging his grave. If we take Faust's illusion and the undetected truth as a whole, a unity, the meaning is that, in the particular position he assumes, the fulfillment of his project corresponds logically and concretely to his death.

This literary image may be taken analogically to reflect the anticipated outcome of one aspect of today's state of *Opus Magnum*. The ecological catastrophes that haunt our world must be interpreted not as a by-product or side-effect of a still imperfect capacity for domination, but as the necessary manifestation of a contradiction, on the logical level, in the present form of domination. Instead of being referred to the image of nature as man's problem-child, or troublesome aging-mother, these phenomena should rather be envisioned as a sort of ghostlike nightmare. On the logical level, this nightmare corresponds to that contradiction that stems, on the one hand, from the lack of full and effective acknowledgment of the dialectical interdependence that unites man, "master of nature," and nature itself. When nature, through being regarded as mere "raw material," is subjected to such an empirically irrational and self-contradictory exploitation, effective acknowledgment of the deep *truth* hidden in the domination drive is missed in the bargain.

This contradiction can only be dialectically sublated in an eco-logical form of consciousness. In order to understand what I mean, we could describe the structure of the dialectical relation between modern consciousness and nature as composed of four logical moments: (1) the initial, unreflected *position*, expressed in the statement "man shall be the master of nature;" (2) the *negation of the position* as seen in the natural obstacles to human domination, as well as in nature's inability to satisfy the true goal hidden in the urge of domination; (3) the *negation of the negation,* which corresponds to the endless extension of the technological domination of nature that results in ecological unbalance and catastrophes, among other self-destructive effects;[1] and, (4) the *restored position*, which enriched by the whole history of technological achievements and the lesson of its disasters or failures, corresponds to the eco-logical form of consciousness. In this eco-logical form of consciouness, the externalized form of domination is interiorized, and the expression "master of nature" is comprehended in the sense of *genitivus subjectivus*: by becoming master in itself, humankind holds the place of mastership *in* the whole nature. Here the "death of nature" does not need to be concretely acted out anymore, reaching its proper meaning as the dialectical transformation of nature in soul, and the opening up of true human space.

In the history of its relation to nature, modern consciousness has reached an effective state that corresponds to the third logical moment described above—*the negation of the negation*. The ecological catastrophes that result from this position force modern consciousness to become aware of its own particular logical configuration, and also give birth to ecological thinking, as a positive reaction against that position. As such, ecological thinking is situated on the same logical level as ecological catastrophes. By this I do not mean that *any* kind of factual or empirical ecological consciousness cannot correspond to a higher logical level. As it is true that all cats are gray at midnight, so we would have to determine if there is a form of consciousness among those constituents of the ecological *nebula* that would meet the specific logical requirements put up by modernity or modern consciousness. This means that a regressive, nostalgic, naïve return to any old and historically as well as logically overcome form of relation between consciousness and nature is not acceptable as an authentic answer to the problem posed by our Faustian modern civilization. Faust could not truly invoke the Earth-Spirit anymore: the magician had been irrevocably sublated in the technological entrepreneur.

Furthermore, naïve forms of ecological consciousness often romantically idealize the relation of man and nature in a supposed archaic state of humankind. This idealization is rooted in the archetypal image of Paradise—a perfect and total reconciliation of all the conflicting elements of the world. Thus they fail to recognize that, as Georges Gusdorf has put it, there is a kind of original sin of human existence as such, inasmuch as the mere presence of man in the world necessarily introduces some degree of disturbance that must be counterbalanced, in order not only to preserve natural order, but also to make possible the survival of the human species. Humankind has *never* empirically experienced the innocence of a life without fractures.[2] By the same reason, the naïve ecological critique of technological domination of nature by man is misplaced. As Giegerich has pointed out,

> the acquisition of the destructive and creative power that is now
> in the hand of man is only quantitatively different from the
> conquest of fire and the invention of bow and arrow by early

> man, not qualitatively. It is not that the prehistoric advance was
> harmless whereas today's is diabolical.[3]

This statement could be disputed, on the grounds of the qualitative difference between simple [premodern] *technique* and modern *technology*. But even if we grant Giegerich's position, the problem lies in the *attitude* concerning the *utilization* of technical powers. Early man pre-reflexively acknowledged his *dependence* on nature, *even while using his skills and powers to transform it in his own benefit*. He also often distinguished clearly the natural dimension from the spiritual one, and conceived the human position as determined *simultaneously* by both dimensions. He expressed this acknowledgment in his mythical and religious representations. Modern man forgot and even denied that dependence and that determination, maybe inflated by the psychological image of "master of nature" (from biblical and Cartesian origins) and its apparent confirmation in the spectacular advancements of technology. But we should insist that this is precisely a *denial* or an *oblivion*, corresponding on the logical level to the moment of negation of negation (and not the final state reachable by modern consciousness). The ecological catastrophes and the recent—and maybe too late— concern of great financial world institutions and governments with ecological problems are a proof of this obvious truth: man's existence is threatened by an irrational domination and exploitation of nature. This threat is both empirical and logical. Empirically, the serious destruction and exhaustion of natural resources speaks for itself. Logically, the confinement to and obsession with domination of external nature impedes humankind from fulfilling its complete notion as a *spiritual* species.

Observed from this angle, archaic man was more reasonable than we are. Let us repeat: the element of irrationality in this modern attitude or form of relation corresponds precisely to the denial of the reciprocal dependence between man with his technological power, on one side, and nature, on the other. Using (and misusing a bit) the famous Hegelian *topos*, in the "slave" lies the truth of its "master:" the master is the slave of the slave. In other terms: nature is a *positive condition* to man's freedom. Logically seen, the modern dialectical relation of man and nature stopped short in the negative moment, in the form of a one-sided will to domination that simply extends itself outwards *ad infinitum*. It calls for not only the reflexive acknowledgment of nature's relative autonomy as a necessary condition for man's own autonomy, but most of all for the application of the notion of domination of nature to itself.

It is not the empirical *capability and perfection* of domination that is at stake here, but the own *logical form* in which this capability is exerted. Empirically, i. e., concerning the external effective acting out of human power, the mere destructive and irrational domination of nature calls for an *ecological* form of domination which recognizes that nature is a constitutive part of our *oikos*, our home. This is not identical with the noble ecological concern with preservation of nature in all its varieties and forms. It means a state of consciousness that reaches the eco-logical status. Ecological consciousness here implies fundamentally the conscious realization of the full dialectical relation between culture and nature, reached by the interiorization of the domination drive.[4] Empirically it tends to foster eco-technological ways of exploring natural resources within a sense of self-limitation. It preserves not only nature, but humankind as well, at least as long as the human being doesn't succeed in becoming a pure spirit, i. e., as long as we comprehend ourselves as *incarnated beings*: our body is the token of our residual but irrevocable kinship to nature.

As body is the home-substratum of human spirit, so nature is the substratum of our *oikos*. Denying this relation is equivalent to inviting catastrophe, or literal self-destruction, which logically pertains to the third moment of the dialectical structure of modern consciousness's relation to nature. Conversely, ecological catastrophes are an invitation—better, an urgent intimation—to consciously acknowledge that relation, and to empirically find a way of life more congruent with its truth. Logically considered, they are the empirical manifestations of a spiritual drive towards a higher level of spiritualization—the eco-logical form of consciousness.

Now I would like to shift the focus of reflection from the level of the *Opus Magnum* of the Western soul to the level of the *opus parvum* as seen in individual soul-making. In order to make this shift, I will present two interconnected dreams of a woman, the second of which displays literally the motif of "death of nature," in the form of the killing of an animal. The dreamer was a successful engineer, completely identified and apparently satisfied with her profession, who came to analysis complaining of a depressive mood after taking several vacations, wishing of course to get rid of it. At the end of our first meeting, she told me, out of the blue, that she would never quit engineering, even if she spent two years in analysis with me.

In the first dream, *she is in a place that reminds her of my consulting room. Someone hunts her, a killer. She runs away, passing by subterranean hallways. In a cave, she finds two deer, a mother and her offspring. She continues to run, up and away, waking in panic.* In the second dream, *she walks through the streets of an old place, with old houses, looking for a tailor who would sew her graduation gown. The tailor was the deceased father of a friend of hers, whose mother (though alive in external reality) had already died in the dream. The gown would be made with the skin of the younger deer. The dreamer plays with both deer. A servant comes in and takes the younger deer to be killed. The dreamer is compassionate and feels full of sorrow, but permits the sacrifice. The deer then begins to transform, to suffer a transformation. It acquires a human shape, and then desperately grasps the dreamer's arms with human hands.*

Let's initially bracket the personal attitude and situation of the dreamer and concentrate briefly on the dream image itself. The two dreams obviously compose a unity, and there is a remarkable difference between them: in the first one, the dreamer herself is the sacrificial victim, and while fleeing in panic she meets the deer, but doesn't realize what this has to do with her situation, whereas in the second dream, the younger deer is the victim experiencing panic, and while the dreamer is full of sorrow for it, the deer starts to metamorphasize into a human being. The fact of both being the target of an act of killing prepared by the soul indicates a profound identity between dreamer and deer, at some level. An evolution has taken place from the first to the second dream. Initially, the dreamer tries to avoid in panic the position of sacrificial victim, what in fact means avoiding her own truth—the whole scene of the first dream obviously refers to the process of analysis.[5] In the second dream she actively searches for the killer/tailor who will perform the sacrifice, and a *differentiation* has occurred alongside with her new attitude: not she, but the younger deer shall be sacrificed, and thus humanized.

The deer will be skinned. The transformation that it suffers is homologous to the transformation of its skin into a graduation gown, meaning the acquisition of a human form. This is precisely its death: the exclusively natural dies in the birth of the human or cultural form.

Consciousness being the specific distinction of humankind, we can say with Jung that it "is now called upon to do that which nature has always done for her children—namely, to give a certain, unquestionable, and unequivocal decision."[6] The human being is an overanimal, i.e., a sublated animal, and this means that animality is dialectically *overcome* and *preserved* in the ontological constitution of humankind. What is left behind in this sublation is the common general form of animality, i.e., the *instinctive natural life*, the merely biological form of existence. In its place comes *spiritual or psychological life*. But what is preserved of animality is *corporeality*: this spiritual life is lived in a body, it is embodied spiritual life. And this is the paradox of the human condition: in humankind spirit meets nature in a dialectical relation—identity of identity and difference.

The evolution observed between the two dreams refers to the conscious recognition of the natural dimension of the deer and its implication in the sacrificial action: in the first dream, the deer are just there, as if by accident, and one can hardly see how they fit in the whole scene; in the second dream, consciousness—the dream-ego— has actively advanced, and now the position of the deer becomes evident —they represent the element to be sacrificed or killed. Consciousness has acknowledged its difference from an exclusively natural status, as well as its relative identity with it, and thus it permits and compassionately suffers the sacrifice. The sacrifice—killing—of the deer is the condition for the birth of human being, the human way of being, a being in the soul. Soul and death of nature come together.[7]

There is a most significant detail in the second dream that comes from the personal context of the dreamer: the tailor in the dream was the father of a friend of hers, who in positive reality had already died. The dream inverts positive reality and represents the father as alive, while her friend's mother (who in positive reality was still alive) is the dead one in the dream. That means that the whole process occurs in the realm of *absolute negativity*, in the underworld, just as in the first dream the action takes place in subterranean hallways. To grasp the dialectical meaning of the movement displayed in the dreams we have to "die" to the positivistic principle of reality and consider the whole process from the perspective of the *inverted world*.

Now let's look at the dreams, considering the personal situation of the dreamer. In her case, the engineering graduation gown was only an external form (*persona*), and not a *logical* form (which would require the "killing" and transformation of the dreamer herself, her wholehearted participation in the sacrifice). Individuality (comprehended as logically including the substantial dreamer-deer relation) was not transposed into a new mode of consciousness. The dreamer sort of "played" engineer, but avoided the implications of the *real* identity she pretended to possess. The neurotic identification with the masculine *persona*, fostered by a deeper possession by the *animus*,[8] had not yet been dissolved by a true atonement with its unsurmountable conditions, which would imply her giving up running away from the invisible assassin that comes after her, and letting herself be killed—and this included overcoming her resistances against analysis. The assassin is homologous to the tailor, and is a kind of initiator to the world of the dead, and thus to the real depths of soul. By not submitting herself to death, or to the sacrificial death, she neurotically externalized death in the graduation gown. But one cannot escape death and truth altogether: the little deer pays the price, and this was the origin of her fits of depression. She did not *live* consciously the sacrifice—she didn't even perceive that there was any sacrifice at all, and that she was both sacrificer and sacrificial victim. The depression was the form taken by the suffering of the deer, a claim for recognition and conscious participation of the dreamer in the sacrificial rite, and also a psychological auto-critique of the brutal, blind, and self-alienating triumphalism of a successful career, which one-sidedly dominated her life.

Moreover, we should notice that it is the offspring that will be sacrificed. The little deer also represents her natural childhood position of consciousness, and so she was running away from her full psychological adulthood. The *animus* figures kill the *anima*-childish element in herself, and this brings forth her full human form. However, although being a successful engineer in the concrete world, psychologically she was only playing the engineer, playing the man, playing with the deer, and she did not want to pay the price of real adulthood: death. (I do not mean concrete death, of course.) This price is encapsulated in her depression, which reveals her truth: she is unconsciously and compassionately suffering the death of nature in the sacrifice of the deer. The attempt to get rid of her depression comes from her neurotic split: she did not want to suffer the sacrificial *rite d'entrée* that conditions the conscious and mature transformation of her natural-childish state into a new mode of consciousness. For that reason, she only played engineer, played the woman-who-can-overcome-men.

The *possession* by the *animus* must reach its inner truth, and that means the transformation of the position of consciousness through analysis. In terms of the dream image, this would amount to the institution of consciousness as a mediating moment between the *animus*/killer/tailor and the *anima*/deer, so that their dialectical unity would be manifested *in* and *through* the dream-ego as the graduation gown. The mere *identification* with the *persona* would thus be dissolved analytically, by being brought to consciousness, but not necessarily the particular *persona* itself. It is up to the individual to choose freely after consciously considering her whole life situation as related to the specific collective role she had once chosen, as well as been driven by unconsciously.

The position of sacrificial victim humanizes the deer, but the dreamer, by avoiding in personal life the same position, fails to perceive the identity of identity and difference of herself and the deer, or nature. In fact, by avoiding her own truth she transfers her responsibility in a split-off way to the deer, and thus transforms it in a scapegoat. This corresponds to her neurotic split, and the fits of depression as well as the dreams both hide and reveal the denied truth: in a way she *is* the younger deer, and she *must* acknowledge this truth.

The empirical one-sidedness of the dreamer's identification with her masculine *persona* of engineer, testified by her defensive remark that she would not quit engineering, represented an amputation of her wholeness inasmuch as it *unsatisfactorily* killed her feminine nature — i. e., her feminine kinship to nature or, in other terms, the *anima* function—by splitting it off from herself, and thus making a mock sacrifice. The deer-nature was not *remembered* and *internalized* (*er-innert*) but only *externalized* in the graduation gown. The empirical one-sided *denial* of *anima-nature* was followed by an alienation of the dreamer's concrete individuality in favor of her collective role, and thus she was reduced to the status of a functionary of the technological paradigm that rules the world.

The deer is negated in the engineering graduation gown. And deer and engineer are sublated in the dreamer (though unconsciously) through the sacrifice. But subjectively this sublation only occurs completely if the dreamer participates in the process with her *consciousness*, otherwise she gets stuck in a neurotic contradiction of opposites, without realizing their fundamental and dialectical unity. Now, once the sacrifice is completed, the dreamer will find herself in a new situation: she is now the engineer *but* she is also the sacrificed deer, which is preserved in the new state obtained by sublation in the interiorizing movement of consciousness towards its truth. As such, she bears a kind of psychological scar that must remind her time and again of the *suffering* of the deer, and of her deep identity in the difference with it. The deer desperately demands *recognition*, and this calls for *compassion*—suffering together the sacrificial act, the immolation. Killing is identical with humanization, as Giegerich has reminded us in his *Killings*, but only when accompanied by suffering this same death,[9] otherwise there is only a split-mindedness with the correspondent institution of a conflict and the repression of one of its terms. If the dreamer does not pay attention to and consciously accept this psychological scar, then there is no true *internalization*, and it may be that a reversion occurs to a mere oblivion or unconsciousness of the whole dialectical structure of the situation. Then, by undialectically negating her relative *identity* with the deer, the *difference* between herself and the *function* of engineer also vanishes: she becomes undialectically identical with it, losing or sacrificing the complexity of her human self, thus being transformed into a mere functionary of the science in which she was trained. The present state of the Western soul's *Opus Magnum* swallows or absorbs completely the *opus parvum* of her individual soul-making, and the real distinction between the two levels is lost. Consciousness reverts to mass-mindedness. Reflexivity is obliterated. Individuality and the eco-logical state of consciousness are aborted.[10]

The dreamer's personal neurotic position corresponds logically to the domination-of-nature world relation that now characterizes mankind at the collective level. In this we can see that the real distinction between *Opus Magnum* and *opus parvum* is not an *absolute* disengagement. The dreamer's subjective *opus-parvum*level depression is perfectly homologous to an objective ecological catastrophe, on the level of *Opus Magnum*. The same logic informs both events, and this is not a mere academic issue. It exhibits the real, concrete correspondence between some "minor" subjective experiences and the major objective configurations of the world. These dreams show undoubtedly that the dreamer is truly a child of her age, a modern subject whose psychology is formed within the logical state reached in the history of modern consciousness. And we should notice that she is not a privileged exceptional individual. Rather on the contrary: she is just an ordinary woman, with ambitions all too common for many women, especially in our age, in which professional accomplishment is legitimately, collectively, and logically included among the authentic forms of a woman's realization. (So it should be clear that when I speak of a "masculine *persona* of engineer," I am not endorsing any sexist position, but just using a traditional distinction between masculine and feminine, while at the same time presupposing that many masculine and feminine roles and traits are equally legitimate for both men and women in our contemporary world. On the logical level, we are not dealing with gender issues, but with the *soul's mode of being*, which can be metaphorically manifested through masculine or feminine images.)

The same possible logical development—the next logical step— on the level of *Opus Magnum* conditions the transformation of the individual consciousness in the present example. Just as a truly modern eco-logical consciousness is logically superior to the present only externalized form of technological domination and exploitation of nature, so in the dreamer's case the acknowledgment of her deep kinship with the natural/animal level *in the very act of killing the deer, or the death of nature*, is called for and signals the real transformation and the finding of her truth, which is also *our* truth and a truth of the world. In fact, this truth is already present both in her depression and dreams (as well as in objective ecological catastrophes). But it is not fully and effectively recognized, it is unredeemed, so to speak, for it has not come home to its final conscious logical form. Therefore, I believe I am aligned with Giegerich in stating that modern catastrophes are not soulless: quite the contrary, they faithfully display the logical life of the Soul, much in the same way as does the dreamer's depression. There is a sort of blind and self-destructive religious ritual sacrifice going on in them. But their meaning is completely immersed in the event itself. The call for recognition on the part of the sacrificed—nature—has not been attended by the sacrificer—modern technological consciousness. The dialectical truth of this contradictory state is reached by moving towards an eco-logical consciousness.

As I have stated before, with regards to their constituting logic, ecological catastrophes are intrinsic to the modern externalized form of domination of nature. They exhibit its self-negation, so that the domination drive may reach its true accomplished final form *by being applied to itself*. Once interiorized, it is no longer entangled in the "bad infinity" that rules its acting out in the domination of positive nature. It reaches the real infinity that corresponds to its infinite movement, and this is the final meaning and logical truth of the "master of nature." The interiorization of the domination drive brings about a negative interiorization of nature. By this movement, the status of nature changes: it becomes sublated in soul, the space of interiority opened up through the application of domination to itself. This is the true "death of nature" corresponding to the birth of soul, and not the literal acted out death of nature displayed in the outward technological domination of positive external nature. The deer becomes human. Re-ensouling nature means logically killing it, humanizing it. In this movement, the modern undialectical dualism between *res extensa* and *res cogitans* is also overcome: now nature is not anymore undialectically split-off from spirit, but is sublated in it.

The result of this movement is what I have called the eco-logical form of consciousness.[11] It no longer stops short in the domination of external nature, but reaches the proper *human place* in nature inasmuch as it opens the dimension of interiority that transcends positive nature, and thus comes home to itself. In this final state, the externalized domination of positive nature is not simply abandoned, but is now governed from a new standpoint: its criterion is not just the noble (and vital) positive preservation of nature, but fundamentally *its correspondence to the human place in nature*. Empirically it implies ecological forms of technological domination of nature, but most of all self-limitation and a conscious recognition of a quasi-reciprocity between humankind and nature. Not the noble preservationist of nature (innocently saving the deer from the sacrifice), but an "eco-logical engineer" as sacrificed-sacrificer would be a good image for the dialectical reconciliation between modern consciousness and nature.

Now we should raise the question as to whether the individual answer to this specific problem has any significance whatsoever to the state of the same problem on the objective level of the *Opus Magnum*. I completely sympathize with Giegerich's position against a megalomaniac inflation of the subjective sphere of *opus parvum*. But, as to the *logical* form of the answer, we should notice that, if the same logic is here operative on both levels (*Opus Magnum* and *opus parvum*), the answer also has the same logical form: an eco-logical form of consciousness. So I would say that the personal answer may have an infinitesimal significance or meaning as related to *Opus Magnum*. Concerning the improbable weight of the personal answer, I would rather skeptically suspend my judgment (make the skeptical *epoché*), instead of declaring categorically that it has *no* weight at all, for we have no means of reaching such an absolute certitude in this case: we just cannot determine either positively *or negatively* the existence of any effect coming from such an infinitesimal scale. At any rate, this academic problem should not concern us empirically. We should only concentrate on the *personal* construction of the answer, in order to avoid the inflation of *opus parvum*.

Finally, the eco-logical form of consciousness corresponds to a possible and legitimate kind of "resurrection of nature," which logically overcomes—i.e., dialectically sublates—the previous moment of "death of nature." This sublation implies a new mode of relation inside which the image of a machine as the root metaphor for nature is no longer *absolutely* valid. This amounts to a radically different form of relation of man to himself, and especially to his body—that residual element of nature in human form. Our body is (still) our link to nature. As such, it partakes, along with nature, in the same "death" that is imposed by the externalized form of its domination: it is reduced to the status of a mere meaningless object, a biological machine subjected to the will and manipulation of its "owner" or "conqueror." Not incarnation, but simple negation of the body is the particular truth (and, dialectically, falsehood) of this specific modern way of being-in-the-world. If we bear in mind that empirically, as well as logically, the conqueror falls under the spell of the conquered and is unconsciously determined by his prey, then we can comprehend that the status of machine attributed to nature should sooner or later come home to its origin in man's psyche, and engulf man himself. This fantasy-reality is displayed in films such as *Terminator*, *Matrix*, *Blade Runner*, and many others of lower quality. It was perfectly presented in *Brave New World*, Aldous Huxley's prophetic novel. It can also be perceived in the apparent regression of consciousness, in the figure of the Web-surfer or any other equivalent functionary of modern technological civilization, to the level of "sense-certainty" described by Hegel in the *Phenomenology of Spirit*, as well as in its (consciousness's) correspondent oblivion of the world.[12]

The mechanical instrumentalization of our bodies, so common and predominant today, is logically overcome on a higher level. In spite of the continuous use of knowledge and technological skills developed in the history of modern science, body and nature, no longer being reduced to the status of a mere machine, are seen as the relatively autonomous basis for the manifestation of life and death. But this means that humankind has to come to terms with its empirical *mortality*. At bottom, this is what is denied in the irrational and one-sided form of technological domination of nature. And here lies the major problem hindering the *effective* empirical transformation of the externalized "death of nature" attitude: will modern humankind be able to calm down its essential and deep-rooted fear of death, and tame its present irrational externalized craving for immortality, finding its proper logical status, and thus coming to its own deep truth in an eco-logical form of consciousness? *This* question only history will answer.[13]

Returning to Faust, we can now comprehend dialectically the relation between his death and the subsequent scene where he is rejuvenated and meets the Eternal Feminine. The realization of his innermost urge lies precisely in his death—and in the beginning he wanted to die concretely, coming close to suicide (which would have been the "wrong" death in his case, because it would have been merely an ego's acting out), and he was stopped by a reminiscence of his early religious atttitude. We could say that the transcendent essence of Faust's urge (see the *Prologue in Heaven*) attracted him to itself, and he could only reach its final destination through his whole saga, mediated by Mephistopheles. Mephistopheles, we should remember, keeps a very friendly relation to the *Lord*, as can be seen in the *Prologue in Heaven*. This means that he is already contained in the absolute position from the outset, and thus his actions belong to the whole process of realization of this original truth in Faust. So the apparent failure of Faust's never-ending mundane project of domination is in fact a success, inasmuch as it opens, by its own failure, the way to the transcendent-negative dimension. Only through his *own* death in the Mephistophelian dimension can Faust finally reach what he had been searching for all along in his quest: the vision of the Eternal Feminine. Mephistopheles is the ruler of this world, *princeps huius mundus*, and all his tricks and illusions may be seen as the prodigious capacity of human spirit to dominate and transform *objectively* the world. But Faust's *soul* is taken from him because its deep essence, manifest in its thirst for the Absolute, does not belong to the same level governed by Mephistopheles, and that's the reason for Faust's confident bet with Mephisto. While wishing and acting out inside Mephistopheles's realm (the realm of positive realities), Faust logically could not find satisfaction. His infinite urge demanded a kind of death, *but not the concrete one similar to the externalized death of nature in its domination.* It was the *logical death of the merely externalized will to power*, if we can so express it, which amounts to the interiorization of the drive of domination. *Mors nostra non est mors vulgi*, said the alchemists.

To conclude, I would like to summarize the main points of my argument: we could say that the higher state of spiritualization logically implied in the modern Faustian form of consciousness lies not in the literal death of external nature, or in its domination, but in the realization of its truth by interiorization of domination itself. We can plausibly conjecture that, once this eco-logical form of consciousness is reached, the empirical death of nature would not need to be acted out anymore, and this would open space for the emerging of positive ecological thinking, and a corresponding transformation of the form of empirical relation to nature: the predatory and annihilating present devastation could give way to an eco-technological form of domination

.

NOTES

1. Along with the ecological catastrophes, we should include overpopulation, exponential violence, and all sorts of socially disastrous results that ultimately have their origin in the externalized will to domination upon which the modern world is built.

2. Cf. G. Gusdorf, *Mito e Metafísica* (São Paulo: Convívio, 1979), 24.

3. Wolfgang Giegerich, *The End of Meaning and the Birth of Man: An Essay about the State Reached in the History of Consciousness and an Analysis of C.G.Jung's Psychological Project,* http://www.beamish.org/Files/Giegerich_EndofMeaning.pdf, 24.

4. Needless to say, this does not mean simple *self-domination*, which would still be a form of domination directed to an object distinct from itself. The logical interiorization (*Er-innerung*) means "domination of domination."

5. The connection between hunting and psychological truth was masterfully exposed by Giegerich in his interpretation of Actaion's myth in *The Soul's Logical Life: Towards a Rigorous Notion of Psychology* (Frankfurt am Main: Peter Lang, 2001), 203-275.

6. *CW* 8 § 750.

7. On this topic, see Wolfgang Giegerich, "Killings: Psychology's Platonism and the Missing Link to Reality," *Spring 54* (June 1993), 5-18.

8. I cannot develop and expose the basis for this statement, for this would require the presentation of additional "case material" that would blur the focus of the argument I develop here. I am also aware that there are other lines of interpretation of the dreams presented here. At the time they were dreamed—some 20 years ago—I myself adopted a traditional Jungian approach, similar to the one I use here when considering the personal situation of the dreamer, with fairly good therapeutic results. I do not think that traditional and dialectical lines of interpretation are merely incompatible, but I do think that the dialectical one is more complex and can better do justice to the complexities of soul life.

9. Jung has developed this point in *Symbols of Transformation*. See *CW* 5 § 659ss, and especially § 668.

10. Jung was deeply concerned with this problem — "the plight of the individual in modern society." Cf. *CW* 10, "The Undiscovered Self."

11. To be more precise, what I have here called eco-logical consciousness is not a new form of consciousness *per se*, but a logical determination *within* modern consciousness as such.

12. See Wolfgang Giegerich, *The World Wide Web from the Point of View of the Soul's Logical Life*. \www-sll.wpd, 15-16.

13. The distance between conscious reflexive acknowledgment of human dependence on nature and its effective empirical actualization (cf.: the failure of the Kyoto Protocol) may be fatal: the self-destructive drive going on at the level of *Opus Magnum* today does not allow any kind of naïve optimistic hope.

AZURE

To be thrown as a ball is thrown,
sometimes lost in a cloud of purple flowers.
Language too gets thrown like a ball game;
meaning tossed between ourselves,
to catch its plenitude. More often we fumble
and it falls from our hands.
If only you would let me fail
when I speak; let me search
in the long grasses of the wild meadow
for the ball we lost at twilight,
tangled somewhere in a thicket of syllables.
Maybe then, just maybe, my fingers
could touch the earth's roundness,
the inexhaustible, unfound meaning
of its azure horizons.

—*Michael Whan*

Nature Writing: Jung's Eco-logic in the Conjunctio of Comedy and Tragedy

SUSAN ROWLAND

The moment one forms an idea of a thing... One has taken possession of it, and it has become an inalienable piece of property, like a slain creature of the wild that can no longer run away.
— C. G. Jung[1]

Even the loneliest meteor circles round some distant sun, or hesitantly draws near to a cluster of brother meteors. Everything hangs together with everything else... This is undoubtedly the same as the idea of an absolute God... But which of us can pull himself out of the bog by his own pigtail? — C. G. Jung[2]

I am going to argue that C. G. Jung is essentially a comic writer. His comedy consists of a conjunctio of tragic and comic cultural forms. In turn, these amount to a new embodiment of myth for a world in desperate need of eco-logic. For Jung's experimental writing styles are an attempt to let the psyche speak in all its native diversity. Jung writes not only from the ego, but also from the mysterious

Susan Rowland, Ph.D., is Reader in English and Jungian Studies at the University of Greenwich, UK, and author of *Jung as a Writer* (Routledge, 2005). She was Chair of the International Association for Jungian Studies, 2003-2006.

sublimity of the self. So much so that Jung's writing aims to be nature writing: the voices of the psychic other dance in his prose.

WHAT IS NATURE?

In an era of global warming and pollution, we imagine nature to be the green world of non-human animate and inanimate reality. This nature suffers from the culture of capitalism and industrialization. Indeed, even politicians such as President George W. Bush speak of "Mother nature's wrath," in the face of devastation from weather that may be linked to human activity.[3]

But what is nature if humans are not part of it? The eco-critical ethos is that everything is connected to everything else. It follows that humanity's behavior as if we were *not* part of nature inflicts reciprocal damage. I particularly like Jung's variation on this theme in the second quotation heading this article: "[e]verything hangs together with everything else...". He improves on the ecocritical cliché for, as we say, those that do not hang together will hang separately.

The eco-philosopher, Kate Soper, has analyzed the paradoxical positioning of the word "nature" in western culture.[4] "Nature" signifies three frameworks for figuring the relation to the non-human. By "the laws of nature," referring to such phenomena as atoms, gravity, cosmic forces, we mean "nature" as a holistic notion that embraces all: it certainly includes humanity. Jung, above, characteristically points out that nature as totality infers an absolute God.

A second use of "nature" is in its habitual opposition to "culture." The nature/culture opposition is a binary structure that is metaphysical: it positions "nature" as an "other" that exists "outside" culture in a system that licenses all sorts of other oppositions and theologies. In particular, the gendering of the culture/nature opposition as masculine/feminine founds a patriarchal hierarchy that could be traced back to a masculine transcendent father god mythology triumphing over goddesses that stem from an ancient "mother" Earth. For "her," the sacred is immanent in/as nature. To this crucial division of reality about the bodying of nature, I will return. For now, it is worth noting that psychoanalysis represents a continuation of this gendered *metaphysic* of nature when it insists upon selfhood as conditional upon suppressing connection to the (m)other, and adopting a transcendent relation to the unconscious under the name of "father."

The belief that consciousness is dependent upon subordination of the other is enacted in cultures where separation and distancing are all too often hardened into dominance and exploitation. Such repulsion of the other may work through gender, or ethnicity, or the casual appropriation of nature as culture's instrument or "resource." Nature/culture as a founding and funding metaphysic begs the question: does consciousness have to be constructed more out of the suppression of the other, than by relating to it? I would suggest Jung's response to this challenge is visible in the first quotation heading this article. Suggestively, his response is in the form of a dawning eco-logic. For he says that absolute transcendence of thought, the complete capturing of an idea, which necessarily means cutting it off from its surrounding matter (its habitat), has all the eco-logic of a naturalist who kills animals in order to study them. Such methods are effective, in that the dead thing becomes wholly the property of the hunter/knower, and can be transported to new epistemological locations. Yet, Jung goes on to say, such attempts to entirely "own" psychological ideas not only "kill," they may fail in their aims: some knowledge may not be amenable to the methodology of the big game hunter. Indeed the hunting skills provided by conceptual thinking may so shape the results that they reflect the being of the hunter more than the natural life of the psyche.

> [T]he psychologist... never suspects that the very fact of grasping
> the object conceptually gives it a golden opportunity to display
> all those qualities which would never have made their appearance
> had it not been imprisoned in a concept.[5]

Conceptual thinking is problematic when it comes to the "nature" of the psyche. Like all attempts to "know" the psyche, it is also an intervention into it. It is, moreover, a methodology with lethal properties, precisely because it is a technique of "knowing" that converts the psyche *into* property. Jung here expresses how some of our valued "scientific" forms of knowing are allied to coercive aspects of modernity in killing, incarceration, and ownership. Nature is trans-formed through the medium of some aspects of science into its "other," culture.

Out of this pervasive metaphysic of nature comes our third usage, argues Soper. The nature we think of as endangered, as in need of protection, is the aesthetically constructed picturesque "outside" and "inside" to culture. If nature as universal "laws" is evoked by science, nature as metaphysical "other" by philosophy, then nature as picturesque and sublime comes to us via art. For as the poststructuralists have shown, we cannot escape language because we cannot conceive of "nature" outside the ideas and conventions inherited through language. There is no such thing as "nature" apart from the cultural ways in which we understand it. As Paul Kugler explains:

> We have come to realize that language of any sort, be it literary, philosophical, clinical, or scientific, does not allow for a transparent view to the so-called empirical world. *Our theories of interpretation have no location outside of language, neither objective nor empirical, and can never be a ground, only a mediator.*[6]

I want to return to this resonant use of "ground" later.

Jung, as I shall show, is a psychologist devoted to expanding the richer possibilities of the artistic legacy of "nature." Indeed, in his works on alchemy, he most overtly demonstrates his model of working with the psyche as a form of organic gardening. Jung's alchemy is about cultivation of the psyche by replacing a repression model of the psychic other with one of relationship. In particular, the alchemy works re-frame the symbolic structures of the European mind so that Christian transcendence of nature allows space for the sacred as garden, as free flying bird, as voices of the non-human, animated. Through alchemy Jung debates and re-frames Soper's three constructions of nature. He considers nature as totality and "laws" in alchemy's location of the sacred/psyche in matter, its metaphysical construction in the making of consciousness *contra naturam* (against nature, culture/nature, but crucially including a relationship *to* psychic nature to which I shall return), and offers a discourse of the aesthetic of nature that allows a sense of relating to it to survive his source material's insistence on Christian transcendence.

The alchemy works show Jung attempting to exceed the limitations of the culture/nature metaphysic while still, to a certain extent, reliant upon its "ground" in the basic adherence to a subject/object distinction as Robert Romanyshyn[7] has pointed out and Wolfgang Giegerich.[8] However, the rest of this article is going to argue that Jung *as a writer* went further than Jung as a psychologist in making an eco-logic. That at the level of *writing*, Jung's own art, he surmounts the limitations of what Giegerich calls his "atomized" modern version of myth as the story of the alienated modern subject.[9]

As a writer, Jung is a more radical architect of consciousness than he is as a psychologist. This is not surprising if we refer back to the initial Jung quotation where he argues that conceptual or theoretical thinking is limited when it comes to the wilderness of the psyche. It is a vital argument made *vital, embodied* in the art of metaphor. As a writer, Jung provides space to do what for him myth always does: connect the ego to the other, the individual to the collective, the human to the cosmos. Jung's writing acts out eco-logic as myth. He does this by drawing freely upon the triple forms that nature wears in our times: as totality, metaphysics, aesthetics. David L. Miller has examined the contemporary persistence of the trinity in *Three Faces of God*.[10] I would like to suggest that nature's triple ontology could be included in Miller's fascinating tracing of trinity through modernity to Christianity, and significantly back to ancient theologies. It is therefore unsurprising to discover in Soper's triune "nature" an echo of the three-formed goddess of nature herself.

To turn to the matter of myth, Giegerich is surely correct to argue that myth in its historical incarnation has been written out of modernity's consciousness by the linear progression of history. In pre-historical times "[m]yth is immediately the truth of nature and life, it is nature's knowing."[11] Much later for the metaphysical man of pre-modernity, nature remained because God was its "ground."[12] Now in modern times of economic globalization, Giegerich says, man is no longer embedded in nature so myth is alienated, can become merely another aid to capitalist production: "[b]ut what it cannot be anymore is myth."[13]

This may work for Jung the psychologist. However Jung as a writer is a trickster with a profound historical sense attuned to what the linear account of modernity leaves out. At the level of theory he argues for a biological inheritance of meaning-producing organs, for archetypes. Whether or not this is regarded as scientifically valid, *as a writer*, Jung offers a plural notion of time and space, one in which consciousness is continually mythically re-made in the discourses of present and past symbolic forms. Essentially, I aim to show that Jung enacts history in his writing in a way that produces a new dialectical "ground" in Giegerich's terms, or myth, in my terms. *Jung as a writer counters the historical "progression" identified by Giegerich in favor of reinventing myth as eco-logic.* So let us turn to Jung's portrayal of "ground" as a bog in the second opening quotation. In order to find out what Jung meant by: "[b]ut which of us can pull himself out of the bog by his own pigtail?,"[14] we need to look at the mythic embroidering of "ground," the genealogy of this evocative term and its relation to comedy and tragedy.

GROUNDS FOR COMEDY AND TRAGEDY

The eco-critic Harold Fromm describes a characteristic modern reaction to his protest about the dire effects of air pollution. He received a letter of complaint containing the question: "[d]o we eliminate many of the necessities of life for the sake of clean air?"[15] He goes on to point out that such an attitude is so common because modern capitalist culture sees "necessities of life" as divorced from biological being.

> *Somehow*, she is alive: she eats food, drinks water, breathes air, but she does not see these actions as *grounds of life*; rather, they are acts that *coincide* with her life, her life being her thoughts and her wishes.[16]

Here, as Fromm shows, we have the environmental consequence of that characteristic of modernity, "the traditional mind-body problem, the view here being that man is his mind."[17] Such a denial of the necessity of the body is a denial of nature as necessity, of humans as embedded in nature, in at least a biological sense. The distinction between body and mind needs to be overcome by a new conjunctio because this distinction has calcified into a blind opposition of interests.

In addition to the body/mind distinction, itself an offshoot of nature/culture and frequently gendered, is the notion of "ground" as a foundation of argument. One of the most important ways of reconsidering such "ground" is Giegerich's re-reading of Hegel in *Dialectics and Analytical Psychology*.[18] Here is Giegerich's description of Hegel's dialectical ground:

> Hegel does not begin with opposites... and does not *look for a creative* solution of their conflict. Rather, the process of deepening thought discovers and reveals that the opposites had been united all along in common Ground...

> So the dialectical movement, instead of seeking a future solution, is a going under; it makes explicit the presuppositions that had unwittingly been behind and inherent in one's initial assumptions; it goes back and down to the deeper Ground that had been there all the time and had merely not been seen.[19]

What is fascinating about this description of dialectics is its anti-linearity, "instead of seeking a future solution," and shows that simple linear progression of thought belies a complex multi-directional movement dependent upon a notion of time and space: the "time" of thought with the positionality of "Ground" to be uncovered. It also portrays "ground" as something discovered rather than made. "Ground" is exterior to, yet integral to, the success of the argument. Such a depiction of "ground" is, on the one hand, common to the metaphysic culture/nature (and behind that to nature as created separately from divine logos). On the other hand, "ground" as integral *necessity* is suggestive of dialectics in the image of the trickster, who has a very different divine lineage as I shall show later. The fact that Giegerich explicitly disavows Jung's privileging of the image makes this dialectics all the more tricky.[20]

I would contrast this complex depiction with Giegerich's apparently more *pointed* portrayal of the evolution of consciousness in "Killings."[21]

> In the spear the male had his self (it was therefore not in himself!). Likewise the blood shed in the hunt was not merely the biological juice of life. Rather, the sacrificial animal's blood was collected by the women in a basket (in which they had *their* selves) and taken into their village, so that from it the inhabitants might "partake of the fullness of power, partake of the sacrificial gain..." *In the hunted or immolated animal man knows himself.*[22]

> Soul cannot be thought of in ontological terms. Soul is *logical* life, and as such is self generating... The soul first made itself through killing. *It killed itself into being.* That is why I consider sacrificial killing as primordial soul-making.[23]

If I describe this as a powerful argument, I mean not only is it persuasive in its logical exactness, but also that it is rhetorically impressive. The force of its language and syntax im-presses itself on the reader, much as the spear pierces the animal. The thrust allows the blood to animate the culture of the prehistoric village. No logical argument of philosophy, science, or history can shake off the rhetorical and creative resources of language, just as initiating human culture required aid from the "basket" of the women as well as the spears of the men. So if killing was the first act of soul-making, does that suggest that the female psyche took on a different relation to consciousness from Giegerich's point of view? What does it mean if man has his self in a spear and woman hers in a basket?

Giegerich's cultural arguments all rest on the assumption that the dominant will always subsume the marginal, that the spear-self will incorporate the basket-self to the extent that the basket will not trouble the essential *thrust* of human consciousness as spear dominated. Such a structure inhabits his argument that nature is elided in modern techno-capitalism: historic remnants of nature and its culture of myth are merely sentimental pretenses within the discourse of modernity. Nature and myth are left behind in the face of the forward thrust of technology allied to money.

This is, of course, a privileging of a one-ness of vision against the many-ness of competing discourses that is explicitly, and indeed is acknowledged to be, monotheistic. For Giegerich, the only myth in modernity is the survival of Christian narrative in technology as the incarnated modern soul. Our hope for psychological health (and the only possibility of the pluralism of the many) rests in the proper embrace of the modern soul's technological nature. Such a union would provide a viable relation to the technological "other" as animism.

Jung is more fundamentally disturbed by the pull between the oneness of his Christian monotheistic European heritage and the many-ness of his psychic nature. Here we might look back at the opening quotation where "killing" is indeed an act of generating consciousness and a sacrifice—but Jung is preoccupied with the *loss* of the other, wanting a soul's logic that does not divorce itself from "hanging together." But before looking at these large mythical structures in Jung's writing, I want to examine a very similar interpretation of psychic history to "Killings," written before it and, one might say, from the point of view of the basket carriers.

Ursula K. Le Guin writes of the origins of human culture (product of consciousness) in the spear and the basket in "The Carrier Bag Theory of Fiction."[24] Where Giegerich concentrates on the origins of culture in the soul's generation of itself, Le Guin sees hunting as the begetter of cultural forms, of storytelling. Like Giegerich, she concedes that storytelling, depending upon suspense and its resolution, will privilege the spear thruster over the basket carrier.

> It is hard to tell a really gripping tale of how I wrested a wild-oat seed from its husk, and then another, and then another, and then another, and then I scratched my gnat bites, and Ool said something funny, and we went to the creek and got a drink...
>
> No, it does not compare, it cannot compete with how I thrust my spear deep into the titanic hairy flank while Oob, impaled on one huge sweeping tusk, writher screaming, and blood spouted everywhere in crimson torrents, and Boob was crushed to jelly when the mammoth fell on him as I shot my unerring arrow straight through eye to brain.
>
> That story not only has Action, it has a Hero. Heroes are powerful. Before you know it, the men and women in the wild-oat patch and their kids... and the songs of the singers are all part of it, have all been pressed into service in the tale of the Hero. But it isn't their story. It's his.[25]

In these two similar legends of the origins of culture, Le Guin's difference from Giegerich is in the last two sentences: "[b]ut it isn't their story. It's his."[26] Giegerich asserts that "killing" became the paradigm of consciousness, the self-generation of the soul in forming the relation to the other *for the whole community*. He sees culture and history based on a dominant "logic," as essentially *unified* or monotheistic. Le Guin produces a tale of the origin of cultural *difference*, highly likely to be gendered. She sees culture as based on a split between hunters and community in which some are positioned as "other." But what if the basket carriers have a cultural form of their own? Prehistory is *dominated*, true, by the genesis of the Hero through killings, yet surely the culture of the spear itself has a prehistory? The earliest archaeological artifacts may be spears, but that does not mean that they were the first cultural objects.

> So you get up and go to the dammed soggy oat patch in the rain, and wouldn't it be a good thing if you had something to put baby Oo Oo in so that you could pick the oats with both hands? A leaf a gourd a shell a net a bag a sling a sack a bottle a pot a box a container. A holder. A recipient.[27]

I have quoted extensively from Le Guin because what is crucial to her argument about the generation of cultural forms as *two*, dominant and marginal, is its embodiment in a *variety* of writing styles. By placing domestic comedy alongside the heroic rhetoric of the spear thruster and the logic of the polemicist, her essay enacts its theme of culture as plural *at the roots*. Where Giegerich enlists forceful rhetorical devices to carry his message of the monotheistic thrust of early man's soul, Le Guin reminds us of language's multifarious capacities. So she traces the legacy of hero culture through hunting, to making epic myths, and finally to their later incarnation in the genre of tragedy. The descent of the basket, on the other hand, with its repetition and deflation of heroic pretence to transcend human limits, produces the literature of comedy, and ultimately the novel. For while novels may have heroes, the form itself forces those inflated egos into a *relationship* with another: "[a] n novel is a medicine bundle, holding things in a particular, powerful relation to one another and to us."[28]

Meanwhile, if the novel inherits the culture of the basket, the dominant science and technology of modernity (or perhaps science and technology *as* dominant) takes the shape of the tragic myth of the Hero. For to found those enterprises upon a promise of capitalist success, "is a heroic undertaking, Herculean, Promethean, conceived as triumph, hence ultimately as tragedy."[29] The narrative end of tragedy is, of course, death, not only for the hero, but also for his world.

Giegerich believes that the only hope for this situation is the fulfilment of the Christian promise of the transcendence of nature in an animated resurrection of the soul in technology. Le Guin, on the other hand, wants conjunction between dominant and marginalized. She sees hope in plurality where Giegerich puts faith in the quest for oneness.

Le Guin sees a possible conjunctio between the tragedy of science and the comic plurality of the novel in the hybrid form, science-fiction, as the attempt to compose or rediscover "other" mythical narratives for modernity. My argument is that Jung's writing constitutes just such a speculative series of experiments in aesthetic-scientific form. It is science as art. I will return directly to his writing by way of the large mythical structures encompassing the topos "nature" and ecocriticism's revaluation of them. I will also argue that the marginalized cultural forms connecting humans to nature have re-surfaced in surprising new "ground:" poststructuralism. First of all, more on comedy and its embrace of nature.

Framing Nature in Comedy, Myth, and Theory

The ecocritic Joseph W. Meeker points out that whereas types of tragedy are culturally specific and far from universal, comic forms are to be found everywhere and throughout the history of human groups.[30] Comedy celebrates the ignoble and the foolish. Comedy laughs at the fine ideals that lead the tragic hero into "his" supreme sacrifice. It privileges survival and sex. So it is therefore arguable that comedy is closer to our blind biological drives than tragedy's indifference to bodily limits. In comedy's opposition to transcendence can be traced an eco-logic. It is ecology critical of the heroic and tragic fantasy of elevating mind so far "above" body as to divorce humanity from nature and necessity.

So if comedy has a biological root, does that mean that we can "frame" nature as comic? Meeker draws on recent discoveries of the incredible complexity and inter-connectedness of natural systems. Nature works by adaptation and accommodation to changing circumstances, key principles of the comic domain. Moreover, nature seems most dedicated to fostering the continuance of life, like the generative instincts of comedy.

> Tragedy demands that choices be made among alternatives; comedy assumes that all choice is likely to be in error and that survival depends upon finding accommodations that will permit all parties to endure. Evolution itself is a gigantic comic drama, not the blood tragic spectacle imagined by the sentimental humanists of early Darwinism.[31]

So we have the long cultural history of the basket giving birth to comedy and the novel. It offers a framing of humans and nature as participants in a comic and cosmic drama. Together humans and nature meet in a dialogue of many voices and interests that have to learn to accommodate one another in *relationship*, not by separating off into a hierarchy of (tragic) transcendence.

It is worth at this point recalling the two great creation myths that each sponsor these varying relations to nature. Whereas Christian transcendence is built upon a sky father myth where the divine is separate from the matter of *his* creation, immanence and animism is owed to an earth mother. For *her*, matter and Earth are sacred and consciousness relies upon connection to the sacred other. In these two myths we have the structuring of oneness (of a transcendent divine) versus the sacred as immanent in nature and so presented as its *plural* voices, as animism. My argument is that Jung and Giegerich have different relationships to the intertwining of these foundational myths: in the difference lies Jung's "nature writing."

An eco-logic for humans and nature requires a balancing of these two mythical, metaphysical structurings of consciousness. The ecological disaster that is western modernity results from the over-valuing of sky father transcendence as the privileging of rationality, discrimination, and separation over connection and relating. The result is that consciousness is dominated by patriarchy, devaluing the other, and its exploitation as feminine, body and nature.

Crucially, this is an argument about dominant versus marginal forms, and ultimately about oneness in tension with plurality, *as mutually constructing and limiting entities.* For Christianity itself is not simply a manifestation of a sky father myth. Rather Christianity must be thought of as a *location* made up of narratives that only has as its *dominant* such an understanding of the divine, and hence has sponsored a human subject as Man, in the image of God as "above" and in charge of nature. Yet within the Christian stories of the sacred garden, the serpent (an ancient goddess image), the iconic picture of the Virgin Mother embracing her divine son, can be found survivals of a sacred feminine Earth.

For the goddess myth of consciousness is of a divine eros, the sexual union of the sacred mother with her son-lover, his death and rebirth. Earth mother consciousness unites sexuality and the sacred. It does not devalue the body, for matter is mater, the sacred origin of all life. The Western world has privileged sky father culture (transcendence of body, separation from messy "feminine" matter of material nature) over earth mother relating, to its own detriment. Such privileging is manifest not only in patriarchy and colonialism, but also in the rationalizing of knowledge and its divorce from matter and irrationality.

For this last issue we need to consider how far modernity's attitudes to knowledge are dependent upon medieval theologians attitudes to

God. Since God is separate from his creation, nature became a secondary product, worthy of study in order to know the mind of its creator. So knowledge was regarded as abstractable and inherently separable from its ostensible "ground." God the creator *made ground as something apart from himself to walk upon*. Eventually the "logos," the abstract knowledge of the natural world, ceased to be identified primarily with the mind of God and became the dominant (and privileged) mode of knowledge as science. It soon produced its own resurrected form of the logos as modern technology, as Giegerich has argued.[32]

We need to look at this eclipse of nature by considering the issue of language again. One of the most pervasive and persistent modes of the metaphysical binary of nature/culture is the belief that language is purely cultural and, indeed, may be the cultural phenomena that divorces us from nature. The most conventional understanding of this tenet is the Lacanian view that the entry into language splits the subject, severing the ego in its very formation from the "nature" and "body" of the mother (another agon of the sky father/earth mother myths entwining to produce modern consciousness).

Eco-critic Christopher Manes points out that when theology separated God from his creation, the cultural practice of animism did not die.[33] Rather it shifted location from nature to texts. Once nature spoke to us, now texts do in "the book says..." etc. Moreover, medieval theologians began to decode the bible for the abstract logos or truth of God, just as they treated nature as a great book "speaking" of divine creation: animism not only shifted from nature to books, but returned to "frame" nature *as* a book. Exegesis was the practice of reading "behind" the surface matter of the biblical text to produce a moral, holy, and rational logos. As Manes describes, here we witness the sky father origin of reason and its elevation.

> Exegesis established God as a transcendental subject speaking through natural entities, which, like words on a page, had a symbolic meaning, but no autonomous voice. It distilled the veneration of word and reason into a discourse that we still speak today.[34]

The separation of nature and the divine is the root of the metaphysical binary of nature and culture, and so also of nature and human language. The Lacanian model of the human subject offers a particularly potent example where language is solely the gift of culture dependent upon suppression of the bond to mother (nature).

From two directions it is possible to argue for a counter to such a "metaphysical" notion of language. Poet and eco-critic Gary Snyder regards language as a dialogue of nature and culture. Language begins as part of our biological being. Since humans are born so helpless, the instinct for language and communication is a necessary part of survival *as connection to* human communities. Language then becomes culture as it is developed in the vitality of social being.

> The grammar not only of language, but of culture and civilization itself, comes from this vast mother of ours, nature...
> Language is basically biological; it becomes semicultural as it is learned and practiced...
> Good writing is 'wild' language.[35]

Secondly, Jung can offer a challenge to language as pure culture, as metaphysically determined. In this Jung provides a vital countering to sky father mythmaking as the dominant structure of subjectivity. Since for Jung, the unconscious is pro-active and creative in making the infant self, and subjectivity needs relationship *as well as* separation from the unconscious other, language and culture similarly require connection as well as separation. Indeed, Jung's well-known privileging of image over words is not, I would argue, a necessary devaluing of *language*. It is more true to say that Jung sees image as the language of the other, a language connecting us to nature and the body. What is archetypally and psychically manifest as image has its bodily root in instinct.

Now I want to explore a third way of rethinking language and nature. It is also a third way of rethinking the human subject into the realm of animism: for if our language is liminal to nature, then nature is articulate and we are part of it.

Manes's point about the shift of animism to texts needs to be expanded upon in an era of poststructuralism. Manes shows how theological reading practices produced, in the construction of the Christian logos as coherent and rational, the oneness of transcendent monotheism from the multiple matter of biblical texts. Poststructuralism, on the other hand, reads texts *for* their multiplicity, for their many discordant voices. It *emphasizes* plurality and diversity. In arguing that meaning is always unstable, that signifiers slip away from their signifieds, poststructuralism is an animistic vision of cultural production. Which brings us to the notion of "ground." For poststructuralism, as Paul Kugler has explained previously, there are *no grounds* as in solid foundations, for an argument, a truth, a philosophy, a knowledge. There are no grounds because there is no external foundation to the system of (unstable) language producing the argument. A "ground" is a metaphysical "other," as Derrida has it, and there is no "outside" text (a better translation of Derrida's "there is nothing outside the text").[36]

Derrida and poststructuralism provide this elimination of "ground" as a philosophical argument. Taking the point that everything is "situated" within the cultural system, and hence cannot control, stabilize, or transcend it, what does this look like from the point of view of eco-logic and myth? The notion of external "ground" to an argument, an idea, a philosophy, is an expression of the transcendent sky father model of knowledge. "Ground," earth, foundation, is the externalizing of matter, mater, mother, and erotic relating in the construction of a logos, whether it be the mind of God or another form of transcendent knowledge. This use of "ground" is the philosophical counterpart to the cultural assumption of nature as a resource, to the body as that which accompanies, frames, and makes possible life, but is somehow not an integral part of it. Indeed, "ground" *grounds* argument because it is not caught up in it.

So there is something very interesting in poststructuralism because it constitutes a fundamental shift of myth. Such a change in the relation of the creation myths can be profoundly eco-logical if it can allow a move away from the metaphysical notion of language as part of a nature/culture binary opposition. If the notion of philosophical ground is sky father othering of nature, then the elimination of "ground" as "outside" and the recognition that we are always caught up in language is a shift to the ontological perspective of the earth-mother. Poststructualism is linguistic animism in the many voices of texts. Its energy drives ever further into pluralism and diversity and away from a monotheistic oneness of meaning. It is earth-mother animism if we follow through the discarding of metaphysical binaries and regard humans as creatures made of the shifting discourses of a culture profoundly imbued with nature. Poststructuralism is animism where nature itself has become cultural, both by material interventions into it and by the fact that our only relation to it is one of our cultural framings of it—two sides of the same inseparable nature-culture phenomena. Alternatively, poststructuralism is where culture has become attuned to the many, non-rational voices of nature. So the poststructuralist human is animated by culture-nature's discourses. We are voices in a cultural system embedded in the ecosystem as an animistic plural whole. Recognizing poststructuralist animism might enable us to pay more attention to the other (nature) that can never be regarded as truly, absolutely "other" ever again.

So I am arguing that the animism that Giegerich calls for in technology, as the summation of monotheistic sky father myth, is already present, sponsored by earth mother in poststructuralist theory and those writings that prefigure it. Unsurprisingly, given the affinity of poststructuralist animism for aesthetics, the lesser cultural domain of art, on the *margins* of culture, harbors this prefiguring of the return of sacred nature animism. Art is animistic where it celebrates plurality of voices in a mutually sustaining web that is part of the ecologic of comedy.

Jung's writing is its own invocation to the arts—specifically, the arts of the two creation myths. It is time to think again of Jung's writing as eco-logic.

The Eco-Logic Myth in Jung as a Writer

Jung is a critic of modernity who recognizes that the characteristic of marginalizing the other is at the expense of relating to it. The consequence is neurosis in both personal and collective spheres. The over-valuing of sky father separation as rationality threatens consciousness itself with a demonic return of the other, blackened by its repression. So despite a bias towards retaining masculine symbolism as dominant, Jung's writing constitutes a major attempt at re-balancing the great creation myths of human consciousness. Like all great aesthetic writers, Jung's drive to redeem the modern soul occurs on a number of levels.

For instance, the goddess returns in three guises, somewhat related to Soper's three frames for nature. "She" appears as a figure for relating and connecting in Eros, enacting a dual relation with her "opposite"

Logos, in the metaphysical binary use of "nature." Here the goddess rests at the heart of Jung's wish to preserve a structuralist binary metaphysic with his delight in organizing the concepts of his psychology in oppositional pairs.

Yet, secondly, as trickster image and myth, the goddess displays something of her mutability, and her "nature" as matter, body, and generation prior to sexual divisions.

> Even [the trickster's] sex is optional despite its phallic qualities: he can turn himself into a woman and bear children… This is a reference to his original nature as a Creator, for the world is made from the body of a god.[37]

Introducing the earth mother goddess in the form of the trickster image is a true moment of trickery for Jung. "He" is described in his narrative mythical mode largely as the figure whose tricks and stories are the aesthetic framing of nature *inside and outside* culture. No surprise that the trickster is the form of the goddess as the architect of poststructuralism. Where Jung becomes trickster himself, as a writer, is in negotiating the trickster between image and narrative.

Jung explores the psychic constitution of time and space as his writing re-negotiates connections between image and its framing narrative. Psychic images such as the trickster need narratives to *signify*. Narratives, whether drawn from folktales like the trickster, ancient mythology, or contemporary discourses, must incarnate in images in order to *matter*. The signifying of psychic matter in the liminal dance of image and narrative is Jung's re-formation of myth for the contemporary psyche. Jung's myth is of the trickster writer whose arts summon earth mother and sky father into mutual fusion, con-fusion, and the rewards of the conjunctio. The matter of the psyche (earth mother) *matters* when it is drawn into the signifying practices of the discriminatory, sifting powers of sky father consciousness. In turn, knowledge has body and soul when its propensity to transcendence has a connection to immanence and the earth mother vision of psyche as a web linked to earth and the sacred.

A third example of Jung's invocation to the goddess as nature is his most overt attempt to reconcile science and aesthetics in synchronicity.

> [Experiment] makes conditions, imposes them on Nature, and
> in this way forces her to give an answer to a question devised by
> man. She is prevented from answering out of the fullness of her
> possibilities.[38]

In the notion of "synchronicity" Jung evokes the nature of "totality;"
the laws that govern the universe and subsume humanity into nature
as one. Synchronicity seeks meaningful connections between
phenomena involving the psyche beyond usual casual mechanisms. It
is therefore the attempt to read reality aesthetically. Suggestively, the
essays on synchronicity try to find a rational and scientific language
for this eros Earth mother (nature as "her" "Nature" goddess) activity.

So we have an eco-logic in Jungian content in Eros, trickster, and
synchronicity. We also have eco-logic in a dialogue of literary style in
which image and narrative mutually make and unmake their
significance. The eco-logic content is bodied in the dialogical writing.
Such writing, I argue, is *eco-logic myth* for today. It is myth because it
draws together the heritage both of sky father and earth mother
signifying in consciousness. As myth, it is woven from narrative and
image, logic and rhetoric, scientific argument and poetic embodiment
in language, the linear understanding of reading as time oriented and
the spatial understanding of reading as image oriented. Moreover it is
myth not only to show the fundamental impossibility of completely
divorcing these two creation myths and their lineage, but also because
Jung's writing places special emphasis on historical incarnation. It is
time to look at Jung's writing as a special form of *psychic history*.

JUNG'S NATURE WRITING AND HISTORY

Jung as a writer generates a special perspective on history, which
can best be understood by comparing it to M. M. Bakhtin's ideas of
dialogics, chronotopes, and the historical novel.[39] Bakhtin very starkly
portrays the tension in modernity between the oneness of monotheism
and the plurality of animism, and seeks its rebalance (of creation myths)
by his notion of dialogics. Here language in social use is a dynamic
interaction between two polarities. A centripetal drive to centralize
power and meaning is always *in dialogue with,* and so structured by,
an opposing centrifugal impulse to pluralize and disperse meaning
and power in the singularities of social intercourse.

Such a vivid portrayal of the tensions between father-god transcendence (of social diversity) and oneness versus Earth-Mother immanence and plurality, not only finds a psychological counterpart in Jung's notion of the centralizing power of archetypes, only ever representable *dialogically* by reaction to the specifics of personal history in archetypal images, it is also powerfully articulate in the *matter* of his writing. Jung is a dialogical psychologist *and* a dialogical writer— between creation myths.

For Bakhtin, the novel is the literary form where the essential dialogical nature of language in social use is most visible. For the novel exploits the diversity of social speech rather than tries to close it down. Bakhtin also thought that language dialogics was built upon more basic structures in culture called "chronotopes." These are unities of time and space such as the "meeting" or phrases such as "the path of life." Language and bodily experience are ultimately chronotopic: culture is the dialogically interwoven fabric of many chronotopic forms. Even history makes sense only as a chronotope, as events in time can only be comprehended via their enactment in defined space.

However, the problem with history for Bakhtin is that as it is generally understood, it is too abstract for full chronotopic realization in consciousness: the time periods are too lengthy for their spatial realization. Hence the more valuable cultural form (to Bakhtin) of the historical novel. For the novel is the most truly dialogical work of art. In its openness to linguistic plurality, it brings the reader into its dialogical processes. *The novel re-makes consciousness* in the chronotopic form of reading: uniting the time of the activity with spatial psychic images. So the historical novel *redeems history* by reconciling the time of an individual consciousness with the historical time that transcends an individual lifespan.

Jung is fundamentally a dialogical writer. Not only does the concept of archetypes work dialogically, he also develops a dialogical relationship between images and narrative. Indeed, Jung's writing is a trickster dialogics of sky father and earth mother forms of representation. And he is a *trickster* writer because he re-frames "history" as modernity's re-formation of the cultural role of the trickster myth. Modernity suffers from its over-separating capacity. Where, in an-other culture the trickster holds up a mirror to social weakness, we have de-natured the myth by turning it into a narrative that can be abstracted from psychic potency. Yes, "history" as a phenomena does have the capacity to "teach" moral values, but it no longer embodies and enacts them for us. Modernity's history is the result of relative separation of myth into components of a time-oriented narrative of events and a space-oriented embodiment in a "personal" shadow image.

Jung explores this problem in the essay, "On the Psychology of the Trickster Figure."[40] In *Aion*, Jung enacts the solution.[41] For this volume of the *Collected Works* is dedicated to re-imagining history as a mode of ethical psychic energy, as myth. The way to make history once more a genre of the psyche is through creating archetypal patterns as chronotopes, forms of time-space, and making them dialogically inter-generating. By putting cultural symbolism in the frame of archetypal matrices, Jung identifies consciousness as structured through a dynamic dialogue of space (image) and time (narrative) symbolism. So the large cultural patterns, such as the alchemical, temporary holding together of sky father and earth mother notions of nature in pre-modern science, provide frameworks for historical events to become imbued with ethical relating because consciousness enters a dialogue of separation from, and relating to, them.

Aion, in particular, is a map of the European self. It is a form by which consciousness reaches back into its past through the inter-animated, co-created symbolism that generates modern materialistic science from Gnostic roots. *Aion* does not describe a history of consciousness because that would be a sky-father-dominated history in which the necessary "separating" quality of consciousness (without which consciousness could not be structured), had hardened into "separating off" and marginalizing earth mother consciousness (connection and embodiment mostly harbored by aesthetics in modernity). Rather *Aion* creates history as consciousness re-made ethically through the act of writing and/or reading. History is re-imaged, re-imagined as the spatial and temporal expanses of being. Consciousness is imaged in discourses that work dialogically with each other and with the psyche.

In this way, Jung's writing is myth. It is myth in a dialogic frame between oneness (in his writing as coherent, as offering a recognizable comprehensible psychology) and many-ness (in the plurality of its structuring forms and images, in its commitment to social and historical embodiment). *Jung's writing is myth because of its dialogical attempt to re-balance modern consciousness.* One incarnation of this radical attempt to re-balance sky father and earth mother resources by writing myth is its dialogical embrace of comedy and tragedy as mutually constituting polarities in cultural production. I am stressing the comic in Jung's writing because dialogics is fundamentally comical in its commitment to on-going survival, to dialogue never ending, however much deflation of transcendent, tragic ideas is required. Dialogics does not choose. It is a method of mutual evolution and change. So, when Jung says, "[b]ut which of us can pull himself out of the bog by his own pigtail?," this comic use of the vernacular counters modernity's tragic vision with an eco-logic comic recognition of necessity and independence.[42]

We do have to leave the "bog" of our mother's womb (as nature and body). Sky father separation is necessary for humanity to assume consciousness, the consciousness of being human. But a comic countering of over-inflation preserves a necessary sense of ourselves as the product of bogs as well as of the leaving of them. Jung's nature writing is a conjuring of animism's many voices in the living habitat of the psyche. Let us regard it as an invitation to re-join the comedy of nature's on-going creation.

NOTES

1. C. G. Jung, *Collected Works of C. G. Jung* (Princeton: Princeton University Press, 1960), Vol. 8, para. 356 [the *Collected Works* are hereinafter referenced as "*CW*," followed by the volume number and the paragraph number].

2. Jung, *CW* 9ii § 221.

3. President George W. Bush speaking at a news conference shortly after Hurricane Katrina devastated New Orleans in September 2005.

4. Kate Soper, "The Idea of Nature," in L. Coupe (ed.), *The Green Studies Reader: From Romanticism to Ecocriticism* (London and New York: Routledge, 2000), 123-6.

5. Jung, *CW* 8 § 356.

6. Paul Kugler, *Raids on the Unthinkable: Freudian and Jungian Psychoanalyses* (New Orleans: Spring Journal Books, 2005), 36.

7. Robert Romanyshyn, "Alchemy and the Subtle Body of Metaphor," in R. Brooke (ed.), *Pathways into the Jungian World: Phenomenology and Analytical Psychology* (London and New York: Routledge, 2000), 27-45.

8. Wolfgang Giegerich, *The Soul's Logical Life: Towards a Rigorous Notion of Psychology*, 3rd revised edition (Frankfurt: Peter Lang, 2001).

9. Wolfgang Giegerich, "The Flight into the Unconscious: A Psychological Analysis of C. G. Jung's Psychology Project," *www.rubedo.psc.br/artingle/flight* accessed 22/09/2005.

10. David L. Miller, *Three Faces of God: Traces of the Trinity in Literature and Life* (New Orleans: Spring Journal Books, 2005).

11. Wolfgang Giegerich, in Wolfgang Giegerich, David L. Miller and Greg Mogenson, *Dialectics & Analytical Psychology: The El Capitan Canyon Seminar* (New Orleans: Spring Journal Books, 2005), 50.

12. *Ibid.*, 58.

13. *Ibid.*, 59.

14. Jung, *CW* 9ii § 221.

15. Harold Fromm, "From Transcendence to Obsolescence: A Route Map," in C. Glotfelty and H. Fromm (eds.), *The Ecocriticism Reader: Landmarks in Literary Ecology* (Athens and London: The University of Georgia Press, 1996), 30-39.

16. *Ibid.*, 37.

17. *Ibid.*, 38.

18. Giegerich, Miller, and Mogenson, *Dialectics & Analytical Psychology*, 50.

19. *Ibid.*, 5.

20. Giegerich, *Soul's Logical Life*, 143.

21. Wolfgang Giegerich, "Killings," *Spring: A Journal of Archetype and Culture, Vol. 54*, 1993, 5-18.

22. *Ibid.*, 9.

23. *Ibid.*, 12.

24. Ursula K. Le Guin, "The Carrier Bag Theory of Fiction," in Glotfelty and Fromm, *Ecocriticism Reader*, 149-54.

25. *Ibid.*, 149-50.

26. *Ibid.*, 150.

27. *Ibid.*, 150.

28. *Ibid.*, 153.

29. *Ibid.*, 153.

30. Joseph W. Meeker, "The Comic Mode," in Glotfelty and Fromm, *Ecocriticism Reader*, 155-69.

31. *Ibid.*, 164.

32. Giegerich, *Soul's Logical Life*, 28.

33. Christopher Manes, "Nature and Silence," in Glotfelty and Fromm, *Ecocriticism Reader,* 15-29.

34. *Ibid.*, 20.

35. Gary Snyder, "Language Goes Two Ways," in L. Coupe (ed.) *Green Studies Reader*, 127-31, 129-30.

36. See Niall Lucy, 'inside-outside,' *A Derrida Dictionary* (Oxford: Blackwell, 2004), 52-6.

37. Jung, *CW* 9i § 472.

38. Jung, *CW* 8 § 864.

39. M. M. Bakhtin, *The Dialogic Imagination: Four Essays*, ed. M. Holquist, trans. C. Emerson and M. Holquist (Austin: University of Texas Press, 1981).

40. Jung, *CW* 9i § 456-88.

41. Jung, *CW* 9ii.

42. Jung, *CW* 9ii § 221.

JUNGIANA

NEWS FROM THE PHILEMON FOUNDATION

STEPHEN A. MARTIN

On the weekend of May 27 and 28, the Philemon Foundation hosted its inaugural donors' seminar on Jung History at the prestigious Georgian rooms of the Royal Society of Medicine, Chandos House, in central London. Thirty-four attended, mainly from the United States and the United Kingdom, and were treated to an unprecedented glimpse into the exciting, if not astounding, projects underway through the auspices of the Philemon Foundation.

Saturday, May 27, began at the civilized hour of 10 AM with coffee and tea and conversation as those assembled met each other. When the seminar formally started, Dr. Stephen Martin, the President of the

Stephen A. Martin, Psy.D., is president and co-founder with Dr. Sonu Shamdasani of the Philemon Foundation. A graduate of the C. G. Jung Institute in Zürich, he is former Editor-in-Chief of *Quadrant: The Journal of Contemporary Jungian Thought*, and former president and founding member of The Philadelphia Association of Jungian Analysts.

Editor's Note: The mission of the Philemon Foundation is to prepare for publication the unpublished works of C. G. Jung that number in the tens of thousands of pages of seminars, manuscripts, books, and correspondences. Having nonprofit status allows the Philemon Foundation to invite tax-deductible support to accomplish this great work. For further information, please visit the Philemon web site at www.philemonfoundation.org or contact Dr. Martin at smartin@philemonfoundation.org.

Philemon Foundation, opened with story of the Foundation's birth and the evolution of its purpose and commitment to Jung's work, imparting to all present the sense of immensity and awe that he first felt when he learned of the scope of C. G. Jung's unpublished material: the tens of thousands of pages of seminars, manuscripts, and letters. One seminar member, a senior Jungian analyst from New York who was visibly moved, said out loud, "this is a virtual Tsunami of Jung," a sentiment echoed by others around the seminar table.

Dr. Martin then introduced Dr. Sonu Shamdasani, General Editor of the Philemon Foundation and Philemon Reader of Jung History at University College London, who delivered a riveting exposition of a previously unknown book length text by Jung on alchemy dated 1937, and listed in the catalogue of the Jung Archives at the ETH in Zürich, the main repository of Jung's unpublished work, merely as *"unpubliziertes Buch"* (unpublished book!). Predating the 1944 publication of Jung's landmark *Psychologie und Alchemie*, this manuscript discusses many subjects including the problem of opposites as well as being, possibly, the first written record and psychological consideration of Jung's immensely influential, early life "phallus dream" known to us from *Memories, Dreams, Reflections*—which in this text he ascribed to someone else. We are delighted to report that this *"unpubliziertes Buch"* is among the first unpublished manuscripts to be transcribed using funds provided to the Philemon Foundation by The Andrew W. Mellon Foundation for this express purpose. In addition to the lively discussion that ensued with Dr. Shamdasani adding additional information about the unpublished Jung, a palpable sense of astonishment at what remains yet to know of Jung's work filled the room.

After a buffet lunch, the program recommenced with a presentation by Dr. Angela Graf-Nold, Research Collaborator at the Institute and Museum for Medicine and History at the University of Zürich, on the reconstruction of Jung's seminal *ETH Lectures of 1933-1941*. These lectures are at the center of Jung's intellectual activity in the 1930s and form a critical part of his work in the 1940s and 1950s. In what seemed like a unfolding mystery story worthy of a documentary film, Dr. Graf-Nold described to the seminar how she was reconstructing Jung's first volume on *The History of Psychology* from as many as five different verbatim transcripts some of which were recorded in an obsolete, nearly indecipherable German shorthand. Were it not for a retired transcriber in her late 70's with macular degeneration who works for the Philemon Foundation, the content of these documents would be lost for future study. From comparison with the various less complete notes and more complete transcriptions of Rivkah Schärf, one of Jung's most gifted students whose later work on Jewish themes, such as *Satan and the Old Testament,* have become classics in Jungian literature, and the extraordinarily complete transcript of Edward Sideler, an underemployed engineer in the public audience with no training or particular interest in psychology but who took it upon himself to record what appears to have been nearly every word of Jung's lectures over eight years (as well as Einstein's early lectures that form the basis of Einstein scholarship), Dr. Graf-Nold is constructing a document that will rival an audiotape of Jung's actual lectures. What struck the seminar was the enormous work that is required to produce a complete, scholarly manuscript, something akin to intellectual archaeology; discovering and rendering the transcription readable, reconstructing its background history, and finally collating this immense amount of data to bring into existence a document. The first publishable volume of an expected eight volumes of ETH lectures is projected for late 2007.

After a congenial intermission, Saturday's intellectual activity concluded with a presentation prompted by the forthcoming publication of the first Philemon Series volume, the correspondence between Jung and Victor White, by Dr. Adrian Cunningham, Emeritus Professor at the University of Lancaster. Dr. Cunningham is the literary executor of Father Victor White, one of Jung's closest friends in the latter portion of his life, and principal sounding board for theological issues, most notably the nature of evil. Dr. Cunningham fleshed out White's analysis with John Layard, the early compatibility of White's own work with Jung's, and the eventual conclusion of a friendship that foundered over irreconcilable differences over the nature of God and evil. What was particularly moving was Dr. Cunningham's willingness to circulate amongst the seminar participants actual letters from Jung in which he wrote about, among other issues, his deep sadness and compassion towards White. Handling these remarkable letters lent an emotional immediacy to this story of failed friendship between two great men.

The next event, an exquisite banquet at the fashionable Blandford Street Restaurant, just off Marylebone High Street convening at 8 PM, cemented the evolving sense of community that the Philemon Foundation hoped would occur when this donor seminar was planned. Between the delicious phases of this meal, accompanied by champagne and carefully chosen wines, many of the participants from the two long tables rose to give toasts: to the Philemon Foundation for beginning this important work, to the continued collaboration between it and the International Association of Jungian Analysts (IAAP), to the donors present who not only were generous but also wanted to be an active part of the experience of the Philemon Foundation, and to the continued financial health and success of our endeavor. Special mention was made of the presence of Carolyn Grant Fay, our founding patron, who at 92 would not have missed the festivities for anything. Needless to say, people lingered late into the night, delighting in the convivial atmosphere.

The seminar reconvened on Sunday morning around 10:30 with people greeting each other like friends after the previous evening's pleasures. At 11:00 Dr. Eugene Taylor, Philemon Foundation Board member and the William James Scholar at Saybrook Institute Graduate School, got the day off to a compelling start with "Philemon: A Prophesy." In this historically wide-ranging, erudite, and visionary presentation, Dr. Taylor resituated Jung in the context of 19th century psychologies of transcendence, debunking the perception that he was merely a student of psychoanalysis, elucidated Jung's early reception and important role in American psychology that predated any personal contact with Freud, and outlined his profound and continuing influence on the American psychotherapeutic counterculture. Dr. Taylor began wrapping up his presentation with thought-provoking reasons for supporting the Philemon Foundation's mission to provide "more Jung." Among them were that Jung's work aids in the recovery of the numinous in our inner lives; that Jung's work helps deepen the spiritual communication between men and women; and that Jung's work helps establish depth psychology as a bridge between science, the humanities, and the experience of transcendence. His concluding thought was that a map of world mythologies, depicting the inward iconography of each culture, might be useful in future discussions about world peace.

After a leisurely lunch break, the seminar concluded with a collaborative presentation about the newly completed English translation of Jung's famous *Children's Dream Seminar*. Participating were Dr. Ernst Falzeder, chief translator of the Seminar and eminent Freud scholar and translator, Dr. Angela Graf-Nold, and Dr. Stephen Martin. The *Children's Dream Seminar* elicited an intriguing discussion among the presenters and the participants where its many angles were examined and, at times, debated, including its text, translation, and structure, as well as its symbolic and clinical import and focus. It became abundantly clear that Jung, with this lengthy seminar of some 28 cases of childhood dreams remembered by adults, contrary to standard belief, paid considerable attention to the psychology of childhood. Moreover, as one seminar participant wrote: "These meetings give a fresh experience of Jung's verbal eloquence, his dexterity and scholarship, and his humor and warmth in a class room context" in contrast to his more scientific writing.

As presenters and participants took leave of each other for further travel, or drinks at a nearby pubs, there was a firm unanimity among all: there is a treasure trove of unpublished Jung very close at hand. By making ever more of it available as the Philemon Foundation is doing, our spiritual, professional, and emotional lives will be deepened and enriched.

FILM REVIEWS

When the Levees Broke: A Requiem in Four Acts. Directed by Spike Lee, HBO Docmumentary Films, 2006.

DAVID BARTON

A few days after the levees gave way in New Orleans, giving millions of television viewers images of the apocalypse, *New York Times* columnist David Brooks declared that Hurricane Katrina was an "anti-9/11" experience for the nation. September 11, after all, gave us a heroic cast—firefighters taking charge of a falling building, Rudolph Giuliani taking charge of a beleaguered city. The images coming out of New Orleans were of an entirely different character—they were, in Brooks' words, a "national humiliation" and "de-legitimizing" of government.[1] September 11, if we can think back to the mood of the nation in those days, filled the heartland with a sense of pride and determination; the flooding of New Orleans gave us images of social and cultural failure, and reminded us of years of bad planning and bad faith by the

David Barton teaches expository writing at Northern New Mexico College. He was founding editor of *The Salt Journal*, which is no longer published.

Editor's Note: *Spring Journal* is very pleased to announce that David Barton will be joining our staff as Contributing Editor and will serve as Co-Editor of our upcoming Politics issue (fall 2007).

government, which had been told the levees would probably fail if even a small hurricane hit New Orleans.

Spike Lee's HBO documentary of the New Orleans flood gives us the whole experience again, this time in the words of those who lived through the storm. Lee, who first saw images of the flood while at a film festival in Europe, spent a year living in The Big Easy, interviewing survivors, and collecting film footage of the flood. The result has been called Lee's best work as a filmmaker and a continuation of the themes of race, class, and gender so evident in *She's Gotta Have It*, *Do the Right Thing*, *Jungle Fever*, and *Malcolm X.*

There is probably a grain of truth in this perspective. Lee himself has said that he was outraged by the images of African Americans abandoned in New Orleans and the lack of an effective governmental response to the disaster. As a storyteller, however, Lee's edginess comes from telling stories that no one else will touch. Class and race may be important components of what happened in New Orleans but only because something deeper is at stake. *When the Levees Broke* is ultimately a story of loss, betrayal, abandonment; race is simply one element, a not-all-that-convincing explanation for the lack of interest in saving the 35th largest metropolitan area in the country.

To see New Orleans as an image of abandonment recalls that other American catastrophe, the one that took place in New York City. In New York City, President Bush visited Ground Zero himself on the Friday after the collapse of the Twin Towers, grabbing a bullhorn to cheer rescue workers. "I can hear you," press reports quoted the president as saying. "The rest of the world can hear you. And the people who knocked down these buildings will hear all of us soon." In New Orleans, the president observed the scene from Air Force One. His mother, touring a stadium where refugees from the hurricane were sleeping on cots, seemed to give voice to the kind of thoughtless flippancy one suspects in politicians who are more careful not to verbalize their inner feelings. "So many of the people here," said the president's mother in a moment caught on tape, "were underprivileged anyway. This is working out quite well for them."

September 11, of course, is the 600-pound gorilla of symbolic events. It's become a cliché to refer to the destruction of the World Trade Center as a turning point in American history; people speak regularly of the post-9/11 world, a phrase reflected in our governmental response: two wars, the redefining of presidential powers, military traditions, and national security. This seemingly heroic and muscular response is all the more odd when compared to the begrudging reaction to the flood in New Orleans. On the fourth day that 80 percent of the city was underwater, the director of FEMA, Michael Brown, said he hadn't been told that 50,000 people were trapped in the convention center without adequate food or water. The federal government didn't bring in troops until the city had been underwater for five days; one year after the disaster, whole neighborhoods (including much of the Ninth Ward) have yet to be emptied of debris, much less rebuilt.

These twin catastrophes—the flooding of New Orleans and the downing of the World Trade Center—seem to have a strangely complimentary relationship in the cultural imagination, as if each is a negative inversion of the other. Both events give voice to the fantasy that what used to be called the American way of life is under attack, by the "terrorist" who doesn't share our values and by Mother Nature. Both events also function as post-millennial images of a fall, amplifying fears of impotence and incompetence, of a haunting suspicion that social, technological, and environmental problems of our own making haunt the future. Seen in this light, the triumphalist response to September 11 and inaction in New Orleans point to the same deep cultural anxiety. Both events speak to a sense of abandonment and both our responses served, in part, to escape the inner terror we dare not face.

One difference between the two events is that the destruction of the Twin Towers allowed us to focus on an external enemy. Unfortunately, there are a limited number of enemies who can take responsibility for New Orleans: Mother Nature and the collective ineptitude of the local, state, and federal governments. Our inability to have a sustained interest in the rebuilding of New Orleans—which is probably the largest national disaster in the nation's history, dwarfing the collapse of the World Trade Center in complexity and social impact—probably lies in the fact that thinking about the causes of the flooding is highly unpleasant.

But as many have pointed out, 2005 was a banner year for Hurricanes and it's probably true that global warming, by increasing temperatures in the Atlantic Ocean, was at least partially responsible for the size and frequency of tropical storms that we can expect to become even bigger and more frequent in the future. As a city sitting below sea level, protected by man-made pumps and levees, New Orleans functions as a wonderfully apt symbol for our increasingly precarious relationship with nature.

As the documentary points out, however, it's not quite accurate to say Hurricane Katrina knocked out the levee system. The irony is that the Katrina missed New Orleans; the winds along Lake Pontchartrain, where the levees gave way, were no stronger than from a Category 2 hurricane. The city was not so much overwhelmed by nature as unprepared, despite the fact that FEMA had listed the breaching of the levees in New Orleans as one of three worst potential disasters facing the country (the others: a terrorist attack in New York City and a violent earthquake in San Francisco).

The inaction before the hurricane, then, functions as still another form of abandonment. Many who watch Lee's documentary will see the failure to build an adequate levee system as a much larger story, a parable for the 21st century. That New Orleans was destroyed not by a hurricane but by poorly designed levees makes the metaphor all the richer.

No wonder, then, that the images of New Orleans are a downer and no wonder that our newspapers and television news channels pay scant attention to the aftermath. Lee's documentary, however, is anything but depressing, in part because Lee tells the story in the language New Orleans loves. The sound track is full of Louis "Pops" Armstrong ("Do you Know What It Means to Miss New Orleans"), Fats Domino ("Walking New Orleans"), and original music from Terence Blanchard, a New Orleans-born trumpeter who also appears in the documentary, with his mother and grandmother, as they return to their flooded home. Lee's own father, Bill Lee, was a jazz bassist and composer, and Lee understands how images and interviews can form their own analog to New Orleans jazz. Its form is that of the jazz funeral, with the long, slow grief-stricken dirges on the way to the cemetery and the up-tempo celebration that takes over once a casket has been laid in the ground: a requiem with a New Orleans twist.

Watching the interviews and the footage from the flood reminds us that if New York City is the financial center of the nation, New Orleans is its sexy and debauched body. New Orleans means Preservation Hall and Mardi Gras; it's a city of exhibitionism, voyeurism, erotic possibilities. Those who were lucky enough to have been born in New Orleans understand something about life's pleasures that the rest of the country has forgotten. Andrei Codrescu, who lives in New Orleans (or did before the flood), was once asked by a reporter from *The Wall Street Journal* to explain why New Orleanians live, on average, almost ten years less than the average American; Codrescu responded by taking the reporter to his favorite bar, where they drank until 3 a.m. "Yes, it's true," Codrescu writes, "that we live statistically less than people who go to bed at a plain hour in the joyless working hells of virtuous towns, but we live experientially twice as long."[2] The association of New Orleans to booze, music, and sex is so powerful that its destruction was seen in biblical terms by fundamental Christians who imagined their Old Testament God had cleaned the streets.

Part of the epic nature of Lee's documentary, then, is the enormity of the loss for both those who live in New Orleans and for the country as a whole. As the mayor of New Orleans keeps repeating, we've never had 80 percent of a major American city sit underwater for weeks at a time. Katrina herself was only the third largest hurricane on record; the breaching of the levees, however, may well be seen by future generations as the greatest natural disaster in American history. More than one million people were evacuated from New Orleans; enough debris has been removed to equal 25 World Trade Center disasters. According to the national Hurricane Center, the flooding killed more than 1,800 people and caused an estimated $81 billion in property damage.[3]

If that does become the storyline that future historians repeat, they will wonder at our dawdling and at our inability to understand the epic story we find ourselves in at the dawn of the 21st century. Lee himself seems to understand the epic with great clarity. In the opening scene of his documentary, amidst the terrible beauty of the flood, the camera pans across a neighborhood that is quickly disappearing under a rush of rising water. We can see only a house or two and a green sign marking the intersection that reads "Humanity Street."

What happens to New Orleans, the image suggests, involves us all.

NOTES

1. "Politics after Katrina," *The NewsHour with Jim Lehrer,* analysis with David Brooks and Tom Oliphant, Public Broadcasting Service, 2 September 2005.

2. Andrei Codrescu, introduction, *Obituary Cocktail: The Great Saloons of New Orleans* by Kerri McCaffety (New Orleans: Pontalba, 1998), 15.

3. Richard D. Knabb, Jamie R. Rhome, and Daniel P. Brown, *Tropical Cyclone Report: Hurricane Katrina,* National Hurricane Center, 20 December 2005.

FILM REVIEWS

"Mutually Mutating:"
A Review of *Grizzly Man*

REVIEWED BY CATRIONA H. MILLER

Grizzly Man is a 2006 documentary directed by German film
maker Werner Herzog. It explores the life and death of Timothy
Treadwell, a self-proclaimed bear expert and eco-warrior who spent
thirteen summers living in Alaska, protecting the grizzly bears who
live there. In 2003, he and his girlfriend, Amie Huguenard, were killed
by one of the bears he sought to protect.

Treadwell is a captivating character, photogenic and extremely
engaging in his enthusiasm for his subject. In the monologues to his
own camera he appears uncensored, raging, crying, and delighting
with equal abandon, drawing the viewer into his world. He left behind
a treasure trove of video footage shot over his last five summers in
Alaska, which Herzog utilizes extensively in his documentary. As Erik
Nelson, the film's producer, put it,

Catriona H. Miller, Ph.D., teaches at Glasgow Caledonian University where her
research interests include the vampire myth in particular and the horror genre in general,
Jungian film studies, and the archetypal dimensions of science fiction and fantasy.

> Treadwell was basically recording everything that was happening
> to him. Inadvertently or purposely, he was filming this Joseph
> Conrad-like epic of an extraordinary thing and, amazingly,
> covered it all. And covered it very well, I might add. He always
> knew where the camera was pointing: he really worked hard at
> making a good movie.[1]

And the images *are* striking. Of course, there are many scenes of
the bears fishing, fighting, and playing, and there are also moving
sequences capturing foxes at play in Treadwell's campsite, but perhaps
the most dramatic element is the Alaskan landscape itself, backdrop
to all Treadwell's footage. Treadwell was a gifted cameraman as well as
an enthusiastic advocate for "his" bears.

However, there is no doubt that Treadwell sentimentalized
Nature—thanking the foxes for being his friend, moved to tears by
the sight of a dead bumble bee in a flower, and above all telling the
bears over and over how much he loves them (to the extent of
rhapsodizing about a recent bowel movement from one of his favorite
bears, Wendy, because it had come from within her body). "*Everything
about them is perfect,*" he says simply at one point.

Treadwell seemed to want something more from the natural world
than to be its advocate. In a letter, Treadwell spoke of his desire to
"*mutually mutate into a wild animal to handle the life I live out here.*"
One of his ecologist friends, Marnie Gaede, speaks in the film of
Treadwell's wish of "*connecting so deeply that you're no longer human.*"
Indeed, bear biologist, Larry Van Daele, also acknowledges the "*siren
song*" of the bears, as he calls it. "*There is that desire to get into their
world,*" he says, before adding, "*but the reality is we never can.*" Treadwell
did not seem to accept that point of view. He needed something more.
For some reason (and Herzog tries to explore the reasons), to Treadwell
the bears were far more than just animals.

The trouble is that Treadwell seems to have become fascinated
with what some might consider a typical Europagan archetypal image
of the bear. As Margaret Atwood aptly put it, the traditional European
attitude to animals in literature is that they are "Englishmen in furry
zippered suits, often with a layer of human clothing added on top."[2]
In this view, the bears are interpreted as somehow humans clothed in
animal skins.

Certainly the way Treadwell talks to and about the bears suggested that he anthropomorphized them to a high degree. He gave them names like Mr. Chocolate and Sergeant Brown, Wendy and Downy. In fact, one of the pilots, who was involved in clearing up the camp where Treadwell and Huguenard died, said: "*Treadwell was, I think, meaning well... but to me he was acting like he was working with people wearing bear costumes out there, instead of wild animals. Those bears are big and ferocious.*"

It is interesting that the film also makes a distinction between European attitudes to bears (and bear symbolism) and the Native American one. Pratt suggests that Native Americans do not make the mistake of thinking of bears as human, pointing out that to them the "bear is completely beyond human control and greatly feared."[3] And in the film Dr. Sven Haakanson of the Alutiiq makes the point that the Native Alaskans have always respected the line between human and bear. Treadwell did not do this and Haakanson says, "*For him to act like a bear the way he did would be the ultimate disrespecting [sic] the bear and what the bear represents.... If I look at it from my culture, Timothy Treadwell crossed a boundary that we've lived with for 7,000 years. It's an unspoken boundary, an unknown boundary, but when we know we've crossed it, we pay the price.*"

Treadwell is a sufficiently fascinating character to warrant extensive discussion in his own right, but it would be a mistake to forget this is a film by Werner Herzog, or to think that such a powerful character had no influence over the telling of this story especially as in this case Herzog is also the narrator.

Comments about Herzog and his work invariably portray him as

> an obsessed, half-crazed auteur willing to risk his life for a film. His protagonists—rebellious dreamers and heretics, fanatics and maniacs—serve as doubles for the independent film maker who seeks to realize his vision against all odds. All of his films explore and validate otherness.[4]

Herzog is certainly a film maker who deserves the term *auteur*, and it is imperative that his perspective on Treadwell is taken into account because in Tim Treadwell Herzog appears to have found an embodiment of his favorite obsessed character, a role once filled by his friend and perhaps arch-enemy, Klaus Kinski, a point noted by a number of reviewers. Phillip French, for instance, reviewer for the British *Sunday Observer* newspaper, notes that if Tim Treadwell had not existed,

> Herzog would surely have invented him, so close is he to the wild protagonists of his movies. With his rantings to camera, his crazy eyes and his long, lank flaxen hair, he's a dead ringer for the director's favorite actor, Klaus Kinski. He is indeed so weird that even Herzog notices it.[5]

While some of his contemporaries from the New German Cinema (such as Wim Wenders) seem to have been fascinated with urban landscapes, Herzog's interests have remained with Nature and "preoccupations with problems of progress, environmental destruction and apocalypse characterize his films."[6] *Aguirre, The Wrath of God* (1972) and *Fitzcarraldo* (1982) both cover this territory, albeit from a fictional perspective. However, the natural world which Herzog sees is very different from Treadwell's anthropomorphized Eden.

In fact, it would be fair to suggest that Herzog, who has spent his own time staring Nature in the face in the jungles of South America, utterly disagreed with Treadwell's view. To Treadwell the bear was an archetypal image of profound significance, and it seems to have been harder and harder for him to maintain emotional or physical distance between himself and the bears, but to Herzog the bear is just a bear. Towards the end of the film, Herzog laments, *"And what haunts me is that in all the faces of all the bears that Treadwell ever filmed, I discover no kinship, no understanding, no mercy. I see only the overwhelming indifference of Nature. To me there is no such thing as a secret world of the bears and this blank stare speaks only of a half bored interest in food. But for Timothy Treadwell this bear was a friend, a savior."*

These tropes of obsessive over-reacher and wild nature perhaps fit quite well under the single umbrella of Romanticism and, for some, Herzog's films, whether fiction or documentary, belong firmly in the Romantic tradition.

> Romanticism has been associated with a naïve longing in the face of nature. In many Romantic narratives, the protagonist yearns for a home in happy harmony with his environment. This tendency to entangle self and nature, in particular through natural landscape... translates into an inscription of the self on an Other.[7]

In Treadwell's story (the eco-warrior who found meaning in the bear Other), Herzog found a real life example of the Romantic loner, pitting himself against civilization and nature and, in the end, being destroyed by that which he desired most. Herzog could hardly have written it better himself. Indeed, as one review put it, the "story is classic Herzog: the celebrated German director practically has copyright on the concept of the half-crazed, obsessive outsider picking a fight with the forces of nature."[8] In fact, Herzog himself has said:

> No matter what, I had to do it. I had the feeling there was something much, much bigger in Treadwell's story. And probably not so much a look at wild nature as a look at human nature: the dark side, the demons and also the exhilarations and ecstasies.[9]

Tim Treadwell was an embodiment of Werner Herzog's own obsession: the hero who is single minded to the point of mania, literally consumed by his passion. If Treadwell had his bears, then perhaps it is only fair to suggest that Herzog had his Treadwell.

Ultimately, the film seems to reflect the obsessions of *two* men. One who views Nature as implacable and inevitably brutal or, as the poet A. E. Housman put it, "For nature, heartless, witless nature, will neither care nor know what stranger's feet may find the meadow."[10] For Herzog, the bears did not care if Treadwell shared their "meadow," having their blank stare which *"speaks only of a half bored interest in food"* and nothing more, but for the director the presence of the all-too-human Treadwell, with his passions and rages, is what gives the landscape meaning. It is Treadwell that obsesses him, not the object of Treadwell's obsession. Treadwell himself, conversely, would have better understood the Romantic Byron's vision of oneness: "I live not in myself, but I become Portion of that around me; and to me, high mountains are a feeling, but the hum of human cities torture."[11] For Treadwell, everything about the bears was perfection and, for a while, he seemed to have found a strange kind of society with the bears that he never quite found amongst humans.

However, the film begins and ends with Treadwell and Amie Huguenard's death, or perhaps it would be more accurate to say that the entire film seems to circle around this moment of tragedy, looking for reasons, but refusing to give easy or obvious answers. In the footage that he left, Treadwell speaks often and sometimes with apparent relish of the danger he is in and almost as often about the potential for death at the "*paws and claws*" of his bear "friends." It gives the film a sense of *schadenfreude* but also an elegiac air, for Treadwell says equally often that there is nowhere else he would rather be, and that he wanted no retribution against the bears should anything happen to him. "*This is it,*" he says mere days before his death, "*this is my life, this is my land.*" In the end, perhaps, the film is less a celebration of Treadwell's life and more a meditation on the inevitability of his death.

NOTES

1. Quoted on www.wernerherzog.com (accessed 6/6/06).

2. Cited in Annis V. Pratt, *Dancing with Goddesses* (Bloomington: Indiana University Press, 1994), 340.

3. Pratt, *Dancing with Goddesses,* 341.

4. Geoffrey Nowell-Smith, *The Oxford History of World Cinema* (Oxford: Oxford University Press, 1996), 620.

5. Phillip French, *Sunday Observer,* 5 February 2006.

6. Tom Cheesman, "Apocalypse nein danke: the fall of Werner Herzog," in C. Riordan (ed.), *Green Thought in German Culture: Historical and Contemporary Perspectives* (Cardiff: University of Wales Press, 1997), 292.

7. B. Prager, "Werner Herzog's Hearts of Darkness: *Fitzcarraldo, Scream of Stone* and Beyond," *Quarterly Review of Film & Video* 20: 23-35, (2003), 24.

8. *The Guardian*, Oliver Burkeman, January 27, 2006.

9. Quoted on www.wernerherzog.com (accessed 6/6/06).

10. A. E. Housman, *Last Poems* (1922), No. 40.

11. Lord Byron, "Childe Harold's Pilgrimage," Canto 3, Stanza 72.

BOOK REVIEWS

CHRISTINE DOWNING. *Gleanings: Essays 1982-2006*, iUniverse, Inc., 2006.

REVIEWED BY DRUSCILLA FRENCH

Could it be that a name functions as a kind of prophecy? By self-admission, James is a "Hill Man," a puer/senex who, despite all his trips to the Underworld, ends up occupying a position on the top of the highest peak. If Hillman is our Peak Guy, then Christine Downing is our Valley Girl. She's always peering under rocks, picking up chaff, looking for meaning in whatever it is the rest of us have dismissed. Such are her "gleanings."

In this collection of essays, Downing directs our attention, over and over, to the examination of our own wounding, in the fervent hope that doing so makes us better healers. She does this, not from the perspective of superiority but with an acknowledgment of her own hemorrhaging. Just as in her other books, she gets so personal sometimes that it brings a blush to this (somewhat Calvinistic) cheek. She exposes, right to an inner core, what it means to be human, and

Druscilla French, Ph.D., is President of the Foundation for Mythological Studies. She serves on the board of the Center for the Study of Depth Psychology and the Women's Leadership Council at the University of North Carolina at Chapel Hill. Currently she is at work on *The Blissless Myth: Cultural Narcissism*.

particularly female. Wielding a sharp scalpel, she incises her own tumors and plops them on the table for dissection. Downing is the "wounded healer" who "gets down" with the rest of us, assuring us that it is important that we grapple with the conditions of existence, the inevitable, discombobulating, deflating discoveries of self-examination, those "discontents of civilization." She reminds us that we must always continue to unabashedly tell the truth to the best of our abilities, keeping alive those stories that humble and nourish us rather than those that feed our inflations.

Gleanings is a diverse collection, written over a span of almost a quarter of a century. Her illumination of Freud, sprinkled throughout the essays, provides balance to the depth perspective, particularly Jungian and post-Jungian. (As usual, when reading Downing's books I find myself wondering, "How does she *know* all this stuff and how does she remember it all?") There is, however, a leitmotif: the movement within the archetypal perspective from personal mythology to a more global viewpoint. In "Turning Again to Athene," she revisits commitment to the welfare of the *polis,* envisioning a much broader perspective than the citizens of Athens might have imagined. She writes, "I believe we need to recognize that the relation between psyche and polis is both inescapable and conflicted....Polis is inside us as well as outside." She warns of the misuse of myth, citing historic examples reminiscent of the kind of abuse of Christian, Muslim, and Jewish traditions used today to justify violence and war. "The danger of succumbing to 'mythological enthusiasm' is real...."

A couple of the essays address 9/11 and the destruction of cities all over the world. In the face of such terrible global madness, she grapples with us about our role as healers, our sense of impotence coupled with responsibility.

> My hunch is that the point is not immediately to DO something,
> in a practical action kind of way.
> Maybe that is not our task, the task of us depth psychologists
> and teachers and writers.
> Perhaps our task is rather to imagine differently.
> To direct our imagining to the world.
> To re-myth the city.
> To recognize that cities are always mythic, always ordered by
> mythic assumption, always in a sense imaginal constructs....

Chris Downing has, for decades, written with amazing candor about the events of her life. Here she gathers bits over the years and packages them with a crone-like wisdom. Like Baubo, she brings both raucous laughter and an excruciating sob when she exposes herself (ourselves) to us.

BOOK REVIEWS

MARION RAUSCHER GALLBACH. *Learning from Dreams,*
Daimon Verlag, Einsiedeln, 2006.

REVIEWED BY ANITA U. GREENE

In *Learning from Dreams*, Marion Rauscher Gallbach, a Jungian analyst
in São Paulo, Brazil, draws from her years of experience working
with Dream Groups and offers us innovative ways of interacting with
dreams through dramatic narrative, symbolic language, and somatic
presence. She has experimented with approaches which allow the
dreamer to remain within the context of the dream experience itself.
Looking somewhat askance at an overly interpretive method in which
mental associations may take the dreamer in the direction of a
premature rational control of the unknown, Gallbach advocates staying
on the stage of the dream, the inner actor not leaving until the drama
is finished. This involves tolerating the tension of not knowing for
longer periods of time than is normative in a more interpretive method
and exploring all aspects of the dream before associating them with
one's present life experiences.

Anita U. Greene, Ph.D., IAAP, is a graduate of the C. G. Institute of New York
where she has taught and served on the Board. She is trained in the Rubenfeld Synergy
Method,® which combines Alexander and Feldenkrais body techniques. Anita has a
private practice in Amherst, Massachusetts, and writes and lectures widely about the
integration of body and psyche.

I cannot do full justice to the experiential process recorded in this book without having immersed myself in her Dream-Experience Groups. All I can do is give some sense of how they work. The groups are made up of three to six participants who are interested in learning how to engage with their dreams. (All of the dreamers are women mainly in their 20s through 40s). They meet once a week for an hour and a half in the analyst's office, and over a period of time, establish an atmosphere of trust that facilitates non-judgmental support for unexpected insights and emotional reactions to dream content. Although not characterized as group therapy, the group has a therapeutic effect, acting as a sheltering place or alchemical vessel for deeper processing of dream material. Greater confidence in understanding dream language, according to Gallbach, leads to a more receptive attitude to the autonomous process of the dream experience as well as to a deeper openness to one's own psychic process. I suspect that many of the women may have little knowledge of Jung or Jungian concepts. Gallbach speaks to them directly and gives explicit directions. She does not speak or write with professional jargon, which is refreshing.

Each participant tells her dream to the group. Then she works on it individually, in great detail, and before reporting her experience of the exercises back to the group. Only then is the dream opened to discussion within the group and comments, associations, and interpretive opinions allowed. By delaying the comments of others Gallbach hopes to avoid premature projections onto the dream material which, she thinks, inhibit the development of one's own oneiric style.

The main approach of Dream Processing is to observe the dramatic structure of the dream as it plays itself out in the present tense on the three-dimensional stage of one's Inner Theater. Gallbach uses aspects of classical theater, as Jung did, to describe the basic structure of the dream: Exposition, Plot, Climax, and Lysis. She encourages group members to write about them in great detail, including the inside/outside spaces—how they are configured, climate, weather, time of day, thorough descriptions of characters—their positions and movement in relation to each other, the actions and feelings of the dream-I and other protagonists, etc., etc. I found these five pages of detailed instructions rather daunting, perhaps relying on the thinking function too much, and wondered how participants managed to answer them within an hour and a half. In the many examples given, I was gratified that in the section on actions and feelings of the dream-ego and other protagonists, both pleasurable and disturbing emotions were, at least, identified.

A significant part of Dream Processing is to describe the dream-I's (Gallbach's term) underlying attitudes and evaluate those which are life affirming and those which are less advantageous to the ego's functioning. Participants are encouraged to play with changing the negative attitude into its opposite, trying it on for size until it can begin to be experienced as more ego syntonic. The last stage requires the dreamer to imaginatively rewrite the dream, staying within the original structure, using all that has been learned, including any positive attitude change that feels comfortable. In the examples, most of the re-creations place the dream-I in a more present and pro-active relationship to the protagonists and dramatic development of the dream.

One might question whether shadowy elements of psyche are adequately dealt with in this process. And yet, who of us, as analysts or working with our own dreams, can be certain any of our methods work long term, shadow aspects being so tricky to manage and to transform? The trust and respect for each other's process that Gallbach fosters in her groups seems to permit acknowledgment of disturbing shadow attitudes and encourages changes in the ego's choice of action. The re-creations strike me as ego strengthening. Evaluations of participants at the end of their group work seem to affirm not only that they have learned new techniques for engaging with dreams but have found new ways of applying insights from those dreams to their daily lives.

Gallbach uses a technique which she calls Body-Active Imagination to relate the dream content more deeply to the somatic experience of the dreamer. In *The Vision Seminars* (Vol. 2), Jung, speaking as much to himself as to others, cautions against the danger of heady immersion in symbolic images: "Whatever you experience outside of the body, in a dream, for instance, is not experienced unless you take it into the body, because the body means the here and now." I am always gratified to discover another analyst who works in an embodied way with symbolic material and is familiar with E. T. Gendlin's book: *Let your Body Interpret your Dreams.*

Beginning with a relaxation method, using breath, which centers participants in their bodies, Gallbach suggests that the participants re-enter their dreams: 1) Enter into the characters, adopt their postures, sense how their bodies move, feel the emotional effect of their actions. Then return to the dream-I and perceive your own experience of the dream; 2) Enter into the spaces, both inside and outside, sense the quality of your emotional response to the dynamics that take place within all the spaces; 3) Enter into the movements and actions of the dream—sitting, running, hiding, attacking, etc.—in the people, in the environment, in the dream-I. Live these movements in your bodies and sense where in your bodies they might feel part of you. Incorporating elements of the dream into one's immediate body experience can soften resistance to acknowledging dissociated and projected aspects of oneself.

The last exercise, Contemplative Dream Experience, also begins with relaxation and centering. The dreamers are invited to compare their present body experience with the body experience of the dream-I. One dreamer worked with a calm ego versus an agitated ego and discovered how the dramatic action and emotional quality of each scene changed as she reentered various parts of the dream with her presently composed sense of self. An enclosed room with no windows opened to the outside world with windows and a balcony. Now the dreamer can experience the outside without the same fear which has enclosed and shuttered her life.

I cannot begin to do justice to the complexity of the research and its findings. Basically, Gallbach moves from an objective to subjective approach to dream processing. 1) She begins with the objective dream in which the dreamer becomes aware of all the scenes, characters, and dramatic action as external to oneself. 2) Before any interpretive or personal associations are allowed, she encourages imaginative dialogue with all of the aspects of the dream, still as other. Everything in the dream has symbolic meaning, the characters and action in the foreground; setting and environment in the background. 3) The next step encourages the dreamer to experiment with the actions, ideas, and emotions in the dream as possible elements inside oneself. At this point the dreamer may become aware of the inner coherence of the dream, the precision of oneiric language—how, for example, the gray, cloudy weather is reflective of the emotional climate both in the dream and in oneself. The participants are ready now for more personal associations and feedback from other group members and an imaginative recreation of the original dream. 4) Re-entry into the dream in terms of incorporating all the elements inside oneself, especially affective bodily reactions, moves the dreamer more deeply into the complexed areas of the psyche and invites integration of projected shadow elements. 5) Reliving the dream from a more relaxed and centered place seems to provide participants with an embodied experience of an alternative way to face life's viscissitudes with equanimity.

Except for passing references to the archetypal dimension of dreams, Gallbach does not write at length about the archetypal themes in the dreams of the participants. I missed this aspect of dream processing. Having commented, I must add, as a Jungian, an awareness that Gallbach touches down into the mytho-poetic level of psyche of her dreamers, inviting them to think and feel into the fantastic and figurative language of the dream. Everything is symbolic in the dream. They are messages from the Self, informing us of what is out of balance in our lives. Beginning with the Ego-Other polarity, Gallbach's dream processing recognizes the dialectical patterns in the dream narrative that prevent us from separating and/or reuniting with dissociated and projected elements of our instinctive, authentic selves. Through imaginal and embodied engagement with all dream elements, Gallbach fosters the development of an Ego/Self axis which engages the larger Self in creative ways.

BOOK REVIEWS

GREG MOGENSON. *A Most Accursed Religion: When a Trauma Becomes God.* Spring Publications, 2006.

REVIEWED BY TIM PILGRIM

Greg Mogenson enjoys turning things upside down. Midway through *A Most Accursed Religion: When a Trauma Becomes God,* he tells the story of a childhood science experiment where a student wears a pair of glasses that reverses perception in such a way that the world appears inverted. The boy is understandably disoriented but after several days the upside-down world appears aright as his perceptual system adjusts. The further twist of the experiment is that when the boy later removes the glasses, he is confronted with a freshly flipped perspective, left topsy-turvy by the removal of the lenses that had originally reversed his worldview. It again takes him several days to get himself right-side-up again.

In examining our notions of god and trauma, Mogenson has us, like the boy in the experiment, put on upside-down glasses. Not only does he flip our thinking by revealing the many ways we turn our

Tim Pilgrim is a Candidate-in-Training and member of the Pittsburgh seminar of the Inter-Regional Society of Jungian Analysts. He is in private practice in Toronto, Canada, as a licensed MFT with clinical membership in the American Association for Marital and Family Therapy.

wounds into gods or our pain into religion, he also inverts many of
our belief systems, most notably Christianity, exposing the pathological
underpinnings of what we revere and worship. However, *A Most Accursed
Religion*, as well as not being about religion, is also much more than
psychologizing—more than demonstrating how gods become diseases,
as Jung put it—because no sooner do we adjust to one of Mogenson's
perspectives, than he removes the experimental glasses, leaving us
metaphorically and intellectually reeling, and even wary for what may
be in store with the next new "spectacle." Like Flaubert who deepened
his perspective by looking though different colored glass, Mogenson
examines trauma and whatever else penetrates our psychological skins
through a variety of lenses: the paradoxical "affliction and loving-
kindness" of the Christian-Hebrew God, the clinical metaphors of
Freudian and Jungian psychoanalysis, the linguistic dimensions of
postmodernism, and the soul-making strains of the Romantic poets.

Mogenson's multi-focal tactic of metaphorically changing colors
or repeatedly turning things around and even inside-out, is by his
own definition an act of soul-making that agitates our perspectives
and stimulates the skin or "crust" of what holds us together
psychologically, culturally, and even semantically. The idea of a crust
"thoroughly 'baked through' by stimulation" (115) is derived from
Freud's seminal biological metaphor about an organism's outer layer
which acts as both a protection against and a mediating receptor for
stimuli. For Mogenson, quoting Jung, the cardinal task is to "break
that spell that binds us to the cycle of biological events" (175) and
peel back the crusty layers of inorganic matter that have become the
empty creeds of vicarious religion or the defunct God terms of the
therapy cult. "Soul-making," Mogenson stresses, "is the human
refinement of the crust-making process, which is present in all living
things." The human refinement to which Mogenson refers is not just
material incarnations like "the animal skins, shirts of mail, hoop skirts,
corsets, jock-straps, mini-skirts, polyester suits, designer jeans, space
uniforms," (119) but the imaginal skin of metaphor, which can escape
the self-referential traps of religion and even the linguistic dogma of
post-structuralism, which is encased in its own solipsistic thick skin:

> Those deconstructionists! What thick skins they have! Imagine
> the luxury of being able to assert that words are not a function of
> the objects they seem to signify, but, rather, of their relationship

> to other words. When the psychotherapist reads these critics he is filled with envy. If only his patients were so linguistically well-constituted. If only they could turn their projection-laden, referential communications into self-reflective texts… If they could only realize that their symptoms are rhetorical, perhaps they would cease to vicariously ascribe blame and salvation to others. (121-2)

However, lest our layers of words become hard and headless like an oyster's shell or impenetrable like a deconstructionist's endlessly self reflecting text, such that they "protect the soul so absolutely from exposure to events that the soul shrivels up for lack of stimulation," the job of metaphor is to become "thinner, finer, subtler and more complex." (121)

Many of the images and much of the energy and edginess of the book are the legacy of the earlier 1989 version, *God Is a Trauma: Vicarious Religion and Soul Making,* which was written when Mogenson was 25. While *A Most Accursed Religion* is extensively revised and expanded, we still experience the feistiness of the youthful Mogenson's kinship with Nietzsche, whose polemical "God is dead" carries the spirit if not the inspiration for the original title. The Nietzschean influences are not only apparent in the persona of the rebel, the iconoclast, and the Gnostic, but also in the book's discursive style which is reminiscent of Nietzsche's aphoristic vignettes. But there is method in this format, since the use of many short essays is a literal enactment of the repetition compulsion (one of Mogenson's presiding metaphors), whereby, when a theme is varied "in a sufficient number of situations, a context may coagulate around it in whose terms the event at its core can be relativized, particularized, and experienced." (18)

The new book's additions, including the revised title, *A Most Accursed Religion: When a Trauma Becomes God*, reflect an enhanced emphasis on the diabolical process of traumatization and its compulsive enchantments. Mogenson goes deeper, using more subtle arguments and images that show how "the outwardness of traumatic events [move] to the inwardness of the subject's proneness to be traumatized." (176) With intensified insights into the paradoxical nature of trauma's interiority, we see how the "sinister company" (173) of the night-room fears experienced directly by children and symptomatically (read: metaphorically) by adults create an "essential tension," which, like the members of our inevitably wounding families of origin, traumatizes us into awareness. Terrors and affliction, like parents and siblings, help shape and shame us into a painful but profound sense of our own individuality. As such, symptoms become "the soul's way [of] discarnating itself from its encasement in the arbitrary order." (189) Injury and anguish shed light on the individual's way out of the religious cult. Bumps, bruises, and bug-a-boos become the *scintillae* or *lumen naturae* of new possibilities. The parapraxes of everyday life offer saving grace.

Mogenson does not dismiss or minimize the powerful effects of trauma or stimuli that are so dangerously split-off and potent that they undermine the defenses of the victim both clinically and figuratively. However, he does not support the thick-skinned God-terms that while holding us, also tragically abuse us (like Kalsched's "internal saboteur"), moving from protectiveness to inflexibility and ultimately to a domineering monotheism that even stifles our groans:

> But the commandment not to cry out forbids the comparison of inarticulate sounds, preserving the awesomeness of the eliciting stimulus and traumatic response. With each cry that is held back in the throat, the event to which it was a response becomes more and more other until, like a God, it becomes wholly other. God is the deferral of cursing and swearing, the deferral of groaning, weeping, howling and shrieking, and the indefinite postponement of whimpering in the dark. He is the inarticulate made Holy, the sanctification of the literally unspeakable, a circumcised tongue. (48-49)

In order to wrestle with such a God and to address Nietzsche's fear "that we are not getting rid of god because we still believe in grammar," Mogenson makes sure that we do not linger long or securely in any structure. He intentionally keeps us verbally thin-skinned and alert, on the lookout for his next chameleon move as he darts and blends into the vernacular background or rhetorical surfaces of revered institutions and their fundamentalist assumptions. His ability to sport the idiomatic vestments of various priesthoods gives him linguistic access to their inner sanctums, which for some might exacerbate the iconoclastic and even heretical treatment of their objects of worship (the first version of the book generated its share of hate mail). Yet wordplay is one of the tools of this "Gnostic analysis" or literary talking cure which strives "to liberate spirit from the contingency of the patient's life [or the reader's] through metaphor:"

> Gradually, the analytic discourse breaks up the patient's account of his incarnational life to the point where suddenly his words are no longer bound to it at all. The couch becomes a subtle couch, a couch of light, a Mount of Olives, a metaphor. Reclining in the repose of metaphor, the patient is released from the prose of his incarnational life. By restating in poetic terms the incidents of his life which the language of prose had preserved as trauma, the patient frees his soul to follow its desires. (79)

What metaphor accomplishes is more than just radical liberation from the deadening worship of trauma-Gods or prosaic patterns. Its skin-thinning stimulation also has an evident corpus and organization—and certainly craftiness in Mogenson's case—which substantiates experience into an imaginal body alongside of its capacity to "dis-carnate."

Metaphor is not just Mogenson's *via regia,* it is the hallmark of his craft. He not only has a way with metaphor, he has *his* way with metaphor, wrapping us in the skin of his book's image-rich body and creating a semantic membrane that allows us to feel and absorb many provocative ideas in meaningful doses. Unlike Freud's biological crust which can have a numbing effect, with Mogenson's spell-breaking and spell-making layers, we are stimulated, provoked, and soulfully enriched.

PHILEMON

FOUNDATION

PHILEMON FOUNDATION is preparing for publication the *Complete Works of C.G. Jung* in English and German. In distinction to the widely known *Collected Works*, it is intended that the *Complete Works* will comprise manuscripts, seminars, and correspondence hitherto unpublished or formerly believed "lost" that number in tens of thousands of pages. ✺ Among our funded projects are Jung's legendary *Red Book*, the Children's Dreams Seminar, the ETH Lectures from 1933 to 1941, and Jung's remarkable correspondence with Father Victor White. ✺ Given the magnitude of our task, the Philemon Foundation invites all those who value the work of C.G. Jung and appreciate its importance to our personal and collective journeys to join us by making a donation. For further information, please contact Dr. Stephen Martin. ✺

PHILEMON FOUNDATION
119 COULTER AVENUE, ARDMORE, PENNSYLVANIA 19003 USA
FAX 610-660-9219 TELEPHONE 610-896-0344
SMARTIN@PHILEMONFOUNDATION.ORG
WWW.PHILEMONFOUNDATION.ORG

Harvesting Darkness
Essays on Literature, Myth, Film and Culture

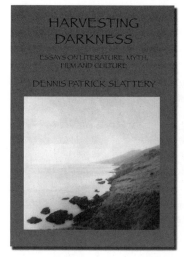

ISBN 0-595-38452-8 • Price: $24.95 (USD) • Paper
Publishers: iUniverse, 2006

Harvesting Darkness gathers essays, both scholarly and cultural, written during the past 25 years, all of which have been published previously in books, journals, and other periodicals. They span a wide arc, exploring subjects as diverse as writing, the imagination, grief, poetry, prayer, loss, and silence, as well as address specific literary works and films, such as Sophocles' *Antigone*, Dante's *Commedia*, Mark Twain's *Huckleberry Finn*, Dostoevsky's *The Idiot*, Melville's *Moby Dick*, Joseph Campbell's mythology, Wim Wenders' *Wings of Desire* and Philip Leacock's *Three Sovereigns for Sarah.* Drawing upon the theories of phenomenology, depth and archetypal psychology, and mythology, these essays develop a theory of mythopoiesis.

A Limbo of Shards
Essays on Memory, Myth and Metaphor

ISBN 0-595-41925-9 • Price: $24.95 (USD) • Paper
Publisher: iUniverse, 2007

Both literature and culture coalesce in the three main arenas of this volume: memory, myth, and metaphor. As Peter C. Phan, Chair of Catholic Social Thought at Georgetown University, writes in the Foreword to this volume, the fields of literature and depth psychology "function for Dennis *as modes of knowing,* or more precisely, *modes of imagining,* and hence *modes of being and acting* in the world." *A Limbo of Shards* is a study of literature, psychology, mythology, culture, and nature in its various shears that, taken together, fashion a single image of the imagination's diverse expressions.

ABOUT THE AUTHOR:
Dennis Patrick Slattery, Ph.D., is Core Faculty, Mythological Studies at Pacifica Graduate Institute in Carpinteria, California. A teacher for 39 years, he is author/co-editor of 9 books, including two volumes of poetry and accompanying CDs. His work witnesses intimate and sustained marriages between poetry, literature, spirituality, phenomenology, and depth psychology.

Order online at: www.amazon.com
or contact Pacifica Graduate Institute Bookstore, (805) 969-3626, ext. 141

In 2007
The San Francisco Jung Institute Library
JOURNAL
will change its title to:

JUNG JOURNAL
culture & psyche

The perfect companion
to your SPRING subscription:
in-depth explorations of culture—
myth, literature, music, visual arts,
history, religion, and cultural conflict

published quarterly
in print & online

Subscribe
or download a subscription form
at www.sfjungjournal.org

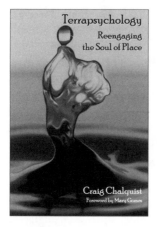

**Foundation for
Mythological Studies (FMS)
&
Spring Journal**

present

*Nature and Human Nature
Changing Perspective*

**March 16-18, 2007, Santa Barbara, CA.
www.mythology.org**

The Nature and Human Nature Conference will explore how the sciences and the humanities can work in tandem to achieve a shift in consciousness with respect to our current environmental ethos.

Scientists, psychologists, and cultural mythologists are increasingly addressing the toughest and most perplexing global issues, yet critical dialogue is required so that we no longer ignore the human factors or the ecological facts.

Experience extraordinary presentations and conversation led by experts in various fields that will increase your knowledge of environmental and human issues seen from a long-term perspective.

The aim of this Conference is to contribute to constructing new worldviews about the interactions between humans and nature. In this way, we hope to motivate educators, policy makers, and entrepreneurs to devise attitudes, policies, and corporate responsibility for the future of our planet and humankind.

Co-Sponsors: Pacifica Graduate Institute, Santa Barbara City College, Joseph Campbell Foundation, International Association of Jungian Studies (IAJS), Sustainable Santa Barbara.

For more information: www.mythology.org